FAKE HEROES

FAKE HEROES

Ten False Icons and
How They Altered the
Course of History

OTTO ENGLISH

WELBECK

Published in 2023 by Welbeck
An imprint of Welbeck Non-Fiction Limited
Part of the Welbeck Publishing Group
Offices in: London – 20 Mortimer Street, London W1T 3JW &
Sydney – Level 17, 207 Kent St, Sydney NSW 2000 Australia
www.welbeckpublishing.com

A CIP catalogue record for this book is available from the British Library.

ISBNs
Hardback 9781802795899
Trade paperback 9781802795905
eBook 9781802795912

Typeset by seagulls.net

Printed in the UK

10 9 8 7 6 5 4 3 2 1

For my parents, Hannah and Peter Scott

CONTENTS

THE MAKING OF A HERO
WESLEY AUTREY

We begin with a miracle – beneath the streets of New York.

It is just before 1 p.m. on Tuesday 2nd January 2007, and Wesley Autrey, a 50-year-old father of three, is taking his two youngest children to their mother's house, before going on to the construction site where he works.

They are late, and Wesley hurries his girls down the steps into the 137th Street Station; they pass through the turnstile, head out onto the concourse and walk straight into high drama. Ahead of them, on the almost empty platform, a 20-year-old film student, Cameron Hollopeter, is having a violent seizure and while startled commuters look on, he falls backwards onto the ground, violently smacking his head.

Cameron just got lucky. Wesley is a navy veteran, trained to respond to emergencies, so he goes straight to the young man's aid, pulls him back from the platform's edge and forces his mouth open with a pen, to stop him swallowing his tongue. Then, with the help of another passenger, he holds tightly onto the student until his epileptic seizure has passed. After a few minutes, Cameron seems to be OK. He rises, unsteadily, to his feet, thanks Wesley and the other passenger, staggers off, tilts sideways and falls straight onto the tracks.

Bang on cue, the silence of the 137th Street Station is broken by the roar of an approaching train. As one passenger shouts for help and another scrambles for the emergency telephone, Wesley stares down at Cameron writhing between the metro lines, with a voice in his head (by his own later account) saying: "Fool, you got to go in and help."

And so it is that this middle-aged father of three leaps into the path of an oncoming train, to save a stranger's life.

Down on the tracks, Wesley tries to lift Cameron up, but he's soaking wet from drainage water and keeps slipping through his hands. The Number One train is now bursting into the station, illuminating the darkness with its headlamp and storming towards them and as it does, Wesley spots a drainage chute between the rails – and calculates that they might just fit in. Grabbing Cameron tight and rolling on top of him he pushes them both down tightly into the gap and as he does, the 190-ton locomotive shoots over them and screeches to a halt above their heads.

The entire drama from Cameron's fall to the train arriving at the station has lasted less than a minute. The locomotive has cleared them by just half an inch (1.27 cm) and has deposited a line of grease right along the top of Wesley's blue beanie hat.

"Am I dead?" Hollopeter asks.

"No, sir, we're under a train!" Wesley replies and then, fearing for the safety of his daughters, yells: "Everybody be quiet! There's two young girls up there, I'm their Daddy, let them know their Daddy is OK!"

As his voice echoes upwards, the now crowded platform falls momentarily silent, before exploding into whoops of joy.

A hero has been born.

* * *

Wesley later told Cara Buckley of *The New York Times* that: "I don't feel I did something spectacular; I just saw someone who needed help and did what I felt was right."

But that was not good enough for those seeking to understand why he had shown such extraordinary bravery. In the years that followed his story was constantly revisited and re-examined as people sought to understand the nature of his heroism.

In 2008, Wesley's story was told in an early TED talk by the renowned psychologist Philip Zimbardo, who held him up as an example of the sort of altruistic, everyday hero that potentially lurks inside us all. In 2012, the Harvard University mathematician and biologist Martin Nowak, author of a book called *SuperCooperators*, considered whether Wesley's act was rooted in evolution, suggesting:

"He showed us all that in the game of life, surviving is as dependent upon the goodwill of others as it is upon personal qualities such as drive, excellence, and so on. He became a living testament to the power of cooperation."

Others, including the American journalist Joe Nocera, argued that Wesley's actions may have been based on more societal factors and was perhaps down to something called the *Bystander Effect*. That paradox, first identified by John Darley and Bibb Latané in 1968, argues that the larger the number of people present at an emergency, the slower anyone is to respond; and conversely the smaller the number, the more likely someone is to act quickly.

In other words, crowds diffuse personal responsibility, but individuals feel obliged to do something.

There might be something to this theory, because five years after Wesley saved Cameron's life, another man, Ki-Suck Han, fell onto the tracks of the crowded 49th Street Subway Station and lost his life while everyone dithered. On that occasion no Wesley Autrey appeared and some of those present even snapped photos of Han's fate on their cell phones as he was hit by the train and then tried to sell them to a tabloid newspaper. There were, it must be said, several important differences between the two events, not least that Han was drunk and aggressive prior to being pushed onto the tracks, but it was significant that the 49th Street station that day was crowded, while on that lunchtime in 2007, the 137th Street Station had been almost empty.

What the *Bystander Effect* cannot do is explain why Autrey ignored every single ordinary human instinct to jump. After all, there was every reason not to. Wesley was with his two young daughters, and ordinarily the primitive parental urge to protect them would override all else. He was also the patriarch of his extended family and not only took care of his elderly mother but also supported his adult son's grandchildren, as well as his nieces and nephews. By risking his life, he was jeopardising the security of all those he loved and what makes it even more extraordinary is that he risked it all for a stranger.

Individuals are significantly more likely to help those who resemble themselves and in 2006, one year before Wesley saved Cameron's life, research led by Stefan Stürmer of the University of Kiel concluded that:

"While all… people [in the study] *felt empathy for someone in distress, they only tended to assist if the needy person was viewed as a member of their own 'in-group.'"*

Wesley was Black, middle-aged and working class; Cameron was a white college kid from Massachusetts. They had nothing in common and had barely met. Wesley had nothing whatsoever to gain by acting. This then was an act of pure, altruistic, heroism, a high bar by which all others can be measured. We shall dub it "The Wesley Factor" and having done so, let's return to New York on that January afternoon in 2007.

Two hours after being freed from beneath the train and having discharged himself from St Luke's–Roosevelt Hospital Center, Wesley was greeted outside by a journalist and photographer from the tabloid newspaper the *New York Post*, who tried to coax him into putting on a Superman outfit and posing for photos. "I'm late for work!" he said and set off to do his shift.

By that evening his face was on every news network in the USA. For some he was the "Subway Hero", for others the "Hero of Harlem" and depending on whether you were a DC or Marvel fan, you could pick between "Subway Superman" or the "Subway Spiderman". By the following morning he was the most famous construction worker in

America and when he left home, TV cameras greeted him at his door, and he was practically mobbed in the street.

Strangers tried to press dollars into his hand, and a woman even told him she had decided against an abortion because she now realised that there was "good in the world".

Two days later Wesley visited Cameron in hospital and met his father, Larry Hollopeter, who thanked him for his "unselfish act". Larry was so overcome, that he began to cry and Wesley, put his arms about him, saying:

"What better way to start the New Year than to save someone's life?"

That afternoon, the Mayor of New York, Michael Bloomberg, gave Wesley the Bronze Medallion, the highest civic award that the city can bestow and threw in an all-expenses paid trip to Disneyworld for him and his girls, Shuqui, 6, and Syshe, 4. The same evening Autrey appeared on the *Late Show with David Letterman* and demonstrated that in addition to being a national icon he was just about as nice and normal as a guy can be.

In January 2007, America was not a happy place. The economy was shrinking, unemployment was rising, the housing bubble had burst, and the nation was mired in an ugly Middle-Eastern war. A YouGov poll that year found the number of citizens willing to describe themselves as "Extremely or Very Proud" to be Americans was at an all-time low. In the words of Bonnie Tyler, America had been "holding out for a hero" and Wesley was the much-needed "streetwise Hercules to fight the rising odds." For a nation that felt it had lost its way, his bravery spoke of another, albeit imagined, age and another, albeit imagined, country. More than anything, he embodied that most potent Hollywood storyline of all: the everyman who comes out of nowhere to save the day.

But there was a problem. Autrey had not planned to be a hero or sought reward for his courage. He had simply acted out of instinct and good intent and that meant that having found him, neither America nor Wesley himself knew what to do next. So in lieu of any other ideas, the United States did what it always does, resorted to factory settings – and tried to turn him into a celebrity.

Things began predictably enough with him being invited onto Montel, Oprah, Ellen and every other *mononymous* chat show in the USA where he was showered with gifts. Ellen gave him a $5,000 Gap gift card and the promise of a Jeep. Hugh Hefner gifted him a Playboy beanie hat (to replace the one that had been greased) and a lifetime subscription to his top-shelf magazine. The New York Film Academy threw in a cheque for $5,000, and property tycoon Donald Trump one for $10,000. You will be shocked I know, to hear that the future 45th President of the USA may not have been entirely motivated by largesse. The previous six months had been very bad for him indeed. Ratings for his TV show *The Apprentice* had slumped and while his wife, Melania, was tending to baby Barron, he had made an embarrassment of himself by telling *The View* that: "If Ivanka weren't my daughter, perhaps I'd be dating her". The same year, on the very eve of the subprime mortgage crisis that would help wreck the US economy, the self-styled business genius had launched "Trump Mortgages", telling CNBC: "I think it's a great time to start a mortgage company; the real-estate market is going to be very strong for a long time to come."

By January 2007 that market was already crashing, and Trump's stock was falling with it. By befriending the Subway Superman, the future president was latching onto the hero of the moment, in the hope that some of the sheen might rub off on him.

Trump was far from alone in that. Everyone wanted a piece of Wesley. Big brands lined up to give him fur coats, trainers and cologne. Beyoncé invited him to one of her concerts and gave him backstage passes, while blues legend B.B. King dropped to his knees and told him: "You don't know what you've done to and for America."

He was even asked to open the New York Stock Exchange and next thing he knew, President George W. Bush was on the phone inviting him to come round to the White House to "hang out". Bush – like

Trump – needed a boost to his ratings. In January 2007 he was the least popular US president since Richard Nixon with an approval rating of just 28%. There were percentage points in Wesley Autrey's heroism and after meeting him at the White House, Bush invited him to be guest of honour at the State of the Union Address on January 23rd. Towards the end of his speech, he paid tribute to his new friend:

"He insists he's not a hero. He says: 'We got guys and girls overseas dying for us to have our freedoms. We have got to show each other some love.' There is something wonderful about a country that produces a brave and humble man like Wesley Autrey."

Even as he spoke, the miracle on 137th Street was beginning to turn into a sort of a curse because with his fame came another sort of attention. Where once people had come up to hand him money, now they began to ask him for it assuming, that he had become rich. His father, who hadn't contacted him in three decades, rang out of the blue and, as Wesley later told Robert Kolker of *The New Yorker* magazine:

"'Like everybody else,' he starts saying 'I need, I want, give me'. Never once did he say: 'Are you alright? Are the little girls OK?' He just said, 'there's a family reunion coming and if you're coming bring me some of that money you've got'."

On Valentine's Day a woman who'd dumped him 15 years previously rang and when Wesley asked why she was contacting him like that, she took umbrage and slammed down the phone. He started getting paranoid about the safety of his girls, worrying that they might get kidnapped – and inevitably perhaps, all the adulation started going to his head.

When Oprah booked him for her Chicago studio on the same day that the makers of *Deal or No Deal* wanted him in LA, he rang his new best friend the American President and tried to borrow a stealth jet. Somewhere along the line he had picked up "business partners" with big ideas. There was talk of a film and a script in which Wesley, played by Eddie Murphy, or perhaps Brad Pitt, would foil a terrorist attack on the subway and there were plans to turn him into a brand. When

Wesley realised that the deals would entitle him to just 50% of any proceeds and that his "business partners" were charging journalists extortionate sums for access, he filed papers.

Aristotle, the polymath of the fourth century BCE, suggested that the role of the tragic hero is always to fall, because only through that fate can heroes reflect the fear and tragedy of mortal human experience – which is in essence – their purpose.

The Greek Gods loathed braggers and were forever bringing down heroes who had ideas above their station. When the hero Odysseus sets off back home after the Trojan Wars, his pride led to a fall – when a journey that should have taken him roughly a week ended up taking ten years and led the crews on all twelve of his ships to be drowned, slain – or eaten.

As Wesley navigated the odyssey of his fame, his own fate in the twenty-first century was to be sealed by the Siren call of daytime TV and the Cyclops beast of empty celebrity.

The moment of his downfall can be traced to 21st May 2007, and that appearance on *Deal or No Deal** hosted by Howie Mandel. The show is a classic "risk it all for the big prize" format and unfortunately, Wesley did just that. Turning down an offer of $305,000 from the "banker" he won just $25. The audience had been expecting an upbeat Spielbergian finale, with Wesley riding off rich and happy into the sunset – they got a super-bleak Lars Von Trier one instead. As consolation Mandel gave Autrey a Chrysler Jeep Patriot, his second Chrysler Jeep Patriot. And the look on everyone's faces said it all – Wesley's 15 minutes of fame were up.

What could not be doubted was that Autrey had done something extraordinary on that January morning in 2007. He had saved another man's life, with no thought for his own safety and no expectation of reward. He was and remains a hero of the highest order. But that moment had been tainted. Powerful people had used him, the American

---

* Case 24 was held by a certain Meghan Markle during much of season two of the gameshow, but she left after episode 34. Autrey appeared in episode 67 of the same series.

media had sucked him in and spat him out him and the news cycle had simply got bored and moved on.

* * *

In November 1872, a self-educated, 32-year-old Assyriologist called George Smith working in the British Museum Library in Bloomsbury made an astonishing discovery.

Smith was unlike any other Assyriologist of his time. Born in a slum in Chelsea to a working-class family he had, aged 14, become a printer's apprentice and banknote engraver in nearby Clerkenwell, but lunchtime visits to the British Museum had led to a burgeoning fascination with the ancient world. George's passion for the subject and self-taught expertise was such, that eventually the Department of Oriental Antiquities offered him a job as a "repairer", piecing together fragments of Assyrian tablets. George quickly demonstrated that his talents stretched beyond elaborate jigsaws and he became indispensable to the museum and Sir Henry Creswicke Rawlinson, as one of his chief decipherers.

Most of the tablets came from a horde that had been discovered at Nineveh and Nimrud between 1849 and 1854 by Assyriologist Sir Austen Layard and later, his assistant Hormuzd Rassam, a Mosul-born accountant turned archaeologist. The finds had once formed part of the Royal Library of Ashurbanipal, a collection of some 30,000 tablets assembled on behalf of King Ashurbanipal himself, the last of the great Assyrian rulers. In 612 BCE the Assyrian capital, Nineveh, was sacked and Ashurbanipal's library was burned to the ground, but in the process, the clay tablets within had been baked and preserved beneath the city's ruins for posterity.

They were written in Akkadian, a language spoken from roughly 2600 BCE to the first century of the Common Era and put down in cuneiform text – one of the earliest known writing systems. In use from 3500 BCE, the very start of the Bronze Age, it was adopted over time by at least a dozen languages, including Sumerian and Akkadian, before falling into obsolescence in the second century BCE.

The text had been deciphered only fairly recently, in 1857 and Smith was one of the first people in millennia to read the contents. Many of the tablets were legal, diplomatic or financial in nature, but Smith had made some amazing transcriptions, including accounts of a solar eclipse in 763 BCE and an invasion of Babylonia in 2280 BCE. His greatest and most famous translation however was to be deciphered that autumn day in 1872.

The tablet told the tale of a "great flood" and a vengeful god, Enlil, who decides to press alt-ctrl-delete on creation. But before unleashing the storm, he tells one man, Utnapishtim, of his plans, urging him to:

"Demolish the house, build a boat!"

And then to:

"Abandon riches and seek survival! Spurn property and save life! Put on board the boat the seed of all living creatures!"

So, he and Mrs. Utnapishtim, construct a ship and stuff it full of food, seeds and baby animals to ride out the rising seas.

"On looking down the third column," Smith later wrote, "my eye caught the statement that the ship rested on the mountains of Nizir, followed by the account of the sending forth of the dove, and it finding no resting-place and returning. I saw at once that I had here discovered... an account of the Deluge."

Smith's interest in cuneiform extended beyond the archaeological value of the tablets. Like many Victorian scholars, he believed that the finds were key to proving the historicity of the Bible and here was an account of the same events as Noah's Ark in Genesis (chapters 6–9) but, crucially, a full thousand years older. Smith was so elated by what he had transcribed that he leapt from his chair and shouted: "I am the first man to read that after more than two thousand years of oblivion!" before stripping off his clothes and running naked around the British Museum Library to the disquiet of his more cerebral colleagues. The following month and by now (thank God) reacquainted with his trousers, he presented his findings to the Society of Biblical Archaeology and an audience that included the Archbishop of Canterbury, Campbell Tait, and the then Prime Minister William Gladstone. It was a huge moment and Smith became history's first and last cuneiform global celebrity.

There was general frustration that a crucial bit of the story was missing, so the *Daily Telegraph*, under editor Edwin Arnold, put up 1,000 guineas to fund an expedition to the ruins of Nineveh, in order that Smith might find the missing chunk.

Fulfilling a lifelong ambition to lead an excavation, Smith travelled to Mosul the following year and, incredibly, on 7th May 1873, discovered the segment. That success led to plans for a further expedition but returning to the Middle East once more, Smith fell ill and succumbing to fever and dysentery, died on 19th August 1876, in Aleppo in what is now modern-day Syria.

In the years that followed, even as the legend of George Smith drifted into obscurity, his astonishing discovery was to become far more important than the questionable "proof" it provided for the historicity of Noah's ark. For the tablet that he had translated was nothing less than Book 11 of the *Epic of Gilgamesh* – the oldest written story in existence.

Put down on cuneiform circa 2700 BCE the poem tells the tale of the eponymous hero, the king of Uruk, in what is modern-day Warka, Iraq. Gilgamesh starts out as a baddie, a sexual predator who insists on *ius primae noctis* (his right as a king) to sexually molest women on their wedding nights. He is a violent oppressor who forces men not only to give up their wives but also to work for him building vanity projects. Inevitably therefore, the gods decide to teach him a lesson and send Enkidu, a hunky wild-man down to Earth to challenge him. To become human, Enkidu must engage in 14 days and nights of (frankly *really* exhausting sounding) lovemaking with a woman called Shamhat and having done so, he is then ready to set out to confront Gilgamesh. But there is a massive plot twist for when they meet, they click and Gilgamesh suggests that instead of fighting each other they should join forces to kill the monsters Humbaba and the Bull of Heaven instead.

Enkidu agrees and, in doing so, enrages those ever-touchy Gods who feel he's upset their plans. In a peculiar foreshadowing of the fate of George Smith 3,000 years later, the wild man catches a fever and dies.

Gilgamesh is so distraught by the loss of his friend, that he sets off to find the secret to everlasting life, which takes him to Utnapish-tim (aka Assyrian Noah) who reveals – after a bit of encouragement from his wife – that there is a sacred plant able to grant eternal youth. Unfortunately, a serpent gets there first and steals it (another trope the writers of Genesis may have plagiarised) and the King returns home empty-handed only to later spring his old friend from the Netherworld, so that they can have a good old natter.

The *Epic of Gilgamesh* has it all: bromance, human folly and redemption; the existential pain of being and the fear of what happens when we die. There's sex and floods and Netherworlds. But at its heart lies the most retold story of all. The one where the hero sets out on a quest, overcomes challenges and returns home changed. It is a tale that has defined our view of "the heroic" from the pre-Hellenic era onwards and one which continues to imprint itself firmly on our cultural land-scape in books, TV series and films.

The American writer Joseph Campbell used the term *monomyth* (hero's journey) to describe this archetype in his hugely influential 1949 book *The Hero with a Thousand Faces* and given that we will encounter many a *monomyth* in the pages ahead, let's take a moment to examine it.

For Campbell, at the heart of a *monomyth* lie three distinctive elements: *separation*, *initiation* and *return*. Separation involves the protagonist travelling from known to unknown worlds, before expe-riencing a transformative experience (initiation) and coming back with a new power or knowledge. That basic arc is found in the works of Homer, the *Rāmāyana*, the four gospels of Christ, Saint George and the Dragon, *The Very Hungry Caterpillar*, *Superman*, *Dumb and Dumber* and even the tale of Wesley Autrey, which I shall use as our example.

The monomyth is cyclical, so let's first consider a clock-face with Wesley standing at the top, setting off clockwise. He leaves the *status quo* of home (12 p.m.) and has the *call to adventure* (1 p.m.) when he witnesses Cameron having his seizure. Seeking *assistance* (2 p.m.) from a fellow passenger he *crosses the threshold* (3 p.m.) and leaves the safety of his *known world* (4 p.m.) by leaping in front of the train. He *solves the riddle* (5 p.m.) of how to save Cameron by *slaying the monster* (i.e. climbing into the drainage chute) (6 p.m.) and *defeating death* before being *reborn* (7 p.m.). That rebirth is his fame which leads him to *rewards and treasure* including the Playboy hat and the Jeep (8 p.m.) before there is a *lesson* (9 p.m.) at the hands of *Deal or No Deal* and greedy business partners, that *returns* (10 p.m.) him back *transformed* (11 p.m.) to his original world with the status quo now shaken up (12 a.m.).

Campbell was a lover of folklore and travelled widely collecting the origin myths of societies and tribes. In the process, he came to believe that the monomyth's prevalence was rooted in our hunter-gatherer past. Palaeolithic cave art in the Salle du Fond, in the Ardèche valley in South-West France, discovered in 1994 hints tantalisingly at a 35,000-year-old version of the same story and it's perhaps not surprising. After all, experiencing challenges, tackling problems, overcoming monsters and returning home triumphant is part and parcel of human existence and likely always has been. Going to the shops is a kind of monomyth. So too is the daily school run, the commute to work or even getting out of bed on a bleak late December morning, having eaten your body weight in cheese over Christmas.

The Hero with a Thousand Faces was hugely influential on Hollywood film makers. George Lucas based the first three *Star Wars* films on the structure, but really Lucas didn't need Campbell's guidance and could have plucked his story from any number of heroes journeys from the tenth century BCE Hellenic-era onwards.

The Greeks believed that their heroes were descended from Gods and thus were imbued with "God-like" qualities that blurred the lines between being human and the divine. But crucially, unlike the Gods, these heroes were mortal and thus destined to die, usually gruesome and early deaths as a result of hubris – or whatever else they had done to upset the Gods. In that sacrifice and the journey towards it they attained something called *kleos*, which roughly translates as "glory". *Kleos* was about not just the glory of heroes in life but the remembrance of them after they were gone, hence the epic poems and ballads that included Homer's Iliad and Odyssey.

Kleos, like toilet paper in a pandemic, was not just handed to you, you had to actively and deliberately search it out, meaning that you had a choice whether to live a long, dull and swiftly forgotten life, or live fast and die young. The ultimate goal was to attain *kleos aphthiton*, aka "eternal renown", and really, if you think about it, that's what all of our heroes still are some three thousand years later.

Most of us are aware of Hellenic "A-listers" like Ajax, Achilles and Theseus, slayer of the Minotaur, striving towards *kleos*, but the Greeks had a busy line in B-listers too and there were thousands of cults to local heroes. These were a critical aspect of Hellenic culture, with the faithful believing, much as ancestor-worshipping cultures still do, that in death these great people would become protectors and defend their immediate locale. Shrines known as *tumuli* were built to them and they became places of devotion. The Christian tradition of sainthood had many similarities with such Greek and later Roman cults, and in addition to the roster of "official saints", "folk saints" proliferated throughout the Christian world from the very start.

The Anglo-Saxons had around 100 unofficial local "English" saints and the tradition of celebrating them continued well beyond the Norman invasion in 1066 and into the sixteenth century. Some figures, like Æthelthryth of Ely, founder of the monastic community in Cambridgeshire, are still venerated today.

Across the Catholic world, local saints proliferate still. In Sinaloa, on the north-western coast of Mexico, offerings are still made to Jesús Malverde, a "Robin Hood" figure said to have lived at the end of the nineteenth century. Malverde is also the "patron saint" of drug traffickers and given the association I wouldn't hold your breath for his official canonisation any time soon.

In recent decades, the secular cult of celebrity has eclipsed the divine one of saints. And once again, in death, many a modern-day icon has gone on to exist in a kind of *kleos* – revered by fans, as their stories are told and retold in biopics and biographies.

As we make our own journey through the pages that follow, we will come across many a temple and place of pilgrimage raised to the recent dead and many a legend propped up on the back of them. The likes of Princess Diana, John F. Kennedy, Dr Martin Luther King Junior and even Winston Churchill all have their *tumuli* and *kleos aphithiton*, while prematurely deceased pop stars make particularly resonant folk saints. Every year an estimated 500,000 people make the pilgrimage to Elvis Presley's grave at Graceland. On the corner of Central Park in New York you can visit Strawberry Fields, a shrine to the late Beatle, John Lennon, and even hear people with guitars annihilate his back catalogue. Cards and flowers are still pinned to the tree outside Amy Winehouse's flat more than ten years after her death and by the B306 near Barnes, a veritable temple has been raised to former T. Rex front man, Marc Bolan – who died there in 1977.

The modern preoccupation with celebrity and political and cultural heroes is really then just a continuation of a 36,000-year-old story and you don't need to look far to see the *monomyth* all about you. Pick up your phone and scroll and you'll soon find advertisers selling you a monomyth. Pop over to Instagram, Tik Tok and Twitter, and you'll encounter any number of influencers and politicians living out their "heroes' journeys" for likes.

When Rishi Sunak sought to become the British Prime Minister in 2022, he put out a video that made no mention of his policies and much more of his family's monomyth. The video began: "Let me tell you a story" before weaving the tale of how his hard-working immigrant grandmother left the *status quo* and *crossed the threshold* by boarding a plane to England *"with hope for a better life"*.

Another hero's journey was at play in the recent war in Ukraine. President Volodymyr Zelenskyy was once a professional writer and actor, so it was perhaps unsurprising that he brilliantly used his mastery of narrative in waging war against Putin, pitting his heroic country (but crucially not himself) as the protagonist, taking on the monster that was the Russian bear.

During the Covid-19 pandemic, as scientists raced to produce a vaccine and as NHS workers fought an invisible beast, other legends were forged and British people, like others across the world began "clapping for carers" to show their gratitude. The attention was not entirely welcome. Writing anonymously in the *Guardian*, one doctor said:

"I really don't need… people clapping. I don't need rainbows. I don't care if people clap until their hands bleed with rainbows tattooed on their faces… the NHS is not a charity and it is not staffed by heroes."

Doctors and nurses, like Zelenskyy and Wesley Autrey, had not actively chosen the glory of *kleos*; rather they had been obliged to behave heroically by circumstances put in their path – and this is critical to everything that follows. The "Autrey Factor" is ultimately, an "innate heroism" and that's very different to societal heroes,* like Achilles, Nelson, Washington, Che Guevara, Captain Scott and even Mao Zedong, who all deliberately chose the heroic path.

Questioning societal heroes can be a risky business tantamount to a kind of heresy because wherever you live you will undoubtedly have been conditioned to believe in the great figures of your nation's history. It can be deeply discomforting and disconcerting to be told that there is another side to the story; one in which that great person did not so great or even terrible things. There is always a very fine line indeed between heroism and villainy and the old cliché that "one person's terrorist is another's freedom fighter" can be applied to many a historical and fictional figure. For many in the West, Mikhail Gorbachev remains a celebrated figure who helped end the Cold War, but in Russia

* Societal heroes are those who have been appointed by historians, politicians, society and tradition as our collective icons.

he is broadly detested for his role in breaking up the USSR and helping spark the chaos that followed.

The same is the case with the Elizabethan English sailor and "explorer", Sir Francis Drake. Known to the Spanish as El Draque (the Dragon), the local, English version of his legend sees him defeating the Armada in 1588, between discovering the potato and circumnavigating the globe. Millions in Britain and across the old Commonwealth grew up with his *kleos* and Drake's reputation, as defender of the nation, is such that he is even the source of a curious supernatural "local hero" legend where his snare drum, housed at Buckland Abbey, is said to beat whenever England is threatened. The sound of the drum is said to be a reminder that he is still protecting the nation from beyond the grave, and the last time it is claimed to have happened was in May 1940, during the evacuation at Dunkirk.

Drake's buccaneering myth is a corker, but the actual details of his life paint a complex and far less flattering picture of the man. While he did indeed circle the Earth between 1577 and 1580, it was not because he had a lust for exploration. His intent was to make himself rich and famous and to that end, he robbed practically everyone he met along the way. He wasn't the first sailor to circumnavigate the Earth either, as Magellan had completed that journey in 1519, 21 years before he was born. While it is true that Drake helped see off the Armada, Lord Howard was the Admiral in charge of the fleet on the day and really, the victory was his. Yes, Drake brought tobacco and potatoes to Europe, but the Spanish had been there, seen it and *patatas bravased* it a full decade earlier.

As for being a "privateer", well that is just a polite way of saying that he was a pirate.

In a 2013 BBC TV series *Britain at Sea*, the broadcaster David Dimbleby told the story of how he had once been involved in a scheme to take Sir France Drake's lead-lined coffin, from its final resting place off the coast of Panama, and bring it back in "great glory" on a Royal Navy ship to be buried at St Paul's Cathedral. But there was a problem:

"There was one group you might have thought would be enthusiastic for it who were completely opposed – the Royal Navy – and why... well, I think it was because, though he is a national hero, Drake was a pirate."

Like all mobsters, brutality and murder were part of his job description and he used it not only against the people he robbed, but also his own companions. While sailing around the world on his ship, the *Pelican,* Drake's brother, Thomas, was caught stealing captured cargo by an aristocratic rival, Thomas Doughty. Fearing a mutiny, Sir Francis brought jumped-up charges of treason and witchcraft against Doughty and he was beheaded on 2nd July 1578. Subsequently, Drake changed the name of his flagship from the *Pelican* to the *Golden Hind* largely to placate the expedition's sponsor, Christopher Hatton, a close friend of Doughty, whose family crest featured a golden deer (or hind).

My childhood history book of Drake made no mention of Doughty's fate any more than my 1978 copy of children's history magazine *Look and Learn* explored the massacre on Rathlin Island off the coast of Ireland on 26th July 1575. At that atrocity, Drake, along with the Earl of Essex and Sir John Norreys, forced their way into a castle being used as a sanctuary by the MacDonnells of Antrim while resisting Queen Elizabeth's attempts to subjugate the local rulers and then butchered 600 people including women and children. Some hero – huh.

When not engaged in piracy and infanticide, Drake helped enslave 1,000 Africans and kill 3,000 more. Early in his career, between 1562 and 1569, he sailed, with his cousin John Hawkins on voyages that established the Triangular Trade (the transatlantic slave trade operating between Africa, Europe and the Americas) and deprived African people of their liberty and lives in a brutal and dehumanising crime against humanity, which nonetheless made Drake rich. During his life, Drake and his deeds were well-known. He was a controversial figure in England and that was in no small part down to his efforts to promote himself as a politician, serving as Mayor of Plymouth and a Member of Parliament three times. But his legend largely persists thanks to the Victorians who turned him into a paragon of English derring-do and a sort of patron saint of Empire. Throughout the nineteenth century, in bestselling books like Froude's *History of England* and Charles Kingsley's 1855 novel *Westward Ho!,* Drake was retrospectively cast as the central male protagonist of the Elizabethan era. And that is why so many of us were brought up believing that he was a great hero.

Westward Ho! was particularly guilty of forging the myth with the once-radical author using his fictionalised account of Drake to underscore his belief that Anglican English values trumped those of the Spanish, that the Empire was the nation's destiny and that we had Drake to thank for making it all possible by defeating the Catholic Armada.

Societal heroes like Drake do not happen by chance. They do not, like Wesley Autrey, spring from nowhere. They are, more frequently than not, carefully selected and their place in the national psyche involves a lot of conniving, self-promotion and mythologising along the way. The real-life Drake was a greedy, back-stabbing, murderous, slave-trading pirate – but his *kleos* is so embedded in England's greater myth that to suggest as much is to take a sledge hammer to our island story.

When the Sir Francis Drake primary school in Lewisham, southeast London decided to change its name to Twin Oaks in January 2023, there was uproar, among the self-appointed guardians of Britain's past. At least one Conservative MP, Alexander Stafford, tweeted:

"Absolute madness. Drake literally saved England from invasion by the Spanish Armada. One of England's finest heroes and one of the reasons we remain speaking English rather than Spanish. When will this cultural vandalism end?"

The Tory peer Lord Frost added: "This is a very bad sign of our cultural decay & of disrespect for our history."

And the historian, Professor David Abulafia, part of an influential Conservative pressure group called "History Reclaimed" told the *Daily Mail*: *"Blotting out names is blotting out the past in all its shades."*

It was nonsense. The school was not "erasing history" but examining and assessing it. To that end, it had revisited the true events of Drake's life, held a thorough consultation with the local community and discussed the proposed name change and reason behind it. In a ballot, 88% of the 450 staff, pupils and locals affected had then voted for the change and in the process, everyone had learned more about Drake than they ever would have done so by walking past his name on a sign outside the school. In renaming the primary school, the teachers and governors were not "cancelling Drake", they were teaching history.

The study of the past and our appreciation of it should never be reduced to the status of an elaborate fan club for the "big names" from it – but all too often it is. In the process, people who were not really very heroic indeed have been lifted up to the status of icons and even gods. These are the people that I have dubbed *Fake Heroes*. That is not to say that all who follow were necessarily terrible human beings. Some sought *kleos*; others were granted it almost by accident; others still, were raised up posthumously by people who sought to ride on the coattails of their legends, for the promotion of their own.

As we undertake the journey, we shall find that many of the "great people who did great things" really did nothing of the sort. Along the way we will discover others, who have been edited out of the narrative, or neglected by it and who are probably more deserving of the heroic epithet than those that stand in their place.

But what became of Wesley Autrey?

Well – 2007, his year of glory, ended with him being shortlisted *Time* "Person of the Year" with his entry (at 48) penned by none other than Donald Trump. Wesley missed out on the top spot that year to a statesman who was ranked first by dint of his "extraordinary feat of leadership" that had taken his country from chaos back to "the table of world power".

His name was Vladimir Putin.

CHAPTER ONE

WAR HEROES
DOUGLAS BADER

Propaganda and the Hero

On 22nd March 1895, two brothers, August and Louis Lumière, demonstrated their invention, *Cinématographe*, to a small gathering at the Société d'Encouragement pour l'Industrie Nationale* in Paris and unwittingly set in motion a chain of events that would change the world.

A year earlier their father, Antoine, had witnessed an exhibition of Thomas Edison's Kinetoscope, a mechanical peephole which, by the turn of a handle, allowed viewers to watch moving pictures. Recognising that more profit could be made if one film was shown to a single, larger paying audience he returned home to Lyon and challenged his sons to find a solution. The result was the *Cinématographe*, a lightweight machine that could both film and project moving images.

Workers Leaving the Lumière Factory, which much like *Snakes on a Plane* (2006) had all the spoilers in its title, was the result and the film shown at that demonstration in Paris in 1895. In December the same year it featured, with nine other 50-second reels, at the first ever public film show at the Grand Café du Paris. That program did not include their most famous work, *Train Pulling into a Station*, which premiered

---

* Society for the Development of National Industry.

the following January. Once again, the short does what it says on the tin. A train arrives at a station, people get off, others get on – the end. But, there is more to it than that – for this 50-second sequence has an artistry that is lacking in the earlier films. As the train comes to a stop and the hustle and bustle of the passengers ensues, we are not just watching "moving pictures" but something recognisably "cinematic".

Legend has it that the first audience fled in terror as the train shot towards them. The event is recreated in *Bram Stoker's Dracula* (1992) and *Hugo* (2011) and appears in many standard texts on cinema, including Mark Cousins' 2004 book *The Story of Film*.

In her 1973 biography of director F. W. Murnau, the academic Lotte Eisner explains: "The spectators in the Grand Café involuntarily threw themselves back in their seats in fright, because Lumière's giant locomotive pulling into the station seemingly ran toward them."

But in 2004 German academic Martin Loiperdinger thoroughly debunked the story and the consensus nowadays is that it is no more than a cinematic foundation myth.

The story persisted because it sounds credible. Millions of us have hidden our eyes behind our hands on visits to the cinema or leapt out in terror at jump scares in horror films. So, it's feasible to believe that people seeing a train heading towards them on a massive screen for the first time, might have been tempted to run for the doors.

Often cited as the first "documentary", the 50 seconds of footage was actually a fix. The Lumières made two previous versions, before getting it right in that third take, and luck played no part in the result. Though the film appears to have been shot spontaneously, many of the "passengers" on La Ciotat station are not hapless passers-by but friends of the filmmakers moving under the direction of Louis Lumière. By their 11th film, the brothers had already worked out an important aspect of the film craft: to make something look convincingly real, you must fake it.

History's first documentary film was in fact, scripted reality.

The curse of innovators is always to be bettered by those who follow, and soon other early film-makers were making much more innovative and interesting work. The Lumières viewed their invention as little more than a novelty, but others saw its immense possibilities. The French theatre director and illusionist Georges Méliès had witnessed that December 1895 demonstration in the Grand Café and soon after tried to buy one of their machines off them. When they refused, Méliès commissioned a copycat device from an English inventor and began making films of his own. They included the first science-fiction film ever made: *A Trip to the Moon* (1902), a triumph of special effects and political satire which went on to become a worldwide global hit.

The Lumières quit the business in 1905 to concentrate on the development of colour film. Both went on to live long lives and in later life were feted for pioneering cinema. Although – in truth – they had done so much more than that.

One of the unintended consequences of the early movie industry was the invention of modern celebrity. In film's infancy in Hollywood, actors had no billing and were known by their looks, with Mary Pickford dubbed "the girl with the golden curls" and Florence Lawrence "the Biograph girl". The reasoning was simple. Some serious actors deemed film-making beneath them and didn't want their names associated with it; at the same time studio bosses feared that if the talent became famous, they might want more money.

But audiences clamoured to learn the names of their favourite actors and eventually the film-makers relented. By the mid-1920s, an estimated 50 million Americans were going to the pictures every week, and many a star was born. Some were elevated to the very heights of Gods.

When the matinee idol Rudolph Valentino collapsed and died, aged 31, in 1926, it was as if Heracles himself had perished and overwrought acts of public mourning ensued. Tens of thousands of people descended on the Frank E. Campbell Funeral home on Madison Avenue in New York to see his body, and mounted police had to disperse the crowd. Sensational news reports heightened the hysteria and at least one woman, Peggy Scott, a 27-year-old British actress, was said to have taken her life on hearing of the actor's death. Scott claimed to have been having an affair with Valentino, but they probably never met, and the testimony of friends suggests she was struggling with a significant mental health episode when she died. Either way, accounts of her suicide poured further fuel onto the raging pyre and Valentino's funeral on 30th August 1926 turned into a frenzy.

A British Pathé newsreel of the day shows massive crowds and even greater melodrama. At the centre of it all is Valentino's bereaved fiancée, the actress Pola Negri.* Dressed in widow's weeds, she is guided unsteadily to a waiting car, clutching a handkerchief, and then whisked to St. Malachy's Actor's Chapel past vast crowds.

Film cameras were not allowed inside the church, so sadly we miss the bit where Negri, whose, once stellar career had hit the skids, "fainted" dramatically three times in front of the assembled throng of movie producers and casting directors. Although fortunately, for posterity, a photo was taken of her prostrating herself dementedly over the coffin, beneath a giant floral tribute that read "POLA" in lettering two metres high.

Her histrionics set off the mourners outside who burst into the church, as Pola wailed: "My love for Valentino was the greatest love of my life. I loved him not as one artist loves another, but as a woman loves a man."

She was married to someone else within the year.

Valentino's final resting place at the Hollywood Forever Cemetery quickly became a shrine and on the first anniversary of his death, a mysterious woman, dressed in a heavy black veil appeared and laid a single red rose. The flower bearer was later revealed to be a studio plant, hired to promote re-releases of Valentino's films, but in the years that followed, another woman, Ditra Flame, took up the mantle and carried on the tradition until she was crowded out by a veritable army of copycat "ladies in black" in the 1950s.

In all the theatrics, few were mourning Rodolfo Pietro di Valentina d'Antonguolla, the Italian-born agricultural student, odd-job man and gigolo who had, almost by chance become an actor. The crowds on the

---

* There is some doubt as to whether Negri and Valentino were actually engaged; the only evidence for it was Negri's not-always-convincing word.

streets, Pola Negri, Ditra Flame, and her imitators had turned out for the *Sheikh** – the "Latin lover" onto whom they had projected all their longing and desire – a man who, was little more than a fantasy, but who, through the power of cinema, had been turned into a latter-day God.

The unique ability of cinema to "make us believe" that what we are watching on the screen is real has long been a source of academic study. In his 1916 book *The Photoplay: A Psychological Study* the German-born American psychologist Hugo Münsterberg noted that when we watch movies, we become more than mere passive observers.

"More than in the drama, the persons in (a film) are to us, subjects of emotional experiences. Their joy and pain, their hope and fear, their love and hate, their gratitude and envy, their sympathy and malice, give meaning and value to the play."

One hundred years later, in 2016, the Mexican film director, Alejandro González Iñárritu put it more succinctly: "Cinema is a mirror, by which we often see ourselves. That's the role we play as filmmakers. If that power is not transmitted on the screens, there's something wrong".

In its use of close-ups, montage and points of view, film comes closer than any other visual medium to replicating human experience and even putting us inside the heads of other people. It mimics life and the experience of it. We have all felt fear, loss, greed, betrayal and envy and through its intimacy, film allows us to relive these emotions in the lives of others. When we watch movies and see those same arcs play out, we are in a sense watching imitations of our own experiences.

But something else might be at play.

In 2008, Tamar Gendler, a professor of psychology at Yale University, coined the term *alief* to describe the cognitive dissonance we experience when we know something is false but at the same time, believe it to be true. Gendler's examples included people being repulsed by plastic poo, despite knowing it to be fake, or fearing they might fall through a glass floor while knowing full well that it is reinforced. *Aliefs* are

---

* His most famous role.

automatic, inherent, belief-like attitudes which defy rational logic. Even if we tell ourselves that it is perfectly safe to walk across that glass-bottomed viewing platform thousands of metres above the Grand Canyon, our palms might sweat as we grip the handrail ever more tightly.

Alief could explain why sad movies make us cry and why *Jaws* (1975) made millions of people too scared to go into the sea, even off the coast of Margate, in fear of being eaten by a great white shark. When we watch *Jaws,* we know "it's just a film". We are aware that the monster is a prop, but all the same – *alief* makes us buy into it.

Gendler's work is controversial, and some critics have wondered why we need a new word to describe what are in essence hard-wired human responses. In 2010, the *Guardian* columnist Oliver Burkeman came to her defence arguing: "She's not concerned with causes... but with capturing the state of mind involved. 'Alief' allows for another possibility: that you can be absolutely, rationally convinced of something, yet also *alieve* – and thus behave – quite differently."

Alief could be another contributing factor to the widespread cognitive dissonance that followed the death of Rudolph Valentino in 1926. Mourners knew he was "just an actor" but they *alieved* him to be the *Sheikh*. It might also help explain why film can be such an effective propaganda tool.

In the early 1900s, the British film-makers Sagar Mitchell and James Kenyon, working in Blackburn, Lancashire, made a series of early "war films", including *The Despatch Bearer* (1901), which they claimed was based on a real incident in the ongoing conflict between South African Boers and the British Empire. In the film, a backstabbing pantomime-esque Boer kills a British soldier before having his comeuppance. This and other films of the time were a sensation and Mitchell and Kenyon augmented the on-screen action with "effects" which included actual gunfire and smoke.

Watching it now, it's hard to believe that anyone could have fallen for such ludicrous slapstick propaganda, but as the Boers continued to give the mighty Empire a lesson in hubris in 1901, emotions were running high and perhaps people needed a lift. The British Army had lost at least 22,000 men, mostly from disease, in a war that was supposed to have lasted just a few months. With British atrocities perpetrated on the civilian population leaking out into the press, people back home needed a cinematic dose of reassurance that they were on the right side and the Despatch Bearer delivered it.

On 4th August 1914, with Germany having breached Belgian neutrality and then failed to respond to a British ultimatum to remove their troops, the United Kingdom and her Empire declared war on the German Empire and in the ensuing bloodbath, cinematic propaganda came of age. A 1916 "documentary", *The Battle of the Somme*, which did more than anything at the time to shape perspectives, is generally considered to be the first masterpiece of the form. The actual Battle of the Somme, which had begun on 1st July that year, failed in almost all its objectives. The British suffered 57,470 casualties and 19,240 dead on the first day alone and the Big Push was in fact a Massive Flop. But the heavily edited version of events, presented in the film, told a more upbeat story, and an estimated 20 million Britons went to see the "documentary" in the first six weeks alone.

The film seemed to be telling audiences "the truth". It did not shirk from the blood, the toil, the mud, the death and the violence but crucially, it ended on an uplifting note that gave the strong impression that the war was being won. But this was altered reality once more and like the *Train Pulling into a Station*, the filmmakers had fiddled with the truth.

What audiences were seeing was not "the war" but a cleverly edited and heavily biased version of it made by War Office filmmakers. The raw footage was shot by Geoffrey Malins and John McDowell, embedded with the 29th and 7th Divisions respectively, but it was intercut with staged re-enactments that were passed off as the real thing. Scenes, including a famous sequence of men running across No Man's Land had actually been shot at a training ground, miles behind British lines.

Audiences believed what they saw and still do. The footage endured long after 1918 and scenes from *The Battle of the Somme* – including that "advance" – are still regularly used in documentary films today. As such the film is one of the most effective and enduring pieces of propaganda in cinematic history as it is still informing our vision of the First World War more than 100 years after it ended.

Britain was not the only country to harness the power of cinematic propaganda.

Throughout the Russian Civil War (1917–1923), Lenin sent *agitation trains* across the countryside, disseminating heavily biased newsreels and short pro-Bolshevik films, influencing the minds of hundreds of thousands of peasants in the process. The USSR went on to make cinema a powerful instrument of the communist state. From the mid-1920s, directors like Sergei Eisenstein turned out visually stunning and emotive films like *Battleship Potemkin* (1925) while the likes of the editor and film-maker Esfir Shub, made "documentaries" including *The Fall of the Romanov Dynasty* (1927) which forged a party-friendly version of Russia's recent history.

In Germany, Adolf Hitler and Joseph Goebbels, both admirers of British propaganda, used the medium to promote their fascist ideology following their rise to power in 1933. Some of those films and most famously, Leni Riefenstahl's Nazi documentaries, including *Triumph of the Will* (1935) and *Olympia* (1938), were hugely effective in giving the impression of Nazi indomitability. They were also – somewhat depressingly – highly acclaimed beyond Germany. *Triumph of the Will*, which showed Hitler as the central hero protagonist amidst the spectacle of fascism in a sort of Nazi wet dream, caused a sensation farther afield than Germany, winning a gold medal at the 1935 Venice Biennale in fascist Italy and praise from critics as far away as America. The US film director Frank Capra, himself a maker of propaganda films, later claimed that while *Triumph of the Will*: "Fired no gun (and) dropped no bombs… as a psychological weapon aimed at destroying the will to resist, it was just as lethal."

Other, less sophisticated, work, aimed squarely at domestic audiences, included a fake documentary *The Eternal Jew* (1940), which set up the dehumanisation of millions of people for the Holocaust that followed.

Goebbels realised that the medium could not simply be used to bludgeon the population into believing in the cause and recognised the need for state-backed movies to thrill and entertain as well. So, throughout the Third Reich reign of terror, the Nazis churned out hundreds of films in multiple genres. The state-funded lavish musicals, pratfall comedies, operettas, historical dramas, escapist romances and dozens of war movies featuring heroic German soldiers taking on the enemy. The last included *Kampfgeschwader Lützow* (Battle Squadron Lützow) made in 1941, which told the story of a daring bomber squadron during the invasion of Poland, and *Stukas* made the same year, which features multiple storylines including that of a fighter pilot, suffering from post-traumatic stress (PTSD) following a crash, who overcomes his fears and wounds to fly again.

In all these films there are more than passing resemblances to the Allied equivalents, the difference being that the films made in Britain in the era are still regularly shown on TV today. A particularly resonant example is 1942's *Went the Day Well?* in which a typical English village is invaded by German soldiers, disguised as British troops, who are unmasked and subsequently defeated by local people.

The best propaganda flatters us, plays to our prejudices and turns the other side into a bogeyman. *Went the Day Well?* does all the above, suggesting that stiff-upper-lipped English country folks with a ready sense of humour are every bit the match for Nazi paratroopers, and that given the chance, matronly housewives can turn into heroes.

In many films of the time, including *Pimpernel Smith* (1941), *One of Our Aircraft is Missing* (1942) and the spy film *Bulldog Sees It Through* (1940), this theme was key, with plucky, urbane, amateurish Brits outwitting dastardly humourless Germans. Some were funded partly or wholly by the Ministry of Information, the government department with responsibility for propaganda. Others were unofficial, freelance agitprop* made to fit the populist, patriotic mood of

---

* A portmanteau of the Russian words *agitatsiya* and *propaganda* (agitation propaganda), from the name of a department of the Communist Party of the Soviet Union.

the time. In war, unifying myths are critical, and given that the Nazi regime was systematically murdering its own people, the country and it's leaderships were already behaving monstrously and the British were understandably and sensibly cast in the role of a latent St George.

To veer from the narrative of cheerful, wise-cracking, indomitable Brits fighting evil Nazis was to invite trouble. When word reached PM Winston Churchill, in 1943, that the director and writer team Michael Powell and Emeric Pressburger were making a film called *The Life and Death of Colonel Blimp*, based on the wartime cartoons of David Low, which satirised stuffy old-fashioned Britishness and, worse, that Austrian émigré actor Anton Walbrook featured as a "sympathetic German", he set out to stop to it. He wrote to Brendan Bracken, his Minister of Information, asking him to: "propose to me the measures necessary to stop this foolish production before it gets any further".

Under pressure, Powell and Pressburger showed a rough cut to censors and the film got the green light. When the movie was shown in 1943, a tag line invited audiences to "come and see the banned film", demonstrating that even in war, PR people see an angle.

The Second World War formally ended on 2nd September 1945, but the makers of war films in Britain and America were only just warming up. In the last four years of the 1940s, US and UK studios produced around 30 wartime-set films and in the next decade the genre became even bigger box office business. In the 1950s, as the immediate pain of the conflict gave way to a sort of nostalgic trium-phalism, British studios alone put out over 50 war movies. Some were fictitious, but many were based on events already familiar to audiences thanks to propaganda efforts by the Ministry of Informa-tion in the war years. That work fed the film industry for decades to come and through constant repeats on post-war television, became central to the retrospective narrative of the Second World War.

There was considerable bleed between truth and fiction. Since these films tended to show the military establishment in a good light, they were welcomed by it and regimental bands even adopted the music. The themes to *The Bridge on the River Kwai* ("Colonel Bogey March") and *The Great Escape* remain part of the repertoire of the Coldstream Guards Band. Attend any military parade featuring the Central Band of the RAF and you will hear the theme tune to *The Battle of Britain, The Dam Busters, 633 Squadron* or *Reach for the Sky*.

While claiming to recreate "real-life" events, most of these post-war films took considerable artistic licence and often left important details and people out.

In 1950, the director Jack Lee began casting a film version of the bestselling book *The Wooden Horse*. The script told the story of a real escape by British prisoners of war (POWs) from Stalag Luft III in 1943, the same camp from which the more famous "Great Escape" took place the following year. In that first breakout, POWs used a hollow gymnastic vaulting horse as cover for digging a tunnel and, under the guise of "exercise", smuggled three men back home to the UK.

While casting the film, Lee auditioned the actor Peter Butterworth, later famous for his roles in many of the *Carry On* series of comedy films for the part of a British detainee. As Butterworth later reminisced and as the National Archives attest, he was turned down for the role on account of being "too fat" and "not convincingly heroic". And that, despite Butterworth having been an actual POW at Stalag Luft III in 1943, who had been involved in the planning of the escape and one of the decoys on the day.

The Dam Busters (1955) is now almost as famous for the racist name of the mission leader's dog as it is for the exploits of Wing Commander Guy Gibson and his men. The film tells the true story of a bombing raid, codenamed Operation Chastise, which took place on the night of the 16th and 17th May 1943, when 19 Lancaster bombers breached two dams and knocked out a power station in the German Röhr using innovative "bouncing bombs" designed by the inventor Barnes Wallis. But in doing so, an awful lot of inconvenient facts ended up on the cutting room floor. For a start, the daring mission was nowhere near as effective as the movie makes out.

The historians Charles Webster and Noble Frankland, whose official four-volume history of the Strategic Air Offensive came out in 1961, were certainly not convinced, believing that the RAF massively overstated the success of the attack and that its impact was short-lived. Using slave labour and putting every available hand to the task, the Germans repaired the dams and had them operational again in just five months; the hydroelectric power station at Herdecke was up and working again in weeks.

In 1972, documents relating to the event were declassified and the journalist Bruce Page wrote: "The truth about the Dams Raid is that it was a conjuring trick, virtually devoid of military significance... The story of the raid is one of sloppy planning, narrow-minded enthusiasm and misdirected courage..."

The attack had undeniably caused the Germans a huge headache, but it was at the end of the day a costly propaganda stunt, which cost the lives of 53 RAF crew. There were other victims too, for as 330 million tonnes of water gushed into the valleys below, some 1,600 people including 1,000 slave labourers were drowned.

Such uncomfortable details of course did not make their way into triumphalist 1950s films – not least because British people had other concerns. Wartime rationing ended only in 1954, one year before *The Dam Busters* was released, and many British cities were still pock-marked with bombsites. Unemployment may have been at an historic low and there were new opportunities of education, employment and even housing – in the shape of the new towns that were popping up everywhere in the Southeast – but Britain was a different country to the superpower of 1939. India and Pakistan had gained their independence in 1947 and other former colonies were following suit. In losing its Empire, the nation had begun to decline as a global player and was starting to lose a sense of who it was and what it was about. Films, which shone a brighter light on the country and its recent victory over the Nazis, made people feel good about themselves. *The Dam Busters* epitomised the wartime fiction of British spirit, and audiences were only too willing to believe.

In a classic example of *aliefery*, that merger in minds between film and reality conflated fictional portrayals with the actual events. Richard Todd* became entwined with the real-life Guy Gibson who he portrayed in *The Dam Busters* and, in another even more famous example, the actor Kenneth More became a sort of *doppelgänger to* the legendary fighter pilot Group Captain Douglas Bader.

Practically everyone who grew up in post-war Britain knew the story of Douglas Bader. The 1956 film of his exploits, *Reach for the Sky*, based on the book of the same name and directed by Lewis Gilbert, did much to cement his legend and was regularly broadcast on TV screens following its first showing in September 1965. *Reach for the Sky* is unusual among post-1945 war films, in that it is the story of one man – and More's portrayal of Bader was to fuse the two men, almost as one in the national psyche.

If you were born after 1980 or did not grow up in the UK, you might be unfamiliar with it – so the story, as told in *Reach for the Sky*, goes like this:

We first meet Bader on his motorbike, shooting through the English countryside on his way to join the RAF in the late 1920s. As a plane swoops overhead, Bader crashes, dusts himself down and arrives at the barracks with a hole in his bowler hat. Much to the mirth of fellow trainee pilots and much to the rage of the company Sergeant Major, the top of his damaged hat keeps flipping up while he is on parade.

He loves RAF life and the camaraderie and there are japes galore, including the time he and his chums loosen a policeman's bicycle wheels,

---

* Richard Todd served in the Parachute Regiment in the Second World War and parachuted into France on 6th June 1944. During the battle to capture Pegasus Bridge near Caen, he met Major John Howard and fought Wehrmacht troops. In 1962 Todd would portray Howard in the D-Day film *The Longest Day*.

after he has had the temerity to tell them off. But, in 1931, disaster strikes when Bader crashes a plane at Woodley Aerodrome, near Reading, while showing off a few feet above a runway. He survives but loses both legs; one just above and the other just below the knee. Told he won't walk again, he proves the experts wrong through sheer bloody-mindedness and takes up golf while romancing his sweetheart, Thelma.

The RAF has no need for a legless pilot, so he goes to work for the Shell Oil company instead but six years later, when war breaks out, he seeks to re-enlist. The recruiting officer meets him with the line: "You're wasting your time, I'm afraid, sir, they'll never let you fly."

Bader won't take no for an answer, proves he can fly and ends up commanding group of battle-hardened Canadians, winning their hearts with an aerial display.

One day – off the top of his head – Bader suggests a new tactic ("Big Wing") to his commander Air Vice-Marshal Trafford Leigh-Mallory in which three squadrons get put in the air at once rather than one, and his idea is quickly put to work by the Duxford Wing under his command. Along the way, as with any good monomyth, there are mentors and teachers, thresholds crossed and even miracles. There is also a rebirth when, instead of killing the Luftwaffe monster, the monster nearly kills him.

On 9th August 1941, a year after the Battle of Britain, Bader's Spitfire is hit over Saint-Omer in North-West France. With one prosthetic leg trapped in the cockpit and his plane hurtling towards the ground, he unclips it and bails out, floating down by parachute before getting captured.

Reunited with both legs, and while still convalescing in Saint-Omer, Bader contacts the Resistance and escapes. He is quickly recaptured, while his French hosts are carted off for questioning, but the tenacious Bader doesn't give up there. Eventually his hosts lose patience and tell him that he is going to be moved to a more "comfortable" camp. Bader refuses but when told by his friend Harry Day that: "You've given them a lot of headaches and we're all on your side… but it only needs a spark to start an incident…" he relents and is sent to Oflag IV-C aka Colditz

Castle, waved off by his cheering comrades. In the spring of 1945, he is liberated but instead of celebrating he seeks immediately to get his hands on a Spitfire. He returns home to Thelma and tells her of his plans to head East to fight the Japanese but much to her relief, VJ Day catches up with him and the war ends.

And so too does the film.

But, of course, Bader's real-life narrative carried on. He was already a well-known figure when the film came out in 1956, and *Reach for the Sky* made him one of the country's most famous war heroes. Despite Bader being wary of the film and not watching it for years, it was a critical and commercial success, winning the 1956 BAFTA for Best Film. Rank, the film's distributor, released it in the USA too but pitted against the big-screen colour movies of the time, including *The King and I*, *The Man Who Knew Too Much* and *The Ten Commandments*, this two-hour black and white picture about a legless British fighter pilot failed to make its mark.

Throughout the 1960s and 1970s, Bader remained a celebrity in the UK and in Commonwealth countries like Australia, South Africa and New Zealand. And as perhaps Britain's most famous disabled person, he also campaigned hard on behalf of others. A few months before his death in 1982, he was surprised by TV host Eamonn Andrews at a charitable event in London's Haymarket for an edition of the ego-massaging biographical show *This is Your Life!* The programme was a staple of the schedules at the time, and it consisted of the surprised guests hearing flattering versions of their life stories, before getting handed the big red book that was, in effect, the show's script. Bader's special guests that night included former comrades from "Dogsbody Section", his fighting unit, an old adversary in the shape of General Adolf Galland of the Luftwaffe, and even Madame Hiecque and Lucille Debacker, the two French women who had tried to help him escape in 1941.

In the preamble to the programme, Andrews describes Bader as: "a living legend, one of the greatest romantic real-life heroes of our time or any time."

And though since his death, the Bader myth has faded, he remains perhaps the best-known hero of that increasingly sacred event called the "Battle of Britain". That Bader's reputation continues to linger is thanks in no small part to the film that cemented his legend and Kenneth More's hugely sympathetic portrayal of him.

In S .P. Mackenzie's *Bader's War* (2008), the author relates a story where the Chairman of the British Limbless Ex-Servicemen's Association introduces Bader mischievously with: "Some of you may remember him as the man who played the part of Kenneth More in the film *Reach For The Sky.*"*

Bader was not comfortable with the association, often telling interviewers variations on the theme of: "Everyone thinks I'm that nice chap Kenny More but I'm not."

But it undoubtedly sealed his legend. Forty years after his death he is still regularly name-checked in podcasts and the pages of the *Daily Mail*. In July 2016, in an interview with *BBC History Magazine*, the then Prime Minister David Cameron named Bader his "greatest hero of all time" and the myth proliferates in shrines and memorials.

His name is enshrined in streets and there are statues too including a bronze one, unveiled by his second wife Joan Bader at Goodwood Aerodrome in 2001. The Douglas Bader Walking school, Bader's Bus Company (a disabled aerial display team) and the Bader Academy, a special school in Doncaster, all keep his name alive, and there are even drinking holes in his honour.

On the site of what was once RAF Martlesham, just off the A12 in Suffolk, sits the Douglas Bader pub, with its ribbon cut by the man himself in 1979. Another local, The Bader Arms, used to stand in Tangmere, West Sussex, and was opened by Bader in 1982. A local legend tells that when asked by a reporter what he thought of the name, Bader is said to have replied: "They could hardly have called it the Bader fucking legs, could they."

---

* Mackenzie, S.P., *Bader's War*, 2008, p165.

The story is typical of Bader and his propensity for swearing. Another, undoubtedly apocryphal, tale has him giving a talk at a girl's school about dogfights: "There were fuckers to the left of us, fuckers to the right of us and fuckers coming out of the Sun!" – until the headmistress interjects to explain that "a Fokker was a German aircraft type of the Second World War, girls!"

"That as may be", replies Bader, "but these fuckers were Messerschmitts".

It is one of the many paradoxes of his life that teetotal Bader should have two pubs named after him, but then he and his legacy are complicated. Wartime propaganda and the subsequent portrayal of his life has left his truth ever more in a tug-of-war with his fictional alter ego. The uncomfortable fact is that a man held up as Britain's greatest war hero was not much of a hero at all. Or at least, not one in the way we remember him.

* * *

It's a blistering hot day in July 2022 and my teenage son and I are driving to the Imperial War Museum at Duxford.

I have set out with an iconoclastic spirit, but almost as soon as we enter the premises a weird transformation takes place and suddenly, I'm Alan Partridge, pointing excitedly at military hardware. For many boys of my age growing up in the 1970s, the Second World War was a big deal. War was everywhere – in our toys and games and across our weekend TV viewing and we all knew who Bader was. This might explain why I am but one of many men, of about my age, wandering about Duxford with children in tow.

The constant *putt, putt, putt* of vintage planes taxiing fuels the atmosphere.

You can ride in a Spitfire at Duxford for £2,950 which is beyond the day's budget, so we opt for the "Spitfire simulator" at a far more affordable £4 instead.

A mum and three young kids hop in and soon we are sliding left and right on a little plastic seat as we "experience" the Battle of Britain from the perspective of a Messerschmitt pilot over the White Cliffs of Dover in 1940. The experience, it must be said, lacks the inherent drama of being in a dogfight at a thousand feet – but at £4 each who has a right to complain? It is all too much for one of our younger pilots and everything shudders to a halt as he presses the emergency stop button and demands to get taken to the loo.

The kindly attendant tells us we can have another go and we are joined by a fellow dad and his sons, who he is chivvying along "to shoot down some Germans." As a battle-hardened veteran of the simulator, I explain, that we are in fact Luftwaffe pilots and a great big smile breaks across his face as he barks:

"You hear zat kidzzz?? Vee are zee Germanz!!!"

Four minutes pass and we emerge into the summer heat, with the commentary telling us that the Battle of Britain pilots had "prevented the invasion of Britain". "That was fun!" says the other dad and I concur that it was. But as we return to the car past the machinery of death and the gift shop selling "Dam Raider" gin, an uneasiness descends. It has been a great day out, but what have we learned?

Duxford has thousands of exhibits and atmosphere galore, but among all the gleaming planes and glass cases there is very little to remind us that we are in the presence of machines designed to kill people. With all the rides and interactive displays, it feels more entertainment than museum – and it's almost as if we have had a day out at the Disneyland of War.

Duxford was well known to Bader. He was posted there to Number 19 squadron in February 1940, and it was here that he first flew a Supermarine Spitfire.

In the pre-war years, Fighter Command had divvied up the UK into different regions and this airbase was the southernmost base for 12 Group which was responsible for defending a huge swathe of airspace from North Wales, across Lincolnshire and down as far as the Fens. Right up to the fall of France in 1940, it was believed that the main threat from the Luftwaffe would come from the east, across the North Sea and consist mostly of bombers. Had that been the case, Duxford would have been right in the thick of the fighting. But instead, following Dunkirk, most of the threat came from the Channel and the action fell to 11 Group, further south, with 12 Group job effectively reduced to defending their bases from attack.

That annoyed the hell out of battle-hungry Bader and 12 Group's hugely ambitious Air Vice- Marshal Trafford Leigh-Mallory. Believing they were missing out on the action, they spent a good proportion of the Battle of Britain lobbying their way to relevance and notice. But in a sense, that journey, for Bader at least, had started long before that.

Douglas Bader was born on 21st February 1910, in St John's Wood, London. The second son of Jessie and Frederick Bader, a civil engineer, he had a wretched childhood in the shadow of his brother – on whom his parents doted. His father fought in the First World War in the Royal Engineers and reached the rank of Major, but was seriously wounded in 1917 and died in 1922* when Bader was 12, partly from those wounds. Jessie swiftly remarried a vicar and, finding they could not handle Douglas's excessive energy, the couple sent him off to boarding school where sport became his salvation.

Bader was not academic but at Temple Grove, or St Edward's in Oxford where he went from the age of 13, he gained notoriety for excelling at games. He was a brilliant boxer, an outstanding cricketer and – above all else – a poet of the rugby ball. Following the death of his father, he would often holiday with his aunt Hazel and her husband Cyril who was in the RAF. It was Cyril who introduced the young Bader to aircraft during a 1923 visit and it captivated the boy immediately, but Bader's first love remained competitive games.

* Many biographies and encyclopaedias have Bader Snr dying at the hospital in Saint Omer from which Douglas later escaped. Some claim he is buried there with the story repeated in Bader's *This Is Your Life*. Not true. Major Bader died in Brussels in 1922 and his grave, in a civilian plot, is situated in the Brussels Communal Cemetery close to the monument at Waterloo.

Having signed up, against his mother's wishes, to the RAF in 1928, Bader joined the Air Force and later the Harlequins rugby squads. Just prior to his crash he was anticipating an invitation to join the England team for the 1932 season. Losing your legs would be a tragedy for anyone, but for sports-mad Bader, it was doubly so. So as soon as he was walking again, he began casting about for an alternative recreation, finding it first in golf, and then from 1939 onwards in war. For the best way to understand Bader and his wartime exploits is through the prism of sport. Every account of Bader's activities has him treating combat like a heaven-bound rugby match. He is frustrated not to be in the A-team – Group 11 – and acts like the captain of the squad even when he is not. He is jealous of fellow teammates and all the time he is itching to get the ball and run with it.

Bader saw action over France during the evacuation at Dunkirk – his first kill was a Messerschmitt 109 on 1st June 1940. Others followed, including a Dornier bomber shot down off the coast of Norfolk on 9th July. There were later successes and reckless moments – including the time Bader ran out of ammunition and considered ramming an enemy plane. But for most of the duration of the Battle of Britain, with his section relegated to a secondary role, he was frustrated by the lack of play.

That changed later in 1940, when he became a celebrity. In fact, Douglas Bader was by no means the only contemporary pilot to be afforded that status. RAF pilots were much the boyband members of their day and as Wing Commander Paddy Barthropp DFC AFC told Channel 4 in 2009: "We were like... David Beckhams... being a fighter pilot... was probably the most glamorous job... in any of the three services."

But Bader stood out. As his sister-in-law Jill Lucas put it: "There had never been a person with no legs flying, commanding a squadron, shooting down German aeroplanes."

Talk of the charismatic, legless fighter ace had first reached Alexander Austin, Senior PR officer at Fighter Command, in the early summer of 1940 and following a briefing on 14th July 1940, journalists went out to interview him and his mother. The *Daily Mail* found Mrs Bader who talked up her boy's "sunny disposition" despite his life-changing accident and, shortly afterwards, the *Daily Mirror* dubbed him: "The Greatest Hero of Them All". The moniker stuck and the *Guardian*, *The Times* and the *Daily Telegraph* all ran gushing pieces about this legless superman.

In the middle of the Battle of Britain both sides were talking up their star players. In Germany, dashing *Fliegerasse* (flying aces) like Hans-Ulrich Rudel and Erich Hartmann were also being spun into massive celebrities for propaganda purposes. Both men were movie-star handsome and both, somewhat uncomfortably, continued to be celebrated after the war. Hartmann, with his 352 aerial kills, is still considered to be the most successful and deadly fighter pilot in history. On that journey he won every decoration going and he and Rudel were two of just 27 German soldiers to receive the Diamond to the Knight's Cross, awarded personally by Adolf Hitler. We shall return to Rudel later on.

Bader won gongs too and in September 1940, was awarded the Distinguished Service Order (DSO) by King George VI and promoted to Flight Lieutenant. With his career in the ascendency and afforded a new authority, courtesy of his fame, Bader began searching for more glory by pushing the strategy known as "Big Wing". In fact, the idea was an old one, which the Italian Air Force had been using for shows of aviation force in the 1930s – but mainly for aviation displays. Big Wing involved sending up three to five squadrons at once, each made up of around 12 planes, to take on the enemy. Bader's boss, Air Vice-Marshal Trafford Leigh-Mallory, had been toying with the idea since January and after conversations, both men began lobbying hard for its use. Leigh-Mallory was the younger brother of the mountain climber George, who had heroically perished in 1924 while trying to conquer Everest – and the loss combined with George's posthumous fame seems to have left Trafford with a Himalayan-sized chip on his shoulder. Like Bader he was frustrated by 12 Group's lack of action and was well-connected and hugely ambitious to make things happen.

In September 1940, the Germans changed tactics and went from bombing airfields and radar stations to attacking London and as they did, Leigh-Mallory believed Big Wing's time had come. With Bader's growing renown and the wind in their favour, the two men used their combined influence, and the strategy was adopted. All good news for Bader and Leigh-Mallory but a dreadful tactical error for the RAF and the nation, because Big Wing was a really stupid idea.

The Luftwaffe attacks on London required a rapid response – and the Dowding Interception System, named after Air Chief Marshal Hugh Dowding, who had helped put the world's first air counter-offensive strategy in place, provided that. Via a network of radar, relay systems and command centres, fighter planes could be scrambled quickly and effectively and sent to take on the enemy. The combination of technology and tactics had worked brilliantly in the Battle of Britain and helped given the RAF the upper hand.

By contrast, the massive complexity involved in amassing 60-odd fighter planes of different types and power over Duxford, before flying south to engage the Germans was cumbersome and time-consuming. By the time a Big Wing had formed, the Luftwaffe were often heading for home. The Dowding System had effectively been hobbled by a self-promoting vanity project. When the Big Wing did manage to engage the other side, there was a huge uptick in collisions and friendly fire and they also made bigger targets for the enemy.

None of this was immediately obvious because in all the confusion, everyone thought it was working and pilots massively over-estimated their number of kills. It was later calculated, based on wreckage and equivalent German figures, that the Big Wing pilots had exaggerated their kills by a staggering ratio of around 7:1. In one raid on 15th September 1940, the RAF claimed a whopping 52 kills and 8 "probables" – but Luftwaffe records show that just six planes were lost.

In the fog of war, a gleeful press leapt on the numbers.

"175 Nazi Planes Shot Down! Raiders Chased Back to the Channel!" the *Daily Herald* declared on 19th September 1940, adding: "RAF triumphs in Biggest Air Battles of War!"

It wasn't true, but with London and other cities smouldering under the assault of Luftwaffe bombs, it was the spin the nation needed, and Leigh-Mallory and Bader's careers went from strength to strength. Even as they did, those of the far more competent Air Vice-Marshal Keith Park and Air Chief Marshal Dowding began to wane.

Both men had been outstanding leaders, true heroes of the Battle of Britain – but they had been trumped by the headline-grabbing Big Wing strategy and the personal ambition of Bader and his high-ranking ally. Park was replaced by Leigh-Mallory and Dowding by Sholto Douglas. The official history of the Battle of Britain would later sideline both Dowding and Park even as it exaggerated the success of Leigh-Mallory and the Big Wing strategy pushed by Douglas Bader. For years it was practically gospel that Bader and Leigh-Mallory's tactic had been a decisive factor in the RAF's success story, and wartime propaganda which bled into *Reach For the Sky* put it centre stage in Bader's 1956 legend.

But the success of Big Wing was a big lie.

Even as Dowding and Park departed, Bader's legend grew courtesy of RAF press releases, friendly reporters and dashing official photos. He was turned into a collectable "cigarette card" series and featured in a mass-produced propaganda postcard, distributed to schools, called "Heroic Deeds of War", which bore his legend: "His name (is) a watchword and inspiration amongst our fighter pilots. Who would have believed it possible that a man so handicapped could do so much?"

On 18th March 1941 the newly promoted Wing Commander reported for duty at RAF Tangmere and from there on in "DB" (callsign "Dogsbody") sought to become the greatest fighting ace of the war. To that end he loved nothing better than leading "rhubarb" operations across the Channel. These were hunting sorties with small groups of fighters seeking out lone enemy planes or hitting targets on the ground.

Most pilots hated rhubarbs but Bader, addicted to the thrill of aerial war, revelled in them. In the words of his friend Squadron Leader Johnny Johnson: "His idea of a Saturday afternoon off, was to take… one or two unfortunates up over the Channel or the Pas-de-Calais in the hope we might encounter [the enemy]."

By August 1941, he had claimed 23 kills – making him, on paper, the fifth biggest ace in the RAF – but there's no medal for coming fifth at games and the ever more competitive Bader began bullying those about him even more than ever. The largely working-class ground crew were a particular target. If his plane wasn't ready when he wanted it, he would fire off a string of "F" and "C" words at them. Officers could get it in the neck too. One pilot, William Walker, returning to his duties after having been shot down in August 1940, reported to his new commanding officer, only to be sworn at for nearly getting killed – "…which I thought was a bit off to say the least," Walker later said. He didn't stay long.

Wing Commander Bader also became ever more unreliable in battle and had the habit of breaking off the moment he saw enemy fighters, in the hope of upping his scorecard – leaving every other man for themselves. In all of it there was no sense of higher purpose; no altruistic "Wesley Factor". Bader did not reach for the skies to save his fellow Britons from the menace of Naziism; he did so because he loved the sport of war.

On 9th August 1941, his recklessness caught up with him.

Flying without his usual wing man, Alan Smith, Bader set off on a rhubarb knowing that the instruments on his plane were not functioning properly. Engaging four enemy aircraft along the northern coast of France, he dived too fast without knowing his altitude or speed. At some point the tail of his plane was shot off, perhaps by friendly fire,* and with his aircraft barrelling towards the ground, Bader detached his leg – and bailed out.

---

* To pamper his ego the Germans later dug out the most dashing Luftwaffe pilot they could find and told Bader it was him.

Bader never blamed himself for what happened, despite it clearly being largely his own fault, and would regularly point a finger at old comrades instead.

The flying ace's capture was a PR disaster for the RAF but provided a bit of a thrill for the Luftwaffe who treated their celebrity POW like a rock star on tour. Showing admirable bloody mindedness and determined to get up on his feet again, Bader demanded that his hosts liaise with the British to drop a replacement leg. General Adolf Galland, who years later would pop up on Bader's *This Is Your Life* appearance, organised the delivery and on 19th August, the RAF dropped a prosthetic limb over Saint-Omer.

Being a POW did not suit the ever-restless Bader and he went on to make numerous, extremely ill-advised escape attempts. Post-war films and documentaries have given rise to the impression that officer POWs at the time had a "duty to escape", a sort of code of honour which obliged them to try to get back home from imprisonment. But it was certainly not formalised in any manner by the British High Command and is something of a post-war myth. Most British, Allied and even Axis POWs simply made the best of a bad situation and sat the war out – and the idea that Bader should have felt obliged to try is somewhat ludicrous. But despite that, try he did. His first attempt at Saint Omer ended not only in his swift recapture, but also in the French locals who had helped him, Maria Hiecque and Lucille Debacker, and their co-conspirator Monsieur Leon being sentenced to death. Thankfully those sentences were commuted to hard labour after an appeal by Vichy leader Marshall Petain but Bader should never have put their lives at risk in the first place. It should have given Douglas a lesson in humility, but the word did not appear in his limited lexicon. Further attempts followed with him always swiftly being recaptured: his walking gait made him instantly recognisable, whatever the disguise. He was posted to a series of prison camps including Stalag Luft III, of wooden horse and "Great Escape" fame, where he made life difficult for his fellow prisoners by constantly pranking the guards.

Bader had determined – as he later said – to be: "a plain (and a) bloody nuisance to the Germans" but in the process of what was known as "goon-baiting", he annoyed the hell out of his fellow POWs as well. Privileges were constantly removed as he fought his one-man campaign against boredom. When he was finally transferred to Stalag Luft VIII-B, the celebratory mood on both sides of the wire, was palpable. One fellow inmate later wrote: "to tell the truth it was a relief to everybody, friend and foe, to see him go."*

Bader didn't last long at the new prison camp and was soon transferred to Colditz, where his antics antagonised everyone around him. His "goon-baiting" got so annoying that even the Germans gave in and suggested that Bader might like to go before a Swiss Repatriation Commission to get himself sent home. He loftily refused – as a matter of pride, because he had not been wounded in action – and stayed in the camp, to the collective disappointment of all. More dispiritingly, he deliberately blocked the repatriation of someone else. Alex Ross, a bandsman with the Seaforth Highlanders, had become his medical orderly, on the grounds that nobody else wanted to do it. It was a thankless task and Dilip Sarkar quotes Ross as saying:

"In all the time I knew him I don't think he said please or thank you to me. I was only a little squirt compared to him… he was the boss. Wherever he was he liked to be the head…. When he shouted you ran to do whatever he wanted."

When, in 1943, the Red Cross told Ross he was eligible for repatriation and that the Germans had agreed to the terms, the thrilled bandsman told Bader: "I'm going home!" to which Britain's greatest wartime hero replied: "No, you're bloody not! You came here as my skivvy and that's what you'll stay".

On 12th April 1944, US Army soldiers arrived at the gates of Colditz and Bader and his fellow POWs were liberated. As the Americans began to process the POWs, Bader pushed his way to the front and made it be

---

* Mackenzie, S.P., *Bader's War*, 2008, p144.

known to Lee Carson Reeves, a celebrated reporter who was embedded with the American forces, that he was a famous fighter ace. Sensing a story, Carson Reeves helped arrange his swift exit from the camp.

Bader had no interest in going back home to Thelma, and much to his long-suffering wife's horror, set about trying to avail himself of a Spitfire. The idea was ridiculous. He had been out of action for three years and the technology had moved on to such an extent that it would have taken weeks of training to get him back in the skies. But like everything else in Bader's war, such considerations flew over his head. Bader was less interested in "doing his bit" than "getting the glory".

He also wanted his spare pair of aluminium legs back.

Some weeks after liberation and having returned to his native Scotland, the bandsman Alex Ross was called to the local post office telephone exchange, only to find Bader on the other end of the line. His former boss wanted to know if he had his spare legs and when Ross said he didn't have a clue where they were, the great fighter ace called him a "cunt" and slammed down the phone.

The war in the Far East ended before Bader could get back in a plane and post-war, he returned to work for Shell Oil. In the years that followed, as books and that famous film sealed his legend, his celebrity rose as did his propensity to back all the worst types of people. In 1953 he was invited to write a foreword to Luftwaffe pilot Hans-Ulrich Rudel's autobiography *Stuka Pilot*. The handsome and charismatic pilot was known as "The Eagle of the Eastern Front" with German military commander Colonel General Ferdinand Schörner once claiming: "Rudel alone is worth an entire division!" Late in the war, he was shot down by Soviet anti-aircraft fire and lost one leg below the knee. Like Bader, he had refused to let it stop him and was soon back up in the air taking on the enemy.

In the introduction, Bader described him as a "gallant chap" and lavished praise on his old enemy. But Rudel was also an unapologetic Nazi, who had fled to Argentina using fake documents in the immediate aftermath of war and then written angry diatribes about those who had

failed Hitler. In Argentina he had co-founded the neo-Nazi organisation "Kameradenwerk" (Comrade's Work) which sought to help fleeing
war criminals escape justice, and his memoir had been published by a
house that had links with British fascist leader Oswald Mosley.

When this was revealed, Bader waved off all criticism and insisted
that even if he'd known Rudel was an unapologetic Nazi he'd have
written the introduction anyway. His stubborn refusal to back down
and the row around the extent of Rudel's commitment to fascism has
rumbled on in geeky military circles ever since with many apologists
insisting that Rudel was "just another pilot" and that no harm was
done. Suffice to say, when Rudel died, in West Germany in December
1982, just three months after Douglas Bader, mourners gave Nazi
salutes at the graveside.

In 1956, the same year *Reach for the Sky* was released, the Suez
Crisis erupted as Britain and France, in an act of aggressive late-
colonial interventionism, sought to seize back control of the nation-
alised canal from Egyptian President Nasser and topple him in the
process. The fiasco would see the Anglo-French operation routed and
Nasser emerge as a hero, not just within his own country but across the
developing world. In response to the invasion and amid the growing
clamour for independence across the African continent, Bader told a
New Zealand journalist that Africans could "bloody well climb back
up their trees".

The outburst was no one-off. Bader had staunchly right-wing and
frequently openly and rabidly racist opinions and backed white minority
rule in Rhodesia, apartheid in South Africa and the return of the death
penalty in the UK. Nowadays we see the "Few" and people like Bader as
defeaters of fascism and upholders of liberal values, who wanted to free
the world from tyranny. But Bader was not afraid to rub shoulders with
his former enemies, write forewords to Nazi books and deny the rights
of African people to determine their own future freed of British rule. It
is hard to escape the sense that in other circumstances, Bader may well
have felt equally comfortable playing the game for either side.

It was not the worst of his crimes, but Bader could also be unforgivably inconsiderate. During a visit to Munich to meet former Luftwaffe pilots, he told them: "My God, I had no idea we left so many of you bastards alive." He was often blunt, opinionated, stubborn and like many ex-public schoolboys from Britain of his era, imbued with a surfeit of self-importance and entitlement. In interviews across the post-war era, there is a sense too of a man acting a part. His liberal use of "old boy" and "old man" was such that when he acted as an adviser on the 1969 film *Battle of Britain*, Canadian actor Christopher Plummer proclaimed himself astonished to discover that "people like that really exist".

He also had his contradictions. The man who thought Campaign for Nuclear Disarmament (CND) supporters should be deported also told a 1965 BBC interviewer that he was "all for the young" and that "every generation" including his had questioned the one that went before. When asked to pick his favourite track on a 1981 appearance on BBC Radio 4's *Desert Island Discs*, he chose the sentimental hippy anthem "I'd Like to Teach the World to Sing" by the New Seekers.

In any biographical account, there is always a temptation to do a bit of amateur analysis on the subject. The early death of his father, his mother's remarriage to someone he didn't like, and loss of his legs must have affected him, and far more deeply than he ever let on. So too must have that loveless childhood. He once claimed that the only time he cried, in his entire life, was when his mother, father and brother took off in the car for the day and deliberately left him behind. It's not much of a leap to believe that the neglected boy, so desperate for love, turned into a man who needed to be celebrated and noticed.

Bader did good works too. As a campaigner, he inspired children who had lost limbs, and throughout his career in the public eye, he showed that a disability, however debilitating, should not put a stop to a full life. His encouragement and example helped changed perspectives and people.

But that is not the reason we remember Group Captain Douglas Bader. His legend endures because in the summer of 1940 a PR man at

Fighter Command thought he might make good copy for the war effort and in the years beyond, people continued to believe in that propaganda. *Reach for the Sky* lingered long in the collective public consciousness because it showed Bader, as portrayed by likable Kenneth More, as a sort of apotheosis of British stiff-upper-lippery in wartime. Witty, defiant, charming and brave, that fictionalised Bader epitomised that line from Alejandro González Iñárritu earlier in the chapter: "Cinema is a mirror, by which we often see ourselves" – or perhaps, in this case, how British people would like to see themselves.

That is the legacy of most British war films from 1940, and it is the reason perhaps why many a war nostalgist is still drawn to them. Well into recent times, films like *Dunkirk* (2017) and *Darkest Hour* (2017) have trotted out much the same gospel in what has become our modern origin story. The Lumière brothers' invention is still misleading audiences 130 years after the train entered the station.

History is much more than a simple series of goody versus baddie tropes and tales of cinematic, heroic derring-do. And in reducing it, as we have done, to just a few big events and the actions of a carefully selected group of individuals, we edit out many another hero from the tale.

* * *

You've probably never heard of Wing Commander Ian Richard Gleed DSO, DFC – so let's rectify that.

Born in Finchley, north London on 3rd July 1916, Ian was the son of a GP, Dr Seymour Gleed, and his wife Florence. Sent to board at Epsom College aged 13, he found, like Bader, that he did better at sport than at his academic studies and, also like Bader, he had a love of pranks including once "borrowing" * a junior master's car, when the boys were supposed to be attending a lecture on "Piltdown Man".†

---

* Franks, N, *Fighter Leader: Story of Wing Commander Ian Gleed*, 1978, p13.
† Piltdown Man was a 1912 archaeological hoax perpetrated by an amateur palaeontologist, Charles Dawson, who claimed to have found bone fragments that were the "missing link". At the time of the lecture, it was still not known that it was a hoax and the truth was revealed only in the 1950s.

Gleed had a love of sailing and owned a boat, *Spindthrift*, which he sailed throughout the 1930s with his friend, Teddy Denham, near his family holiday home in Herne Bay on the Kent coast.

Gleed also had an almost unquenchable thirst for adventure and, as an active member of the Public Schools Exploring Society, went on expeditions organised by Surgeon Commander Murray Levick RN, who had been a member of Scott's *Terra Nova* Antarctic expedition in 1910.[*] On one trip, to Newfoundland in 1934, one of Gleed's companions was a young Roald Dahl, who was also destined to become a fighter pilot. During the expedition, Gleed got lost in the wilds and was stranded for three days, living off nature, before finding his way back to camp. His calm in the face of what was a life-threatening event, was typical of him.

In March 1936, having already learned to fly, Gleed was commissioned into the RAF where he was nicknamed Widge supposedly on account of him being, at 5 foot 5 and a bit, a "wizard midget" although "widge" was also a 1930s' slang word for a penis.

Gleed had an energy about him. The playwright Beverley Nichols, who met him in the late 1930s, found him hugely enigmatic and possessed of a pair of steely grey eyes that "seemed to be scanning far horizons".

He had an absolute passion for sailing and Gleed would spend most of his leave and weekends in Kent, and his friendship with Teddy, who he had initially hired to look after his boat, became something of a sailing partnership. In *Fighter Leader*, Norman Franks' 1978 biography of Gleed, he describes how: "Gleed and Teddy Denham got on well together, Gleed giving him much of his time…" – but come 1939, there were other matters to attend to.

The start to Gleed's war was inauspicious. In February 1940 he was nearly killed when his Spitfire broke up, knocked him unconscious and threw him out of the cockpit. He came to, mid-air, in an utterly confused state, as he explained in his memoir, *Arise to Conquer* (1942):

[*] Levick studied the penguins in the region and witnessed that some of the males engaged in relationships with each other. His report was considered so shocking that it was not published in his lifetime. Levick himself was gay.

"'Where am I? When did I land... Christ I must be in the air! Where's the ripcord?' It was very strange, there was no dropping sensation, it was absolutely dark and I couldn't feel any rushing air... I tugged hard, felt a jerk and then nothing."

He survived but was seriously injured and, unsurprisingly, shaken up by the event – and he turned to drink. Weeks spent recuperating, and more spent convincing the RAF that he was mentally fit and sober enough to fly again, saw a return to the cockpit. On 17th May 1940 he was assigned to 87 Squadron, based in France, as Squadron Leader. Gleed flew a Hurricane in combat missions against the Luftwaffe during the Fall of France and later in the Battle of Britain, proving himself to be not only a brilliant pilot but also an outstanding leader.

His DFC* citation in *The London Gazette* in September 1940 described him as taking on "his task with energy and discretion he won the confidence of his flight and led them with skill and success. Throughout, he showed great courage in the air and was on duty almost continuously."†At 25, Gleed was a hardened combat veteran and after being promoted to Wing Commander he was sent to RAF Middle Wallop in November 1941. The following year, on 22nd May 1942, he was awarded a DSO‡ for leading "his wing on 26 sorties over enemy territory. He has always displayed a fine fighting spirit which, combined with his master leadership and keenness have set an inspiring example. Wing Commander Gleed has destroyed at least 12 enemy aircraft two of which he shot down at night". It was the most awarded British gallantry medal of the war with 20,354 given out.

---

* DFC – Distinguished Flying Cross – RAF gallantry medal for "an act or acts of valour ...against the enemy."
† Bourne, S, *Fighting Proud: The Untold Story of the Gay Men Who Served in Two World Wars*, 2017, p100.
‡ DSO – Distinguished Service Order – given to higher ranking officers and generally considered to be the medal just beneath a Victoria Cross in terms of gallantry. Just 4,880 were awarded in the Second World War – by comparison 10,776 Military Crosses were given.

That same year, *Arise to Conquer*, his account of his experiences in the Battle of Britain, was published and became an immediate best-seller in both the UK and the USA – which had newly entered the war.

The book is very much a *Boy's Own* type of page-turner and is full of thrills and spills, all delivered with wit and polish. While Franks puts that talent down to Gleed's brief encounter with the author Somerset Maugham, the journalist and author John Strachey, who was later to become Minister of War in the Atlee administration, did most of the work and based it on interviews with the credited "author".

Given the time it was written and the purpose of the book, there's a fair bit of bombastic propaganda on the pages and a hatred of Naziism comes shining through. Describing his visit to Buckingham Palace to receive his DSO, he writes: "It was one of the most impressive ceremonies that I have ever attended. It gave me courage and increased my morale. Nazis, you may blow London and every town in our country to smithereens if you can. You shall never rule the British Isles."

Gleed also describes his fiancee, Pamela, and romantic moments with her while he was on leave: "Off to Kent I went to stay a weekend with the girlfriend. It was grand being with Pam again. We went to all the old spots together to Herne Bay, where my boat, *Spindrift*, was laid up. With the help of several old boatmen friends, we had her outside the Sailing Club, rigged ready for launching. We went for our first sail on a rough, blustery day, and loved it."

Later he describes an evening out with her in Canterbury in which they drink a lot of beer. Later still, following the loss of a comrade over France in a dogfight, he drifts off to sleep with "my sailing-boat floating before my eyes... (and) Pam laughing as I got a wave over me as we launched her."

All of this surprised his family and friends, who did not know that he was engaged, had never heard of Pamela, or heard of him going sailing with her near Herne Bay. There was a reason for that. Gleed had invented Pam, on the insistence of Strachey and his publisher, because he was gay.

In 1942, homosexuality was still illegal in Great Britain and would remain so for the next 25 years. Same-sex relationships of course existed in the armed forces – as they did everywhere else in life and had done throughout history.

Emma Vickers, author of *Queen and Country – Same Sex Desire in the British Armed Forces 1939–45*, estimates that: "of the 6,508,000 million men and women who served between 1939 and 1945 in the British armed forces, 1,179,000 million experienced some form of same-sex intimacy."

But despite that, open and outward demonstrations of love could spell disaster.

There was a belief among many, and one which prevails in some quarters to this day, that LGBTQ+ service people were ineffectual and worse that they might be "distracted". It was only, disgracefully late, in 2000, that openly gay men and women were allowed to serve without fear of losing their rank and careers.

Gleed did not fit the standard model of what a dashing hero should always be – straight – and so Pam had been conjured up.

Ian's homosexuality caused problems for publishing houses long after the war. Norman Franks' *Fighter Leader* dances around the subject of Ian's private life, but you do not have to read very far between the lines to realise that Gleed was a member of a friendship group comprised of some of the most famous gay men of the time. Almost everyone outside of the RAF who gets namechecked, from the playwright Beverley Nichols, who noticed his eyes, to Murray Levick, who led the expedition to Canada, were as openly gay as the times allowed. Later in the book, Franks talks about Ian befriending a group of men in the south of France, which includes writers Somerset Maugham and Hector Bolitho and Brooklands racing legend Raymond Mays. Franks calls them the "in scene" but they were in fact very much the "out" ones in their immediate circle.

All of this might have gone over the heads of readers in 1978, but Norman Franks does drop hints including that friendship with his boating companion Teddy Denham, which may have been the most significant love of Ian's life. For comparing Gleed's account in *Arise to Conquer*, with the one Franks gives in *Fighter Leader*, it soon becomes apparent that when co-writing his own book, Ian turned Teddy into "Pam". Those long sailing trips off the coast of Herne Bay in the halcyon summer days before 1939, the nights out in Canterbury and him drifting off to sleep thinking of "Pam" all happened. Only it wasn't Pam but Teddy. Even with homosexuality having been decriminalised in 1967, a full decade before his biography came out, Franks skirts that obvious truth and treats it as nothing more than a "friendship between two amateur sailors" – and perhaps that is what it was for Teddy who was then still alive. But Gleed was quite clearly in love.

How open Gleed was about his sexuality is a matter of debate. Wartime propaganda photos, shot to promote his celebrity, show the pilot in the cockpit of his Spitfire with the character Figaro – smashing a Nazi swastika – painted on the side. Figaro is the "little kitty cat" in Disney's 1940 film *Pinocchio* and Gleed kept the image on the sides of all his (6) subsequent Spitfires and Hurricanes. None of his biographers are entirely sure why he picked the cat, but many interpretations of the film point out Figaro's innate campness, and more, that he is quite obviously besotted with the eponymous wooden boy. Was Gleed's choice of art a subtle nod to his identity? A middle finger to an enemy which – even as he fought them in the skies – was rounding up members of the gay community and throwing them in concentration camps. Or perhaps an act of defiance too against his own society that deemed homosexuality to be wrong. We shall never know.

Gleed's sexuality might have remained publicly a secret but in a 1997 interview for a BBC2 series called *It's Not Unusual*, one of his junior wartime officers, Chris Gotch, described their affair. Gotch, who was then 74, described the moment his eyes met Gleed's in the mess room and how, later, the senior officer seduced him in his billet. The two men continued to have a relationship for the remainder of their posting together.

Tragically, aged 26, Gleed was killed in action in April 1943 in what was – again – quite probably a friendly fire incident over the Tunisian desert in the North African campaign.

In the immediate post-war years, he like many other RAF pilots who had once been celebrated as poster-boys of the conflict, slowly slid into obscurity until there was only space left for one Spitfire pilot in the Pantheon of fighter pilot Gods – Sir Douglas Bader, CBE, DSO & Bar, DFC & Bar.

There must be a suspicion that Gleed was forgotten because he did not fit the mould. Even today, 75 years after its end, we continue to view the Second World War as a straight man's war. The field brims with strapping monomythic heterosexual heroes with space reserved for only the occasional women, like Violette Szabo and Odette Hallowes who fought in the Special Operations Executive (SOE) and a rare token homosexual, Alan Turing. The contributions of millions of other Allied LGBTQ+ men and women who existed, who were there, who fought and died and did heroic things, just like everyone else – have largely been edited out. Perhaps it's time to start celebrating those lives as well and to re-examine our view of that conflict, free from the propaganda and heavy edits that still define it. In short, perhaps it is time to start telling the stories of everyone and not just the few.

CHAPTER TWO

POLITICAL HEROES
JOHN F. KENNEDY

Truth Behind the Image

On that Friday morning of 22nd November 1963, Air Force One touched down just before 11.30 a.m. at Love Field, Dallas, having flown the short distance from Fort Worth. The presidential couple emerged a few moments later. The First Lady, Mrs Kennedy, was wearing a bright pink Chanel suit and hat; President Jack Kennedy was dressed head to toe in his irresistible political X factor.

Despite a midterm dip, Jack Kennedy was still riding high in the polls and with the 1964 US presidential election one year away, he was out on the campaign trail early. In Texas, Vice President Lyndon B. Johnson's home state, there was an ongoing beef between the Democratic Senator Ralph Yarborough and the ambitious Governor Connally (also a Democrat), who already had one eye on the presidency.* The feud was spawning negative headlines nationally and Kennedy and Johnson had decided to make the visit, alongside both men, as a show of unity.

---

* To that end, in 1974, in the wake of the Watergate scandal, Connally changed parties and joined the Republicans in the hope of becoming a Republican presidential candidate. The bizarre move led Yarborough to quip, "It's the first time in recorded history that a rat has swum toward a sinking ship."

It had been raining earlier in the morning, but the sun was out, and it was a warm day, so the plastic bubble top of the Kennedys' Lincoln Continental had been removed. The newly elected Governor John Connally and his wife, Nellie, were already seated in the car and warmly greeted the movie-star President and First Lady, Jackie. as they got in.

Vice President Lyndon B. Johnson and his wife, Claudia, known to all as "Lady Bird", climbed into a car behind with Senator Yarborough. With everyone now in place, the procession set off through the streets of Dallas, driving inexorably towards its place in history.

It was a 10-mile ride to the Trade Mart where JFK was scheduled to give a lunchtime address, and as the cavalcade of vehicles and outriders passed through the streets, tens of thousands of Texans turned out to catch a glimpse of their president and his glamorous wife. There was a carnival atmosphere and ticker tape rained down from buildings. Cheerleaders in bright blue outfits danced, marching bands in smart uniforms played and children waved flags as the parade passed by. Just over two miles from their destination, at around 12.30 p.m., as the motorcade passed into the Dealey Plaza, Nellie Connally turned around and shouted over the din: "Mr President, you certainly can't say that Dallas doesn't love you."

Almost as soon as she had turned back, three shots rang out. One bullet entered the president's neck; a second passed through his skull. Governor Connally was hit in his back but went on to survive. John F. Kennedy would not be so lucky.

The Continental took off, driving at speed to the nearby Parkland Memorial Hospital.

A priest was summoned to the operating theatre, but the president was already dead. By 1.20 p.m., Lyndon B. Johnson was being escorted back to Love Field airport. He waited aboard Air Force One for Jackie Kennedy to arrive with her husband's body and then at 2.38 p.m. was sworn in as the 36th President of the United States of America. Mrs Kennedy, still dressed in her blood-splattered pink Chanel suit, was standing at his side as he took his oath. She was to continue to wear the suit until she went to bed the following morning.

The entire drama, from the arrival in Dallas to Johnson's swearing in, had played out in just three hours and while all of this was going on the assassin, Lee Harvey Oswald, was on the run.

Having shot Kennedy, he discarded his rifle and covered it with boxes, before racing out of the Book Depository store and hopping on a bus. When that got caught up in traffic, caused by the mayhem surrounding the assassination, he changed to a taxi and went to his boarding house. There he grabbed his jacket and a handgun and headed to a bus stop where he was spotted by a patrol cop called J.D. Tippit. Witnesses saw the two men exchange words and at roughly the same time that Lyndon B. Johnson was heading back to the airfield, Oswald pulled out his gun and shot the police officer, before fleeing into the nearby Texas Movie Theater, where he may – or may not – have taken refuge on a seat three rows from the back.

Quickly identified on account of his strange behaviour, he was then arrested outside the theatre on suspicion of killing Tippit. It is testament to the depth of the conspiracy which followed, that to this day, arguments still rage in some corners of the internet, over whether he went into the cinema, which seat he sat in and even whether he bought a box of popcorn.

Two days later, while being taken to the County Jail, he was shot and killed outside Police Headquarters by a local nightclub owner called Jack Ruby. Even before his body hit the ground, conspiracy theories were proliferating.

In his book *Voodoo Histories*, David Aaronovitch notes that just: "One week after Kennedy's murder a major US poll showed that less than a third of those asked believed that Oswald had acted alone and within four weeks such doubts were being theorized."*

Struggling to make sense of the notion that a lone gunman had killed their president, Americans were looking for something bigger to blame, and in the meantime, the USSR's "active measures" Disinformation Unit

---

* Aaronovitch, D, *Voodoo Histories*, 2009, p120.

went to work. In 1994 the Russian President, Boris Yeltsin disclosed in his memoirs that a day after the assassination, while Lee Harvey Oswald was still in custody, a letter was sent to the Central Committee of the Communist Party of the Soviet Union by KGB Chairman Vladimir Semichastny. It recommended the publication in a "progressive paper in one of the Western countries" of disinformation that would expose "the attempt by reactionary circles in the USA to remove the responsibility for the murder of Kennedy from the real criminals" and pin it on someone else.

This was how Soviet active measures worked back then. A story would be planted in a pro-Soviet foreign publication in the hope that its disinformation would spread like a virus into public consciousness and create fear and distrust. It was a methodology that the Soviets used for decades and in 1983 they pulled off an extraordinary disinformation coup when an anonymous letter by a "well-known American scientist" was printed in an Indian newspaper called *The Patriot*, claiming that the AIDS virus had been manufactured in a US military lab and then leaked out. It was so effective that many people still believe it today and continue to fall for many of the same tricks in this social media driven disinformation age.

Two months after the death of Kennedy, the British magazine *Labour Monthly* published an article describing Oswald as a fall guy and, without supplying any evidence, pinned the assassination on "far right" elements in the USA. The magazine's editor was Rajani Palme Dutt, the privately educated one-time General Secretary of the Communist Party of Great Britain. Dutt was an unrepentant Stalinist, who was receiving a "pension" from the USSR and continued to do so until the time of his death in 1974. The *Labour Monthly* piece did its work and soon everyone was cooking up Kennedy conspiracy theories and whispering them in bars across the Western Hemisphere. Dutt was very far from being the only useful idiot in the game, and over the next two years the Soviet Disinformation Unit would propagate many a lie about the assassination, including a carefully planted piece in the *Paese*

Sera, an Italian newspaper that would eventually lead to the arrest of a man called Clay Shaw, to whom we will return in a moment.

The bestselling book *Oswald: Assassin or Fall Guy*, published in 1964, also played a part. The author Joachim Joesten claimed that Kennedy had been against the escalation in Vietnam and that the CIA had been essentially a rogue outfit. As the *Washington Post* revealed in 2003, it was not until "the notes of a former KGB archivist named Vasili Mitrokhin were published in 1999" that it was appreciated "that Joesten's publisher, the small New York firm of Marzani & Munsell, (had) received subsidies totaling $672,000 from the Central Committee of the Communist Party in the early 1960s."

The existing and understandable climate of paranoia in the wake of the assassination, fuelled by Soviet disinformation, led millions to believe that the murder of JFK was a massive conspiracy and opinion only shifted, albeit briefly, with the Warren Commission findings in September 1964. That report into the assassination and the accompanying 888-page report set out in forensic detail what had happened, and it went as follows.

Lee Harvey Oswald was not, as he had claimed "just a patsy".* A 24-year-old former Marine with pro-Castro sympathies, he had been designated a "sharpshooter" during his time in the army. At some point Oswald had become a Communist and aged just 20, in 1959, he had defected to the USSR. There he met Marina Nikolayevna Prusakova, a Russian pharmaceutical student, and swiftly got engaged. Six weeks later, the couple got married and settled down in Minsk. They had a daughter, June, but in 1962, Oswald gave up his job as a lathe operator and the young family headed back to the USA, with Lee claiming he missed bowling alleys and hamburgers. Oswald had an almost pathologically high opinion of himself and believed his return would make national headlines, but it warranted just 24 lines in an AP release. Unable to readapt to life back home, he became the classic outsider.

---

* Slang for scapegoat.

In February 1963, the couple were befriended by a Quaker called Ruth Paine, to whom they were introduced by George Sergius de Mohrenschildt, a Belorussian émigré. Ruth was studying Russian and was drawn to the small community of Soviet exiles to improve her conversational skills. She was separated from her husband Michael and, as a Quaker in conservative Dallas, she was something of an outsider. She felt sorry for Marina, living in the shadow of her peculiar and domineering partner, and took her under her wing.

In January 1963, Oswald had bought a Smith & Wesson handgun. In March 1963 using the name "A. Hidell" he bought a rifle and telescopic lens via mail order and hid it in Paine's garage. Later he posed with the gun for a photograph taken by Marina and then, on 10th April, in an act conveniently ignored by most conspiracy theorists, used the carbine to try to shoot the retired right-wing US Army General Edwin Walker. Walker was a white supremacist and had campaigned to be the Democratic candidate for Governor of Texas. A veteran of both the Second World War and Korea he was a controversial figure despite having won the Silver Star, Croix de Guerre and even a British OBE for his gallantry. Walker was involved in right-wing political fringe movements and had sponsored a leaflet demanding that JFK be arrested for treason.

But Texan Democrats didn't want Walker, and he lost the nomination to John Connally; death didn't want him either and Oswald's bullet missed, shattering a window frame in his office instead. The would-be assassin made off before he was apprehended. Texan detectives were left scratching their heads and had no suspects until Oswald was later apprehended for the murder of Kennedy.

Walker spent the rest of his life fighting right-wing causes and libel battles with the American press. He was arrested in 1976 for propositioning a male undercover police officer in a public toilet in Dallas and having been given a suspended sentence and a $1,000 fine disappeared from public life.

Walker's near miss in 1963, and Lee's subsequent bizarre behaviour, so perturbed Marina Oswald that she and her young daughter moved in with Ruth Paine. It was Ruth who helped Oswald find a job at the Texas Book Depository and Ruth who would later answer the door to an FBI agent, James Hosty, who came looking for Oswald a month before the killing.

Hosty was keeping tabs on the would-be assassin on account of his recent return from the USSR and suspicions around his pro-Cuban activities, but his timing – shortly after Lee's attempt on Walker – could not have been worse.

The visit so unnerved Oswald that he went to the FBI bureau in Dallas and tried to confront the agent. Hosty was at lunch, so the young man left a note which, according to the agent read: "If you have anything you want to learn about me, come talk to me directly. If you don't cease bothering my wife, I will take appropriate action and report this to the proper authorities."

That visit may have been a trigger – pushing Oswald to the endgame that would see the murder of the president – but his discontent had been running high long before and the evidence against Oswald was overwhelming.

Oswald's notebooks, written in the summer of 1962, demonstrated his hatred of the Establishment and his belief that "the destruction of all authority" was the only solution to the world's woes and he had proved his violent intentions in the attempt on Walker.

Marina thought Lee was guilty and told the Warren Commission as much.* Ballistics showed that the gun used to kill JFK was almost certainly the same one used on Walker, although the fragmented bullet left room for doubt. Oswald worked at the book depository store and his rifle was found there with spent cartridges. In addition to the original photograph of him holding the weapon, which Marina admitted she had taken, more photos of him with the gun and holding two Communist newspapers emerged.

---

* In later life, Marina changed her mind and, becoming ever more paranoid, she believed that her phones were tapped and that the CIA were following her. As of writing she is still alive and lives in rural Texas.

He was the only member of staff unaccounted for after the shooting. Subsequently he murdered J.D. Tippit, that Texan police officer – firing five bullets at him – because the cop approached him on account of his matching the description of the wanted man. Oswald might as well have had "JFK's assassin" tattooed on his forehead, with a big neon sign reading "killer" pointing down at him from the sky.

The commission concluded that Lee Harvey Oswald had acted alone and that while it "could not make any definitive determination of Oswald's motives" everything pointed at him. Warren assessed that Jack Ruby had acted alone too. The nightclub owner was an unstable individual, with a long record of acting impulsively and violently and was known to have a hankering for attention and fame. One associate described him as "a complete psycho". This was no deep state conspiracy. It was an angry lone gunman, taking out his self-loathing, paranoia and failure on the most popular politician in America. And another lone gunman taking out his on him.

In the wake of the report and in the face of such a body of evidence, many Americans changed their minds. By November 1964 Gallup found that 87% of Americans now thought that Oswald had acted alone. But memories are short, and the Vietnam War was long, and as more conspiratorial books and films appeared, the pendulum began to swing back the other way.

One man did more than any other to poison the well of certainty. His name was Jim Garrison, and he was District Attorney for Orleans Parish, Louisiana. Garrison was obsessed with the Kennedy assassination and in 1966 announced that he was launching an "investigation" into the killing himself. His theory hinged on a story told to him by a private investigator, Jack Martin, who had recently been assaulted by an associate called Guy Banister in an argument over a missing file. Martin, probably out for revenge, began telling people that Banister and his friend David Ferrie were responsible for the murder of JFK, and Garrison was gullible enough to believe it.

In July 1967 NBC gave Jim Garrison a platform, allowing him to air his ideas: "Tonight, I'm going to talk to you about truth and about fairy tales..." he said in his opening statement, "you are going to learn that although you are citizens of the United States, information concerning the cause of the death of your president has been withheld from you."

The appearance made him look like a crusading hero and turned him into a media star, and the famous 26.6-second silent 8mm film, shot by businessman Abraham Zapruder which captured the moment the President was shot, was to become critical to his theory and spawn an estimated 40,000 books.

Conspiracy theories are not new. Athenian and Roman people saw them everywhere, and in a sense, society and the politics of the eras often consisted of little else. Fear of Christians in the Roman Empire was in large part down to mistrust about what this secretive sect were up to. When Rome burned down in the Great Fire of 64 CE, Nero blamed the Christians and three hundred years of persecution followed. Just over 1,600 years after the fire in Rome, the Great Fire of London ravaged the capital in 1666. On that occasion Londoners blamed the Jews, Catholics, Dutch and French and lynchings and murders ensued.

On the other side of the Atlantic, seventeenth-century Puritans saw their world entirely through the prism of a massive conspiracy in which Native Americans and their religious enemies were working in concert with witches to destroy their new Jerusalem. People saw signs every-where and it was that paranoia that led to the Salem witch trials between February 1692 and May 1693, although the terrible events at Salem, which saw 25 innocent people killed, were far from an isolated incident.

The murder of Abraham Lincoln, in April 1865, spawned a veritable cottage industry of conspiracy theories which variously blamed the killing on Catholics, in a plot hatched by Pope Pius XI or Secretary of State for War Edwin M. Stanton, or even Mrs Lincoln herself. Mary Todd Lincoln had often behaved erratically while her husband was alive, and things only worsened after his death. In 1875 she was briefly committed to an asylum, by her only surviving son, Robert. She later escaped and managed to "prove" her sanity, but rumours abounded that her peculiar behaviour was in some way associated with guilt connected to the death of Abe.

One thing the tin foil stovepipe hat brigade could agree on was that despite John Wilkes Booth, a well-known actor, having shot the President in front of 2,000 theatre-going witnesses – he was not to blame. Well into the twentieth century, Abe's Vice President (later President) Andrew Johnson was getting the finger pointed at him in books such as 1960's *The Web of Conspiracy* by pulp fiction writer Theodore Roscoe. You might be unaware such theories ever existed for the simple reason, that since 1963, they have been eclipsed by those associated with the death of Kennedy.

There is an existential element to conspiracy theories. In times of uncertainty, people want answers and sometimes the truth can be complicated, random, scientific or unsatisfying. JFK's assassination, at the hands of a bullying, attention-seeking loner, is almost terrifying in its banality. If the most powerful and best protected man on Earth can get taken out by someone like that, then what hope is there for the rest of us? So, it makes sense to believe instead that he was just a patsy in a huge web that was spun by the deep state. There is something almost comforting about it.

Shocking events spawn giant conspiracy theories, and little has changed since the time of Nero.

In the years following the death of Princess Diana in a Parisian underpass, millions of people refused to believe that it was just an accident. How could the most famous woman in the world have died as a result of not putting on her seatbelt? Clearly MI6 or lizard space aliens were to blame. A string of claims by her late boyfriend's father Mohammed Al-Fayed and others in tabloid newspapers caused many to question the official findings of French and British inquests which simply kept coming up with the same unsatisfying "car accident" explanation.

A YouGov poll in 2013 found that 38% of Britons thought there had been a conspiracy.

Twenty years after 9/11 some 23% of Americans either strongly or "somewhat" believed that the attack on the Twin Towers was an inside job and in early 2020 as COVID-19 rampaged across the world, millions sought to make sense of something that was beyond any of our control. For some that meant connecting random dots between great resets, 5G roll-out, bats in soup and Bill Gates' vaccine programs. It was easier to blame the "Deep State" or the Microsoft co-founder or any other number of lunatic notions than to grasp the terrifying truth that pandemics happen, have happened throughout history and are largely beyond our control.

Something else lies at the heart of conspiracy theories. *Pareidolia* (Greek for "beyond form or image") is the human tendency to see things that aren't there. The human brain is hardwired to recognise people and sometimes, in that process, it experiences glitches and sees faces in clouds, or Jesus or Elvis on a piece of toast by mistake. Pareidolia belongs to a wider phenomenon known as *apophenia* (aka patternicity) where the brain maps connections where there are none. The term was coined by German psychiatrist Klaus Conrad in 1958 to explain why patients with acute schizophrenia link up otherwise unconnected things, but subsequently apophenia has come to be seen to be a common part of human experience. It explains all sorts of things, including "Gambler's fallacy" where the guy at the slot machines keeps putting his coins in the slot, believing he is sensing a pattern and losing it all because the whole pattern thing is unscientific nonsense.

From an evolutionary point of view, apophenia makes sense. That shape in the trees may be a shadow, but equally it could be a hungry tiger or a member of an enemy tribe, so better to run just in case.

Apophenia alone cannot explain why your cousin on Facebook believes that 5G caused the pandemic, or that Prince Philip murdered Princess Di, but it does go some way to explaining why so many people fell for the guff being spouted by District Attorney Jim Garrison in the late 1960s about the murder of JFK.

Stare at anything long enough and you begin to see things that aren't there. Subject the 26.6-second Zapruder film to forensic scrutiny over weeks and months and years, and you start to see conspiracies in every frame. Much was made by Garrison, for example, of the mysterious "umbrella man", who opened his brolly as "a signal" just as the presidential limousine was passing and it is critical to Oliver Stone's massively successful and hugely influential 1991 film *JFK* too. On the face of it that's not unreasonable – 22nd November 1963 was a warm day in Dallas, with clear blue skies. Many of the people pictured are in T-shirts and summer dresses. So why was a guy in a raincoat opening an umbrella as the motorcade went by? It's weird and suspicious and remains so right up to the moment when you discover who he was. His name was Louie Steven Witt, and he wasn't signalling a gunman on the grassy knoll but demonstrating against the Kennedy family.

"Umbrella protests" had been a common symbol of anti-appeasement movements in the 1940s on account of Neville Chamberlain having held one when he returned from Munich declaring "peace for our time". John F. Kennedy's father, Joe, had long been accused of sucking up to the Nazis, and following the erection of the Berlin Wall in 1961, his son was accused of doing much the same with the East German Communist regime. And that is what Witt was doing in Dallas on the morning of the assassination in November 1963; he was protesting against the Kennedys. Telling his story to the US House Select Committee on Assassinations in 1978, he later said: "If the *Guinness Book of Records* had a category for people who were at the wrong place at the wrong time... I would be No. 1."

Oliver Stone, who by 1991 must have known the truth of Witt's actions, makes no mention of the umbrella man's identity in his film. Nor does he explain that Garrison's main thesis, rooted in a repellant homophobic trope, hinged on a theory that had been placed by the Russian Disinformation Unit in an Italian newspaper. That theory would have the world believe that gay men, with CIA links, had taken part in the murder as part of a "homosexual thrill kill".

"They had the same motive as Loeb and Leopold* when they murdered Bobbie Franks in Chicago," Garrison told reporter James

---

* The infamous murder of 14-year-old Bobbie Franks by two students at the University of Chicago who were obsessed with Nietzsche, which inspired the 1948 Alfred Hitchcock film *Rope*.

Phelan in the 1960s and in what amounted to an anti-gay witch hunt, he brought his chief suspect Clay Shaw to trial.

In the apophenic masterclass that is Stone's *JFK*, Shaw is played by the actor Tommy Lee Jones as a predatory homosexual lowlife. He holds gay orgies while watching Hitler Youth films and might as well have "MURDERER" tattooed on his forehead. The depiction is nothing like the real-life Shaw, who never acknowledged his sexuality, probably for fear of persecution.

Shaw had served his country with distinction and won the Croix de Guerre, Legion of Merit and Bronze Star in the Second World War. He was a published playwright, a lover of old buildings and a professed fan of John F. Kennedy. He had no motive whatsoever.

Garrison suspected him for no other reason than that he acted suspiciously when questioned. But quite obviously, he wasn't covering up a conspiracy, but rather hiding his sexuality. The idea that Shaw had hatched a plot with the CIA to kill the president was absurd and at the end of the 1969 trial the jury agreed, taking less than an hour to clear him of all charges. Shaw was broken by the ordeal and died five years later. Meanwhile, the conspiracy bandwagon rolled on.

In 1975 the Zapruder film was aired on ABC's *Goodnight America* and the attendant apophenia led to the formation of the United States House Select Committee on Assassinations (HSCA) in 1976. Their remit was to investigate the killings of both Kennedy in 1963 and Martin Luther King in 1968 with the hope it might restore a little trust in government, but things backfired spectacularly. For while the HSCA concluded that MLK had been killed by James Earl Ray, the evidence in the JFK case did "not preclude the possibility of two gunmen firing at the President" and suggested that there was probably a conspiracy.

The HSCA findings and Stone's later trial-by-patience movie spawned a whole new era of conspiracies and "alternative theories". A 2018 poll found that 60% of Americans still believed that the state or other actors had been involved in Kennedy's death.

That belief and the conspiracy theories surrounding the death of JFK matter. And the assassination itself matters too. Because the event and its place in the global collective consciousness is critical to his myth. Fifty years after Kennedy's assassination, a Gallup Poll found that by far the first thing people thought about when remembering him was his murder, with "Cuba", "inspiration", "Camelot", "Civil Rights", "adultery" and "space" coming in as distant runners-up – in that order.

Almost a decade after his racist, self-serving "Rivers of Blood" speech in 1968, the British politician Enoch Powell wrote a biography of his political hero, the nineteenth-century statesman Joseph Chamberlain. Describing Chamberlain, Powell said, "all political lives, unless they are cut off in midstream at a happy juncture, end in failure, because that is the nature of politics and of human affairs".

John F. Kennedy's career did not exactly end on a happy note, but it was cut off with him riding high in the polls. A Gallup Poll taken between 8–13th November 1963 showed that he enjoyed a 58% job approval rating, better by far than any US president apart from George W. Bush in the immediate aftermath of 9/11. Americans were upbeat in 1963. And that's why 68% of poll respondents were happy with their income and thought the president responsible. For most of his last year in office JFK maintained a huge lead over his rivals and the impact of his death saw that popularity passed on, boosting the standing of his successor, Lyndon B. Johnson, and leading to the biggest electoral margin in US history, in which Johnson secured 61.1% of the popular vote. That was partly down to the Republican challenger, Barry Goldwater, running an extremely right-wing campaign, but also because the ghost of Jack Kennedy haunted the polling booths.

Had Kennedy lived we would undoubtedly remember him differently and while "What-ifery" can be a dangerous game, let's briefly consider what might have happened.

Despite the conspiracy theories that suggest otherwise, Kennedy was committed to the escalation in the Vietnam War and as it played out, it would undoubtedly have damaged his reputation just as it did for Johnson. Moreover, if he hadn't been killed, the Civil Rights movement that gained so much impetus from his death would very likely never have reached the consensus that saw landmark legislation passed by Johnson in July 1964. Kennedy, as we shall see, was not always committed to the cause – and had he served his two terms, one of the things most associated with him might never have come to pass.

The assassination, in short, bolstered Kennedy's legend and forged a legacy that would likely not have come to pass so quickly if he had lived. The manner of his death and the attendant conspiracies that followed created a sort of cult. It turned him into the great liberal martyr of the twentieth century. The good guy of American politics. The latter-day King Arthur, slain by wicked, nefarious forces, just as he is about to fling open the doors on the future.

It's a nice story, but it is a fiction worthy of Oliver Stone.

* * *

The JFK legend was being forged even as he lay in his coffin. His funeral, orchestrated and starring his grieving widow Jackie, was held on 25th November 1963 and it was a send-off worthy of an emperor.

On Sunday 24th, Kennedy's body was carried by gun carriage to the Rotunda of the Capitol, where almost biblical sounding eulogies were given. Mike Mansfield, Majority Leader of the United States Senate said: "A piece of each of us died at that moment. Yet, in death he gave of himself to us... a profound wit, from which a great leadership emerged. He gave us of a kindness and a strength fused into a human courage to seek peace without fear."

John W. McCormack, Speaker of the House of Representatives added that Kennedy had now "taken his place among the great world leaders of history."

Overnight 250,000 mourners filed past the coffin.

The following day mass was held at St Matthew's Cathedral. Representatives of 82 countries, including French President Charles de Gaulle, British Prime Minister Alec Douglas-Home and the Ethiopian Emperor

Haile Selassie attended. Mrs Kennedy, wreathed in a black veil which did not hide her beauty, clutched the hands of her two young children, Caroline and John Junior. Millions across the world, including citizens in the USSR, watched live on TV as John Junior, whose third birthday fell that day, saluted his father's coffin as it was carried away across the Potomac River. Later, 50 USAF jets flew in formation over Arlington Cemetery, as an eternal flame sprung to life above the grave. Gloom, high drama and grandeur hung across it all.

Several days later, Pulitzer Prize-winning journalist Theodore H. White was summoned from the dentist's chair back to his office at *Life* magazine. When he arrived, Jackie Kennedy was on the line. She had a message for the American people, and she wanted White to be the errand boy. White drove to meet her at the Kennedy Compound at Hyannis Port, the Kennedy family's fortress of solitude on Cape Cod. Mrs Kennedy gave White her interview – and he rang the copy through from a maid's room while *Life* editors literally held the presses. The piece caused a sensation and gave birth to the Camelot myth.

The musical *Camelot* was the *Hamilton* of its day. Written by lyricist and composer partnership Alan Jay Lerner and Frederick Loewe, it is a witty romp through the myth of King Arthur and Guinevere and their eponymous utopian castle kingdom. Arthur and Guinevere are more than just a King and Queen – they are a sixth-century celebrity power couple. Liberal, good-looking folks, they're the sort you might find weekending in Martha's Vineyard. Sure, at the end everything goes horribly wrong and civil war ensues, but there are some great tunes along the way and, very clearly, Arthur and Guinevere are Democrats.

Prior to JFK's death nobody had associated him with the musical, but Jackie's interview lodged the perception in the public mind.

"When Jack [as everyone called her husband] quoted something, it was usually classical," Jackie told White, "but I am so ashamed of myself, all I keep thinking of is this line from a musical comedy. At night, before we'd go to sleep, Jack liked to play some records; and the song he loved most (was) at the very end of the record. The lines he loved to hear were: 'Don't let it be forgot, that once there was a spot, for one brief shining moment that was known as Camelot.'"

For someone so deep in mourning, it must be said that Mrs Kennedy was playing a PR blinder. The original cast recording of *Camelot* was a massive hit record in the 1960s. Millions of people across America owned a copy and knew the words. Jackie knew that and she also understood the newspaper industry inside out. Prior to marrying JFK in 1953, Jackie Bouvier had worked as a journalist for the *Washington Times-Herald* on the "Inquiring Camera Girl" column. The feature required her to pose random questions to passers-by in the street and to secure witty vox pops. Jackie, like no First Lady before or since, knew how to work the press and understood that to propagate the Kennedy legend she needed to be in full control of the message from day one.

She had identified Theodore White as a tame, client journalist and 17 pages of yellow paper in the John F. Kennedy Presidential Library in Boston suggest she chose well. Those pages, which contain White's interview notes, show Mrs Kennedy's neat red markings and additions at the side. *Life* editors tried to cut down the *Camelot* references, but Jackie, via White, insisted they stay. This was an act of very modern image management.

JFK's devoted secretary Evelyn Lincoln later dismissed the notion that Kennedy would have listened to *Camelot* before going to bed and claimed his favourite song was "Bill Bailey, Won't You Please Come Home". But you can't really build an enduring myth on "Bill Bailey, Won't You Please Come Home".

Theodore White later regretted being Jackie Kennedy's "instrument in labeling the myth" and said that he had done so because he felt sorry for the First Lady. But by then, it was too late. The first draft of Kennedy's legend had been penned.

* * *

One of the most remarkable things about the cult of John F. Kennedy is the sheer number of shrines in his honour. Literally hundreds of memorials dot the world, from a plaque on Runnymede Island in the Thames to the massive Yad Memorial near Jerusalem, Israel, which is built in the shape of a giant felled tree.

America's most famous airport is named after him and so too is a NASA base. Hundreds of subways, bus stations, roads, districts, colleges and libraries bear his name, and not only in America. France has 32 Kennedy streets and Brazil two Kennedy municipalities. There is a JFK college in Mauritius and a Kennedy City in Honduras which though not actually a city is still a massive district of the capital, Tegucigalpa. You can drive down a Kennedy Avenue in Fiji and a Kennedy Way in Clacton-on-Sea, Essex.

There are "Kennedy" schools in Berlin, Coventry, Faridabad and Guam.

His face features on postage stamps. Bob Dylan wrote music about him and so too did Dick Holler and Igor Stravinsky. Kennedy got his face on the half dollar, a diesel locomotive named in his memory by British Rail and even his own GI Joe action doll.

But what, apart from his early and unplanned death, did he do to deserve it all?

To understand Jack, you first have to understand his father, Joe.

Born in East Boston, Massachusetts in 1888, Catholic Joe was the scion of a wealthy Irish-American business family and the son of a politician – Patrick. Sent to the elite Boston Latin School and onwards to Harvard, young Joe loved sports, money and beautiful women in no particular order. In 1913, aged 25, he made himself famous by borrowing enough money to secure the Columbia Trust bank, in which his father had a significant share, and became the US's youngest ever bank President. He went on to make a fortune through a series of canny investments and deals that nowadays would have landed him in jail, but in those days kept him just on the right side of the law. Kennedy was not, as is often claimed, either a bootlegger or a mobster, but he did have dealings, as almost all contemporary businessmen did at the time with them both.

Possessed of an almost supernatural sixth sense for buying and selling at the right time, he made millions on the 1929 Wall Street Crash and even more by anticipating the American thirst for strong liquor in the post-Prohibition era. During a 1933 trip to the UK with his wife Rose, eldest son Joe Jnr. and latest mistress Kaye Halle in tow, he secured the rights to sell Haig whisky, Dewar's whisky and Gordon's gin in the USA with the help of no less a figure than Winston Churchill. When Prohibition ended two months later, Kennedy made a killing, later selling the concession for $8.2 million (roughly $100 million in 2023 money). All of this made the already-rich family almost unimaginably wealthy, and, throughout his political life, JFK never drew a dollar from the taxpayer, letting it be known that he donated his entire salary and expense account to charity.

When Joe died in 1969 *The New York Times* estimated his net worth to be around $500,000,000 ($4.3 billion in 2023).

Throughout the 1920s and early 1930s, Kennedy invested in Hollywood. He bought up studios on the cheap and then, like any good venture capitalist, refinanced and reorganised them before selling them on. He gambled on talking pictures and it paid off when he sold his company in a merger that created the studio RKO. Bette Lasky, daughter of Paramount Studio head Jesse Lasky, once said of Joe that he was the "only outsider to ever fleece Hollywood."

Joe loved the movie business, not only because it made him money, but because it gave him plenty of opportunities to cheat on his wife. He had affairs with Gloria Swanson and dozens of other Hollywood stars and later encouraged his own sons to sleep with as many women as possible. Joe viewed women as trophies, but the prize he hankered after most of all was the White House.

To that end, Joe poured money into Franklin D. Roosevelt's 1932 campaign and was handed the job of heading the Securities and Exchange Commission in return. In 1938, Roosevelt sent Joe to London as Ambassador to the United Kingdom and the glamorous Kennedy clan proved to be a sensation in the pre-war capital. Two of the daughters, Rosemary and Kathleen, were presented to King George VI and Queen Elizabeth at court and the family was to be seen at every hot ticket in town. But Joe was no friend of Britain, and when it became clear that he wanted the USA to stay on friendly terms with Hitler, the honeymoon ended.

Joe viewed communism, not fascism, as the great threat to the world and saw the Nazi leader as the natural bulwark against it. He was only too happy to express those views, informing the newly appointed German Ambassador to Britain, Herbert von Dirksen, that Roosevelt was a victim of "Jewish influence" and suggesting in correspondence with his friend, the American-born Tory MP Nancy Astor, herself a Nazi sympathizer, that US Jewish journalists were intent on setting a "a match to the fuse of the world".

Following Kristallnacht, in November 1938, Joe was more worried about Hitler's optics than the murder of 91 innocent Jewish Germans. Writing to another fake hero, the Nazi-sympathising American aviator Charles Lindbergh shortly after the event he asked: "Isn't there some way to persuade (Hitler) it is on a situation like this that the whole program of saving western civilization might hinge? It is more and more difficult for those seeking peaceful solutions to advocate any plan when the papers are filled with such horror."

Joe's own answer to the "Jewish Question", reported in *The New York Times* in 1938, was to ship all the German Jews to Africa and other colonies under the protection of the USA and the United Kingdom.

It was Joe's devotion to appeasement that inspired the 39-year-old Louie Steven Witt, 25 years later, to head to Dealey Plaza for history's worst-timed one-man demonstration.

Even after Chamberlain had declared war on Hitler in September 1939, the American Ambassador continued to communicate with the Nazis and sought to meet the Führer. At the same time, he tried to block US aid to Britain, stressing US neutrality, which made him extremely unpopular with his hosts. Things came to a head in November 1940 when he told reporters from the *Boston Globe* that: "I'm willing to spend all I've got left to keep us out of the war," adding "there's no sense in our getting in. We'd just be holding the bag."

Later, Joe suggested that if the Nazis won, the USA should continue to trade with them – and in a line that would haunt him for the rest of his life added: "Democracy is finished in England. It may be here. Because it comes to a question of feeding people. It's all an economic question."

Kennedy was obliged to resign and his chances of ever running for the White House were scotched, so he passed the baton to his eldest son, Joe Junior, instead. Joe Junior was a chip off his father's block and had a massive political crush on Hitler in the 1930s. Travelling to Germany in 1934, he wrote home gushingly of the Nazi leader's eugenics policies adding that the German "dislike of the Jews" was "well-founded". Joe Junior was killed, over Blythburgh, Suffolk, on 12th August 1944, when the experimental drone bomber he was flying prematurely exploded. He was the first of the siblings to die in what has been dubbed the "Kennedy Curse". His sister, Kathleen, also died in a plane crash in 1948 while flying on route to the French Riviera and with the murders of Jack in 1963 and Robert in 1968, four of Joe and Rose Kennedy's nine children were to predecease them.

Another daughter met an equally awful fate, at the hands of her father. The third child and eldest daughter, Rosemary, was considered "different" by her parents. She was prone to mood swings and slower to read and write than her brothers and sisters, which the Kennedys sought to explain as an accident at her birth or "high spirits". As she grew up, her behaviour became more erratic, and her parents sent her away to Catholic boarding schools from which she frequently escaped.

The morally incontinent Kennedy patriarch became convinced that Rosemary was a ticking bomb and that it was just a matter of time before she got pregnant and spoiled his family's wholly undeserved wholesome image. Taking matters into his own hands, in November 1941, when she was 23, he arranged for Rosemary to have a frontal lobotomy without informing his wife or other members of the family. The operation was a disaster and Rosemary lost the ability to speak and walk. She was hidden away and cared for by nurses, and Jack and Bobby never saw her again. Indeed, it was only with Joe's death in 1969 that the rest of the family fully acknowledged her existence and set about trying to make amends. Rosemary died in 2005, aged 86.

With the death of his eldest son, in 1944, Joe poured all his efforts into the spare, or rather one of the three spares – John, and in time through him, was to fulfil his fantasy of having a President Kennedy in the White House.

Jack had already done some of the groundwork himself. His great hero was that towering figure Winston Churchill and throughout his adult life, Kennedy saw him as a political guiding spirit. His admiration was such that when he later became president, he bestowed honorary American citizenship on Britain's wartime leader. But Winston's influence stretched back some 20 years before that and in the early 1940s Kennedy was already using him as a sort of career template. There were strong similarities between the two men. Like Churchill, Jack was from a powerful and well-connected family, and, like Churchill, he had grown up in the shadow of a famous and successful politician father.

Jack also sought, as Winston had done, to burnish his image as a scholar king by writing books and his first, *Why England Slept* (1940) even plagiarised the title of Winston's 1938 work *While England Slept*.

Why England Slept had been JFK's Harvard thesis and was originally titled "Appeasement at Munich". In it, the young Kennedy argued that it was flaws in the British political system that had caused the UK to be slow to respond to Hitler's regime and that Chamberlain had been unfairly blamed. The thesis had been awarded *magna cum laude* (the second highest grade in a US university) and would never have been turned into a book if it hadn't been written by the son of such a high-profile individual, but Joe saw it as a way of raising his boy's profile and he was not a man to be put down. To that end he hired Arthur Krock, a two-time Pulitzer Prizewinning journalist, to add some polish. Arthur was firmly in Joseph's pocket in the 1930s and only too happy to oblige.

Krock probably rewrote the whole thing, and on publication it became a modest commercial hit, shifting a respectable 80,000 copies in 1940. The war was to raise JFK's profile in other ways too.

Following the attack on Pearl Harbor in December 1941, Jack failed the medical for both the army and navy. Fearing that his son might end up behind a desk, Joe pulled every string that he could to get him to the front line. Sent to the South Pacific in the spring of 1943, the 25-year-old Kennedy was put in command of torpedo boat *PT-109* and proved himself an able leader. On the night of 1st August 1943, while taking part in an action against the enemy, his command was rammed and cut in half by the Japanese Naval Destroyer *Amagiri,* killing two of his men. Subsequently Kennedy led the ten surviving crew members on an epic swim between nearby islands until they were rescued six days later. Kennedy won the Navy and Marine Corps medal for his actions and the Purple Heart for the injury he sustained to his back. But his father Joe felt that he was deserving of something better and lobbied for a Silver Star. The War Department didn't agree, and the medal never came – but it didn't really matter because already Joe was using his son's military heroism to mutual advantage.

Those adventures in the South Pacific were to become critical to Kennedy's profile as a courageous war hero and leader of men. In 1944, Joe used his considerable influence to make sure that the story made its way into the *New Yorker* and a later longer article in *Reader's Digest,* then the most-read publication in the USA, brought it to a wider audience. The article appeared in August 1944, the very month that Joe Junior was killed, and portrayed Kennedy as "a youth who has enormous bravery and energy" and who had used his skills of leadership to save the lives of his *PT-109** crew. It made Jack a household name, turned him into a national hero and propelled him onwards to his political career.

* * *

* In 1963, JFK became the only president in history to have a biographical film made about him while in office. Starring 39-year-old Cliff Robertson as the young lieutenant, the 140-minute movie, which got "final approval" from the White House, is notable for one thing: none of the Black actors get credit.

Not much is made of Rosemary's tragic life, or Joe's appeasement, or Joe Junior's Nazi sympathies at the John F. Kennedy Museum on Main Street, Hyannis. But the volunteers are obviously very proud of their local celebrity family and beam at visitors who queue up to buy tickets reminding us all, several times: "The museum only occupies the first floor."

The exhibition consists mostly of photographs of a smiling JFK, a smiling Jackie and the extended photogenic family – smiling. At times the effect is to make you feel that you are in an interactive toothpaste commercial. It's not all veneer. There is mention of his work to improve Civil Rights, a passing nod to his handling of the Cuban Missile Crisis and a properly enormous Kennedy Family Tree which includes Arnold Schwarzenegger, whose wife, Maria Shriver, was JFK's niece – demonstrating that the political legacy goes on. But soon we are back in the gift shop looking at "reusable Kennedy drinking straws" and birdhouses, made from pieces of the one and only Kennedy Compound, which are being flogged off for $175.00 each.

"The museum only occupies the first floor!" one of the volunteers reminds us helpfully, "but you are welcome to go around again."

So, we do.

"Didn't Marilyn Monroe sing happy birthday to him?" my daughter pipes up. "Why are there no pictures of her?" she asks, and I explain that she's probably not included here because she had an affair with him while he was married to Jackie and so it probably isn't something she should be saying so loudly. This is the life of Jack Kennedy with all the bad bits cut out. Which is perhaps why it occupies just that one floor.

It's not just Monroe who has been edited out. There is no mention of Anita Ekberg or Marlene Dietrich, or Marion Fay Beardsley, his 19-year-old intern, or the actress Angie Dickinson with whom he had an ongoing affair, or indeed any of the hundreds of women JFK slept with. Everyone is dimly aware of Kennedy's affairs, but to read about the scale of them is mind-boggling.

"I get a migraine if I don't get a strange piece of ass every day," he once told his strategist Bobby Baker, and during his 1,036 days in office, he did everything he could to fight those headaches while his gatekeeper, his brother Bobby Kennedy, tried to keep his secret.

Against the better instincts of both Jack and Bobby, they even kept J. Edgar Hoover, the legendary Director of the FBI, on side and in office on the basis that you keep your enemies close. JFK had been on Hoover's radar since 1942 when he had had an affair with a Danish journalist called Inga Arvad, who was suspected of being a Nazi spy. Arvad had conducted three interviews with Adolf Hitler, and he had taken something of a shine to her, so when she arrived in the US and started sleeping with Kennedy, son of the former Ambassador to Britain and himself a naval officer, they got suspicious and started bugging them both.

By the time JFK entered the White House, Hoover had a file on both him and his brother, Bobby, as thick as an elephant's leg, and as Tim Weiner wrote in his book, *Enemies, A History of the FBI*: "Hoover's knowledge of JFK's private conduct and RFK's political conspiracies were potentially lethal political weapons. He brandished them now. He let the president and the attorney general know that he knew they had committed moral sins."

But long before he even got to the White House, JFK was dodging potentially career-ending scandals and, in 1958, a woman called Florence M. Kater posed a particular problem.

Kennedy had become a Senator for Massachusetts in 1953. In 1958 he started an affair with Pamela Turnure, one of his secretaries. Late one night, Kater who was Turnure's landlady, snapped pictures of Jack leaving her tenant's apartment and subsequently began a one-woman campaign to expose the Senator's infidelity. She sent copies of the picture to 50 newspaper journalists along with a lengthy anonymous letter detailing his activities, but to her immense frustration, nobody took any interest and at the Hyannis Museum the same is true today. Anything that shies from the toothy myth of the movie-star-handsome president is ignored.

Just one relic in the museum, a rocking chair, on loan from the Waldorf Astoria in New York, hints at something more honest.

In the mid-1940s Kennedy was diagnosed with Addison's disease, a crippling degenerative illness, caused in part by a failure of the adrenal glands which leads to the body not producing enough hormones. Symptoms can include a darkening of the skin, significant lower back pain and bouts of vomiting, weakness, weight loss and abdominal pain. In Kennedy's case the back pain was particularly acute and in 1954 he undertook a life-threatening operation in the hope of improving his mobility, telling one doctor: "I'd rather be dead than spend the rest of my life on these goddam crutches!"

Nobody beyond the young politician's tight network of family and friends knew about the illness and, throughout his life, his back problems were blamed on those war wounds or old football injuries. The truth was hidden because it sat at complete odds with his image as a "vigorous", youthful politician, who, when he came to power in 1960 aged 43, was the youngest elected president in the nation's history. Vitality was critical to the Kennedy USP and, during the 1960 campaign, he fought his Republican rival Richard Nixon, who was in fact just four years his senior, largely on that basis.

But Jack Kennedy was very far from being a healthy man.

In his book *President Kennedy, Profiles in Power*, Richard Reeves' forensic day-by-day study of JFK's time in office, the author spells it out:

"He had trouble fighting off ordinary infections and suffered recurrent fevers that raged as high as 106 degrees. As candidate and president, Kennedy concealed his low energy level, radiating health and good humour, though he usually spent more than half of most days in bed. He retired early most nights, read in bed until 9:00 a.m. or so every morning and napped an hour each afternoon."

Given that terrible back condition, it is fairly extraordinary that Kennedy managed to have sex with so many people – on top of his exhausting day job. When he had another brief tryst with Marlene Dietrich, in a White House bedroom, she was astonished to see that he was wearing an elaborate back brace and bandages, which he first had to remove.

JFK wore that tightly laced brace to keep his back upright, and it might have directly helped his assassin. The first bullet that hit him on 22nd November 1963 did not kill Kennedy who did not slump because the corset kept him rigid, meaning that Oswald was able to take that second fatal shot.

In addition to the Addison's, JFK suffered from other illnesses, including recurring bouts of STDs which he passed on, unapologetically, to the women he slept with. One of those women, Hjordis Niven, wife of the actor David Niven, who gave the president "a quickie" on the night of his 46th birthday in May 1963, claimed that she caught chlamydia as a result.

Despite his outward charisma, inward Jack was not a well man and, away from the cameras and throughout his presidency, he would often walk with a stick or crutches. So, when not "getting a strange piece of ass", resting was a big part of his day – and the specially designed rocking chair, in the Hyannis Port Museum, enabled him to sit and work comfortably. Drugs helped too. For most of his presidency he was treated by the high-profile "celebrity doctor" Max Jacobson, known universally as "Doctor Feelgood" on account of his reputation for administering "vitamin shots" that contained highly addictive amphetamines.

Kennedy took the shots and gave himself daily injections of gamma globulin, in the thigh, to help beat off infections in his weakened immune system.

In 2002, the historian Robert Dallek, a professor at Boston University who studied JFK's medical records, estimated that the president was on roughly 12 medications a day including codeine, Demerol, methadone, Ritalin, meprobamate and steroids. He took barbiturates to go to sleep and for two days during the Cuban Missile Crisis in 1962 was put on a powerful anti-psychotic drug, trifluoperazine, after showing signs of violent mood swings.

But even now, 60 years after his death, the museum at Hyannis Point, which is dedicated to his memory, shies away from the illness as it does the affairs and all the other dirt and talks up his family, his heroism and brilliance as a man of great speeches and words instead. That is perhaps understandable as Kennedy's reputation as an erudite intellectual is critical to how he was and is still viewed. In many respects, for all his acknowledged flaws, he is still seen as a sort of more handsome, less alcoholic, transatlantic remake of his hero Winston Churchill. Unfortunately, quite a lot of that reputation rests on the hard work of other people.

In 1954, 14 years after Arthur Krock had turned his thesis into *Why England Slept*, and while recovering from spinal surgery on his back, JFK had an idea for a sequel and mapped out the idea for his most famous work, *Profiles in Courage*. The book was a nod to Thomas Carlyle's *On Heroes, Hero-Worship, & the Heroic in History*, in which the nineteenth-century Scottish essayist had argued that "the history of what man has accomplished in this world, is at bottom the History of the Great Men who have worked here". Kennedy's modern take picked eight American heroes (all white men) who at some time or other in the nation's history had taken a principled but unpopular political stand that had subsequently damaged their careers.

Published on 1st January 1956, the book was a bestseller and won Kennedy the 1957 Pulitzer Prize for biography. The Pulitzer board at the time included a chap called Arthur Krock and a rumour spread that Joe had got to Krock and Arthur had got to the jurors. But the problem with that conspiracy theory was that Krock was not on the actual panel, and it seems unlikely that a distinguished group of academics would have been swayed by one man anyway.

Even so, the book is problematic for a number of reasons, not least because Kennedy didn't write most of it. Now it is hardly a big secret that politicians don't always write the words they utter, or the tomes that bear their names, but words and ideas are critical to the Kennedy myth and so it comes as a shock to discover that many of them were penned by other people. Or specifically – one man. Kennedy did acknowledge in the introduction to *Profiles in Courage* that he had been helped by Ted Sorensen, a 24-year-old lawyer, who had become his chief legislative aide, but the suspicion is that Ted wrote pretty much the whole thing.

Trained as a lawyer, Sorensen wrote like a poet and during the decade he worked for JFK he penned most of his greatest lines. In *Kennedy*, his 1965 biography of the President, Ted acknowledged the partnership, saying:

"As the years went on, and I came to know what he thought on each subject as well as how he wished to say it, our style and standard became increasingly one… we tried repeatedly but unsuccessfully to find other wordsmiths who could write for him in the style to which he was accustomed. The style of those whom we tried may have been very good. It may have been superior. But it was not his."

Forty years later, while discussing JFK's inaugural speech with the author Richard Tofel, Sorensen suggested that the myth of Kennedy and the preservation of it, was more important than the truth of who had written what and when.

"I recognize that I have some obligation to history, but all these years I have tried to make clear that President Kennedy was the principal author of all his speeches and articles. If I say otherwise, that diminishes him, and I don't want to diminish him."

The softly spoken Sorensen went on to see his words attributed to the man who uttered them. Think of any of those famous lines from "Ask not what your country can do for you; ask rather, what you can do for your country" to "Do not pray for easy lives. Pray to be stronger men" and Ted probably penned them, along with that famous book.

The suspicions were there from the start. In December 1957, during an appearance on ABC's *The Mike Wallace Interview*, the journalist Andrew "Drew" Pearson claimed that Kennedy was "the only man in history… who won the Pulitzer Prize for a book that was ghostwritten."

The Kennedys were furious, and Bobby Kennedy turned up, that night at ABC with lawyers in tow, demanding a retraction. Wallace and Pearson refused to back down, but panicked executives did.

Paperwork on display at the John F. Kennedy Presidential Library in Boston suggests that Jack did have input and probably wrote the outline notes for most of the chapters and perhaps a little more for the John Quincy Adams one. But writing a book is hard work and JFK was a busy man in the years 1954–56. The idea that he sat down and wrote out the rest of it with his debilitating bad back is a fairy tale.

It used to be said that behind every man, there was a great woman and that was certainly true of Jack Kennedy. But, equally as important, there was a great Ted Sorensen too.

Whoever wrote what, the subject matter of *Profiles in Courage* has aged very badly indeed. Three of the eight heroic subjects were "owners" of enslaved people. One, Daniel Webster, is included on the basis that he went against public opinion to support the Fugitive Slave Act (part of the Compromise of 1850) which made it a criminal offence in the Northern States of the USA to give refuge to fleeing enslaved people from the south.

Following JFK's assassination, *Profiles in Courage* was expanded into a TV series which ran to 26 episodes from November 1964 to May 1965 on NBC. Joe McCarthy, a Kennedy family friend, who had taken a recent unpopular stand of his own, didn't get an episode, but the TV show did at least benefit from finally including some women and people of colour. The various Kennedy museums make a big deal about it still and the Kennedy family dishes out "Profiles in Courage Awards" to this day to keep Jack's reputation alive. Recent recipients, who get a Tiffany Lamp in recognition of their courage, have included Barack Obama, Volodymyr Zelenskyy and George W. Bush, who got his lamp for being brave enough to go back on his election pledge not to raise taxes. Honestly, I am not making it up.

On his birthday on 8th March 2009, Edward Kennedy, the last surviving brother, was given the award at an event hosted by Bill Cosby. "Ted", who in 1969 had left a 28-year-old campaign worker, Mary Jo Kopechne, to drown in the car he had crashed into the sea at Chappaquiddick, off the coast of Martha's Vineyard, seems to have received the honour as a sort of consolation prize for being the least significant Kennedy brother.

As he took possession of the Tiffany Lamp, a choir sang *The Best Is Yet to Come* but it was another, albeit unintentional, Kennedy fantasy for within five months, Ted was dead.

* * *

Having secured the Democratic nomination for the 1960 US Presidential Election, Jack ran the glitziest campaign American politics had ever seen. Frank Sinatra, Ol' Blue Eyes himself, sang his campaign song and other members of the Rat Pack, including Jack's brother-in-law Peter Lawford, who had married younger sister Patricia in 1954, lined up to endorse the man of the hour. Kennedy had panache in abundance, a ready wit and a mountain range of easy charm. On 26th September he brought all of it to the fore, as he faced his rival Richard Nixon in the first-ever televised presidential debate.

A much-repeated myth has Nixon winning with radio listeners and the telegenic Kennedy winning with TV viewers, but that isn't true. The story springs from the results of just one poll, heavily biased in Nixon's favour, that was conducted by Sindlinger & Company on the night. In all other polls, across both media, JFK won. Vice-President Nixon looked sweaty and awkward on camera, but he sounded equally ill at ease on the audio. He appeared pale in comparison to the healthy-looking Democratic rival and nobody watching could have known that Kennedy's "tan" was in fact a symptom of his Addison's disease.

In the weeks that followed, JFK charmed his way across America, honing his message to "Get America Moving Again" and suggested that under the Republican Eisenhower the country had become economically and militarily weaker than the USSR. Kennedy promised that his "New Frontier" politics would win the Cold War by "levelling up" the United States and demonstrate America to be freer, happier and wealthier than the Soviets. There would be healthcare reforms, increased social security payments, a global "Peace Corps", a radical housing agenda and free candy for all. Kennedy would defeat communism with the magical power of American optimism and close the "missile gap" to make sure that everyone could sleep soundly in their beds at night.

Come 8th November and enough Americans bought it, although Kennedy won by the slimmest margin in US electoral history, gaining just 49.7% of the vote to Richard Nixon's 49.6% and 303 Electoral College votes to Nixon's 219. The result was so close that the Republicans cried foul, and accusations of voter fraud dogged Kennedy's victory. There were suggestions of gerrymandering in 11 states including Texas, the home state of Kennedy's running mate Lyndon B. Johnson, and Illinois. Illinois was home to the powerful Chicago Mayor, Robert Daley, a close associate of Joe Kennedy and it had been won by just 8,000 votes.

As Nixon tactically distanced himself from the accusations of fraud, a recount was held in 863 precincts of Illinois, which showed that yes, Tricky Dicky's votes had been undercounted, but only by 943. Somewhat inconveniently for the Republicans, his vote had actually been overcounted in 40% of precincts and, either way, it didn't make any difference to the result. Kennedy had won the popular vote as well as that all-important Electoral College vote too. There is nothing new under the sun.

On coming to power, Kennedy was, at 43, the youngest person ever to be elected* president and he took over from Republican Dwight Eisenhower, who at 70, was then the oldest. In his inaugural address, the following January, dressed in a morning suit in a wind chill of -7°F, the new president delivered his now famous speech. It was rich in Churchillian rhetoric and climaxed with Ted Sorensen's famous lines about asking what Americans could do for their country.

But Kennedy, like so many leaders before and since, was about to discover that famous backers, big words, crazy promises and impressive rhetoric, albeit written by other people, are not enough to lead a country.

---

* Teddy Roosevelt was 42, but took over the job after the assassination of William McKinley, whose death in March 1901 inspired the inevitable conspiracy theories.

The United States was facing multiple challenges on a head-spinning number of domestic and international fronts in 1961. Mired in recession, US GDP was falling and in May, unemployment was to hit 7.1%. The growing anger and sense of injustice among Black Americans around Jim Crow segregation laws, particularly (but not exclusively) in the South, was already a national issue – and one that no president could ignore. But despite that, Jack tried his very hardest.

Deep-rooted institutional racism meant that millions of Black Americans were unable to vote and their exclusion from everything from juries to places at "white" colleges was deliberate and perpetuated, depressingly, by white Democratic politicians in the South. The issue haunted Kennedy's presidency and for most of his term, JFK would be no friend of the movement. This was not exactly unexpected. He had made half-hearted commitments to improve the lives of Black Americans on the campaign trail but only in places where he thought it judicious. In January 1960, the concerns of Black Americans were very low down on his agenda indeed. Kennedy had won by a whisker and was a hostage to a Democrat-dominated Congress that was unwilling to play ball on the "New Frontier" politics he had promised, let alone Civil Rights, which they believed would cost them white votes in the South.

The conservative-minded Kennedy brothers were not natural radicals and were unnerved by movements like the Freedom Riders, who were challenging segregation through direct action. They wanted the Civil Rights movement to pursue their activities through the courts – or in other words "kick the issue into the long grass". Despite his later reputation as a champion of Black rights, Bobby, now Attorney General (Joe Senior insisted) and the second most powerful man in America, told aides that he was "determined to keep (Jack) out of this Civil Rights mess". The Catholic Kennedys, already paranoid that their faith might alienate non-Catholic voters, certainly did not want to attach themselves too closely to Martin Luther King who they – and most of America – viewed as a dangerous radical with even more dangerous friends.

They were particularly concerned about his relationship with Stanley Levison, an activist and lawyer who was King's "Ted Sorensen" and who helped to finesse many of his works including, in 1963, his "I Have a Dream'" speech, perhaps his most famous. Appeasing Hitler was fine on Planet Kennedy; fraternising with Civil Rights activists who might lose them votes was not.

Throughout the 1960s and up to his death in 1968, the FBI, under consecutive Democrat administrations, harassed King and tried to discredit him. He made it easy for them, not least because despite being America's best-known Baptist Pastor, he was almost as libidinous as JFK and slept with dozens of women. On 8th November 1963, just two weeks before Jack was killed, Robert Kennedy gave written approval to wire and bug MLK's office and home. FBI boss J. Edgar Hoover wished to neutralise King and destroy his reputation and uncomfortably for the JFK faithful, it happened on the Kennedy brothers' watch.

That is disconcerting for anyone who grew up believing the myth. In many a mind and at this distance from the period, Martin Luther King and Jack Kennedy are almost entwined as one. It's an association that the cathedrals to JFK – whether they be the Hyannis Museum or the John F. Kennedy Presidential Library and Museum, on the perimeter of the University of Massachusetts in Boston – seek to underline. But while MLK and JFK shared an era, they never shared a vision and certainly never saw eye to eye. Although they spoke on the phone, they met just once, on 28th August 1963, following King's "I Have a Dream" speech when he and other Civil Rights leaders were invited to the Oval Office.

Back in that freezing January of 1961, things were far frostier. MLK was deeply frustrated by the lack of action and, in June 1961, challenged the president to follow Abraham Lincoln's lead and pass an executive order that would effectively be a second Emancipation Act. Jack sat on his hands and did nothing, and anyway, he and Bobby had what they considered to be far more pressing concerns.

Jack and Bobby had long been a double act. The *Saturday Evening Post* columnist Stewart Alsop called it a "sweet-and-sour" performance with JFK deploying "his charm and (waving) the carrot" while "Bobby (waded) in with the stick". History and broader public perception have come to view them both as liberal reformers, driven by high ideals, but in truth the Kennedy brothers' main motivation was to seek and gain high office and achieve their father's ambitions. They were driven by their loyalty to the Kennedy family, the Kennedy family legacy, the Catholic Church and the Democratic Party – in that order.

They also, and this really cannot be understated, *really* hated communists, and their commitment to that loathing was to have a number of far-reaching consequences. The "in tray" of 1961 was collapsing under a ton of international crises, from Vietnam to Berlin and Cuba. But as the brothers took on the challenge of office, they were to blunder from one massive fuck-up to another.

During his campaign, JFK had taken a tough line on the Castro regime that had seized power from President Fulgencio Batista in Cuba in January 1959. JFK inherited a Joint Chiefs of Staff plan cooked up by the CIA in the dying days of the Eisenhower years and instead of questioning it, simply deferred to senior advisers and gave the operation the green light. And so the "Bay of Pigs" invasion began on 17th April 1961 and ended three days later in carnage.

A hundred of the Cuban exiles sent to overthrow Castro were killed and a thousand more were captured, and the diplomatic repercussions and the failure of the operation would haunt JFK's presidency. Kennedy's Cuban cock-up emboldened the Soviet Union's Premier Nikita Khrushchev, who viewed the ingénue president's unwillingness to see further military action through as proof that he was "all profile and no courage."

Khrushchev decided to test the waters. For a decade, a flood of 2 million East Germans had been heading into West Berlin, then effectively an enclave of West Germany in the middle of East Germany (DDR), and they consisted of many of its most highly educated and productive citizens. Something obviously had to be done to stem the tide and, sensing, from Cuba, that Kennedy was out of his depth and unwilling to act decisively, the Soviet leader made his move.

Soviet confidence was high. In the post-Stalin years, the Soviet economy had grown faster than that of the United States. They were also winning the Space Race and had both put the first satellite, Sputnik 1, into orbit in October 1957, and the first Soviet Cosmonaut Yuri Gagarin into space just a few days before the Bay of Pigs fiasco. Cowed by the success, NASA had rushed to put astronaut Alan Shepard up there too, three weeks later, but Shepard had not gone into orbit – merely dipped his space boot in the atmosphere. The Americans were very aware that they were playing catch up and so on the 25th May, Kennedy upped the stakes and in his second State of the Union address in a year, promised to put an American on the Moon by the end of the decade. It was to cost the nation $25.4 billion (roughly $194 billion in 2023) and become another of JFK's posthumous legacies.

What is often forgotten, is that in the same speech, Kennedy also declared the "whole southern half of the Globe… a great battlefield… of freedom" and in so doing effectively set the stage for the deadly Cold War proxy conflicts that followed.

In early June, Kennedy flew to Austria, via Paris for a conference in Vienna. In the French capital he met President Charles de Gaulle, who warned him about the Soviet leader's abrasive style, but his friendly words only gave Kennedy the jitters and from the moment he met Khrushchev things went disastrously south. The 66-year-old Soviet leader was tougher than Stalin's old boots and a formidable and seasoned opponent.

Khrushchev was seeking to tear up the 1945 Potsdam Agreement. That was the consensus between Attlee, Truman and Stalin at the end of the war that divided the European theatre of war among the three major powers, the USA, UK and USSR. Germany itself was subdivided into four occupation zones (affording France a role) with the German capital, Berlin, which sat in the Soviet zone also split between the four nations. In the years that had followed the end of WW2 the agreement was seen by the West as critical to keeping the peace. But now, the Soviet premier wanted to sign a separate treaty with the Communist DDR (East Germany), in part because he wanted to extend the USSR's sphere of influence but also because he knew it would undermine US and other Allied interests and power. The DDR leadership were keen too, not least because it would enable them to put in a border and stem the flood of immigration.

As Berlin sat in the centre of East Germany, the new deal would see the sections of the city controlled by France, the USA and UK effectively cut off and isolated from the rest of West Germany – a situation that was obviously untenable.

Khrushchev's threats had huge ramifications and Kennedy failed to stand up to him. The inexperienced new president had massively underestimated his counterpart and Khrushchev treated the younger man with lofty, barely concealed contempt. The Soviet premier essentially told Kennedy that if he objected to the separate deal, he would do it anyway.

The British Prime Minister, Harold Macmillan, later noted that: "For the first time in his life, Kennedy (had) met a man who was impervious to his charm."

Kennedy flew back to the United States with Jackie at his side, pumped full of Novocaine and broken confidence; by the time he saw Bobby, he was said to be on the verge of tears.

In July, trying to claw back his advantage, Kennedy delivered a speech promising a $3.25 billion ($32.5 billion 2023) addition to the defence budget and 200,000 more US troops. He added that any threat to West Berlin would be seen as an attack on the United States. The tough words were a ratings hit with Americans and Kennedy's popularity surged in the polls, but Khrushchev didn't blink and the following month, on 13th August, the East German authorities started building their wall, claiming it was an "Antifascistischer Schutzwall", or "antifascist bulwark". The Berlin Wall would see Germany's most famous city divided for the next 38 years and became the defining symbol of Cold War hostility.

As crisis mounted on top of crisis, a curious and perhaps slightly counter-intuitive thing started to happen. Instead of denting his popularity, JFK's star rose with the American people as he came to be seen as a sort of wartime president. Indeed, over the course of his presidency he was to score an unparalleled approval rating of 70.1%, comfortably making him the most popular post-war president. Americans grew to love their tough-talking, handsome leader with the beautiful wife but the Kennedy Show belied the policy mistakes he was making left, right and centre.

Having failed to properly confront the USSR and having overseen the disaster at the Bay of Pigs, JFK determined to "draw a line in the sand" and turned his attention to South-East Asia. The crisis in Vietnam had its origins in the legacy of French colonial rule and a communist insurgency led by Ho Chi Minh which had started in 1946 and lasted eight years. In 1954 the nation had been divided along the 17th Parallel following the Geneva Accords, but incompetent leadership in the South and the growing threat of communist insurgency led to deeper US involvement in the twilight of the Eisenhower years.

Kennedy began to escalate military assistance to the South Vietnamese government under the leadership of Ngô Đình Diệm. Washington didn't trust Diệm, President of South Vietnam since 1955, and as the next two years played out Kennedy found him increasingly difficult to work with. Among other things, they feared he might be planning to make a deal with North Vietnamese leader Ho Chi Minh. But the line in the sand had been drawn and Vietnam would become a new front in the Cold War, whether the South Vietnamese leadership wanted that or not.

Khrushchev meanwhile was opening up a new front of his own and hoping to bring the Cold War to America. The Bay of Pigs fiasco and Kennedy's timidity at Vienna had emboldened the Soviet premier, while simultaneously seeing Cuba become a sphere of Soviet influence. Kennedy had taken the Bay of Pigs failure personally and was now ploughing millions of dollars into Operation Mongoose – a CIA mission to disrupt Cuba and its economy, which included sabotage and attempts on the life of the Cuban leader. Mongoose was a failure for JFK and encouraged Cuba once again to forge a closer relationship with the Soviets.

During his presidential campaign, Kennedy had repeatedly and dishonestly talked up the so-called "missile gap" and in the process stoked tension on both sides. He was now nakedly involved in an arms race while simultaneously trying to undermine and possibly kill the Cuban leader.

The Soviets were hardly an innocent party either and were forever rattling their nuclear sabres. There was, in short, considerable grandstanding and beef on both sides. The Americans had missile bases in Italy and Turkey that were a source of ongoing humiliation to Khrushchev. Soviet missiles, with a maximum range of just 4,500 km, had no hope of hitting key targets in America. In fact, in 1962, the Soviets had just 20 intercontinental ballistic missiles capable of reaching the USA, putting them at, what they believed to be, a serious tactical "first strike" disadvantage. By building bases in Cuba and arming Castro, the Soviets believed they could play a stronger negotiating and strategic hand.

Khrushchev began building those bases long before the Americans detected them and poured an estimated 43,000 Soviet troops, surreptitiously, into the Caribbean nation – dressed in civilian clothes.

By the time the Americans woke up to the plan, courtesy of U-2 spy planes, most of the chess pieces were in place and the most dangerous game of the Cold War was already afoot. Kennedy was told to act. He knew he had to act, and he knew too that he had to be seen to be acting, but he was poleaxed with fear and appreciated, rightly, that if he made one false move it might lead to his impeachment – or worse, all-out war.

Unbeknown to the Americans at the time, the Soviet had shortrange tactical nuclear weapons in place and so the threat was very real.

Courtesy of expletive-filled conversations conducted in the Oval Office, captured on secret wires* that JFK had installed in the autumn of 1962, we know that the National Security Council were in favour of an all-out pre-emptive strike and/or an invasion of Cuba.

Thankfully and to his immense credit, Kennedy ploughed a more cautious furrow and imposed a blockade on the island while seeking a diplomatic solution. Behind the scenes, as the world teetered on the

---

* There are conspiracy theories galore, but he probably installed them to ease Ted Sorensen's task in writing his memoirs.

edge, a frantic deal was being hammered out and following several near misses, including an incident on B-59, a Soviet submarine, where panicked sailors – came within a whisker of launching a nuclear torpedo – a compromise was reached. It was agreed that the Soviets would dismantle the bases, on the condition that the US remove its missiles from Turkey and Italy and promised not to invade Cuba.

Kennedy had undoubtedly played a blinder. His part in averting disaster and perceived heroism in the diplomatic stakes saw his popularity soar to an all-time high of 77%. The president was hailed for his restraint and brilliance across the world and there was much truth in it; but among all the plaudits few pointed out that the crisis was in very large part his making in the first place.

The belligerent anti-communist rhetoric and campaign promises to build more missiles had worried the USSR and upped the ante. Repeated attempts to kill Castro and overthrow the regime had laid the groundwork. The diplomatic failure in Vienna had emboldened Khrushchev. And it had mostly been for nothing, since there was no missile gap and the weapons that had so riled the Soviets on their Turkish border had been superseded in strategic value by the submarine-based Polaris missile system. Kennedy had kept them there simply to rile Moscow and when the USSR had played the same cards back at him, he had taken the world to the brink of the Third World War. The crisis had ended because the wily Soviet leader had the guts to compromise and the sense to appear to back down. And why would he not? The Soviets and Cubans had achieved all their objectives.

Kennedy's determination to turn political disaster into personal triumph had far-reaching consequences. The perceived humiliation of the Soviet leader contributed to his downfall in 1964. Nikita Khrushchev, for all his bombast, was a premier that the West could do business with a full two decades before Gorbachev came along. His fall from grace saw a return to a harder line of leadership in the Brezhnev years and all the mutual mistrust that perpetuated the Cold War for many years longer than it should have lasted.

JFK may have been wreaking havoc, but it was all going down very well indeed with audiences at home. By mid-1963 and riding high on a popular wave, he set his eyes on the prize of a second term and at the same time, realising that the Civil Rights issue could no longer simply be ignored, began doing things he should have been doing two years previously. In June 1963, he made a direct and long overdue intervention in the politics of Alabama, when the Democrat Governor, George Wallace, tried to block two Black students, Vivian Malone and James Hood, from taking up their places at the State University. On 11th June, the same day that Wallace was obliged, by National Guardsmen, to stand aside and let the students in, Kennedy delivered an extraordinary speech known as the "Report to the American People on Civil Rights" – in a simultaneous live TV and radio broadcast.

In that moment, the great liberal hope of twentieth-century America finally hit the ball out of the park. Addressing events earlier in the day, he praised the two Black students and their peers for the "constructive" way they had comported themselves and then invited all Americans to examine their conscience: "This Nation was founded by men of many nations and backgrounds. It was founded on the principle that all men are created equal, and that the rights of every man are diminished when the rights of one man are threatened..."

Kennedy said that it "ought" to be possible for Americans of any colour to go about their lives without discrimination.

"But this is not the case... one hundred years of delay have passed since President Lincoln freed the slaves, yet their heirs, their grandsons, are not fully free. They are not yet freed from the bonds of injustice. They are not yet freed from social and economic oppression. And this Nation, for all its hopes and all its boasts, will not be fully free until all its citizens are free. We preach freedom around the world, and we mean it... but are we to say to the world, and much more importantly, to each other that this is a land of the free except...." for Black Americans.

Ted Sorensen may have excelled himself, but the power of Kennedy's delivery was in a class of its own and inspired Martin Luther King to fire off an approving telegram to the White House.

This was probably the bravest moment of his presidency, but his resolve did not last long. Overnight Kennedy's popularity nosedived in the South with his 52% approval rating tumbling to just 33%. A week and a half later, Civil Rights leaders met him and told him of their plans to lead a National March on Washington for Jobs and Freedom, but already the dip in popularity had seen him lose his nerve. Those approval ratings and his own fears that the demonstration might turn ugly had spooked him, and he offered only behind the scenes support. In time he might of course have rediscovered his nerve and become the president that we all think he was. But the world was never to find out.

On 2nd November 1963, President Diệm of South Vietnam was overthrown and executed on the orders of the Kennedy administration – in an act that was to lead to a massive escalation of American intervention in the Vietnam War. Two weeks later, while trying to smooth out an ongoing disagreement between the senator and governor of Texas, JFK's life was cut short by a disaffected man called Lee Harvey Oswald.

* * *

In life, Kennedy promised more than he ever delivered; in death his legend grew.

His presidency lasted just 1,036 days, the eighth shortest term in US history. British Prime Minister Theresa May (1,106 days) led her country longer and so too did Gordon Brown (1,048). But it is unlikely that Britons will be building gigantic libraries, or local museums to the Cult of May or Brown any time soon. Kennedy was undoubtedly hugely popular, but in part that was because he became the saviour against the very monsters he created. And it's impossible to escape the suspicion that his popularity in office was down largely to his good looks and immense personal charm.

Kennedy was the first television president, and the small screen turned him into a star, but his death which turned him into a sort of political God is the reason that he remains so embedded in our collective apophenic memory. The truth is that on close examination he was neither a great man nor a properly great president. His prep-boy arrogance and incompetence took the world to the brink of nuclear annihilation, and his legacy was the blood of young and innocent people in the fields and cities of Vietnam.

Beneath the smiling image, Jack Kennedy was, in the end, an entitled, alpha male, who treated his wife with contempt and who did very little that was good or meaningful in his brief presidency.

And yet and … yet… as I walk around the sacred temple that is the John F. Kennedy Library and Museum in Boston, I find myself wanting to believe the lie. I know it's a fairy tale, just like the one about King Arthur and the knights of the Round Table; but it is a beguiling and beautiful one, nonetheless. Who wouldn't want to put their faith in this charismatic man and his handsome family? Who wouldn't want to believe that there are good people out there, in pursuit of a dream who are trying to make our world a better place?

* * *

By its very nature, politics makes fake heroes of anyone who tries to climb the greasy pole. There are, of course, idealistic people who set out with higher motives, who seek an electoral mandate because they want to make the world a better place. And very occasionally good women and good men get into office or make a principled stand and a difference for us all. But it's hard to think of anyone who made it to the very top by being an altruistic, selfless leader – perhaps because no such person exists.

Nobody reaches the upper levels of politics without a good bit of image management, conniving, ditching of values and backstabbing along the way. Becoming a prime minister, chancellor or president requires compromise, self-belief and ruthless ambition. But it also takes Machiavellian degrees of ruthlessness. We forget that because all too often, in death, many a significant politician – whether they be William Pitt, Churchill, Thatcher, Reagan, Lenin, Clement Attlee or even Nelson Mandela – gets turned into a gigantic fiction. There are no selfless heroes in the upper echelons of political history and there never have been.

But the same is perhaps not the case, further down the ladder. Take the remarkable Shirley Chisholm, the first Black American woman to be elected to Congress, in 1968.

Born in New York in 1924, Shirley was one of four daughters of Ruby, a Barbadian-born seamstress, and her father, Charles, a factory worker from Guyana. Her parents were ambitious for their children and, struggling to make ends meet in 1930s America, sent the girls to Barbados to live with their maternal grandmother, a redoubtable matriarch called Emaline Seale. She became Shirley's role model and in 1972, Shirley would tell *The New York Times* that she had given her "strength, dignity and love... (and the belief) that I was somebody."

Shirley returned to New York as a teenager and in 1939 enrolled at Girls' High School in Brooklyn, a mixed-race establishment made up half-and-half of white and Black American schoolchildren. There, her teachers recognised her talents and her passion for politics, which she had inherited from her father, Charles, a politically active unionist and an early admirer and supporter of the Jamaican activist, orator and divider of opinion Marcus Garvey.

In 1942, she left high school and went on to the all-women Brooklyn College, where she became a leading figure on campus and a powerful force on the debating team. She campaigned for Black History to be included on the syllabus and became a supporter of union rights.

Graduating in 1946, she took an MA at Columbia University, working as a teacher and marrying a private investigator called Conrad Chisholm in between. Later she became the director of a childcare centre in Manhattan and then, aged 36 and in the burgeoning dawn of the 1960s Civil Rights Movement, she began to take the first steps of her political journey.

"Fighting Shirley" had none of the privileges of the mega-rich Kennedys or most of the other predominantly white male politicos around her – but she didn't let that stand in her way. She joined the League of Women Voters, the National Association for the Advancement of Colored People (NAACP), the Urban League and became a member of the Democratic Party club in Bedford-Stuyvesant, Brooklyn.

In 1964, a year after the death of John F. Kennedy, she became only the second African American to be elected to the New York State Legislature. Four years later, she became the first Black woman in history to be elected to Congress, running on her campaign slogan "Unbought and Unbossed". From the very outset, Shirley did things her way. In her first term she refused to accept her assignment to the Agriculture Committee, and instead informed Democratic Party leaders that she wanted to be appointed to the Veterans' Affairs Committee where she could better serve her Brooklyn constituents, many of whom were former African American servicemen.

As a congresswoman, she campaigned against the Vietnam War, spoke out against gender inequality and fought for the poor and the dispossessed while paving the way for ground-breaking legislation that included a bill which would see cleaners and domestic workers become entitled to unemployment benefit.

In July 1971, Chisholm informed the annual conference of the National Welfare Rights Organization that she was considering running for president. Shirley envisaged a new politics that would transcend old party lines and see a broad coalition of individuals that could change the existing political status quo, insisting that "this nation must be turned around". The speech brought her a standing ovation and she greeted it with a clenched raised fist. That worried the party hierarchy and as soon as she declared her candidacy in January 1972, the machine began irrevocably to turn against her.

While she had stayed on the margins, Chisholm had been something of a novelty – a Black woman on the fringes of the political establishment. Now she was declaring her intent to run for the highest office in the land and it worried the party hierarchy. As soon as she declared her candidacy in January 1972, the machine began irrevocably to turn against her.

Some decried her announcement as a self-promoting act of political symbolism. A sideshow to the main event. But Shirley wasn't having it: "I am for real, and I am very serious about what I am doing," she said and set about being as good as her word. Chisholm wanted to smash the hierarchy, the *whitearchy* and the patriarchy and make a new America for all. In her opening campaign address she declared: "I am not the candidate of black America, although I am black and proud. I am not the candidate of the women of this country although I am a woman and I'm equally proud that. I am the candidate of the people of America."

But specifically, Shirley was the candidate for the downtrodden and dispossessed people of the USA. The people without money, without power or a voice – and as such, she never stood a chance. Despite her efforts and on a shoestring budget, she failed to make it beyond the primaries.

Chisholm took no quarter and could be a divisive and combative figure even in her own caucus. As time went on, she increasingly split opinion, making a lot of enemies as she blazed her trail across the 1970s. Many of her old allies even accused her of turning her back on everything she claimed to stand for, as she increasingly sided with her Democratic bosses against marginalised factions within the party. Nobody is perfect.

Chisholm quit politics in 1983, four years after her second husband, Arthur Hardwick, was seriously injured in a motoring accident. He predeceased her in 1986 and she died 19 years later in 2005. In the Obama years she began to be cited as a significant political figure and in January 2018, the New York State Governor announced plans for a Shirley Chisholm State Park. A year later a monument in her honour was proposed at the southside entrance to Prospect Park in Brooklyn, and in time, her name might become as widely known as that of her childhood hero, Harriet Tubman.

Shirley Chisholm could be seen as a classic "catalyst for change" – one of history's stalking horses, who prepares the ground for those that follow. But that was certainly not how she saw herself. Chisholm wanted to reach the top and didn't seek the validation of the establishment to get there. Her friend and colleague Muriel Morisey once said of her: "I don't think she ever actually asked anybody's permission to do anything."

That inner instinct – best summed up as "I don't need your permission" – was never her campaign slogan; it defined everything she was.

CHAPTER THREE

REVOLUTIONARY HEROES
CHE GUEVARA

The Icon on Your Bedsit Wall

It was 8th October 1967, a Sunday morning, and as the sun rose over the Rio Grande, in the mountains of Bolivia, dozens of US trained Army Rangers took up their positions on a ridge overlooking a valley. The military had been tipped off about a party of foreign guerrillas by a local peasant and through their binoculars, they could see the shadows of men darting about, down by the river, in the scrub below.

The small group, made up of just 22 men, had in turn heard the troops arriving. They knew they were heavily outnumbered and knew too that the only way out – was to fight.

Just after 1 p.m., the guerrillas made their move and the Bolivians opened fire. Mortars and bullets rained down into the valley, thudding into the thicket and splintering the earth. One rebel was killed immediately, and two more met their fate as they scrambled along the riverbank. From behind a rock their leader fired blindly into the air, emptying his carbine until it got hit by enemy fire, rendering it useless. Unable to find the magazine for his pistol and with a bullet wound in his leg, he escaped, supported by his comrade "Willy". Somehow, they managed to evade the enemy and as they neared the top of the ridge, it may have felt that – not for the first time – they had defeated the odds. But if so, they were mistaken because as they cleared the peak of the valley's walls, government soldiers sprang out of the bushes and the two men wearily raised their arms in surrender.

"Don't shoot," the taller man said. "I am Che Guevara, and I am worth more to you alive than dead."

The legendary guerrilla leader was searched and found to be carrying two Rolex watches, a rucksack, an aluminium pan containing six eggs, his pipe, several thousand US dollars, documents, maps and a set of handwritten diaries, which the patrol commander, Captain Gary Prado Salmon, put in a bag. There were said to be at least three suspected "Che Guevaras" in the area at the time, so Prado identified the rebel from known scars, one behind his ear and another on his right cheek, sustained as result of an accident during the Bay of Pigs invasion in April 1961. Prado quickly established that he had caught the most famous revolutionary in the world and 50 years later would tell the *Financial Times*:

"He presented a pitiful figure, dirty, smelly and run-down. He'd been on the run for months. His hair was long, messy and matted, and his beard bushy. Over his uniform he was wearing a blue jacket with no buttons. His black beret was filthy. He had no shoes, just scraps of animal skins on his feet. He was wearing odd socks, one blue, one red. He looked like those homeless people you see begging in the cities pushing a supermarket trolley."

Salmon began calling in reinforcements until his prisoner told him: "Don't worry, Captain. This is the end. It is over."

Guevara's hands were bound with his belt and he and "Willy" were taken to the nearby village of La Higuera and locked in the schoolhouse. There Guevara was interrogated by Prado's senior, Major Selich, who asked the Argentinian why he had chosen to fight in Bolivia instead of his native homeland.

"Maybe it would have been better," Che replied and proceeded to give an impromptu lecture on the benefits of world communism, until his captors asked him to shut up.

Guevara looked depressed, but that was hardly surprising. Two of his dead comrades lay bound on the floor next to him, he was wounded in the leg and in captivity. The circumstances were hardly convivial.

That night he and Prado continued the conversation that Selich had begun in the afternoon. Prado could not understand why Guevara's had come to his country. Bolivia had seen significant land reform after the 1952 revolution and in 1967, albeit under the dictatorship of René Barrientos, the peasants had enjoyed reasonable prosperity. Nobody had rallied to his cause because there was no incentive to fight. Che concurred and said he had been given "the wrong information".

Early the following morning, a military helicopter swept into La Higuera and a Bolivian colonel, Joaquin Zenteno Anaya, and a CIA agent, "Captain Ramos" (aka Felix Rodriguez), stepped out. Rodriguez was carrying a state-of-the-art field telephone and a camera. The two men went into the schoolhouse and tried to speak to Guevara, but he simply lay there, wheezing heavily on the floor.

Prado and the others were transfixed by the enormity of the moment. Che Guevara was a living legend. The Argentinian poster-boy of global revolution who French philosopher Jean-Paul Sartre would later dub "not only an intellectual" but "the era's most perfect man". He had played a critical role in the Cuban Revolution that overthrew the dictator Fulgencio Batista in 1959 and had gone on to become Cuba's Economic Minister; for a decade he had been a thorn in the side of the United States of America, snubbing his nose at the administrations of Kennedy and Johnson. He had led a guerrilla uprising and defied all attempts to capture him until now. He was bigger than the sum of his impressive guerrilla resume. He was 'Che Guevara' the rockstar of Marxism, and now he lay there, wretched and broken.

Rodriguez photographed Guevara and his diaries and belongings before sending a coded message on his field radio to his masters in Washington. He tried to question Che but received only gruff responses until Guevara, sensing that he was Cuban, asked where he was from. Rodriguez confirmed he was Cuban and that he worked for the CIA.

He was present at the Bay of Pigs and had been on the Marxist's trail for months.

"Ha!" Che replied.

At around 12.30 p.m. a message came through to Colonel Anaya with orders from the Bolivian President. Sentence had been passed and Anaya ordered Selich's commanding officer, Major Ayoroa, to "proceed with the elimination of Senor Guevara".

Selich and Anaya then boarded the helicopter and flew away.

Rodriguez tried to dissuade Ayoroa from executing the Argentinian. The CIA wanted to interrogate him and was willing to whisk him out of the country by plane. But Ayoroa wasn't having it and insisted that the order had to be carried out – as it came from the very top. As the two men argued, gunfire rang out from the schoolhouse. A guard had killed "Willy", claiming he was trying to escape.

As Willy's body was dragged from the school, Rodriguez asked Che Guevara if he would pose with him for a photo. The dishevelled and bound Che obliged and went outside to stand with his captor and some Bolivian soldiers.

Fifty years later, Rodriguez told the Spanish newspaper *El Pais* that he then said: "'Comandante, look at the birdie' (and) he started to laugh because it's what we say to children in Cuba: 'Look at the birdie'".

Rodriguez put his arm about Che, almost as if they were old college friends posing at a reunion, and the photo was snapped.

Ayoroa had orders to kill Guevara by 2 p.m. at the latest and that hour was ticking to its conclusion. The CIA agent told Che he was "sorry" and asked him if he had any last requests. In his definitive biography of Guevara, Jon Lee Anderson relates that Che told him to "tell Fidel that he will soon see a triumphant revolution in America. And tell my wife to remarry and... be happy."

As they spoke, Ayoroa sought an executioner from among the ranks of his men. Just one volunteer came forward. His name was Sergeant Teran. Accounts differ as to how eager he was to do the task, but most agree that he was probably drunk. Taking a semi-automatic, Teran marched purposefully into the school before hesitating. According to Anderson, Guevara ordered him to:

"Shoot, coward, you are only going to kill a man."

Teran opened fire but botched it, hitting Guevara in the legs and arms. The guerrilla writhed on the floor in agony, trying not to scream in pain. Accounts again differ as to how many times the sergeant fired his weapon. Some say two bursts, others as many as nine, but at some point, a bullet passed through Guevara's throat, and he was dead.

The Bible tells that after the death of Jesus, the soldiers took his clothes and shared them – and much the same thing happened following the execution of the Marxist Messiah.

Teran took his smoking pipe, Prado took one of his Rolex watches (Selich had taken the other) and Anaya the damaged carbine. The money was divided between the other men. It's unclear who got the pan of eggs.

The body was strapped to the underbelly of a military helicopter and flown to the nearby city of Villegrande, where his corpse was tossed onto a concrete slab in the local hospital's washhouse. Over the next 24 hours, curious locals crowded in, to gawp. To ward off flies and the stench of rotting flesh, the body was injected with formaldehyde.

Photographs were taken and quickly shared around the world by the Bolivian authorities and the CIA. The goal was to demystify Guevara, to demonstrate that he was just another dead guerrilla who had suffered an inglorious end. But the effect of the lightbulbs in the darkness of the Villegrande washhouse gave his body an ethereal quality and comparisons to Jesus began to come thick and fast.

Once the crowds had been ushered away, Guevara's hands were cut off and sent to Havana to prove that he was dead. Some had wanted to cut off his head too, but sense prevailed. The body was removed from the hospital and buried unceremoniously on the edge of a runway at the nearby airport – where it remained until it was located and exhumed in 1997.

News of the death, like Kennedy's four years earlier, reverberated across the world. But it was not met with the attendant ceremony and offers of condolence that came in the wake of the JFK assassination. The official, diplomatic response was muted. Romanian dictator Nicolae Ceaușescu and a handful of communist leaders sent messages to Cuba, but that was it.

Elsewhere, in the West, the reaction split on largely generational lines. For some, mostly young, Western activists and students, it was seen as a tragedy; for many of their parents it came as something of a relief. In Cuba, Fidel Castro declared a state of national mourning. On 18th October he delivered a lengthy tribute to his fallen comrade in front of an estimated crowd of one million Cubans.

"If we want a model of a man, a model of a man who does not belong to this time, a model of a man who belongs to future times... that model is Che!... To victory always, fatherland or death, we shall win!"

It was followed by a 21-gun salute.

The US government said little publicly but privately was glad to see the back of him.

In a declassified memo to President Lyndon B. Johnson on 11th October, the national security adviser, Walt Rostow, told the president "we are 99% sure" that Guevara was dead. It was long rumoured that the CIA were responsible for the killing, but Rostow's memo proves otherwise saying that the Bolivian Armed Forces Chief had "ordered him shot. I regard this as stupid, but it is understandable from (their) standpoint given the problems" they had previously had. Rostow believed the death of Guevara had three immediate implications. It would mark "the passing of another of the aggressive romantic revolutionaries... will have a strong impact in discouraging would-be guerrillas... and shows the soundness of 'preventative medicine' assistance to countries facing... insurgency."

A report the next day for US Secretary of State Dean Rusk, by Thomas Hughes, a specialist at the State Department's Bureau of Intelligence, made many of the same points. Acknowledging that Guevara would probably "be eulogized as the model revolutionary who met a heroic death" his capture was "a feather in the cap" for the Bolivian authorities. Hughes believed that Che's end could see a change in Fidel Castro's efforts "to foster insurgency abroad".

What Hughes, Rostow and perhaps almost nobody else at the time could possibly have appreciated was just how much Che's legend would live on well beyond his times.

Central to all of that was the iconography. Think of John F. Kennedy and you immediately picture him riding in that Lincoln Continental. Think of Che Guevara and the famous photograph known as *Guerrillero Heroico*, taken in March 1960 in Havana by the photographer Alberto Korda, instantly springs to mind. It is generally considered to be the most widely reproduced commercial photograph in history and perhaps only the Mona Lisa comes close to it in ubiquity, although this is impossible to quantify.

In the 56 years since, *Guerrillero Heroico* has become so corny and over-killed that one could be forgiven for forgetting why it was so famous in the first place. Korda's photo is extraordinarily evocative. Che's pensive, handsome face seems to embody the romantic, revolutionary idyll in a single take. He looks defiant, thoughtful, rebellious all in one.

In his lifetime, the picture was not widely known but in the wake of Guevara's death it was to become his posthumous trademark. The image first came to light when it was turned into an enormous banner and hung in Revolution Square in Havana. But it was through the publication of Guevara's Bolivian diaries the following year, that it entered the mainstream. Like a meme, it soon went viral and throughout the uprisings and student occupations of 1968's year of revolution, Korda's photo cropped up everywhere.

An article in *Time* magazine in May 1968 observed: "Portraits of Che have been carried in practically every student riot in Europe this spring" and "in Brazil, mythmakers have circulated thousands of copies of a photograph of the dead Che captioned 'A Saint of Our

Time.' Italian students have christened him Angela della Pace – 'Angel of Peace'."

It was spotted in the streets of Paris during the uprisings and demonstrations that same month and appeared in the streets of London at anti-Vietnam War demos. John Lennon and Yoko Ono, those other icons of the age, even put a version of it up on their wall, and like millions of others, even took to donning berets and fatigues, sales of which went through the roof.

That same year, a two-tone red and black version of the Korda image, dubbed *Viva Che*, was made by Irish artist Jim Fitzpatrick. In a nifty bit of pre-digital photoshopping, Fitzpatrick slightly altered the picture, sending Guevara's eyes skyward, and the effect turned him into the modern incarnation of Heracles, Alexander the Great or Christ – depending on your favourite male paragon.

Viva Che was first printed in the British satirical magazine *Private Eye* in 1968 and subsequently millions of copies of the Fitzpatrick version were disseminated worldwide. That version, even more than the Korda original, led to its ubiquity, and even Andy Warhol got in on the act – of which more, later in the book. In cities across the world, you will Che staring out at you from street art or stickers posted to lamp posts today. The boxer Mike Tyson has Che's face tattooed on his stomach, the footballer Diego Maradona had him tattooed on his arm. Che T-shirts proliferate still and have been sported by everyone from Johnny Depp to Madonna, from Ricky Gervais to Prince Harry. In some left-wing circles "Che chic" is never out of fashion. At the Labour Party conference in 2018, you could buy "Corbyn-Che" T shirts and cufflinks too.

Online markets flog Che watches, pendants, necklaces and carriage clocks. A Che Guevara Louis Vuitton travel bag currently retails for around £2,000.

Guerrillero Heroico is more than a brand – it is an eternal phenomenon and undoubtedly the best-known thing about Guevara. Undeniably, the potent nature of Guevara's extraordinary good looks, propagated by that image, still plays a huge part in the perpetuation of his legend. Would he still be remembered if there was no *Guerrillero Heroico*?

In 2003 the author and former Marxist Christopher Hitchens told the *Guardian* that Guevara belonged "more to the romantic tradition than the revolutionary one. To endure as a romantic icon, one must not just die young, but die hopelessly. Che fulfils both criteria. When one thinks of Che as a hero, it is more in terms of Byron than Marx."

Che is the pin-up guerrilla and the closest thing Stalinism ever had to a pop icon, and that romantic legend continues to inspire artists. There are poems, paintings, books and many film tributes of varying degrees of quality. Within a year of his death, Richard Fleischer, the multi-genre-tackling Hollywood director, had made *Che*, with Egyptian actor Omar Sharif horribly miscast in the title role and Jack Palance as Fidel Castro. It was universally panned. Other films, biographies, documentaries and comedy sketches followed. Che has been played by everyone from Monty Python actor Michael Palin to Antonio Banderas, who played him in a film adaptation of the musical *Evita*. In 2003, the film *The Motorcycle Diaries* told the story of his legendary youthful adventure. In 2008, a two-part biographical film, starring Benicio del Toro, told his life in full.

Guevara was very much a pre-internet mass influencer although instead of dissembling that influence through a mobile phone, he did it through the barrel of a gun. And like all the best phenomenons – he still massively divides opinion even 55 years on.

Russell Brand is a famous fan and at an event in 2015 read out Che's last letter to his children in which he tells them to be "good revolutionaries".

In sharp contrast, the online conservative influencer Ben Shapiro has called him a "genocidal murderer", while ranting Canadian academic Jordan Peterson once dubbed him "just another ideological killer".

Che Guevara remains a figure of considerable loathing among many Republican American voters today, and particularly in the State of Florida where so many Cuban exiles live.

There are social media fans and there are haters. A Facebook group called *Che Guevara was a murderer and your T shirt is not cool* has 4.4k likes. Another called *Che Guevara Fans* has 77k followers.

And of course, there are shrines.

The village of La Higuera, in Bolivia, is now a place of pilgrimage. His face dots the whitewashed walls of the settlement and visitors scatter offerings of coca leaves at the feet of the statue that stands prominently in the town square. Nearby, at the spot where he was captured, there is an enormous bust to *Santo Ernesto,* for in rural Bolivia, the avowedly atheist Ernesto "Che" Guevara is now a quasi-religious "folk saint". Miracles are ascribed to him at the site of his martyrdom and at other secular temples, including the giant mausoleum that holds his exhumed body in Santa Clara in Cuba.

In death Che went on to have an extraordinary afterlife, inspiring fashion, politics and murals across South America. But beyond the enigmatic image that adorned the walls of a million student bedsits, beyond the merchandise, the controversy and the myth – who was this, Santo Ernesto?

* * *

Ernesto "Che" Guevara was born in Rosario, Santa Fe, Argentina on 14th June 1928.

He was the first child of Ernesto Guevara Lynch and Celia de la Serna y Llosa, bourgeois intellectuals, who had eloped when the 20-year-old Celia fell pregnant.

In the endemically classist and racist Argentinian society of the time, where people of Spanish and European ancestry were deemed "superior" to everyone else, Celia was very much a product of the white "upper class". Her family claimed they could trace their roots back to Spain and had a royal Viceroy and a famous Argentine General in their ancestry. Ernesto Senior (known to all as Guevara Lynch) had similar pretensions, claiming he was a descendant of Patrick Lynch, an Irish-born immigrant who had become one of the biggest landowners in Argentina in the eighteenth century.

Two years after Che's death in 1969, Guevara Lynch told an interviewer: "The first thing to note is that in my son's veins flowed the blood of the Irish rebels."

Celia's family were as deeply unimpressed with her choice of partner as they were with the unplanned pregnancy. Guevara Lynch was seven years older than his bride and despite that famous antecedent, on paper, he wasn't much of a catch. He had poured his money into a yacht-building firm in Buenos Aires and was struggling to make a success of it.

Perhaps seeking to repeat the glory days of his landowning ancestor and make something of himself, shortly after the birth of Ernestito (as Che was then known) in 1928, Guevara Lynch bought a plantation, with Celia's money, in Misiones, a remote region in northeastern Argentina. It was a moment of marital and familial bliss but spelled disaster for the family yacht business. Left in the hands of a cousin, the firm hit the rocks and one year after buying the ranch, Lynch was obliged to give it all up and head back to Buenos Aires. The business was on the brink of collapse but worse was to follow; soon after his return, the shipyard was destroyed by fire, wiping out his assets.

Despite being completely broke, the couple refused to accept their reduced circumstances. They carried on living beyond their means, forever pushing themselves to the brink of bankruptcy and spending money they did not have on fripperies, entertainment and nice things.

Ernestito was a sickly child and suffered a severe case of bronchial pneumonia in his early months, which almost took his life. Aged three, he developed a cough after paddling in a river, and when it didn't go away, was diagnosed with chronic asthmatic bronchitis. The condition would plague him for the rest of his life, frequently leaving him wheezing and in need of medical attention. Fears about his health constantly hung over his parents like a great big black cloud and Celia claimed that one of the first words he learned to say was "injection".

When he was four and on the advice of doctors, the growing family left Buenos Aires and moved to the spa town of Alta Gracia in the province of Córdoba, hoping the climate would improve Ernestito's health. When the time came to go to school, his protective mother kept him back, fearing he might suffer a potentially fatal asthma attack, and it was only when the inspectors literally began hammering on the door, that he was sent out into the world.

Those early pre-school years had also forged an extraordinary bond between mother and son. Celia was a remarkable woman. A fiercely independent spirit, she was an atheist and an intellectual who loved her boy unconditionally. Even when things got very difficult for her in Argentina, because of her son's activities, she remained loyal to Ernestito.

Ernestito had a far less functional relationship with his father. Guevara Lynch's bouts of depression, accentuated by his financial worries, were made worse by heavy drinking. He could have a volcanic temper and was repeatedly and unashamedly unfaithful to Celia. Domestic rows were common, and the police were sometimes called. But peace of a sort arrived with the advent of the Spanish Civil War in 1936. In the febrile atmosphere of the times, Guevara Lynch had found politics and, as Republican refugees fled across the Atlantic, he became obsessed with their plight and even took in the two refugee children of a Spanish Republican, Dr Aguilar.

Lynch followed events in Spain assiduously and would plot troop movements on a gigantic map. On one occasion, he even built a model of Madrid in his back garden and re-enacted the siege of the city with his children, injuring Ernestito in the process.

At the start of the Second World War neutral Argentina kept out but Lynch became ever more politically active and joined an antifascist group called Acción Argentina, which lobbied the government on behalf of the Allies. He travelled the country making speeches and even engaged in a little light spying, which consisted of him stalking people with German names through the windows of their homes until the police were called and told him to go home.

All of this must have influenced his son, but for the moment, Ernestito had his mind on other things. In 1942, he entered the public Colegio Nacional Dean Funes, in Córdoba.

The college, like Argentina at large, was macho, but Ernestito was remarkably bookish. By 14 he had devoured hundreds of novels, poems, scriptures and theses and drawn up vast inventories of his reads, which included everything from Jack London to Rudyard Kipling, Kafka, H.G. Wells and Adolf Hitler.

Despite his asthma, Ernestito was a keen rugby player too and known to be extremely aggressive on the pitch.

Hugely attractive to girls, he was socially hamstrung in tango-obsessed Argentina on account of being completely tone deaf. His first biographer, Aldo Isidron, wrote that, "He did not have an ear for music. He couldn't even identify a tango. He had to learn dance steps by rote." He was scruffy to an almost legendary degree. Contemporaries noted that Che would wear the same shirt for weeks at a time and never seemed to wash. This slovenliness earned him the nickname *chancho* meaning "pig" but he wore the badge with pride.

When not playing rugby, reading or lounging about, adolescent Ernestito had sex with maids. In Argentina at the time, where people of dark skin were viewed as little more than third-class citizens, this was considered a privilege of white boys. Maids existed to wash and clean and provide sexual services in what was, by any measure, a culture of widespread sexual abuse against society's poorest people.

Carlos Figueroa, his childhood friend in Alta Gracia nicknamed him the "Fast Rooster" in their teenage years "because he was eating in the dining room, and immediately, when the mucama (maid) entered the room he forced her to climb on the table and had sex. After he had finished, he would carry on eating, as if nothing had happened…"

Guevara's behaviour was not unusual for the time, but that does not forgive it. It is an unfortunate truth that the man who would one day become famous for fighting for the rights of the dispossessed, spent his youth abusing women on the bottom rung of the Argentinian social hierarchy.

Young Ernestito was a rampant capitalist too. For much of his teenage years he spent considerable time cooking up "get rich quick" schemes alongside his friend Figueroa. One of these involved taking a locust insecticide called Gamexane and watering it down with domestic talcum powder to sell as a cockroach killer. Ernestito initially planned to call it "Al Capone" but told that he might be infringing the late gangster's "copyright" opted for "Vendaval" instead.

His entrepreneurial spirit impressed his parents – especially when Guevara secured a patent. But soon the production line in the back garden started to poison everyone and asthmatic Ernestito most of all. The plug was pulled on the nascent chemical empire but not on his desire for money. Figueroa and Guevara ploughed their efforts into a door-to-door footwear-selling business instead, but poor planning saw them end up with hundreds of odd shoes and any gains they had made killing cockroaches were lost in the process.

Meanwhile, beyond the world of his home, his college and his hair-brained, money-making schemes, Argentina was changing fast.

In 1943, the democratically elected government of Ramon Castillo was overthrown in a populist military coup. A year later, the new regime suspended all diplomatic relations with the Axis powers and while his left-wing parents were overjoyed, Ernestito was furious. In *Che Guevara: A Revolutionary Life*, John Lee Anderson quotes Che's friend Pepe González Aguiler: "I couldn't understand how he, who had always been so anti-Nazi, didn't share our happiness."

Ernestito, he guessed, was angry because: "the decision had not been made on principle, but because of US pressure, and he shared Argentine nationalists' sense of shame that their country had buckled under to the Americans."*

Guevara's all-consuming hatred of the United States of America would shape his life and it first sprang to life in the war years from what he viewed as his homeland's bended knee to the Roosevelt administration. Young Guevara wanted his country to be more than just a US client state.

---

* Anderson, J. L., *Che Guevara: A Revolutionary Life*, 1997, p33.

Two years later the war ended and Guevara Lynch was proud to receive a certificate from General de Gaulle, thanking him for his efforts in aiding the Allied effort.

The following year, Colonel Juan Perón became President of Argentina. Perón was a populist who had formulated his political outlook in Benito Mussolini's Italy while studying alpine warfare there in 1939. Back in Argentina, he had become a member of the GOU (United Officers Group), a secret society that had helped overthrow President Ramón Castillo in 1943. As Secretary of Labour and Welfare, Perón built a platform and gained support from workers by implementing reforms and garnering support from unions. His political philosophy, known as "Perónism", explicitly rejected both communism and capitalism and sought a third way instead that would remove tensions between workers, business leaders and government.

Peronism drew inspiration from both the far left and far right but had a strong authoritarian streak, and Perón would repeatedly stamp down on civil liberties and perceived enemies of the state. His philosophy was essentially an Argentine version of Mussolini's Italian Fascism but without the "f" word.

In another off-brand moment, 17-year-old Ernestito Guevara liked what he saw and was enraptured by the charismatic leader. The Colonel's rise to power, more than anything, heralded his early political awakening. Guevara joined a Peronist movement and even told his maids to vote for the Colonel. His enthusiasm was driven in part by Perón's cult of personality but more so by his unabashed "Anti-Yankee" agenda.

Perón's rise to power was initially backed by the Catholic Church, whose conservative outlook was broadly aligned with the military interests that the Colonel represented. Perón's government reaffirmed the influence that the Church had regained following the 1943 coup, which had seen the reintroduction of religious education and a closer alignment of Catholic Church and state. But as time went by, Perón and his second wife Eva (Evita) grew wary of the arrangement. As the Peróns encouraged the propagation of their own personality cult and began to promote avowed anti-Catholics to positions of power, they put themselves on a collision course with the Church.

That would come to a head in 1954, when in his second term and following the death of Eva in 1952, Perón legalised divorce and prostitution. The move saw the Argentinian Catholic Church seek to excommunicate him and, as he tried to take on priests and bishops, his fall from popularity and power became inevitable. But for much of his time in power, the avowedly atheistic Ernestito Guevara approved of all of the above. Of Perón's removal in 1955, Che would write: "I will confess with all sincerity that the fall of Perón deeply embittered me... Argentina was the Paladin of all those who think the enemy is in the North."

In the early 1960s, when he had political power of his own, Che struck up a correspondence with Perón and strangely, given the polarity of their political differences, he seems to have remained deeply sympathetic to the deposed president. It might seem strange that the most famous Latin American Marxist-Leninist guerrilla of the twentieth century had a bond and a sense of common cause with the most famous regional fascist of his time, but there was a curious asymmetry. Both men were populists, both had egos the size of the Atlantic coastline, both hated the United States, both were in love with their own mythos, both saw themselves as mouthpieces of their people and both had strong autocratic tendencies.

Many atheists seek an alternative to faith and Ernistito had yet to find his church. But in much the way that John F. Kennedy copied Winston Churchill, Che had found a role model in Perón. In his later political trajectory, Che Guevara would poach many of Perón's ideas.

But back in 1948 he was still just a nascent rebel out looking for a cause. That year, the young Guevara enrolled as a medical student at the University of Buenos Aires and shortly afterwards was drafted into the army, only to fail the medical on account of his asthma.

Around the same time, his parents briefly separated and, feeling rootless and hungry for adventure, young Ernestito took off in 1950 and spent several months cycling through northern Argentina and a further six working as a medical orderly on a ship. Two years later, with his former rugby coach, Alberto Granado, he embarked on a far more ambitious adventure. Granado, at 29 some five years older than his companion, was seeking one last hurrah before settling down as a biochemist. Che wanted to see the continent beyond his limited horizons and perhaps find that cause he was looking for.

His "gap year to end all gap years" would change his life forever. Although, it very nearly didn't happen. Worried that their son was frittering his life away, his parents briefly reunited to try to talk him out of it, and he only secured their agreement to go on the promise that he'd finish his studies when he returned. He was to be true to his word, but the carefree twenty-something who set out on the road to Chile in January 1951, was to return a changed man. Everything that followed, in a sense, was like the realisation of the worst nightmares of any parent whose child ever went backpacking.

In Chile, the motorcycle gave out and the two men fell back on hitch-hiking. At the vast US-owned Chuquicamata copper mine, widely viewed in South America as a symbol of American imperialist oppression, their eyes were opened to another world.

As Lee Anderson writes: "While these companies reaped huge profits, Chile's economy was hugely dependent on the revenues it received from them, which varied from year to year depending on the fluctuations in the copper market. Resentful of the terms of this deeply unequal partnership, many Chileans particularly on the left were lobbying for the nationalisation of the mines. In response, the United States had actively pressured Chile's recent governments to break up the mining unions and outlaw the Communist Party."*

On the edge of the mining complex, Che and Alberto met a worker and his wife. The man had just been released from prison for belonging to the outlawed Chilean Communist Party and was unable to find a job as a result. The couple had been forced to give up their children

* Anderson, J. L., *Che Guevara: A Revolutionary Life*, 1997, p77–78.

to neighbours and were planning to head to a sulphur mine deep in the mountains where conditions were so dangerous that no questions were asked.

Guevara was struck forcibly by the injustice of it and, more, by his own sense of middle-class liberal guilt. He and Alberto were travelling through Chile for the hell of it, while these people were living through hell. In Peru, the inner rage grew. On 22nd March, Guevara wrote of the desperation and poverty: "These people who watch us walk through the streets of the town are a defeated race. Their stares are tame, almost fearful, and completely indifferent to the outside world. Some give the impression they go on living only because it's a habit they cannot shake."

It's a moment of awakening in his motorcycle diary, but this legendary, coming-of-age revolutionary bible, like all religious texts, has deeply uncomfortable moments too. Guevara still saw the world through a white man's eyes and his views on people of colour – written in the same diary in which he despairs at the poverty around him – are sometimes troubling. The man who had once been called a "pig" by his own friends for his slovenly ways, wrote:

"The blacks, those magnificent examples of the African race who have maintained their racial purity thanks to their lack of an affinity with bathing, have seen their territory invaded by a new kind of slave: the Portuguese...

The black is indolent and a dreamer; spending his meagre wage on frivolity or drink; the European has a tradition of work and saving, which has pursued him as far as this corner of America and drives him to advance himself."

Unsurprisingly, in the weaponised atmosphere of the twenty-first century culture wars, these lines are manna to right-wing politicians and pundits seeking to dismiss Che as nothing more than a "racist". In 2013, when rapper Jay-Z went to Cuba, having been spotted earlier that same year in a Che Guevara T-shirt, right-wingers went to town. Marco Rubio, the Republican senator for Florida and himself the son of Cuban exiles, lambasted the rapper and his wife Beyoncé, telling ABC:

"Well, I won't rap it, but I'll say, first of all, I think Jay-Z needs to get informed. One of his heroes is Che Guevara. Che Guevara was a racist. Che Guevara was a racist that wrote extensively about the superiority of white Europeans over people of African descent. So he should inform himself on the guy that he's propping up."

This notion that Che was a racist remains popular in the very right-wing corners of the internet where modern racism itself prevails. The lines from the diary are frequently deployed in Twitter spats and anti-Guevara blogs as slam-dunk proof of it. But is it fair?

Responding to the Jay-Z incident, Mark Sawyer, a UCLA professor of political science, told PolitiFact, the fact-checking website at the US Poynter Institute, that Rubio's remarks were a "gross exaggeration". Sawyer argued that they reflected "a Che whose views evolved on the issue of race and who eventually saw black liberation as synonymous with ending oppression."

Sawyer perhaps has a point. As deeply uncomfortable as Guevara's youthful writings on race are, they are not really borne out by his later actions. As "Che", he would repeatedly condemn Western intervention in Africa and the fully formed adult had Black Cuban comrades and advisers. Rubio and other Guevara haters have picked on the quotation and others written in the Congo over the years because they make a good stick with which to beat the Argentinian revolutionary. That does and never can forgive the offensive remarks or those made in the wake of the revolution when he said: "We're going to do for blacks exactly what blacks did for the revolution. By which I mean: nothing."

But Guevara would go on something of a journey in the years to come and openly espouse anti-racist sentiments in his famous UN speech in 1964. Whatever his failings, the motorcycle diary mostly shows a thoughtful young man, trying to come to terms with the inequalities and hardships around him. In a sense there's a sort of pilgrimage going on, with the final goal being the acquisition of wisdom. That meeting on the outskirts of the Chilean copper mine has a surreal, almost quasi-religious flavour to it and was perhaps his

Road to Damascus moment on a path of destiny that would lead to that schoolhouse in Bolivia.

Young Guevara's awakened sense of injustice was justifiable and very real. His determination to get out and to do something about it was even more admirable. Most of us who despair at the state of the world, do so from behind our computer screens or from the comfort of our homes – he was willing to get out there and risk his life if necessary to forge a better world.

At the end of his journey, he wrote in his diary of his intention to "dip my weapons in blood and crazed with fury... cut the throats of my defeated enemies. I can already feel my dilated nostrils savoring the acrid smell of gunpowder and blood, of death to the enemy."

Those words, the fighting talk of romantic youth, were to come to very real fruition.

In *As You Like It*, Shakespeare's character Jacques sets out the seven ages of man from mewling and puking baby to the "mere oblivion" of old age. Guevara never made it to his dotage, but in his 39 years, he lived several and often contradictory lives. The first of those ended in 1952 with the conclusion of the motorcycle diary.

Bourgeois Ernestito's journey was over; the monomyth of revolutionary Che was about to begin.

* * *

Having completed his medical studies, as he had promised to his parents, Ernestito set out to travel again in 1953 and found his way to Guatemala in late December. By now he was firmly identifying as a communist of a particularly Stalinist bent. The Soviet leader had died in March that year and the attendant fuss might well have piqued his interest.

Jon Lee Anderson quotes a letter he sent to his aunt, Beatriz, at the time claiming: "I have sworn before a picture of the old and mourned comrade Stalin that I won't rest until I see these capitalist octopuses annihilated."

Stalin was one of the most egregious dictators of the twentieth century, responsible for the deaths of an estimated 9 million people in his own country alone and the imprisonment and torture of many millions more. The scale of his tyranny would become apparent in the years that followed and in 1956, Premier Khrushchev would condemn the former tyrant and his crimes against humanity. Despite that, Che Guevara remained a lifelong fan. In 1960, four years after Khrushchev had begun the "De-Stalinisation" of the Soviet Union, Che visited Moscow, and against the express advice of the Cuban Ambassador insisted on laying a wreath at Stalin's tomb. And four years later, he was still defending one of history's worst dictators.

In 1964 he blamed opinions of the "so-called mistakes of Stalin" on a "revisionist attitude. You have to look at Stalin in the historical context in which he moves, you don't have to look at him as some kind of brute, but in that particular historical context. I have come to communism because of Daddy Stalin and nobody must come and tell me that I mustn't read Stalin. I read him when it was very bad to read him. That was another time. And... I keep on reading him."

By 1964, Che Guevara was 36 years old and had served as the Finance Minister of Cuba. The excuse of "youthful naivety" could no longer be applied, not least because by then the scale of Stalin's crimes were widely known. The unfortunate truth for even his staunchest defendants is that for most of his adult life, Guevara was an out-and-out Stalinist, in thrall to one of the worst people in history. Politics is often a religion by another name, and locked in the cult of his belief system, Guevara lost the ability to think critically. Instead of accepting the truth of his late hero's many atrocities, acknowledged and recorded by the USSR itself, he began to dig down and entrench his belief in him instead. And in any assessment of the life of Che Guevara, that complete lack of intellectual and moral rigour and that willingness to defend a mass-murderer and tyrant is a stain on his legend.

It was in Guatemala, in 1953, that he met Hilda Acosta, a Peruvian economist who had links to officials in the Árbenz government.

Jacobo Árbenz had come to power as the democratically elected 25th President of Guatemala, in November 1950 on a 60% electoral mandate, promising sweeping reforms. Guatemala's economy was dominated by the United Fruit Company (UFC), a multi-million-dollar, US fruit and sugar conglomerate which had concerns across the continent. UFC had built roads and infrastructure to facilitate its business and, as such, many poor Latin American nations and politicians depended on its apparent largesse, while being trapped in a Faustian pact with the capitalist behemoth.

When Árbenz sought to seize unused land and redistribute it to peasant farmers, UFC hit back, turning to US President Dwight Eisenhower, and insisting that something should be done.

Guevara was impressed by Árbenz's stand against the Yankee corporate monster and began making plans to move permanently to the country. As such, he was witness to the coup d'état that followed, and it further radicalised him. As the new US-backed junta swept to power, he took his first steps as a revolutionary and joined the militia movement. He made an immediate impression, and that drew the attention of agents of the new order who sought to hunt him down. Taking refuge in the Argentine Embassy and, with his lover Hilda under arrest, he fled the country.

The nascent revolutionary wrote in his diary that the United States was the "enemy of humanity" and henceforth dedicated himself to killing the monster. It was a hugely ambitious, one might say, deluded mission, but in the five extraordinary years that followed, Guevara could perhaps have come to believe that anything was possible. In Guatemala, he had befriended a group of Cuban revolutionary students and been introduced to Raúl Castro. The two men hit it off. At some point, one of his new friends nicknamed him "Che" on account of his habit of using the interjection all the time, and the sobriquet stuck.*

Che found work at the General hospital in Mexico City and was joined by Hilda. The two married in September 1955 after she told him she was pregnant.

---

* Che roughly translates as "mate" or "buddy" but can also be used to mean "hey".

Around that time Raúl Castro introduced Che to his brother Fidel, the 29-year-old leader of the 26th of July Movement[*]. Fidel and his brother were not yet communists and saw themselves simply as "freedom fighters" intent on overthrowing the Batista regime in Cuba.

Fulgencio Batista had once been a hero, of sorts. Mixed-race and with indigenous Cuban ancestors, he came from an extremely poor background. His rise to political prominence came when he was one of the leaders of the "Sergeant's Revolt" in September 1933, which overthrew the US-backed regime. As the new head of the army, he established himself as "kingmaker" and power behind the throne of the Cuban presidency, until becoming president himself in 1940.

He introduced women's suffrage and worked hard to promote the interests of non-white Cubans, by encouraging them to join the army. His efforts were endorsed by the Cuban Communist Party, and he was hailed as a populist strong man of the people who would Make Cuba Great Again – or words to that effect.

Prohibition in the USA had turned Cuba into the playground of the world and with it had come casinos, money, prostitution and the Mafia. Some Cubans thrived from the new economy and even after Prohibition ended in 1933, it was boom times for tourism and organised crime. Little of it benefitted ordinary Cubans.

By the time Batista left office in 1944, he was a suspiciously wealthy man and he headed for a life of luxury of hedonistic luxury in the United States with second wife Marta. Had he stayed there and remained out of politics, history might have regarded him differently, perhaps even heroically. But, in 1952, with the encouragement and support of the American crime bosses Lucky Luciano and Meyer Lansky, who were meeting unwelcome impediments to their profits in the new Cuban political climate, he ran again for the presidency.

---

[*] Named after one of the most amateurish attempts in history to overthrow a regime, when in 1953, Fidel Castro, a candidate in the elections that had been cancelled by Batista, led a badly organised and largely spontaneous attack on an army barracks using a hospital opposite it as their base.

Three months before election day, his United Action Coalition was running a poor third in the polls and so, with the backing of the army, he launched a coup, overthrew President Carlos Prío Socarrás and seized power. Under Batista, the Cuban economy boomed and on the back of healthy exports, international trade flourished. By the end of 1952, the island nation had a GDP roughly akin to that of Italy and, while the very poorest rural peasants lived well below the poverty line, workers in the cities earned relatively high salaries compared to neighbouring nations.

But at the same time, American organised crime was back. Batista gave carte blanche to the Mob and it fed off Cuba like a rabid parasite. Brothels, casinos and the drugs trade prospered once more and, in their wake, came a malfeasance of corruption, greed, state-sanctioned violence and murder. Batista took a very sizeable cut of the business, receiving between 10% and 20% of all the casinos' takings and Meyer Lansky poured money into his Swiss Bank Account like a pipeline of Cuban rum.

The Castro brothers wanted to topple Batista, and Che was willing to help. And this was undoubtedly a courageous aspiration. After all, if ever a corrupt regime deserved to be overthrown it was that of Fulgencio Batista, and the ambition was as heroic as the men who set out to do it. It remains striking too just how young they were: Fidel was 30, Che 28 and Raúl just 25.

The guerrillas underwent intensive combat training in Mexico and then, on 25th November 1956, set sail in a ship they had purchased called the *Granma,* with 79 comrades bound for the south-western tip of Cuba. They arrived ten days later but Batista had been tipped off and his army was waiting. A fierce gun battle ensued, and it was to prove another turning point in Guevara's life story. Che was ostensibly the group's medic but, having been shot in the neck, abandoned his medical satchel and picked up a carbine in its place. It was a defining moment in his hero's journey and Che crossed the threshold into another world.

Two-thirds of the rebels were killed or captured, and the 17 survivors headed for the mountains of the Sierra Maestra. There, they won over suspicious local people by stealing cows for them, educating their children and promising better times to come.

The rebels became known as "los barbudos" (the bearded ones) because they were all busy growing beards. At first this was a matter of practicality; razors and soap were quite hard to come by in the remote region. But over time, as Castro would explain in his autobiography, it turned into a badge of identity: "In order for a spy to infiltrate us, he had to start preparing months ahead – he'd have had to have a six-months' growth of beard, you see. So the beards served... as protection."

Castro was still insisting, to all who would listen, that his one objective was to topple Batista.

Guevara, by contrast, was now a hardened Marxist. Until then, like student revolutionaries throughout time, it had mostly been all talk. His admiration for Stalin, his violent thoughts (penned down in his diaries) and his naive hopes for a global communist revolution were just ideas. But there, in the Sierra Maestra, all the dreaming came true. Che Guevara was a dynamic figure – a hugely articulate, intelligent, charismatic and handsome man – and people listened to him. Fellow revolutionaries sat before him as he preached and read them Marxist tracts. He became a prophet, a teacher and a zealot.

Che also had power. He had proved himself as a leader of men and was now firmly ensconced as Castro's number two. Unafraid to throw himself into the middle of the fighting, he had proved his mettle as a warrior and somewhere along the line, it awoke a taste for violence. When a peasant farmer called Eutimio Guerra, who had been working as a messenger for the guerrillas, was identified as a spy, Castro sentenced him to death.

In a foreshadowing of events in the Bolivian village of La Higuera, a decade later, volunteers didn't exactly line up to shoot one of their own – but Che did, writing in his diary that: "The situation was uncomfortable for the people and for (Eutimio) so I ended the problem, giving him a shot with a .32 (calibre) pistol in the right side of the brain, with exit orifice in the right temporal lobe. He gassed a little while and was dead."

It may be reminiscent of the sort of clinical description one might expect of a doctor examining a dead body – but all the same, something about it comes across as nothing short of psychopathic. Desperately poor peasant farmer Eutimio represented the very people that Che was supposed to be liberating, but at his end no quarter was given.

Having killed him, in another peculiar augur of things to come, Che stole his watch and possessions. Later Che was to write a pious, self-aggrandising account of the execution in one of his canonical letters dubbed "Death of a Traitor". The preachy, patronising tone of the epistle, veritably revels in the events surrounding the execution, turning them into something akin to a Marxist revolutionary parable full of biblical omens.

"A heavy storm broke and the sky darkened. In the midst of the deluge, lightning streaking the sky, and the rumble of thunder, one lightning bolt struck followed closely by a clap of thunder, and Eutimio Guerra's life was ended. Even those compañeros standing near him could not hear the shot."

In the essay, Che has Eutimio begging the "revolution (to) take care of his children" and Guevara menacingly ends the account by boasting that while the revolution had fulfilled that promise, he trusted that his children had forgotten their father's name and that theirs too had been changed. There is a disquieting sanctimony to "Death of a Traitor". The moral of this Stalinist parable could perhaps best be summarised as "don't fuck with us". Worst of all, it sounds like he's getting off on it.

By the beginning of 1958, the excesses of the Batista regime were such that even the USA had turned their backs on the dictator. Eisenhower had initially given the regime guns, planes and napalm to fight Castro's uprising, but now, as news of his atrocities against his own people seeped out, they imposed an embargo.

Batista's diminishing band of supporters were now made up of the army, a few wealthy landowners and the Mob. The young insurgents, by contrast, were winning friends and, under Guevara's guidance they were winning the propaganda war too.

In February 1958, Che set up the pirate radio station Radio Rebelde (Rebel Radio). It was not a new idea – radio had been used for the purposes of propaganda in the Second World War by both the British and the Nazis as a means of circumventing the "official broadcasts" of the enemy. Che took the idea from the CIA-backed radio station La Voz de la Liberación in Guatemala. Rebel Radio used the same techniques, broadcasting news bulletins from the "bearded rebels of the Sierra'", playing music and reading bits of literature in between.

It was a hit and support for the 26th of July Movement grew, even if the number of actual guerrillas still numbered only 350 men.

On 28th June, Batista launched Operation Verano (aka the Summer Offensive) and sent some 20,000 troops to surround the Sierra Maestra and finish off the rebel movement. It backfired. The Cuban high command was riven with incompetent leadership and many of the Cuban soldiers were poorly trained. The rebels were agile, familiar with the terrain and by now seasoned combat soldiers, who had mastered the art of stealth; they ran rings around the government troops. Che and Fidel proved to be something of a double act. Che had the tactical know-how, Castro the diplomatic skills. Both were evidenced at the Battle of Las Mercedes in late July. After he and his men had been lured into a trap, Che managed to rout the enemy long enough for Fidel to negotiate a ceasefire. When hostilities resumed, Batista's men advanced only to find there was no enemy to fight. They had fled under cover of darkness.

On New Year's Eve 1958, after receiving reports that Che Guevara's forces had seized the critical city of Santa Clara, just three hours from the capital, Fulgencio Batista ran away, flying to Madeira where the Portuguese dictator, António Salazar, offered him asylum. Batista took hundreds of millions of dollars with him and left behind a legacy of corruption and murder. Thousands of Cubans had died on his watch. The low estimate is usually put at around 4,000, the top at 20,000; the truth – as ever – probably lies somewhere in between.

The tyrant was gone, and hope filled the streets of Havana. Fidel Castro and his men arrived in the city on 8th January 1959 and received heroes' welcomes. Batista had been corrupt, to the very dials of the solid gold telephone gifted to him by American telecom giant ITT, and surely anything that replaced him would be better. Around the world and even – cautiously – in Washington, the fall of Batista was celebrated.

US Secretary of State John Foster Dulles wrote to Eisenhower suggesting that the provisional government in Havana was "free from Communist taint" and that there were "indications that it intends to pursue friendly relations with the United States". Castro was still insisting that he was not a socialist theocrat but a freedom-fighting guerrilla, that his intentions were democratic and that democratic elections would follow, so this was a reasonable set of assumptions.

On 10th January 1959, Castro told a BBC News reporter that Cuba would have "free elections within 18 months", adding that he had no intention of cutting off his beard, because he had asked the Cuban people and they had said: "No, no, no." Castro stayed true to his facial hair commitment, but no free elections ever came.

The new leader immediately conferred Cuban citizenship on his Argentinian friend Che, making him eligible for a post in the new revolutionary government.

The hope of those early days was a false dawn for the people of Cuba. In time, for all its original good intentions, the 26th of July Movement would become as bad as the regime it replaced. The great paradox of revolutionary heroes is that all too often, they end up becoming the very archetype of the tyrannical monster that they first set out to slay. Or as the Victorian Liberal Lord Acton put it, "power tends to corrupt, and absolute power corrupts absolutely. Great men are almost always bad men…"

If you were cynically inclined, I suppose the same might be said of any politician. It is impossible to think of any great leader in history who was not tainted by their time in political office. And it is most certainly true of famous revolutionaries throughout history whether they be Lenin and Trotsky in Russia in 1917, Mao Zedong in China in 1948, or Mugabe in post-independence Zimbabwe. Tragically, it was also to be the case in Cuba.

Castro's new regime came armed with a dangerous cocktail of reckless naivety, hubris and stupidity. And in Che Guevara, the self-appointed high priest of Latin American Stalinism, it now had at its heart that most dangerous of things – an enigmatic ideologue with power.

On 27th January, Che made a speech called the Social Projections of the Rebel Army, in which he made it very clear indeed, that Cuba was just the start: "The revolution is not limited to the Cuban nation... The revolution has put the Latin American tyrants on guard because these are the enemies of popular regimes... the victory against the dictatorship is... the first step to the victory of (Latin) America".

It put the fear of God into Washington.

Che was appointed Governor of La Cabana, a castle-fortress outside Havana, and charged with defending the city and serving (what were presented as) Nuremberg-style judgements on the facilitators of the Batista regime. Evermore the moralising Marxist puritan, Che banned cockfighting, the most popular amusement at the military base, and set up classrooms where soldiers were encouraged to play chess and read instead. Having done so, he and his fellow "liberators" turned on the defeated enemy. Batista and his senior henchmen had fled, so most of the "war criminals" they caught were low-level henchmen of the regime: police officers, soldiers, informers and government bureaucrats.

As "supreme prosecutor", Che was in command of the mission to "cleanse" the taint of the Batista years. In that role, alongside the head of the "Cleansing Commission", Duque Estrada, Che oversaw nightly show trials and, in the first 100 days, about 55 people were executed by firing squad.

Over the next five months, thousands more were arrested, and Che Guevara's military tribunals heard the cases in an increasingly frenzied environment of braying mobs shouting out for justice. Some 151 people were executed at La Cabana alone and by April at least 600 other Cubans had been shot.

One detainee, Luis Rodriguez, a sergeant in the Batista-era army, described the atmosphere:

"...all of a sudden you heard the discharge of several rifles and after a few seconds... the single shots [coup de grâce], sometimes one, sometimes two... even four. All this time we saw Che... calling us criminals... he would say 'all you guys will end up the same way. You deserve it.' We were wondering why is this guy here, he was not even a Cuban... He was very arrogant and cold."

In the middle of it all, Che's friends and family arrived on a visit from Argentina.

His parents, briefly reunited, took the trip together. A photo of them with their son looks like any other picture of proud parents attending the graduation ceremony of a favourite child. Guevara Lynch and Celia are smartly dressed, while their Ernestito stands beaming in between them. But far from being able to enjoy their boy's successes, Guevara Lynch quickly became appalled by what he found. The young man who he had waved off on his motorbike just six years earlier, was now the emcee at a grand carnival of retribution and mass execution, and it was too much for his father to bear.

"It was hard for me to recognise the Ernesto of my home, the normal Ernesto," Lynch later wrote in his autobiography.

He also observed, first-hand, how power had gone to his son's head. On one occasion, while waiting to meet Che, he witnessed him grab a rifle from a youthful guard and order his immediate arrest on account of his looking tired. The boy appeared terrified, and Lynch confronted his son, only to have his concerns brushed aside.

"He was transforming into a man whose faith in the triumph of his ideals reached mystical proportions," Lynch wrote.

Che's former friends were unnerved by his transformation too. David Matrani, an old colleague from Guevara's time at the Mexico City Hospital, told Che bluntly what he thought of the killings, only to be told: "You kill first, or else you get killed", an answer he found far from satisfactory. On hearing of the La Cabana executions, other old friends were similarly revolted.

Revolutions by their nature are almost always bloody and often followed by purges as the old order is erased by the new. But these idealistic young men were not meant to be like other revolutionaries and oppressors. They were supposed to be liberators and better than those who had come before. Che himself was meant to be a new kind of revolutionary, the person that Sartre would dub, after his death as: "not only an intellectual but also the most complete human being of our age", "the era's most perfect man".

Could that be squared with his thuggery and killing in the wake of the revolution?

It was to be expected that some prisoners would be tried and executed perhaps, but a lot of ordinary people ended up in front of firing squads and it continued for years. A *Wall Street Journal* article in 2005 estimated that at least 22 children were shot by firing squads.

Che Guevara was dismissive of his friends and families' objections to the violence and even more dismissive of his wife Hilda. When she arrived in Havana with their young child Hildita, he bluntly told her he was now with a revolutionary called Aleida Torres, and that he wanted a divorce.

Hardly the act of the era's most perfect man.

* * *

On a visit to the island in 1960, Sartre, who was mostly optimistic about the revolution, had noticed something else. The new regime was actively persecuting gay men and it led Sartre to compare the situation with that of Nazi Germany: "In Cuba there are no Jews, but there are homosexuals."

As Che and Fidel's revolution sought to rid Cuba of the hedonism that had defined the Batista years, it was turning on minorities. Gay rights had been non existent before they came to power and the community had suffered bullying, intimidation and imprisonment – but rather than improve things in the dawning of the new era Castro and Che went on the offensive.

The new leaders saw same-sex relationships as a symbol of US moral decay – an un-Cuban corruption that had tainted the island nation. So, they set about making gay people's lives hell. Gay men were routinely arrested and sent to re-education camps where they were forcibly converted. By the mid 1960s the state-sanctioned homophobia was such that any boy deemed "effeminate" was taken out of school and sent off to a military college.

Guevara was already touting his idea of "El Hombre Nuevo" (the New Man), which he thought would bring a fresh notion of post-colonial equality to the island. People were told to view each other as equals, regardless of gender and race, but gay people were most definitely not invited to the party.

In the immediate aftermath of the revolution, thousands of gay men were detained, many betrayed by neighbourhood vigilante groups. In a paper entitled "Gays and the Cuban Revolution", academic and author Rafael Ocasio relates the fate of Virgilio Piñera, a well-known writer who was arrested by the police at his home.

Piñera was sent to the "infamous El Príncipe, where they were stripped [and then] dressed in the appropriate uniform: a striped suit with a P on the buttocks. Capital P: pederast, prostitute, pimp."

When the US poet Allen Ginsberg visited the island in 1965, he tried to disrupt proceedings by making a stand against the state-sanctioned homophobia and was bundled out of a press meeting when he compared communism to homosexuality. Ginsberg later complained that "the worst thing I said was that I'd heard by rumor that Raúl Castro was gay. And the second thing that I said was that Che Guevara was cute."

Neither went down well in homophobic communist Cuba.

* * *

Even before the dust had settled on the revolution, the USA's initial 'laissez-faire' attitude to the new Cuban regime was hardening. Seeking to allay any fears, Castro toured America for 11 days in April 1959, getting treated much like a movie star. Eisenhower was wary and didn't want to meet him, though, sending Vice President Nixon in his place. Castro made all the right noises and gave reassurances to Nixon, who thought him "sincere". He then returned to Cuba and did something else entirely.

To their credit, when not persecuting minorities and shooting their enemies, the new administration was focused on making lives better for ordinary people, and that meant building schools, hospitals and roads, improving sanitation and implementing childhood vaccination programs. Unfortunately, all of that cost money and, having cancelled income tax, the coffers soon ran dry. The regime had inherited about $10 billion, but with all the building and investment, it was soon gone and that meant the country needed a new ally; inevitably that meant cosying up to the USSR, which in turn led to all manner of problems with the neighbours. Castro further riled the US by nationalising oil refineries and seizing assets from US businesses. America responded by ending its import quota of Cuban sugar and announcing an embargo.

The nation's perilous financial woes were made a whole lot worse when Che was made head of the National Bank and Minister of Industry in 1960. It was like putting a stoned, hungry fox in charge of a particularly full coop of chickens, and he blew it. Marxist Guevara, a confessed hater of capitalism, treated the appointment with the contempt he felt it deserved and, to the horror of what was left of the island's financial industry, he began signing the state banknotes with his nickname "Che". It was an act tantamount to sticking a childish middle finger up to capitalism and it shredded the last vestiges of faith in the Cuban economy.

The Cuban peso was never taken seriously again.

The problem, essentially, was that Guevara was a dreamer and not a doer and the Cuban economy was simply not robust or productive enough to implement all that he wanted it to achieve. Putting someone in charge of such a fragile economy whose business expertise didn't extend much beyond a teenage start-up that sold odd shoes and another that poisoned everyone in the immediate vicinity was not the smartest of moves. But worst of all, the Marxist ideologue could not shift his guerrilla mentality or make the compromises necessary to carry out the very important job of running the economy. Instead of doing the best thing for the people of Cuba, he treated the island nation like a giant political petri dish where he could finally put into practice all that he had read.

The economic and social hardships which followed, and which affected the lives of generations of Cubans, never affected him or his fellow revolutionary elite; it was, as always, the "little" people who suffered.

Once the immediate revolution had passed, Guevara was bored by the dull old details of making the country work and began casting about for something more thrilling to fill his time.

On 4th March 1960, *La Coubre*, a Belgian ship carrying arms to Cuba, exploded in Havana harbour, killing around 100 people. The famous *Guerrillero Heroico* photo was taken at a memorial event for the victims, attended by all the revolutionary big hitters. Among them was William Morgan, a 32-year-old American chancer turned dedicated member of the movement.

Morgan swiftly got blamed for the explosions on the evidence of another American who had fled the island and he was a very good scapegoat. Morgan had risen to a position of some prominence during the days in the Sierra Maestra, but from 1960 as Castro started to reveal his pro-socialist sympathies, the American had turned critical. He made an easy and convenient patsy, ended up in front of one of Che's courts – and then a firing squad. The revolution was beginning to eat its children.

The explosion was probably an accident and ultimately the fault of Che Guevara himself, who had overall responsibility for the port. Everyone knew the risk. Explosives were supposed to be unloaded onto barges away from the harbour and not on the quayside. The deaths were the result of sloppy management. But it was much easier to blame it all on American saboteurs instead. Guevara may also have been paranoid. After all, the Americans really were plotting to kill his boss and invade the island, so it was not beyond the bounds of reason that they might have caused explosions in the harbour.

Three weeks before the avowedly anti-communist John F. Kennedy took office in January 1961, the US closed their embassy in Havana and cut off remaining diplomatic and trade ties with the country. With Kennedy in the White House, the Bay of Pigs fiasco followed, and the revolutionary government, like Khrushchev, was delighted by the display of American incompetence on show. In a further demonstration of his inept skills of diplomacy, in August 1961 Guevara sarcastically passed on his thanks for the operation directly to Robert Goodwin, a close adviser to Kennedy and part of the US delegation at the Inter-American Economic and Social Council meeting in Uruguay.

In a secret memo to Kennedy, Goodwin told the president how Guevara: "Went on to say that he wanted to thank us [the United States] very much for the invasion – that it had been a great political victory for them – enabled them to consolidate – and transformed them from an aggrieved little country to an equal."

Che was – to use modern parlance – trolling Kennedy and it further aggrieved the already needled JFK. The failure of the Bay of Pigs invasion had haunted and humiliated him, wounding US pride, and Kennedy's determination to exact revenge led to him investing time and considerable energy into Operation Mongoose, the CIA plan to destabilise Cuba. That operation of disruption and attempted assassination was responsible for pushing the Cubans further into the arms of the USSR and helped spark the Cuban Missile Crisis that followed.

None of it benefitted the actual Cubans or the ordinary people of the USA or those in the rest of the world come to that. The billions who sat on the edges of their seats while the peace of the world hung in the balance were but pawns in a game of nuclear chess. Lab rats in the Marxist-Leninist experimentations of a privileged Argentinian dreamer, his similarly privileged friend Fidel Castro, the Russian bully Khrushchev and the prep-boy John F. Kennedy.

Despite it all, the romance of the Cuban Revolution has remained a left-wing cause célèbre for decades. In the UK, figures like the former Labour MP George Galloway have long continued to praise Che and Fidel after others have begun to think twice. In a 2007 piece for the *Independent*, Galloway praised Che as the man who "could have lived a prosperous bourgeois life as an Argentine dentist" but became a revolutionary instead, who inspired other revolutions from Chile to Venezuela.

It's not just old diehards like Galloway. At times, Russell Brand, the social media influencer who once identified as a comedian, has seemed to be little more than a mockney tribute act to the Argentinian revolutionary. On the front cover of his tour DVD, *Messiah Complex*, in 2013, Brand imitated Che's famous look. In his 2014 book *Revolution* he namechecked Guevara and, while accepting his "dark side", did not go into the wider context of Guevara's activities. The following year he read out in full the revolutionary's letter to his children in a video that has been seen by millions. At the time of writing, Brand has 9 million Twitter followers and a huge platform. Che remains relevant.

The UK "Cuba Solidarity Campaign" is still active too, and its website even has a quotation from the late Labour MP Tony Benn prominently displayed, saying that: "Cuba has inspired millions across the world who are still living in poor conditions enforced by US policies. We all have so much to learn from Cuba."

And yes, if you blinker yourself to its excesses, there are things to celebrate in the revolution Che helped foment. The famously high literacy rate stands at 100% according to the World Bank as of 2021. UNESCO figures from the same year show a life expectancy of 81 for women and 77 for men, at birth, that rivals many Western nations. The revolution brought the infant mortality rate crashing down and healthcare remains world class. With eight doctors per thousand head of population (World Bank 2019), it ranks higher than Britain with just 5.8.

But despite those successes, 75 years after Che and the Castro brothers swept to power promising elections, the country remains a one-party state. In 2022, the World Press Freedom Index compiled by Reporters Without Borders ranked the nation 173 out of 180 countries in the world, saying: "Cuba remains, year in and year out, the worst country for press freedom in Latin America."

In 2020, an NGO, the Cuban Observatory of Human Rights (OCDH), based in Madrid, reported about 1,800 arbitrary detentions of peaceful dissidents during that year alone.

The isolation of the country, led by the United States, has played a huge part. Kennedy's anger at the failure of the Bay of Pigs invasion in 1961 had long-term ramifications and in the decades afterwards there were no diplomatic or cultural ties. Indeed, it was only in 2014 that President Obama and President Raúl Castro announced their intentions to normalise relations, but a decade on that has not amounted to much more than the opening of a US Embassy in Havana. For the most part, the USA continues its 60-year-long embargo against the island, and it remains illegal for US corporations to do business there.

So yes, modern Cuba's woes are not the fault of the Cuban revolutionaries alone. The United States of America and its allies must bear some of the blame as well. Matters have been made considerably worse because the island and its regime have become a cause célèbre among some of the most malignant and vociferous right-wing voices in the USA, who like nothing more than to pour gasoline on an already raging fire. But that does not let the Castro brothers and their enablers off the hook because responsibility for the island's post-war history must rest ultimately with the people who seized power in 1959 and then stubbornly ploughed the same furrow while the world about them changed. Che and Fidel had the greatest of ambitions and intentions, but they were morally and ideologically corrupted by their victory. They bullied and tortured and killed in its immediate wake and then set about making enemies and friends of all the wrong people. As Minister for Finance and Industry, Che almost single-handedly wrecked the economy and, in clinging to youthful dreams and ideology over realpolitik, brought misery in his wake. That dawning of hope in Havana in January 1959, was the high point of Che Guevara's life and work. In that moment, when evil and corruption were defeated, a better future briefly beckoned. But he and the Castro brothers blew it.

It's a lesson that is bigger than Cuba. Leadership matters. Democracy too. The choices that are made can turn good nations bad, make bad nations worse and suffocate the potential and the aspirations of millions for the sake of a few stubborn dreamers and their ill-fitting ideology.

The Cuban people deserved so much more.

* * *

In December 1964, Guevara travelled to the UN summit in New York and on the 11th addressed the assembly. Having spoken out against South African apartheid, he laid into the USA, attacking its "imperialist" domination of Latin America even as it denied African Americans basic rights. "How can those who do this consider themselves guardians of freedom?" He asked.

He then returned to a familiar refrain, suggesting that the people of South America would soon rise up against their oppressors.

"Now in the mountains and fields of America, on its flatlands and in its jungles, in the wilderness or in the traffic of cities, on the banks of its great oceans or rivers, this world is beginning to tremble. Anxious hands are stretched forth, ready to die for what is theirs, to win those rights that were laughed at by one and all for 500 years."

Later that evening, dressed in full military fatigues, he was interviewed on a late-night CBS chat show called *Face the Nation*, and looked visibly bored with it all.

The following year, he gave a singularly ill-judged (even by his standards) speech in Algeria and turned his verbal guns not only on the imperialist West but also on the USSR – now Cuba's key trading partner. It was a disastrous intervention that enraged the Soviets.

Guevara was tiring of the responsibilities of being a politician and may have been seeking a way out. Pragmatic Castro gave him the boot – while presenting it as an opportunity to take his revolution out into the world. So, the Missionary Marxist took the word of Karl to the Congo – believing with an imperial arrogance that had thus far been rivalled only by Cecil Rhodes and other Empire builders that he alone could unite Africa and improve its people.

It was utterly delusional. Members of the Simba revolutionary army, while grateful for the guns and supplies, weren't that interested in the Argentinian communist's lofty ideas and remained wedded to a local belief system called *Dawa*, which infuriated the decidedly atheistic Guevara. The increasingly entitled Argentinian failed to grasp that he was the guest not the boss and, in the midst of his miserable and failed experience in the Congo, plagued with dysentery and worsening asthma, he received word that his mother Celia had died.

The endgame was about to play out. Che left Africa and flew to Spain, where he met his one-time hero Juan Perón. The former Argentinian President tried to convince Guevara to give up on his dreams of global revolution and return to his family – but it fell on deaf ears although Che did fly onwards to Cuba for a brief, secret, reunion with his wife, Aleida, and their four children. The kids did not recognise their papa and were told he was an uncle in case word leaked out to the CIA of his presence on the island. Guevara wrote that farewell letter to them, later to be recited by British comedian Russell Brand, just in case he lost his life fighting the cause. Despite what inspiration Brand might have later taken from it, the missive bulges with self-importance and quasi-religious sanctimony.

"Grow up as good revolutionaries. Study hard so that you can master technology, which allows us to master nature. Remember that the revolution is what is important, and each one of us, alone is worth nothing."

As he approached his next project, the fanatical Pastor Guevera was preaching to his heirs, in the hope perhaps, that if he failed, they might finish what he had started.

Having failed on the African continent, Che had turned his attention back to South America and picked Bolivia as the place to start the Latin American revolution. In elaborate preparations, prior to his departure, the Cuban Secret Service plucked every hair individually from the top of his head, to make him look convincingly bald for the purposes of disguise and an assumed identity.

Che arrived in Bolivia, on 3rd November 1966, posing as a Uruguayan businessman, and travelled to La Paz, a rural region in the South-East of the country. There he rendezvoused with supporters, loyal to him since the days in the Sierra Maestra, and set about planning a revolution that he hoped would lead to the entire continent uniting as a communist utopia. Despite his extraordinary successes in Cuba and despite having written a book on guerrilla strategy, Guevara was in fact a man of few ideas.

And there was one small but rather significant problem. Nobody else wanted to join in.

Guevara called his movement the *Ejército de Liberación Nacional de Bolivia – or National Bolivian Liberation Army* – but this grand-sounding grassroots movement was nothing more than astro-turf. Half his 50 men and women were not from Bolivia. Many had never even been there. Guevara had expected support from the local Bolivian communist party, but it never materialised.

There were hapless manoeuvres and a bizarre raid on a chemist shop to get asthma medicine, but once again Che treated the local people, who he was supposed to be liberating, with something verging on lofty contempt. The few locals he had in the movement deserted him until just a handful of diehard Cuban supporters were left.

Che's health was deteriorating and when he was eventually captured on 7th October 1967, clutching that tin of eggs, this lover of adventure books must have realised that he had reached the final page of the story.

In time, Che became a martyr, a socialist saint and, for others, a figure of considerable hate. Right-wing Americans still vilify him. For them he is the bogeyman of left-wing extremism, a mass murderer and war criminal. And they are right, to an extent, because as the final acts of his life played out, there was nothing "heroic" about the *Guerrillero Heroico*. Che's ever more fanatical beliefs, excesses and that growing sense of divine right rode roughshod other people's freedom and happiness and lives. He became, in short, a fanatic – and left a legacy of tyranny and injustice that still haunts Cuba today. That Che really has no place on your bedsit wall.

But the same cannot be said of Ernestito Guevara – the idealistic young medical student, who motorcycled through Peru and Chile, who witnessed the excesses of imperialism and was appalled by it. The young man who did more than hope for a better world; he set out, with good intentions to overthrow tyranny and try to make it happen. The world needs dreamers and doers and Ernestito was certainly both of those.

In a strange way, he is the unsung hero in the Che Guevara story.

CHAPTER FOUR

RELIGIOUS HEROES
MOTHER TERESA
OF CALCUTTA

Why We Create Saints

For years there had been rumours about the strange goings-on at the farmhouse on the edge of Lake Eildon, 200km (125 miles) north-east of Melbourne in Australia.

There were tales of curious comings and goings and ghostly, blonde-haired children glimpsed in the woods beyond the barbed wire fence. There was talk of a cult and a report of a custody battle and, in 1985, a Channel Nine journalist, Marie Mohr, even approached the house to discover what was going on inside. It was to no avail, and it wasn't until an August morning, late in the Australian winter of 1987, when Federal Police raided the property, that the bizarre truth was revealed. Behind a secret door, in a backroom cupboard, police found 14 children in identical outfits and bleach-blonde hair huddled together – in a windowless room – in fear for their lives.

The kids, ranging in ages from 3 to 18, were dressed in outfits that made them look like the Von Trapp family, as portrayed in the 1965 musical film *The Sound of Music** by way of the 1960 horror movie the *Village of the Damned*†.

They had been raised believing that the "police existed to shoot people" and that they were the children of a glamorous and wealthy yoga teacher called Anne Hamilton-Byrne, who was Jesus Christ, they were told, and her husband Bill. Anne had told them that they would be the inheritors of the post-apocalyptic world to come but instead they were taken into care.

Even more alarmingly, the children soon found out that most of them weren't even Anne and Bill's offspring. They had in fact been taken from their real mothers or been offered up for adoption by members of the cult over the years. But that wasn't even the start of it.

Anne Hamilton-Byrne's story and those of her victims reads like some crazy conspiracy theory, dreamed up by 4chan users in the darkest recesses of the internet. The difference is that everything you are about to read is true. It is a tale of greed and wholesale abuse and a powerful example of how deranged people with malignant intent can end up being viewed as saints.

Anne was a congenital liar and by way of proof of that she wasn't even called "Anne". Born in December 1921 in the Victoria town of Sale, east of Melbourne, she was christened Evelyn Grace Victoria Edwards. Her father, Ralph, worked on the railways and her mother, Florence, claimed she was a medium. With the rise of spiritualism after the First World War, talking to the dead was big business. Families who had lost their loved ones in the war and the "Spanish Flu" pandemic, which killed five times as many people as the conflict, were desperate

---

* In real life, Maria Von Trapp and the Captain had been married for 11 years when Germany invaded Austria and in 1938 the "children" ranged in age from Eleanore aged 8 to Rupert aged 27 years old.
† A film in which local women become pregnant by parasitic aliens and start producing identical offspring. In 1983, the Bonnie Tyler hit 'Total Eclipse of the Heart' paid homage to it. Honestly, when I set out to write this book, I had no idea that the Welsh singer would feature so prominently.

to speak to their deceased relatives. But despite having plenty of gullible customers, Florence failed to make money from it. Suffering from schizophrenia, which led to a psychotic episode in which she set fire to her hair, she was eventually sent to live in a psychiatric hospital.

Ralph struggled on his own and Anne and her siblings were farmed off to an orphanage.

Carole M. Cusack, an Australian historian specialising in religion at the University of Sydney, who wrote a definitive 2017 academic paper on the Hamilton-Byrne cult, speculated that these formative experiences: "…appear to have acted as a psychological motivation for the life she later created as the venerated leader of the Family, and – with her third husband Bill – mother of 14 children and possessor of a glamorous jet-setting lifestyle, which was unusual in Australia in the 1970s and early 1980s."

Later, Anne was to fake her backstory altogether, claiming that she was descended from Franco-Scottish royalty and that her parents had been wealthy and successful people. She insisted she had grown up in a grand mansion with rolling lawns, had attended prestigious schools and that her father had been a successful inventor, who had been friends with that other fantasist T.E. Lawrence of Arabia. She may have meant D.H. Lawrence, who briefly lived in New South Wales from May to August 1922, but it didn't matter either way because it was all a lot of old dingo-shit.

By the dawn of the Second World War and now calling herself Anne, she married and had a daughter, Judith. Her husband died in an accident, and she went on to raise the child by herself.

By 1959, the year Cuban revolutionaries overthrew Batista, she had reinvented herself as a Yoga teacher and begun gathering clients among the wealthy housewives of Melbourne.

Anne was extremely attractive and was to "keep" her looks with the help of regular cosmetic surgery throughout her life. She was also incredibly, almost supernaturally, charismatic and possessed of a pair of steely grey eyes. People who met her said she seemed to stare into your very soul. On top of it all she had an uncanny knack of reading people and would flatter individuals, telling them that she had noticed an "aura" about them or that they were "special" in order to lure them into her circle. Like all bullies, she was also highly adept at playing human beings off against each other.

Yoga then had become something of an alternative religion for many people in economically advanced countries like Australia. The Cold War era of H-bombs and chemical weapons, along with the rise in technology, had seen a hankering for a simpler world. As church attendance began to fall away, many sought out answers elsewhere and it was boom times for "Eastern" beliefs, alternative medicine, gurus and charlatans, including a very famous one, called Mao Zedong.

Having seized power in October 1949, Chairman Mao had a problem. Socialist heaven may have arrived on Earth, but the Communist Party of China (CCP) had no means of delivering it. The population of 540 million was being served by just 40,000 trained doctors.

Mao solved the problem by declaring that traditional Chinese methods would henceforth be incorporated into general medical practice – in a process of "grand unification" – and in 1952 a state apparatchik proclaimed that: "This One Medicine, will possess a basis in modern natural sciences (combining) the ancient and the new, the Chinese and the foreign, all medical achievements – and will be China's New Medicine!"

The West's fascination with the East in the 1950s led to traditional Chinese medicine becoming fashionable among movie stars and celebrities, and soon it was being hailed as a new dawn of healthcare. A decade later, following a 1972 article in *The New York Times* claiming it even worked as an anaesthetic, there was a clamour for it to be incorporated into mainstream Western practice.

Acupuncture is pseudoscience. Peer-reviewed studies have demonstrated, beyond all shadow of doubt, that it does not work in any conventional medical sense – although it may have a placebo effect. It does not matter where the needles are placed – there is no scientific grounding in it at all and it certainly cannot be used as an anaesthetic. The scientist David Colquhoun has dubbed the practice a "tax on the stupid" and yet millions of people, from Pitcairn to Tunbridge Wells, still believe in it along with other traditional Chinese medicine remedies.

Ironically, Mao didn't believe in his own mandated medicinal practices either, telling his personal physician that: "Even though I believe we should promote Chinese medicine, I personally do not believe in it." And why would he? Chinese medicine is not an ancient traditional system, but a lot of random practices cobbled together around the time Elvis Presley recorded 'Heartbreak Hotel'.

It's the same story, to some extent, with the "five-thousand-year-old science" of yoga. Yoga is not five thousand years old, nor is it a science. Millions of people do quite obviously benefit from the practice and in terms of giving us all space, peace of mind and exercise, it is clearly a good thing. Unfortunately, as with any poorly understood practice, there is also a long and inglorious history of quacks, fakers and nascent cult leaders latching on to it.

Yoga is a huge industry. The world-wide market in 2023 is worth roughly $161 billion and will reach $215 billion by 2025. Many a teacher and guru has become a celebrity and this has long been the case.

If – as claimed – yoga was indeed "five thousand years old" that would make it roughly the same age as the very first civilisations and about two thousand years older than the Hindu religion itself. It isn't. It was only in the eleventh century CE that the concept of a mind and body Hatha-yogic tradition began to be taught and practised in South Asia, but we have a 1930s Swedish-Russian-Latvian actress called Eugenie Peterson (who had changed her name to Indra Devi) to thank for its modern proliferation.

Devi-Peterson moved to India in the 1920s after converting to Theosophy.* In 1930, she starred in a film and married a Czech diplomat called Jan Strakaty before becoming interested in the teaching of an Ayurvedic yoga-practitioner called Tirumalai Krishnamacharya, who eventually took her on as his first female student. When she left with Strakaty for a new posting in China in 1939, she began teaching it in Shanghai. Strakaty thought yoga was "nonsense" and tried to discourage his wife from doing it but in Shanghai, Devi became a nascent "influencer" and managed to get Soong May-ling, the wife of Chinese nationalist leader Chiang Kai-shek, to be her most famous follower. Staying in China through the Japanese occupation, Devi is said to have taught the entire American consulate during their incarceration in a hotel. With the war's end, she separated from her husband and, in 1947, moved to San Francisco. Soon she had a raft of celebrity clients including Greta Garbo, Yul Brynner and Gloria Swanson, all of whom were willing to buy into the fashionable new-ancient practice of yoga.

The popularity of her books, which included *Forever Young, Forever Healthy* in 1953 and *Yoga For You* in 1959 spawned interest across the States. In 1953 she married a physician called Sigfrid Knauer, who set her up in business on an expansive estate in Tecate, Mexico. There, Devi dressed in a sari and appearing for all the world like an Indian woman, taught yoga.

It was Devi who was responsible for the modern popularity of yoga and she too who turned what had once been an almost entirely male, South Asian practice into one that is largely a female meditative pursuit. Beyond India, it is estimated that in 2023, 72% of yoga practitioners are women. Devi's work spread throughout the 1950s and in time her books reached suburban, conservative, Melbourne, Australia, where Anne

---

* Theosophy is unusual in that it is one of the few religious movements in history ever to have been created by a woman – a Russian mystic called Helena Blavatsky. Theosophy is a faith based on a mixture of elements of spiritualism, Buddhism, Brahmanism and reincarnation. It has no actual belief system beyond faith in a "universal creed" of brotherhood that will bond people of all races, faiths and sexes.

Hamilton, who had been dabbling in a number of "alternative religions" including, like Devi, Theosophy, picked up a copy of *Forever Young, Forever Healthy* and found her calling. By the early 1960s, Anne's esoteric mix of ideas, combining yoga with bits of Buddhism, Hinduism, astrology, Ouija boards and whatever else popped into her head, had turned her into a suburban guru. But her influence went to another stratosphere when, in December 1962, she met Raynor Johnson, the British-born Master of Queen's College, at the University of Melbourne.

Johnson was a graduate of Balliol College, Oxford and had a PhD from the University of London, where he taught between 1927 and 1933. Moving to Australia the following year to become the Master of the conservative Methodist Queen's College, he remained in post until 1964. Throughout the period, in parallel with his research work, he became transfixed with the notion of a higher meaning to life. A man of remarkable academic prowess who wrote hundreds of scientific papers and dozens of books, he was also, it has to be said, a complete fruit loop. Wedded to the theory of psychical research, he was convinced that physics was a gateway to a higher plane, and his meeting with the 41-year-old yoga teacher was a turning point in both of their lives.

Anne was dating Johnson's gardener, a man called Michael Riley, and having heard that the professor and his wife were planning to visit India, she arrived on their doorstep claiming to have had a series of premonitions about the trip. Johnson was ostensibly travelling to meet the newly appointed President of India, Dr Sarvepalli Radhakrishnan, who was a philosopher, and to give a speech to the two houses of parliament. But his greater purpose was to hang out with some notable Indian mystics, visit ashrams and open the doors of perception between heaven and hell. Matters took a decidedly peculiar turn however, when many of Anne's 'predictions' about the trip seemingly started to come true and when Johnson's wife, Mary, became seriously ill with food poisoning, Raynor became convinced that the yoga teacher was some sort of seer, possessed of psychic abilities, and returned home.

Anne's visions were less "divine premonitions" and more like sound guesswork. After all it is not unusual for Westerners who visit Asia to develop stomach problems, and the likelihood of a middle-aged, middle-class person who had never been there before getting some sort of tummy bug was high. But the credible Raynor fell for the "premonition" and on his return, he, Mary and their daughter Maureen visited Anne and Riley, ate magic mushrooms (dubbed "sacred manna"), got seriously off their heads and subsequently decided, as you do, that Anne was a reincarnation of Jesus Christ.

From this bizarre soup of yoga, chance encounters, premonitions, stomach upsets and psychedelic hallucinations sprang the cult of "The Family" with Anne at its head and her inner circle of followers, including Raynor, believing themselves to be reincarnations of the Apostles of Jesus Christ.

The involvement of Raynor – a leading figure in Australian society and a renowned academic to boot – was key to what happened next. Soon afterwards, Johnson introduced Anne to a psychiatrist called Dr Howard Whitaker, who ran the Newhaven private clinic in Kew, a suburb of Melbourne. Like Johnson, Whitaker had impeccable connections and a high standing and was using the hallucinogenic drug LSD to treat his patients. In 1965, Whitaker joined the cult that Anne had begun, then known as the Great White Brotherhood (shortly to be known simply as "The Family"), and Anne then inveigled her way into the clinic and began using her own unorthodox treatments on patients while recruiting more followers. According to Lex De Man, the Melbourne detective who was to later spend five years investigating the extent of Hamilton-Byrne's activities, these treatments included giving patients acid before locking them in darkened rooms.

In an appearance on a May 2021 edition of the podcast *Profiling Evil*, De Man explained what happened next: "The door would open and there was this figure (Anne Hamilton-Byrne) in a white flowing gown with dry ice in a bucket, to make it look as if smoke was coming up from behind her and when they came out of the trance, they'd believe they had seen the Messiah."

As the extraordinarily narcissistic Anne gathered more followers, she grew in confidence.

In 1968, she met William (Bill) Byrne, a handsome British immigrant, whose son was being treated at the clinic for depression. Anne was soon involved in a relationship with him and at one point his wife ended up, against her will, being confined to the facility in Kew. Bill and Anne adopted the surname Hamilton-Byrne and henceforth, with Anne now being called "The Master" by her followers, she started to proclaim that the world was in its final cycle, that the rapture was coming and that only true believers would be saved. Plagiarising ideas from the rival (although much larger) cult of Scientology, which was making in-roads into Australia at the time, she began to conduct "audits" on her cult members, convincing them that she could liberate them from an endless stream of reincarnations and find them happiness in time for their salvation. Much of this stuff is par for the course for any doomsday cult, but what was almost unique about "The Family" was the nature of its leaders and membership. As Cusack noted in her 2017 paper:

"Anne (was) an unusual leader of a new religious movement (NRM) for three reasons: she was female, her followers were drawn from the educated middle and upper professional classes and were middle-aged rather than the traditional student and youth converts to NRMs."

The main problem with being in a cult is that if you are in one, it is almost impossible to recognise the fact.

In 1988, Dr Steve Hassan, a former member of the Unification Church aka the Moonies, wrote a celebrated book called *Combating Cult Mind Control*.

Sixteen years previously, in 1972, and aged just 19, Hassan had gone, within a few weeks, from being a New York poetry student to a radicalised member of Sun Myung Moon's Unification movement. His faith in Moon – who he thought was the Messiah – was such that at the height of the Watergate scandal, he had been willing to storm the Capitol building in Washington in the belief that President Richard Nixon was an archangel sent by God. Hassan had only escaped the cult following a major car crash in 1976, caused by fatigue, which saw an intervention by his family and him being deprogrammed of his beliefs.

The experience led to a lifelong study of the nature and lure of cults, and his 1988 book introduced the "BITE" model, a useful acronym that can be used when both defining cults and deciding if someone has fallen prey to one.

BITE stands for:

- **B**ehaviour control – *where you live, how you live, who you live with, what you eat, who you sleep with, how you spend your money and who you give your money to (the group).*
- **I**nformation control – *is information withheld from you, is your information monitored, are you allowed to source information from outside the group?*
- **T**hought control – *there is only one reality; it is "us" and "them"; loaded language and little phrases used to bond the group; a mantra and a collective "group think" belief system; rejection of critical thinking; and a religious element.*
- **E**motional control – *a divine leader; cult members made to feel like they are failures, or weak who need to be cleansed to become better people. New members are "love bombed" and then gaslit.*

From the mid 1960s onwards, as the yoga classes morphed into something altogether different, "The Family" came to tick every box in the BITE model. Anne began to control all aspects of her followers' lives, telling people who to marry, who to sleep with and who to divorce.

One cult member later told Channel 9: "I was told to leave my first wife and go up to the hills and I did. I was told I was going to have a baby with another woman and I did."

Meanwhile, Anne began separating people from their money. Followers were told to give a minimum 10% of earnings to the cult and Anne paid for nothing herself. She worked everyone hard so that they didn't have time to stop and think. And from the late 1960s she added child kidnapping into the mix. Between 1969 and 1987 she took 28 children into the cult, with half being "given" to Anne and Bill by followers and the other 14 procured from unmarried, teenage mothers at clinics in rural Victoria. The girls were told that their babies would be given to "respectable" families, but some of those working in the clinics were members of the cult and they simply took the children away. Anne's growing network of followers led to a situation where, in the words of Lex De Man: "Babies born in cult hospitals, delivered by cult midwives, [were] handed over to cult social workers."

Documents were forged, names changed, dates of birth made up and, in a bizarre turn of events, Anne, now advancing into late middle age, started faking pregnancies in preparation for the new arrivals, by stuffing clothes in her jumper. A group of nurses, known as "the aunties", who were paid nothing, looked after the growing brood of children and Anne and Bill spent ever longer periods abroad. The aunties worked in shifts so that they could earn salaries from local hospitals which they then handed over to Anne, who used that and other money she received to buy a substantial house, Broom Farm, near Tunbridge Wells, England.

When contracts had been exchanged, she sent cult members to renovate it, at their own expense. Later she did the same thing in upstate New York. At its peak, the cult had about 500 members and, after Anne acquired Kai Lama farm (otherwise known as Uptop) at Lake Eildon in 1971, she used it not only as a home for the kids but also as a spiritual centre where she preached to her devotees.

The cult's motto was: Unseen, Unheard, Unknown.

Few dared to question it and those who did were expelled. But the main victims were the children, who were bullied, tortured, humiliated and at age 14 initiated into the cult by being fed LSD and locked in a dark room.

Followers were expected to be vegetarian and eat a bland and innutritious diet. Anne was obsessed not only with the way she looked but the way her followers and in particular the children looked too. The control drove many to eating disorders and other children would often be so hungry that they would try to steal food. In 2009, during a trip to the farm with Australia's *60 Minutes* show on Channel Nine, Sarah Hamilton-Byrne, expelled from the cult by her "mother" with the suggestion that she "go and die in a drain", told journalists what would happen if they were caught.

"They put a bucket here and one of the aunties would push your head into the bucket and hold it there for 20 or 30 seconds then say 'did you do it did?' and you'd say 'No' and they'd push it back in again… Anne said it was better to be drowned than to be a liar."

Another of Anne's favoured punishments, known as "zebra stripes", was to hit children with the stiletto of one of her designer shoes.

Her plan was for the children to go on to be lawyers and doctors and get jobs in government and powerful positions in the land. She had the farm designated as a school and got a well-known and respected private school headmaster to set the curriculum. But investigative journalism was catching up with her, and Marie Mohr's persistence paid off. When Sarah was expelled from the cult, the teenage girl bravely told the truth about what was going on there, and a raid on the property followed in August 1987.

Raynor Johnson had died in May and was not alive to have justice catch up with him. The case was initially handled by social welfare and it wasn't until Lex De Man got involved and set up "Operation Forest" in 1989 that the extent of the crimes became known. Thanks to De Man's tireless work and a joint operation with UK and US police in 1993, Anne and Bill were eventually arrested at their house in the Catskills in New York State and sent back to Australia.

But, despite it all, the Hamilton-Byrnes were fined just $5,000 (Aus) each on a minor charge of making a false declaration on an official form, and lived out their lives insisting they had done nothing wrong. Lex De Man was of another opinion, telling Channel Nine: "She is the most-evil person I ever met."

The real victims in all of this – the children – endeavoured to come to terms with what had happened, and Sarah perhaps suffered most of all. Changing her name to Sarah Moore, she struggled to reconcile her heroic act in breaking up the cult with her childhood faith and love of her "parents". She attempted suicide multiple times and ended up losing a leg, below the knee, after a failed attempt. Determined to rise above the circumstances of her childhood, she trained to become a doctor and set up a charity called Barefoot Basics, which sought to help children in India.

Working in practice in Australia she would often visit Thailand and India to volunteer, working with children and war refugees on the Thai-Burmese border.

In 1995, Sarah wrote a book about her experiences called *Unseen, Unheard, Unknown* about the cult that had ruined her life. Her estranged "mother" continued to gaslight her from a distance, calling Sarah her "favourite daughter".

Sarah sought to find logic and reason to a childhood of abuse which, by any measure, defied it. Eventually she chose forgiveness over hate, and reason, but the scars she carried were too much to bear and she became addicted to the opioid pethidine and started forging prescriptions for herself. In 2015, she was caught and charged with the offence, before later being diagnosed with PTSD and bipolar disorder.

Still, this remarkable woman fought on. Reunited with her birth mother, she continued to represent her "brothers and sisters" against the Hamilton-Byrne lies and eventually, in an extraordinarily selfless act of reconciliation, met Anne and forgave her.

This extraordinary, brave and heroic woman died of heart failure in May 2016, aged just 46.

* * *

Anne succeeded for so long because her cult was enabled by powerful, intelligent, ostensibly "respectable" people. In her lifetime (she died in 2021 of Alzheimer's), she was never held to account and, indeed, insisted that her critics were the real criminals and that she had just been trying to make the world a better place. It is an appalling story and all the more so because the psychopathic Hamilton-Byrne was no one-off. Throughout history, abusive individuals with Messiah Complexes have portrayed themselves as "saints" and committed crimes in plain sight.

Following his death in 2011, the eccentric British entertainer and DJ Jimmy Savile was widely mourned. Celebrities, members of the public and even politicians took to social media to express their sorrow.

Savile had not just been a TV and radio legend – he was almost as well known for his charitable work and was famed for running 212 marathons, 300 professional bike races and dozens of fell runs and walks for charity. He once cycled from John O'Groats to Land's End and was also extremely generous with his time, popping up at old people's homes, cancer wards and children's hospitals to cheer up the patients.

In 1969, he joined the part-time staff at Stoke Mandeville hospital as a volunteer porter and three years later, in 1972, he began fundraising for them as well. Over the next few years – with help from volunteers – he managed to raise £10 million for a spinal cord unit and when it opened, in 1983, he was made the patron. The hospital then set up The Jimmy Savile Stoke Mandeville Trust in recognition of his efforts.

Savile volunteered at Broadmoor Psychiatric Hospital, too, where he became "voluntary assistant entertainments officer". Jimmy was so respected that he had keys to its secure unit and in 1988 was appointed to lead a taskforce overseeing the management of the hospital.

Savile was widely praised for his charitable works in his lifetime and in death the press gathered to celebrate his achievements, especially when it became known that he had left significant amounts of money to charity. The *Daily Express* was typical, declaring in its pages, just days after his death: "Ow's about that! Sir Jimmy Savile raised £45m for charity and left another £5m in his will"

His death attracted acres of obituaries and was something of a cultural event in his home county of West Yorkshire. In the days before his funeral, he lay in state at the Queen's Hotel in Leeds and thousands came to pay their respects. According to a report by the *Guardian* at the time many were "in tears" and filled a huge book of condolences with reminiscences. Around 5,000 people passed the coffin on the first day and the city of Leeds and town of Scarborough raced to erect a statue to him first.

Savile's funeral on 9th November 2011 at Leeds Cathedral was attended by thousands of people, including former minister Lord Tebbit and the boxer Frank Bruno. Prior to the service, the hearse carrying his golden coffin drove past all of the significant places of his lifetime – including Leeds General Infirmary (LGI). He was later buried in a prime plot in Scarborough's Woodlands cemetery. Savile went into the ground wearing his green beret, the Royal Marine cap, presented to him by the corps in the 1970s for his tireless efforts to raise money for charity, and a Help for Heroes wristband.

His massive, three-part headstone listed his life's achievements:

PHILANTHROPIST, TV PRESENTER, DJ, MARATHON
RUNNER, CYCLIST, WRESTLER, CHIEFTAIN OF
LOCHABER HIGHLAND GAMES.
FRIEND AND SUPPORTER OF: STOKE MANDEVILLE
SPINAL INJURIES UNIT, LEEDS GENERAL INFIRMARY,
BROADMOOR PSYCHIATRIC HOSPITAL, LITTLE SISTERS OF
THE POOR, THE ROYAL MARINES AND MANY OTHERS

There wasn't enough room perhaps for "paedophile" and "rapist". But that is what Jimmy Savile was. For decades – under the cover of his good deeds, charitable works and TV gigs – he had been abusing often very vulnerable children, women and even some men on an almost unimaginable scale. A total of 214 specific offences have since been identified, but Savile was almost certainly responsible for hundreds more.

Nobody talked about due diligence back in the 1970s and 1980s, but there was a sort of assumption from the public in the era that even eccentric characters like Savile had somehow been checked out. If not, then he surely would have been exposed by the self-appointed guardians of morality: the tabloid newspapers. Or, failing that, been removed from our TV screens by those in authority. And more than that – Savile must have been vetted at some point because he had friends in very high places and honours galore. He received an OBE in 1972 and in 1990, following persistent efforts by Prime Minister Margaret Thatcher, was knighted by the Queen.

That same year, Pope John Paul II gave Savile (a Catholic) a Papal Knighthood of the *Ordo Sancti Gregorii Magni*. How was it possible that a man of such standing, who rubbed shoulders with the great and the good could be such an evil human being?

In 2000, when Savile was 74, the film-maker Louis Theroux made one of his off-beat documentaries about him. Having drawn him into his confidence Theroux asked Savile directly:

"Jimmy are you a paedophile?" And Savile replied: "Yes."

Watching now it is unclear whether he is joking – and that was clearly deliberate. By admitting his sins, he swept them under the carpet.

Twenty years later a 2022 Netflix documentary, *Jimmy Savile – A British Horror Story,* demonstrated that for decades he had been doing much the same, "making jokes" on camera and even at one point, openly groping a young girl during the filming of the TV show *Top of the Pops.* But Savile had remained in the public eye throughout, making himself untouchable by doing "good works". The potency of his fame let him befriend powerful and influential doctors and officials and by doing so, he eased his way into hospitals, where he abused patients. Savile even had his own grace-and-favour flat at Stoke Mandeville Hospital.

At LGI and Stoke Mandeville Hospital between 1972 and 1985, he carried out dozens of assaults on people aged 5 to 75. Those patients and staff who were brave enough to make complaints had their concerns dismissed. Savile's victims included little girls, old women, boys and anyone else that he encountered. He was obsessed with hospital morgues and once boasted about having sex with dead bodies at LGI. His fellow porters assumed he was joking, but another witness at Broadmoor claimed to have seen him interfering with dead bodies. Two independent witnesses later claimed he had rings made up of glass eyes he had stolen from dead bodies.

The barrister Kate Lampard, who carried out the Department of Health investigation into Savile's activities at Stoke Mandeville, said that: "He used the opportunities that that access, influence and power gave him to commit sexual abuses on a grand scale."

When Broadmoor introduced a new security system in 2004, he immediately stopped going.

The full extent of his crimes will never be known and even in death there were attempts to protect Savile, perhaps in part to protect others from guilt by association. A *Newsnight* investigation into his crimes by the journalists Meirion Jones and Liz MacKean, which revealed a police investigation into Savile in 2009, was canned before it was broadcast. It was not until October 2012 and an ITV investigation called *Exposure: The Other Side of Jimmy Savile* that the truth was dragged into the light.

Savile was the perpetrator of these acts, but, like Anne Hamilton-Byrne, he was facilitated in no small measure by powerful enablers who basked in the reflected glory of his celebrity. He groomed princes and princesses, prime ministers, popes and the BBC – but more than that, he groomed millions of British television viewers. He dished out his own awards too – a medal which said "Jim Fixed it For Me". The medals were originally props, bestowed on participants in his BBC show, which ran from 1975 to 1994 and arranged for the dreams of the children who wrote in to come true. But Savile continued to 'award' them for years afterwards, even when the cameras were not rolling. He gave them to celebrities, patients and politicians.

The medals were critical to his cult and gave him a sort of regal power – a man capable of dispensing gongs like some flamboyant track-suit wearing Emperor-saint. A twentieth-century St Nicholas. A bringer of gifts and bestower of miracles through the magical mystery of TV.

In retrospect it's clear that Savile was a monster, incapable of feeling anything for anyone, apart from his mother, himself and God. Many of us who grew up with him on our childhood TVs felt some-thing was not quite right, but his fame and his faith acted as a sort of protective force field. He was, after all, a committed Catholic and his most treasured possession was the crucifix given to him by Pope John Paul II when he was made a papal knight. Savile used his religion as his "serious side" and even campaigned for a Scottish nun, Margaret Sinclair, to be made a saint but only, because she had played a part in his own origin story.

When he had been seriously ill at the age of two, his mother's prayers to Margaret had brought him – saintly Jimmy believed – back to the land of the living and set him up on his mission to bring his tacky medallions and sexual depravity out into the world. The campaign, like everything else in his life, was about himself.

God was as key to the Savile public image as his show and his props. While he lay in state, he had already arranged for the two red books from *This Is Your Life* to be put next to his coffin, along with a cigar and the papal crucifix. Savile even co-wrote a 1979 book about his beliefs titled *God'll Fix It*. The blurb reads:

"Jimmy Savile is an enigma. His job forces him to clown, bamboo-zle, and pull the wool over our eyes. In this book he comes clean. He talks frankly about his relationship with God and his commitment as a Christian, showing what this demands of him in his day-to-day life as a disc jockey, TV personality and, most dear to his heart, hospital visitor. His joy in being involved with other people, many of whom are seriously ill, shines through the book.

A strong faith and a sense of humour makes him trust that, come what may, God'll Fix it."

It was all cant; lies dressed up as religious piety for the benefit and promotion of the human being at its core.

While Savile is one of the most egregious examples in modern history of a truly awful human being using faith and charity as a cover for his appalling behaviour, he is far from alone.

"God told me to do it!" has been used as an excuse by criminals, psycopaths, predators and dictators throughout history and the notion of a 'Just War', waged in the certainty that a divine ruler is backing a bad cause, has been deployed since long before the days of Saint Augustine.

Throughout the savage slaughter of the First World War – both sides used the argument to prop up their case for killing other people.

During the sacking of the Belgian town of Louvain in late August 1914, there was universal outrage at German brutality and the murder of at least 248 innocent people. Germany justified the atrocity and deployed 93 German intellectuals, academics and Catholic theologians to draft a manifesto to "protest to the civilized world against the lies and calumnies" of the Allies. Thirteen of the academics were religious figures and chief among them was Adolf von Harnack – a personal friend of the Kaiser.

The 93 argued that Germany was acting in self-defence in a just war and used a mixture of scripture, precedent, half-truths and lies to prove their point. The original dodgy dossier.

Faith, then, can be a powerful protective force field – allowing purportedly "holy" people who support or do really bad things to get away with it on the basis that a broad mass of others deem them to be "saintly".

And that brings us, neatly, onto Mother Teresa.

* * *

From the 1970s until her death on 5th September 1997, one day before Princess Diana's funeral, Mother Teresa was a ubiquitous presence on the world stage. In the last decades of her life this diminutive woman, in her simple blue and white sari, she stood alongside Pope John Paul II as one of the towering religious and moral figures of the century. Hailed as a living saint, she was held up, almost universally, as an example of sacrifice and humility: she was, we were told, a friend of the poor and an example of Christianity at its best. For many, Mother Teresa was in short, "the altruist's altruist" – a woman who gave up her life in selfless dedication and service to others.

On her passing, tributes poured in from around the world. "This evening, there is less love, less compassion, less light in the world" said President Jacques Chirac of France. In Washington, President Clinton called her "one of the giants of our time". Indian PM Inder Kumar Gujral added: "Words fail me to express my sorrow. An apostle of peace and love." And in Britain, HM the Queen released a statement saying, "She will continue to live in the hearts of all those who have been touched by her selfless work."

Two years after her death, in December 1999, a US Gallup poll ranked her first in a list of "Most Admired People of the 20th Century", beating Martin Luther King (2) and John F. Kennedy (3) to the top spot.

In dedicating her life to the poor, Mother Teresa had made some very famous friends, been hosted by presidents and prime ministers and was the recipient of at least 120 awards, including the first ever Pope John XXIII Peace Prize (1971), the Nobel Peace Prize (1979), the British Order of Merit (1983) and the Presidential Medal of Freedom and Honorary US citizenship (1985). But through it all, Teresa affected humility. On being told that she had won the Nobel Peace Prize, she replied: "I am not worthy" but was humble enough to travel to Oslo first class and accept it anyway.

Teresa gave good epithet and many of her quotations about love, empathy and humility dot Pinterest, Facebook and the pages of glossy magazines to this day. Her most famous quotations include, "A life not lived for others is not a life", "I'm a little pencil in the hand of a writing God, who is sending a love letter to the world" and "I know I am touching the living body of Christ in the broken bodies of the hungry and the suffering".

Something peculiar happens to words when they are attached to the names of famous prophets. On their own and of themselves, many, like those above, might seem a little banal – trite even. But put a famous name like Mother Teresa's beneath them and they are transformed into something of value. The same is true of good deeds. The heady mix of fame, global esteem and the approval of kings can, as Jimmy Savile knew, turn even monsters into saints – and that halo's light can blinker us all to the murkiness that lies beneath.

Mother Teresa was certainly no Jimmy Savile, but behind her gleaming blue and white sari and her heroic saintly image lay another, far more human story. And another much darker truth.

* * *

Anjezë Gonxha* Bojaxhiu was born in Skopje (then part of the Ottoman Empire but now the capital of North Macedonia) on 26th August 1910 in troubled times. Turn-of-the-century Albania was riven by ethno-political turmoil, which was all made considerably worse by a prevailing culture of violence. In the years before her birth, Anjezë's great-grandfather, great uncle and grandfather were all killed in blood feuds.

---

* Meaning "rosebud" in Albanian and perhaps given to her by her nationalist parents as a bit of symbolic protest. Either way, Orson Welles would have approved.

Ottoman rule, which had begun in the fifteenth century, ended in 1912 with Albanian nationalists declaring independence. But as the country blinked briefly into the light of a better future, more violence followed. Bojaxhiu's nationalist businessman father, Nikolle, was caught up in events and his activities made him enemies. In January 1919, while visiting Serbia, he was poisoned and died.

With his death, Anjezë, her mother Roza and her two siblings were in serious trouble. Albanian society then, even by the low standards of the time, was deeply, deeply misogynistic and women had no rights. They could not inherit money or own property and were viewed as second-class citizens – despite making up over 50% of the population.

If the father of the house died and you were a woman, you were basically on your own and risked destitution or worse. Fortunately, Anjezë's Uncle Mark took on responsibility for the widow, her daughters and son Lazzaro, but it was to be but a brief respite. In one of those cruel twists of fate that history has a habit of dealing, no sooner had he done so, than the third wave of the "Spanish Flu" pandemic arrived in Albania and by the year's end, Mark, three of his four children, his wife and mother had all died of the virus. The one surviving child, Filomena, came to live with the women – adding another hungry mouth to their burden. The once relatively prosperous family got by only thanks to the kindness of neighbours and their belief in God.

In the official versions of her life, including the biography by her friend Lush Gjergji, these early tragedies are turned into "tests". Young Anjezë finds solace in her faith and in 1928, aged 18, experiences a "religious calling". She feels compelled to serve God and to dedicate her life to good deeds.

The "call" is critical to her narrative arc as it is to anyone who seeks to devote their time on Earth to God, but was there perhaps a less spiritual and more practical motivation behind it. Taking vows was in some ways the "best-worst" option available to her. The youngest daughter of three in patriarchal Albanian society had very few prospects and no dowry;

becoming a nun provided a ticket out to a better life. Throughout her childhood, Anjezë had been fascinated by stories of India and the work of missionaries there. We don't really think of nuns as having heroes, but much as a teenage fan of pop music might go crazy over K-pop stars, she, like many devoutly religious people, had her favourite missionaries and saints and wanted to follow in their footsteps.

If you remove the language of faith and scrape away the veneer of destiny narratives, there is very often a very human motivation beneath the journeys of saints. In essence Anjeze's origin story can be boiled down to a young woman, with limited prospects, having a thirst for adventure and a more interesting life.

In 1928, aged just 18, she left Albania to join the Sisters of Loreto at Loreto Abbey in Rathfarnham, near Dublin, Ireland. She was not to return home for 60 years and never saw her mother again. In Ireland, she learned English and prepared for her mission to India, which came the following year when she became a novice in Darjeeling, taking the name Teresa after the French nun Thérèse of Lisieux who had been beatified* just five years earlier. Saint Thérèse was a bit of a Catholic superstar in the early and mid-twentieth century; since her tragically young death, aged just 24, from tuberculosis in 1897, a considerable cult of devotion had grown up around her, particularly among devout young women, and she was essentially fast-tracked to sainthood by 1925 (in a manner that Teresa's own beatification would later mimic).

In 1937, Teresa made her Profession of Vows and was missioned to Entally, Calcutta (now Kolkata) in West Bengal. She taught divinity and geography at Loreto St Mary's School, attached to her convent, and became fluent in Bengali.

As we have seen already, one of the great enablers of fake heroes is that *aliefic* medium, film; whether they be Bader's *Reach for the Sky*, Kennedy's *PT 109* and *JFK*, or *Che!* as portrayed by Omar Sharif in the

---

* In order for beatification to take place, "heroic virtue" first has to be established by the Vatican – that is, proof of divine or superhuman qualities.

1969 Fleischer film. Mother Teresa's life is no exception and has spawned some truly "so bad they are good" hagiographical accounts. Among the more recent offerings is a 2004 animated film called, imaginatively enough, *Mother Teresa*. In the movie, Teresa is characterised very much as rebel nun, operating on the margins of her order, fighting against the regime of housework and devoted above all else to the work of Jesus and the poor who live beyond the gates. Teresa's convent is surrounded by an enormous shanty town, the Motijheel, and the disparity between the clean and ordered Christian life inside and the misery and deprivation beyond its walls eventually drives her to her greater calling.

In real life, Teresa rose to become the head teacher of the school and did not spend every waking moment ranting at irons and wandering out into Motijheel to repair people's wheelchairs (as happens in the film). She considered it to be the happiest time of her life and, long after leaving, she hankered after St Mary's, writing on the 150th anniversary of the school that: "Although now I am a Missionary of Charity, deep down that Loreto joy is still there. Nothing can separate me from the love and gratitude I have for Loreto."

Had she stayed there, the world would probably never have heard of Mother Teresa, but just as Che Guevara had his road to Damascus moment on the edge of the Chuquicamata mine so she was to have hers on the railroad to Darjeeling, in 1946. During a train ride to that hill city, she experienced what she described to be a "call within a call". Perhaps sparked by the appalling poverty and distress she witnessed through her train window, she decided to break ranks with the Loreto order and dedicate her life to the poor.

In the animated film, this sacred moment comes almost out of the blue. It is portrayed as a sort of divine rebel nun moment, but Teresa was no nascent punk, with a habit, operating on the margins of society. For one thing she did it all by the book, with the full encouragement of those around her and despite the wheels of the Vatican turning with the speed of a three-toed sloth, she never really had any obstacles in her way.

To start the new order, she had to prove herself to her spiritual adviser, Father Celeste van Exem; the Jesuit Archbishop of Calcutta, Ferdinand Perier; and the Pope, Pius XII. She was a well-connected woman and was adept at networking, had already established herself in India and her path was quickly smoothed, but even so it took until 1950 before she could formally open her Diocesan Congregation of the Calcutta Diocese.

Her motivation, by her own account, was that "call within a call', but at the risk of going all "Richard Dawkins", what exactly did that mean? Let's examine it with the forensic eye of a Human Resources manager.

Teresa loved teaching but by the late 1940s she was in something of a career rut. She had been in the same job for almost 20 years, and she was entering middle age with nowhere to go in terms of career advancement. The "call within the call" might very well have been what recruiters dub "a search for a new challenge". There was no possibility of climbing further up the ecumenical ladder for a woman then or now – there are, after all, no women priests or bishops in the Catholic Church. By creating her own order, in effect a religious "start-up", she would have influence she could never have had as a teacher of girls in a Calcutta convent school and become a powerful and influential figure within the church. This might sound cynical, especially coming from someone, who I freely admit, no longer has faith, but nobody rises to the top of anything by chance. And despite its higher aspirations, at its heart, the Catholic Church is an organisation like any other. It has its CEO, its senior management, its career ladders, rising stars and rivalries.

Teresa – for all her humble, meek and mild outward schtick – was a careerist who was forever jostling her way to the front and taking on leading roles. She had not been appointed the head teacher at Loreto by luck or divine intervention. She had actively sought the role, and that same innate leadership would see her go on to be the founder of an order of nuns.

Her decision may also have been driven by a far darker crisis inside her. For in the late 1940s, as Teresa set about establishing her order, she began to question the existence of God.

Many devout people and particularly those who give their entire lives over to faith, often come up against a phenomenon known as the dark night of the soul. What sounds, unfortunately, like a DC Comics spin-off, or an early Blue Label Jazz album, is in fact a spiritual crisis in which the devotee begins to question their calling, or the promise of eternity, or worse – the most critical aspect of their faith – their belief in God. The term was first coined by sixteeenth-century Spanish monk (later Saint) John of the Cross, who rose to prominence during the Counter-Reformation when the Catholic Church was fighting back against the rise of the Protestant faith. In his poem "Noche oscura del alma" (Dark night of the soul), he writes metaphorically of losing his "house" (faith) in the darkness and then trying to find his way back to it – and concludes that, "If a man wishes to be sure of the road he's travelling on, then he must close his eyes and travel in the dark". Or, in other words, simply submit to their faith once again.

It is a remarkably common phenomenon for the faithful. Even Jesus himself seemed to experience it, in his dying moments on the Cross, with the gospels of both Matthew and Mark describing how he cries out in pain: "My God, My God, why have you forsaken me?"

Throughout the subsequent history of the faith, many a Christian has found themselves asking the same question. Indeed, even Mother Teresa's hero, Thérèse of Lisieux, suffered this crisis of faith around the time that she started to get very ill with tuberculosis. Facing death, she felt "far from all suns" and as she plunged into spiritual darkness, she wrote that "a fog surrounds me and becomes more dense; it penetrates my soul". That feeling was with her to her end and at least one biographer has argued that Thérèse died without faith.

It is often said that for those living in religious communities it is not really a question of *if* someone will experience the dark night of the soul, but *when*.

Losing faith in anything, whether it be Father Christmas, the reliability of your iPhone battery or the promises of Boris Johnson is tough enough, but if you have committed your life to faith absolutely and fundamentally, then that is something else altogether. Teresa had been a nun since the age of 18. Her entire identity, everything she had known and everything she did, was wrapped up in it. Her home, her security, her status were all predicated on her faith; losing trust in it was catastrophic on every level and this sparked a prolonged existential crisis.

In the early 1950s and for the five decades that followed, Mother Teresa experienced a very dark night indeed and for many of those years claimed in letters and conversations that she felt absent from God. There is a very real sense that, like her namesake, she may have stopped believing in him altogether. In 1961, for example, she told her spiritual Father Josef Neuner that while she was leading her own sisters into a love of God, her own love had been "wiped out" and she "lived in total emptiness".*

Aware, perhaps, that all of this might posthumously dent her saintly image, Teresa would later request that all her letters be burned. But Neuner preserved them, as an inspiration for others, and the collection formed the basis of a book *Come Be My Light,* which was published after her death. Five of the thirteen chapters are taken up with this crisis of faith and it makes startling reading for anyone who grew up in an era when she was God's best-known, late twentieth-century messenger on Earth.

"The place of God in my soul is blank – there is no God in me," she tells one correspondent, and to another she writes: "I feel nothing before Jesus and yet I would not miss Holy Communion."†

There is a deep yearning for the simple faith of her childhood, and she pleads with priests to "teach me to love him again". On another occasion she writes, "He does not want me – he is not there."

The cognitive dissonance that Teresa was suffering was not really addressed because all the people she was writing to were members of the church. She was effectively in a vast echo chamber and unsurprisingly, at

---

* Come Be My Light, 2008, p209.
† Mother Teresa was obsessed with, one might almost say addicted to, communion and took it at every opportunity.

no point did anybody ever say, "Hey wait a minute, what if you're right and what if God really does not exist? These are good questions." The assumption is that God is there, and she simply needs to find her way back.

If we apply the BITE model here, she was experiencing both *Information control* – in that she was getting access to information only from within her group – and *Thought control* – in that the "group think" of her belief system and her circle of correspondents was rejecting other possibilities. There was *Emotional control* too – because her loss of faith would have made her feel like a failure and lead, at its extreme, to her leaving the only world she knew.

In slightly more earthly terms, Teresa was experiencing the religious equivalent of a phenomenon known as the sunk cost fallacy (SCF), which happens when an individual or organisation becomes reluctant to abandon a project because they have already invested heavily in it. If you buy a house, a car or a religion and then subsequently discover that you've made a massive error of judgement, you are more likely to keep throwing more money or effort into it than walk away. To admit defeat is to admit you made a mistake in the first place and human beings are loath to do that.

I wanted to try to understand the stress this must have caused Mother Teresa. Finding people who have experienced the dark night of the soul is one thing. Finding someone who is willing to let you quote their story in a book, quite another. So, I am very grateful to a former novice (a trainee nun) who shared her experiences with me. I shall call her Christine.

Christine entered her order aged 17 in 1966. Like young Anjezë, she had grown up in a deeply devout family and was unquestioning of her faith. When she announced her calling and declared that she wanted to be a nun, her parents were extremely proud of their daughter and saw it almost as a badge of honour within their community.

Christine takes up the story:

"I was a postulant at 17, then a novice for a year. During my two years I began to see that the life was not what I thought it would be.

To be honest I don't know what I expected it to be like, maybe (I believed) that after putting the religious habit on I would feel something; a change (perhaps) but no, I felt nothing. I tried so hard to feel the faith, the calling that the other 65 young women were feeling – or at least I thought they were feeling.

The doubts crept in and were shocking – especially for one so young... I (realised) that I didn't believe in God but was too scared to voice it. That was just awful – having to keep telling yourself you must believe in your faith, in God (when it wasn't there) really screwed with my head."

Christine had grown up in an environment that controlled her beliefs, what information she received, what thoughts were allowed and what emotions were permitted. She had taken the decision to become a nun and – suddenly having the chance to think about it freed from home – she was starting to have serious doubts. Anyone who has ever lost their faith will be able to relate to and sympathise with that inner journey and the loneliness of it. But most of us have never set out on the path to become a nun and Christine was now trapped in a life she didn't want to lead.

When she finally plucked up the courage to tell the convent that she wanted to leave, she faced resistance.

"I asked a few times but got talked out of it (on the basis that) they needed teachers. It was horrible, I was treated like I had something wrong with me. I was 19 when I left and was not welcomed home, but that is another story."

Christine found the inner strength to walk away, despite it having huge personal ramifications. But she was still very young at the time and not herself part of the Catholic establishment. By contrast, Teresa was much further down the path – a veritable pillar of the Catholic Church in India – when her doubts arose.

Teresa later claimed that her own darkness began "aged 49 or 50", but her letters contradict this. On 18th March 1953, when she was 42, she wrote to Archbishop Perier, a Belgian, Jesuit priest in India saying: "there is a terrible darkness within me, as if everything was dead", and by the time she voiced those concerns it had clearly been that way for years.

In trying to claw back her belief in God and feel the raw faith of her childhood again, Teresa found solace in suffering. It is no exaggeration to say that she was morbidly obsessed with it.

She called "pain, sorrow and suffering... the kiss of Jesus – a sign that you have come so close to him". Elsewhere, she encouraged believers to think that "suffering is nothing by itself. But suffering shared with the passion of Christ is a wonderful gift, the most beautiful gift, a token of love."

As Mother Teresa could only feel God's love through pain, she decided to surround herself with it, and that was why she set up her hospice.

Brian Kolodiejchuk, the advocate for her later canonisation and editor of *Come Be My Light*, put it like this: "The reality of her relationship with Jesus was truly a paradox... At prayer she would turn to Jesus and express her painful longing for him. But it was only when with the poor that she pushed his presence vividly. There she felt him to be so alive and so real."

Yes, this was her belief system and, yes, pain and Christ's death on the Cross are fundamental to the faith – but to this non-believer, it sounds ever so slightly psychopathic.

Her new order opened its doors on 7th October 1950, with 12 members made up of her former pupils, and it began administering help to the sick and dying of Calcutta. Soon aspirants (people who are considering joining) were drawn in and the mission began to grow and with it, Teresa's reputation.

In 1968, Malcolm Muggeridge was drawn to her work and in 1969 he made a BBC TV documentary about her called *Something Beautiful for God*. Muggeridge was a complex and contrarian figure. A well-known British journalist, satirist and former intelligence officer, who had suffered his own, very protracted dark night of the soul, he had spent decades cartwheeling between belief, agnosticism and atheism.

A one-time socialist radical, he was also one of the few people brave enough to express republican sentiments during the 1953 coronation of Queen Elizabeth, sparking outrage by calling it a "soap opera".

But he was very far from heroic and among other things, was a committed sex pest who, the historian Jean Seaton, later wrote, "groped (women) incontinently" at the BBC. As his libido waned in old age, his interest in things spiritual rose in its place. By the late 1970s "Saint Mugg" would be a pillar of the religious establishment and in 1979 famously lambasted John Cleese and Michael Palin live on TV for daring to make the "blasphemous" *Life of Brian*.

But the root of his horrible sanctimony lay a decade earlier in the hedonistic 1960s. The era of free love had turned grumpy old Muggeridge into everything he had once despised; seeing decadence and licentiousness at every turn, he chose to denounce it and in the process he turned into the very worst kind of insufferable, unctuous God-botherer. It also took him, at the BBC's expense, to Teresa's mission in India. There he claimed that there was a visible glow around the nun which was "proof" of a "divine light" and "heavenly aura". His reputation was such that he convinced a broad swathe of the public that they had witnessed the first TV miracle and that Teresa was some kind of living saint. In 1988, in his book *Confessions of a Twentieth-Century Pilgrim*, Muggeridge wrote:

"I at once realised that I was in the presence of someone of unique quality... her shrewdness... her manifest piety and true humility... There is a phrase in one of the psalms that always, for me, evokes her presence: 'the beauty of holiness' – that special beauty, amounting to a kind of pervasive luminosity generated by a life dedicated wholly to loving God and His creation."

There was in fact a slightly less divine explanation for Teresa's "aura" – dust. Knowing they would be filming in dim light, the camera crew had brought hi-resolution film stock with them which captured the sprinkles of dirt that dotted the air.

Muggeridge was told as much but chose to believe otherwise, just as he chose to believe that Teresa was engaged in saintly works.

In fact, despite all the plaudits and the praise, there were some very serious problems with her mission – both in the way it was run and the treatment of those who lived and worked there. Perhaps Muggeridge was too blinded by the light of her dusty, hi-resolution halo and his new-found sanctimony to care. Either way, the documentary made her world-famous. And in the subsequent years her saintly myth was forged as she went on to be celebrated and turned into a global figure.

Though the praise for her seemed to be almost universal at the time, not everyone was convinced and there were iconoclasts, most famously the atheist Christopher Hitchens, to whom Teresa once said:

"There is something beautiful in seeing the poor accept their lot, to suffer it like Christ's Passion. The world gains much from their suffering."

Hitchens was, however, very much a lone voice and as her order spread out across the world, eventually encompassing 517 missions in 100 countries, millions of dollars flooded in from all sorts of bene-factors, and some of them were very disreputable indeed. Even as he embezzled hundreds of millions of pounds from his employees' pension pot, the corrupt newspaper tycoon Robert Maxwell, who later mysteriously disappeared off his yacht *Lady Ghislaine* (named after his daughter), handed her cash. She gladly accepted at least $1.25 million in donations from Charles Keating, an American businessman, and made use of his private jet to fly to the USA.

When he was charged with fraud in 1990, for selling worthless junk bonds, she came forward as a character witness, writing to the judge, Lance Ito (who later presided over the O.J. Simpson murder trial), to tell him: "I only know that he has always been kind and generous... and always ready to help whenever there was a need.... Jesus has told us whatever you do to the least of my brethren YOU DID IT TO ME. Mr Keating has done much to help the poor, which is why I am writing to you on his behalf."

Ito handed down a sentence of ten years.

Teresa didn't seem to care who the money – or for that matter the awards – came from and in 1980, she accepted the Haitian Legion of

Honour from "Baby Doc" Duvalier, one of the most brutal tyrants of his era. Duvalier was even then being accused of corruption, embezzlement, murder, torture and extrajudicial killings in a reign of terror. Mother Teresa chose not to see the suffering and instead, according to Hitchens, told journalists that when she accompanied the dictator's wife on excursions she had "never seen the poor people being so familiar with their head of state as they were with her. It was a beautiful lesson."

Mother Teresa also hung out with a guru called John-Roger Hinkins. Hinkins ran a cult called the Movement of Inner Spiritual Awareness, or "MISA" (pronounced Messiah), and frequently claimed to have a higher spiritual consciousness than Jesus Christ. Despite that, Teresa accepted a gift of $10,000 from him, along with a MISA "Integrity Award".

Five years later, Teresa died, leaving behind a huge fortune in her charity's name which some estimates put as high as $100 million. In his 2017 book *Peccate Originale* (Original Sin), Italian journalist Gianluigi Nuzzi claimed that Teresa had "by far the most cashed up account" at the Vatican bank, and that if the money had been withdrawn, the institution would probably have collapsed. This begs the question: Why was it in the bank and not being used to alleviate the suffering of the poor?

Practically the only person to ask that in her lifetime was Christopher Hitchens, but Hitchens himself was part of the problem: his belligerent style and at times obsessive pursuit of her may have been counterproductive. Hitchens rarely minced his words, and his bellicosity gave ammunition to her defenders who were able to dismiss him as a lone, obsessive voice and a celebrated atheist, who had skin in the game of taking her down.

Of course, by any measure it was not acceptable to take cash off some of the very worst people of her time. But having done so, it was perhaps even more criminal not to put the cash to good works.

In her lifetime, Teresa's most famous project remained her "Home for the Dying" in Calcutta.

Teresa claimed she wanted to provide comfort to the very poorest people in their last hours in a manner given only to the very rich. That was the purpose of this hospice which had the slogan "I am on my way to heaven" above the door. But despite all the cash pouring in, conditions were desperate and the usual rules of sanitation were not applied. Bodies were sprawled out on old beds and across the floor filling every inch of the premises.

In the 1995 documentary *Hell's Angel*, a former volunteer, the author Mary Loudon, claimed that many people suffered agonising and needless pain in their last hours:

"There were no drips and the needles they used and reused over and over and over. You would see some of the nuns rinsing needles under the cold water tap and I asked one of them why she was doing it and .. why (she was) not boiling water and sterilising the needles and she said: 'There's no point, there's no time.'"

This was at the height of the HIV-AIDS epidemic, but nobody seemed to care about the risk of infection, despite India then suffering its peak in infections with 250,000 new cases being reported in 1995 alone.

Despite it being ostensibly a hospice, many who came were seeking help in this life rather than guidance to the next. One study by the University of Montreal found that: "Two-thirds of the people coming to these missions hoped to find a doctor to treat them, while the other third lay dying without receiving appropriate care. The doctors observed a significant lack of hygiene, even unfit conditions, as well as a shortage of actual care, inadequate food, and no painkillers. The problem is not a lack of money."

Mother Teresa did not believe in painkillers, lest they dull the suffering and break the presence of Christ and, as such, they were rarely used. Many people died in abject and needless pain. Others died unnecessarily and Loudon claimed to have witnessed a young boy lose his life because the hospice did not want to take him to hospital to receive life-saving antibiotics.

When Robin Fox, the British editor of the medical journal *The Lancet*, visited Teresa's Home for the Dying Destitutes in 1994, he was appalled by what he saw. Treatment was "haphazard" and the medically unqualified nuns clearly did not know what they were doing, sometimes using guesswork to treat those in their care.

The conditions remained equally appalling in the years following Teresa's death in 1997. The journalist Donal McIntyre, who worked undercover for a week in 2005 at *Daya Din*, one of the charity's flagship children's homes, was shocked by what he saw. Writing in the *New Statesman*, he revealed that in one overcrowded dormitory he saw the "hunched figure of a boy in a white vest. Distressed, he rocked back and forth, his ankle tethered to his cot like a goat in a farmyard."

His concerns were later brushed off by the nuns, one of whom told Prime Asia News: "Physical restraints are used only when absolutely necessary for the safety of the child and for educational purposes for limited periods of time…"

But why, given that there was so much money available, were medicines in such scant supply – and more to the point, why were no proper facilities being built?

One reason might have been that as the mission grew to a total of 517 sites, the money was spread too thinly. But that does not account for all the money that was left in the Vatican bank. Teresa was notoriously tight-fisted. A paper written by Canadian academics Serge Larivée, Genevieve Chenard and Carole Sénéchal in 2013 suggested: "Mother Teresa was generous with her prayers but rather miserly with her foundation's millions when it came to humanity's suffering. During numerous floods in India or following the explosion of a pesticide plant in Bhopal, she offered numerous prayers and medallions of the Virgin Mary but no direct or monetary aid."

She was happy to spend it on herself, though, travelling first class when not borrowing private jets from her famous friends.

When her own health deteriorated in the 1990s, she did not suffer the indignities that those in her Home for the Dying Destitutes endured. Falling ill in Mexico in 1992, she was not left to the care of local doctors but instead flown to the Scripps Clinic in San Diego, California, where she was treated by some of the leading heart specialists of the day.

By the account of one of her doctors, Dr Patricia Aubanel, she was "a terrible patient" and "the worst patient I ever had". Suffering may have been a conduit to Christ, but that did not include her suffering.

Mother Teresa, unfortunately, had one rule for herself and another for the Indian poor. For at the root of how she was perceived and perhaps how she saw herself was that old trope, the White Man's Burden – the notion that "advanced and civilized" people of the Western hemisphere were put on Earth to save black and brown people from their perceived savagery. In many ways this white European woman was a late twenti-eth-century incarnation of that very nineteenth-century phenomenon. The colonial, Christian do-gooder bringing light (supposedly) to the darkness of the undeveloped world. But in truth, she was bringing an awful lot of misery in her wake.

During a trip to the White House in 1981, she openly boasted of liberating babies from the poverty of Calcutta and while, of course, it is possible that some had been (as she claimed) abandoned, under what jurisdiction and authority was she operating? Her mission was behaving in a manner that transcended the laws of adoption, and it would have caused considerable consternation anywhere else. But because it was happening in India, the world continued to celebrate her as a saviour.

It's hard to shake off the conclusion that in the end it was all little more than a giant trip predicated on suffering and engineered so that this very lost woman could feel she was connecting with God.

The suffering was not restricted to orphan children, though – many of her nuns suffered too.

This was acknowledged in Calcutta at the time. In an otherwise sympathetic piece in a 2016 *Guardian* article, Mari Marcel Thekaekara, who grew up volunteering at the Shishu Bhavan orphanage, wrote: "It upset everyone greatly that the nuns were forbidden even a chilled juice on a sweltering summer's day. Absolutely nothing happened without Mother Teresa's permission. Young sisters walked miles in the scorching sun, often barefoot, on burning hot pavements, because Mother Teresa decreed it had to be done. A precocious 12-year-old, I hated this unfair, petty autocrat."

But much worse was going on behind the scenes. Nuns were expected to self-flagellate, daily, with a sheath of knotted cords. Punishment and pain were taken to extreme levels and one ex-nun, Mary Johnson, described it thus in an interview with journalist Valerie Tarico: "This is a religion in which nearly every house of worship, classroom, and private home has as its most prominent feature the image of a bloodied, tortured man. We were taught that wearing spiked chains and beating ourselves allowed us to share in his work of redemption."

In 2021, another ex-member, Mary, told the podcast *The Turning: The Sisters Who Left* that: "Beating yourself every day is a stark reminder that you are a sinner, taking away any sort of pride. You are someone who needs to beat yourself".

Another ex-nun, Colette Livermore, told the same podcast that letters from family and friends were withheld and that they were not allowed to visit loved ones even if they were dying. Those who stepped out of line were isolated. Those who left – and in some cases ran away – were cut off altogether. The sisters were obliged to wear the same clothes as their leader and in the process nullify their individuality. Their lives were strictly ordered. They were woken at 4.30 a.m. and expected to get straight to work. There was no time to question or doubt the work or the reason for it, as just half an hour of recreation time was set aside per day. Nuns were not allowed to go anywhere by themselves and had to travel in pairs under the watchful eye of each other. Private conversation was banned beyond prayer. Daily life was measured out in flagellation and work. Washing and personal hygiene were looked down on, windows were bolted shut to keep out the fresh air and devotees were told to kneel on the stone floor to pray so that even in prayer, that all-important suffering could be felt.

It reads like the fictional world of Gilead in Margaret Atwood's *The Handmaid's Tale*. But there is also an uncomfortable parallel with the very real world of Anne Hamilton-Byrne's "The Family" in 1970s' Melbourne.

All of this was going on in plain sight, and that is perhaps the most troubling aspect of the story. Hitchens claimed that Teresa even encouraged her followers to baptise the dying despite their Hindu and Islamic faith. By the late 1990s, he was no longer her only critic, but Teresa was a global icon and nobody took much notice. Mother Teresa's worldwide fame protected her, in the same way that Jimmy Savile's reputation for good works protected him. And yes, that is a deeply uncomfortable parallel, but it's there and it would be remiss not to point it out.

Her fame also blinkered the world from her truly abhorrent views on women and their rights over their bodies. Her 1979 acceptance speech at the Nobel Peace Prize ceremony was little more than an anti-abortion rant:

"Let us here make a strong resolution, we are going to save every little child, every unborn child, give them a chance to be born. And what we are doing, we are fighting abortion by adoption, and the good God has blessed the work so beautifully that we have saved thousands of children, and thousands of children have found a home where they are loved, they are wanted, they are cared."

As she took her award at the ceremony in Oslo, she returned to her seat to an enthusiastic round of applause.

* * *

Following her death in September 1997, Mother Teresa was immediately lined up for sainthood, but it first had to be proved that her virtue was "heroic". Her friend Brian Kolodiejchuk conducted hundreds of interviews and compiled a dossier of documents to prove she was.

Eventually a miracle came along, when a woman called Monica Besra in Bengal claimed a divine light had come out of a photo of the late nun and cured her of cancer.

She was beatified in 2003 and, in 2015, Pope Francis recognised a second miracle with claims that a man in Brazil had been cured of a brain tumour in 2008 by dint of the nun's intercession. In 2016, she was declared a saint, and in the years since her name has become a byword for – well – saintliness. In 2007, even before her canonisation, construction of a cathedral in her honour began in Kosovo and the building was consecrated a decade later. The Missionaries of Charity, her living, breathing monument, continues to thrive and has some 5,167 members operating orphanages, hospitals and clinics across six continents.

Mother Teresa's fame came about in part because it spoke to our need for saintly people. In this world of pain and suffering, we want to believe that there are "good" spiritual people, who will channel peace and bring light to the darkness. Individuals who, in desperate times, will cling to their values and not shirk, even as horrors unfold, from doing the right thing. But though she enjoyed that moniker, that was not what Anjezë Gonxha was about.

Hitchens called Mother Teresa "a fanatic, a fundamentalist and a fraud" and it is hard to disagree.

But likewise, you would have to have a heart of stone not to feel some sympathy for the young girl who lost her father in terrible circumstances and who wanted to escape the limited options of her world by travelling to India. There's a certain tragedy too in the fact that for much of her life, she was trapped in an environment predicated entirely upon the worship of a God, in whom she struggled to believe.

But that does not let her entirely off the hook. And anyway, at the very root of her story is a tale of unrestrained ambition, faux humility and a barely disguised determination to become immortal by achieving the ultimate accolade. Teresa after all, spent her entire life in pursuit of sainthood, just as her hero Thérèse of Lisieux had been.

Throughout later life she acknowledged that she might day become one and once wrote: "If I ever become a Saint – I will surely be one of 'darkness.' I will continually be absent from Heaven – to light the light of those in darkness on earth." This sounds very much like a pitch and leaves the strong impression that she wanted to make sure it happened. For all her humble exterior, this was one very ambitious human being and sainthood was her goal. For someone so famed for humility there was, paradoxically, a deep hubris at the heart of Anjezë Gonxha. She actively wanted to be venerated and in pursuit of it, she stomped over a lot of other people's lives while failing to spend the hundreds of millions in her Vatican bank account on the very people she was supposed to be helping.

She was not, of course, as deliberately cruel or evil as Anne Hamilton-Byrne and her sins did not come close to those of the violent sexual depravity of vile Jimmy Savile. But like them both, she was a fake – who actively encouraged the veneration of her myth. Quite apart from the money, taken from criminals and dictators and the abuse visited on the young nuns in her care, that makes her a hypocrite.

Sometimes in creating saints, society creates terrible monsters instead.

* * *

On 6th April 1941, under Adolf Hitler's Order Directive Number 25, the Wehrmacht invaded the Kingdom of Yugoslavia.

A week earlier, the predominantly Serb military junta had overthrown the Regent Prince Paul, who had been reluctantly dragged into the war by the Nazi leader, and put his cousin's 17-year-old son, King Peter II, on the throne. This was a poke in the eye for the preening, fanatical German Führer and now he sought to exact revenge.

But as the Axis armies stormed into Yugoslavia from neighbouring Hungary, Romania and Bulgaria, it wasn't quite the pushover they had been expecting. Initially at least, they faced stiffer opposition than they had anticipated and responded by bombing Belgrade and other major cities in the country into submission. On the night of 12/13 April, the Luftwaffe launched raids on the Bosnian capital, Sarajevo, destroying hundreds of homes and business premises and killing 90 people, rendering thousands homeless and among them a family called the Kabiljos who fled for the hills.

Josef Kabiljo was a successful businessman who owned a factory that manufactured sewage pipes, but the unexpected turn of events and the tide of war had now left him and his wife and children homeless and destitute. However, shortly after setting up camp outside the city and quite by chance he ran into an old business associate called Mustapha Hardaga, who insisted that he, his wife and children come and stay at his home until they could find somewhere to live. The grateful Kabiljos gathered up their salvaged possessions and followed him to his house where they were welcomed in by Mustapha and his relatives.

This act of decency in a time of such fear and uncertainty was remarkable enough, but it was perhaps even more so, on account of Mustapha and his family being strictly observant Muslims while their new house guests – were Jews.

Islam had come to Bosnia during Ottoman rule in the fifteenth century and in 1940 the Sunni Muslim population of roughly 718,000 made up about 30% of the population. Sephardic Jews had first arrived from Spain following the Alhambra Decree in 1492 and represented a much smaller minority at the start of the war, numbering just 14,000 people.

There were of course huge cultural differences between the two families and so in order to make the Kabiljos feel at ease, Zejneba and her sister-in-law Bachriya decided to stop wearing their hijabs in the presence of their Jewish guests.

"You are our brother, and your children are like our children. Feel at home and whatever we own is yours," Mustapha told Josef. Despite their religious and cultural differences, the families swiftly became close friends, but the tides of politics and war were catching up and were soon to engulf them all. By the late summer of 1941 Yugoslavia was firmly under Axis domination and the Germans had ceded a large part of Bosnia to the fascist movement, the Ustaše, under the puppet leader Ante Pavelić, Head of the newly established Independent State of Croatia.

In a time of extreme evil, the utterly degenerate Ustaše and Pavelić thrived, and realising that he and his family were at risk of ending up in a concentration camp Josef made plans to flee.

They were all perhaps more aware of the ongoing horrors than most because across the road from Mustapha's house there was a political prison and at night the families could hear the agonising screams of victims being tortured there. One day, the Secret Police turned up at the front door to make a routine inspection of documents and the Kabiljos were obliged to hide in a cupboard under a giant stack of coats.

Hearing that conditions were better for Jewish people in Italian-controlled Mostar, in southern Bosnia, Josef made the necessary arrangements and managed to relocate his family there in the late summer. But this was far from the end of their problems because the Kabiljos needed money and Josef could get that only by liquidating his business back home in Sarajevo. He had no other option but to leave his family in Mostar and return to his home city in order to sell his interests. With nowhere to stay and not wishing to impose on the Hardagas, he posed as a wounded soldier in a military hospital. Unfortunately, he didn't escape detection long and was betrayed to the Ustaše, who sentenced him to detention at a nearby forced labour camp.

At about the same time, in August 1941, the Ustaše had begun arresting what they viewed to be "undesirables" and shipping them to the death camp at Jasenovac near Zagreb, where they began systematically murdering some 60% of the nation's 12,000 Jews along with its Roma population and an estimated 90,000 Serbs. Time was, once again, running out for Josef, but one day while he was clearing snow from the roads, his luck changed when he noticed a Muslim woman in a veil observing him from afar. It was Mustapha's wife Zejneba, and she was so overwhelmed by the sight of her friend's predicament that she determined to do something about it.

At considerable risk she smuggled food to Josef and his fellow prisoners along with a message telling him that if he was able to escape, he should return to the sanctuary of her family home. With little to lose Josef managed to do just that and the Hardagas hid him in their basement once more.

If they had been caught, Zejneba and Mustpha along with their in-laws would have been arrested and sent to the Jasenovac camp, where they would undoubtedly have met their fate. Josef knew that, not least because he had seen signs and bill posters across the city warning citizens against harbouring Jews. So after ten days in hiding, he slipped away and returned to Mostar, where he was reunited with his wife and children.

Once again, the brief respite in fortunes did not last long. The Allied invasion of Italy in 1943 resulted in the dictator Mussolini fleeing north, to run the Italian Social Republic, a Nazi-controlled puppet regime, while the new Italian government in the south made peace with the Allies – and a power vacuum emerged in the Balkans. It was filled by the Ustaše, who seized Mostar and from October 1943 onwards began rounding up the city's Jews.

The Kabiljos fled once more. Josef joined an anti-fascist partisan movement and fought for the liberation of Yugoslavia, and he and his family managed to survive to the end of the war. In 1945, they returned to Sarajevo in the hope of rebuilding their lives and taking back their business and once again their friends, the Hardagas, welcomed them in.

It was only then that Josef learned the fate of Zejneba's father, Ahmed Sadik, who had been caught harbouring a Jewish family called the Papos. Sent to the concentration camp at Jasenovac, he had been murdered shortly afterwards and it was evidence, if evidence were needed, of the enormous risk that the Hardagas had taken.

In the immediate post-war era, Bosnia's surviving Jews faced further indignities, persecution and uncertainty at the hands of Tito's new communist regime and in 1950 the Kabiljos made their way to the newly founded state of Israel to build new lives. But they never lost touch with their old friends and in time the Kabiljos lobbied the Yad Vashem Holocaust Museum to honour the Hardagas for their wartime heroism.

That recognition came in 1985, when they were honoured by Israel as being *Righteous Among the Nations.**

---

* Non-Jews honoured by Yad Vashem for saving Jews during the Holocaust.

There was to be a final twist in the tale. When Yugoslavia collapsed in 1992, war came to Bosnia-Herzegovina once more. This time it was a group of Serbian extremists who turned on their neighbours and the Bosnian Serb Army, under the political leadership of Radovan Karadžić, embarked on the systematic ethnic cleansing of the region's Bosniak Muslims and Croatians. In the genocide that followed, there were numerous atrocities, including the infamous massacre at Srebrenica, which saw 8,000 men and boys murdered.

The wider ethnic cleansing saw tens of thousands of Bosniak Muslims forced from their homes and sent to camps and state-sanctioned rape and torture on a mass scale. Many families, including the surviving Hardagas, sheltered in their homes in fear for their lives or sought to leave the country.

When the Kabiljos got word that Zejneba, her daughter, son-in-law and granddaughter were hiding out in a basement, they immediately went to work to help them. With the aid of the Holocaust Museum, they lobbied the Israeli government to give the family sanctuary and when safe transit was initially denied, the Israeli Prime Minister, Yitzhak Rabin, personally intervened. The Hardagas left their homeland and arrived in Jerusalem in February 1994.

It sounds like a modern parable, doesn't it? One in which "Good Samaritan" Muslims save a Jewish family at enormous risk to themselves only to have the debt repaid years later. But it is much more than a tale of unambiguous heroism and a favour returned. At its heart this is a story of extreme selflessness and extraordinary human decency. A demonstration of unambiguous altruism in the face of terrible evil and personal risk. The Hardagas did not seek plaudits or statues, rewards or fame for their actions – they simply did what they believed was right.

That they did so, when so many millions of other people looked the other way, is not only highly unusual – it makes them heroes.

CHAPTER FIVE

ARTISTIC HEROES
ANDY WARHOL

The Importance of Brand

Few painters have reached the heights of posthumous fame as the great American artist Nat Tate.

Born on 7th March 1928, he was the only child of Mary Tate (née Tager), who told him (to hide his illegitimacy) that his father was a Nantucket fisherman who had drowned before Nat was born.

Having flunked his way through school, Tate enrolled at some point in the 1940s at an art college in Provincetown, Massachusetts – just a few miles down Cape Cod from the Kennedy summer home at Hyannis – and in 1950, aged 22, he began work on his famous "bridge" sequence of paintings. By 1957, he was mixing with fellow Abstract Expressionists in a crowd of artists that included Rothko, Jackson Pollock and Willem de Kooning and was creating a prodigious body of work. But while he was admired by his contemporaries, he always doubted his own talent, and during a trip to Paris in the fall of 1959 it all started to go wrong.

Loftily dismissed by both Picasso and Georges Braque during the trip, he lost faith in his art and after returning to New York on 8th January 1960, he burned everything he had ever produced bar just 18 paintings.

On 12th January 1960, aged 31, this fragile, haunted, talent jumped off the Staten Island Ferry into the frozen morass of New Jersey's Upper Bay and disappeared into inky oblivion. A man of few friends, he left scant trace of a life lived and indeed, in time, it was almost as if he had never existed at all.

All of that changed, some 35 years later, when the rock star David Bowie stumbled across some of Tate's works in a gallery in Lower Manhattan and subsequently became obsessed with his brief, doomed career. A year or two later, at a lunch given for the board of *Modern Painters* magazine at The Ivy in London in 1997, Bowie fell into conversation with the novelist William Boyd and to his amazement, discovered that Boyd was not only a fan of Tate but had been planning to write a book about the artist. Bowie had just started a company called *21 Publishing* and pretty much commissioned him on the spot.

On 31st March 1998, *Nat Tate: An American Artist 1928–1960* was launched at a glitzy party in Jeff Koons' Manhattan studio. Guests included the artists Frank Stella and Julian Schnabel, the deputy editor of *The New Yorker*, Bill Buford, the celebrated novelists Paul Auster and Jay McInerney as well as Jeff Koons himself. The blurb, written by Bowie, read as follows:

"The small oil I picked up on Prince St, New York must indeed be one of the last third panel triptychs. The great sadness of this quiet and moving monograph is that the artist's most profound dread – that God will make you an artist but only a mediocre artist – did not in retrospect apply to Nat Tate."

Boyd was not there, so Bowie went on to read out excerpts from the slim biography.

It was a resonant tale of the archetypal *lone genius* (though adored by art collector Peggy Guggenheim, with whom he had a brief, unfulfilling relationship), who is dismissed by almost everyone else in his lifetime and finally broken on the cartwheel of commercial indifference and personal and public failure. Here was an artist whose name, in the words of Boyd by way of Keats' own epitaph, was "written in water". As Bowie read out extracts, his eyes visibly "misted over".

Later, as New York's art world glitterati reappraised Tate's surviving paintings, drinks in hand, the Arts Editor of the *Independent*, David Lister, mingled with the crowd. Lister, by his own admission, had never heard of Nat Tate, but it seemed that he was almost alone in that and many of the people present were familiar with the artist and his work. One critic told Lister that Tate was "interesting but not terribly well-known". Others reminisced about meeting Nat – or having glimpsed him on the edges of parties and exhibitions – much as, poetically, he had been on the margins throughout his life.

Only they couldn't have, because Nat Tate had never existed, and Bowie and Boyd had made the whole thing up.

Lister was probably not the only person to smell a rat, but he was the only expert present brave enough to follow it down the drain. The next day he went looking for the New York art galleries mentioned in the book and found that none of them were real. There was no mention of "Nat Tate" anywhere in art literature and Lister suspected that the name had been cobbled together from those of London's two best-known galleries, the National Gallery and the Tate.*

The book, the paintings and Nat Tate's very life were an artfully created fiction. The picture of Tate on the cover of the biography and all those inside it were photos that Boyd had found in junk shops or in his own collection. The paintings had been executed by Boyd himself.

There had been clues but most people had missed them. Although held on 31st March, the party had spilled into 1st April and clearly that too was no coincidence. And the slim volume itself was peppered with hints. Boyd's book repeatedly suggests that Tate's artistic talent wasn't fully formed (or even very good) – and comical motifs, such as

---

* Boyd insists that the "Nat Tate" name was a happy coincidence and not deliberate. In recent years he has also claimed that Lister was "in" on the prank but Lister very creditably denies it and insists it was a scoop.

the Nantucket fisherman father who may or may not have existed – suggest a wry sense of the absurd on Boyd's part.

On Monday, 6th April, Lister's scoop landed in the *Independent* and the New York art scene went into paroxysms of collective blushing, while others – including the *Sunday Telegraph*, which had published extracts of the books – scrambled to claim, somewhat unconvincingly, that they had realised it was a spoof all along.

Pretending to be "in" on a practical joke is actually a very common reaction to being pranked. On 1st April 1957, the BBC broadcast a fake Panorama documentary about the bumper spaghetti harvest that year and showed footage of Italian farmers up trees gathering strands of pasta. Millions fell for it and the BBC was inundated with letters requesting information on how to farm the Italian foodstuff, but when the story was exposed as an April Fool hardly anyone would admit they had been duped. The event was later seized on by celebrated Hungarian behavioural psychologist Professor Ivor Fuldya, at the University of Sussex, and his paper "Panorama, pasta – and the British tradition of Tomfoolery" (1978) led to the term "spaghetti treed" becoming shorthand, in the field of psychology, for victims of a hoax insisting they knew it was a joke all along. It's a surprisingly common phenomenon in the age of the internet and one we shall return to in Chapter 10.

In the months following the Nat Tate launch party, "spaghetti treeing" ran rampant in art circles, but beneath the faux bravado and cries of "yes, we knew all along" it was patently clear that many in the art world had been seriously spooked. Boyd, Bowie and their representatives all sought to assure that there had been no "malicious intent" but the stunt had unnerved the contemporary art* industry whose very existence, after all, is built upon collective consensus and belief. Much of the "meaning" of modern art and in that, its value, comes not only common accord but also upon the willingness of the public to buy in. Regardless

---

* Contemporary art is defined by the market as any art produced after 1945 – so everything from Francis Bacon to Tracy Emin and beyond.

of the talent and aesthetics at its heart, art and art heroes are essentially brands, and branding defines everything about their commercial value and – to a very large extent – how we the public therefore perceive them.

The Boyd-Bowie stunt, perhaps inadvertently, sent shockwaves through the industry. If it was possible to con experts and critics into believing that some wobbly bridge paintings knocked up by a novelist were lost masterpieces, then what did that say about the art world's critical faculties, contemporary art itself and the whole billion-dollar bubble that is the market?

At its subversive heart then, Boyd and Bowie's hoax was much more than a pricking of bourgeois pomposity – it posed an existential threat to the very world of contemporary art itself.

* * *

You may know that mid to late 1990s Britain was a happening place to be, but you might be unaware that the moment got its name from an ice cream flavour.

In 1995, at the height of Britpop, as UK bands like Blur, Oasis and the mighty Radiohead rose to global supremacy, Ben & Jerry's brought out their latest creation, a vanilla ice cream with strawberries and fudge-covered shortbread, which they dubbed "Cool Britannia". The term caught the zeitgeist and soon British pop, British fashion, British theatre, British film and even British food were all getting swept up in the phenomenon.

British art too underwent the most extraordinary resurgence, helped in no small measure by the intervention of millionaire advertising tycoon Charles Saatchi, who began snapping up the works of every garret-dwelling artist with a paintbrush in Shoreditch.

Bright new talent started popping up like Van Gogh sunflowers, seemingly from nowhere – on an almost daily basis.

The Young British Artists (known by the initials YBAs) whose number included Sarah Lucas, Gary Hume and later figures like Tracey Emin and the Chapman brothers, had, in fact, been around since the late 1980s, with their roots in the Freeze exhibition of Goldsmith's

College of Art graduates, curated by the artist Damien Hirst in 1989. But by the mid to late 1990s their work, and Hirst's, in particular, had come to dominate the contemporary art scene and Saatchi had become arguably the most influential art benefactor since, well, if not Lorenzo de Medici in the fifteenth century, then certainly Peggy Guggenheim. In the frenzy of this artistic gold rush, a lot of crap got made and bought, but very few people dared to whisper it, for fear of being dubbed snobs, heretics or fuddy-duddies who couldn't see the power inherent within the latest set of invisible Emperor's clothes.

If you aren't part of the world and simply like looking at art and visiting galleries, it's quite easy to forget that the art market is, at its heart, a market – and as such, it has speculators, bubbles, fads, supply and demand issues and crashes. One thing a market is not and never can be is an arbiter of quality, and it was that all-domineering, all-pervading "market" and the decreasing returns – as perceived by Bowie and Boyd – that led to the invention of Nat Tate.

Talking to the *Daily Telegraph* in 2011, Boyd confessed: "The air was full of Hirst and Emin, Lucas, Hume, Chapman, Harvey, Ofili, Quinn and Turk. My own feeling, contemplating the unending brouhaha, was that some of these artists – who were never out of the media and who were achieving record prices for their artworks – were, to put it bluntly and perhaps a little unkindly, 'not very good'."

That same year Boyd put a Nat Tate up for auction at Sotheby's, ostensibly to kill off the monster he had created. *Bridge No. 114* was bought for £7,250 – twice its estimated value – by Anthony McPartlin, better known to the UK public as one half of Ant & Dec, and the money was donated to charity. As the story did the rounds once more, David Lister contemplated the legacy of Nat Tate and what it all really meant:

"Unlike in any other art form, the words 'I've never heard of him' are outlawed in the visual arts. At any private view, at the Frieze Art Fair, at the Venice Biennale, the throngs of people all feel they have to show a superhuman knowledge of hundreds of years' worth of art and artists. We will all admit to not having seen certain plays, or to not having heard certain symphonies; but who would dare to admit to never having heard of a famous abstract expressionist?"

Lister's wish was that Nat Tate's real legacy might be to make the art world take itself a little less seriously.

But a decade and a bit on, it looks like faint hope. For years, critics have been predicting that the contemporary art bubble would burst, and yet prices continue to defy gravity. With the most valuable art bought, more than ever, for investment and with Russian money continuing to feed that thirst right up to (and beyond) the invasion of Ukraine, it is an area that continues to fly in the face of all the usual rules of market forces. But that does not mean that the art that is changing hands for millions of dollars is actually worth anything like the sums it reaches and anyway, as art critic Ben Lewis put it succinctly in his 2009 documentary *The Great Contemporary Art Bubble*: "The most expensive artists are (not) necessarily the best."

Now, before we go any further, I feel duty-bound to make it clear that I am no authority on art whether contemporary or otherwise, but then – as the Nat Tate saga shows – neither are many of the experts. And when it comes to the matter of how art is appraised and valued – well you enter a mysterious realm which, for the lay-person, is almost impossible to fathom.

Three years after the Nat Tate mini retrospective, the highly respected YBA Martin Creed had *Work No. 227* (2000) shortlisted for the Turner Prize (2001). It consisted of an empty room with a light that went on for fifteen seconds and then went off for fifteen seconds, plunging the room into darkness. In 2013, Tate Britain purchased the work for an undisclosed sum, but given that it had been valued at around £110,000 one can assume that they paid something around that figure. For a light. That goes on. And off.

The Tate explained: "This work challenges the traditional conventions of museum or gallery display and, consequently, the visiting experience. Creed plays with the viewer's sense of space and time and in so doing he implicates and empowers the viewer, forcing an awareness of, and interaction with, the physical actuality of the space."

Maybe I was missing something – but in all honesty, I took something else from it. I just found it deeply annoying.

* * *

What is art? stands alongside *Does God exist?* and *Name one Brexit benefit* as one of life's fundamentally unanswerable questions. Defining where art starts and ends is a bit like trying to juggle gravy, in a mask, in space, with your hands tied behind your back – which in and of itself could, I suppose also be a sort of art.

There is no art equivalent of the International Bureau of Weights and Measures. There is no Universal UN Declaration on Art. No regulator or governing body certifies art movements or hands out lobster-shaped accreditation to surrealists. So, in its loosest sense, anything can be art. And that can lead to all sorts of hilarity.

In a celebrated incident in 2015, a dropped glove at the MOMA gallery in New York caused considerable consternation for visitors who began to step carefully around it in case it was a priceless masterpiece. It wasn't. It was a glove which someone had dropped, and it was eventually retrieved and taken to lost property. In May the following year, during a trip to the San Francisco Museum of Modern Art, a 16-year-old student called Kevin Nguyen and his friend TJ Khayatan started leaving random objects around the museum to see if anyone could distinguish between them and the works on display. A baseball cap dropped in a corner didn't elicit much interest, but when TJ placed his glasses on the floor the response was far more encouraging and soon folks were gathering round to photograph the spectacles and to look for a caption explaining their meaning.

Now weirdly, in doing so, the glasses became, unintentionally or intentionally, what the US Fluxus* artist Allan Kaprow dubbed

---

* Founded in 1960 by Lithuanian-American artist George Maciunas, Fluxus (meaning both "flowing" and "effluent") was a loose international group of experimental artists, musicians and poets with work often characterised as being both critical of art itself and unfinished.

a *happening* – that is, a performance or situationist piece of art that disrupts the space between the work and its environment.

It's an interesting concept but one that is rife with hazards because by removing the line between art and life, almost anything can become art. Is that soup on your beard or chewing gum on your shoe a happening? Is roadkill a happening? Does it have to be deliberately left there to have been so? And what about when art gets mistaken for rubbish and is thrown in a bin? Because that goes on, you know, and with wearying frequency.

In 1999, Tracey Emin's *My Bed* – which consisted, as you might suspect, of her own unmade bed – was, well, "made" by museum attendants who thought it had been vandalised. Carefully removing cigarette packets and condoms from around it, they made everything nice and neat again, meaning that the artist was obliged to come back and mess up the space once more. In 2001, an untitled and impromptu piece by Damien Hirst featuring piles of beer bottles, ashtrays and coffee cups was cleared away by a janitor, Emmanuel Asare, at the Eyestorm Gallery in London – supposedly because he thought it was the leftovers of the launch party. In fact, it was indeed the party trash, but at some point, Hirst had declared it art and assembled it as such, and by dint of his acclaimed status as an "artist", it was henceforth, magically transformed into an artwork.

Hirst declared the mistake "fantastic" and "very funny" and underlings were dispatched to fish it out of the bins. But Charles Thomson, co-founder of the Stuckist art movement, which was fighting back against the YBAs and contemporary art movement, was unimpressed and told the *Guardian* that: "The cleaner (should) be promoted to (the post of) art critic of a national newspaper. He clearly has a fine critical eye."

In 2004, it happened again when a cleaner at Tate Britain mistook a bag that made up part of a Gustav Metzger installation for trash and threw it away. The priceless work of art was later retrieved from an industrial wheelie bin but was said by the artist to be "beyond repair", so he had to make another one.

Were these mistakes, as claimed, the fault of hapless cleaners who didn't realise that they were working in an art gallery? Or deliberate provocations by the artists? Or simply tried-and-tested PR stunts that ensured press and publicity and increased the visibility of people's work? Because – and call me a cynic here – this all sounds like a very good way to generate column inches and some viral PR for the artists involved. But then is that process art too? Is creating a viral story about a binned "work of art" itself a work of art?

The line – like the work of the Impressionists – is forever blurred.

In their brilliant 1961 satire *The Rebel*, the British writers Galton and Simpson sent up the pretensions of the art world and its hangers-on. In the film, the comedian Tony Hancock plays a city clerk who longs to be an existential artist and who whiles away his free time knocking off versions of a sculpture called *Aphrodite at the Water 'ole* in his bedsit room. Tired of the rat race and his interfering landlady, Mrs Cravat, Hancock jacks it all in one day and heads to Paris's Left Bank to live out his dream. There, despite having no discernible talent, he swiftly becomes established as the leader of the "Infantile" movement and sets about haranguing his far more accomplished flatmate Paul, whose work he dismisses on the basis that the "colours are all the wrong shape". Believing himself to be a failure, the Nat Tate-like Paul quits art and leaves his paintings to Tony. But when an art dealer mistakes them for Hancock's own works, while dismissing Tony's actual paintings as rubbish, a Faustian pact is struck.

Tony's subsequent attempts to smuggle his own paintings into an exhibition, where he is passing off Paul's work as his own, end in failure, and when his former flatmate reappears on the opening night, worse follows. Paul has begun imitating Tony's "Infantile" style and when he reveals them to the attendant critics, he gets instant acclaim for works that look almost identical to Hancock's.

In despair, Hancock vents his fury on the assembled crowd: "Ladies and gentlemen, I shall now bid you all good day. I'm off! ... YOU'RE ALL RAVING MAD!! None of you know what you're looking at."

And though the line was written over sixty years ago – it feels like a comment for the ages.

* * *

The lone creator myth – the notion of one artist taking on the world from their garret and (even if they fail in life) defying all expectations to become, that most feted of things, a genius – is extraordinarily potent.

Nick Drake, the brilliant, doomed, songwriter is almost as good an example as you can get. During his brief career, Drake produced three almost perfect albums, *Five Leaves Left*, *Bryter Layter* and *Pink Moon*, that were all infused with a melancholic, very English, wistfulness but which in total sold fewer than 12,000 copies.

Drake died aged just 26* in 1974 and it was not until at least a decade after his death that his name became well-known and his work appreciated.

But that wasn't for want of his label, Island, trying and, in his lifetime, they had thrown everything at it. He was given collaborators and orchestrators and some of the best producers and backing musicians in the business. On his second album *Bryter Layter*, the personnel included John Cale of the Velvet Underground, Beach Boys' drummer Mike Kowalski, and Dave Pegg and Dave Mattacks, both members of the hugely influential British band Fairport Convention.

Despite the commercial failure of that record, Island continued to invest in Drake and when his third album, *Pink Moon*, was released in 1972 they spent huge sums promoting it in the music press. This was not someone labouring in solitude against the forces of indifference.

---

* The myth of the "27 club" that would have us believe that a preponderance of great talents die at or around that age. Yes, some famous pop stars and artists do, but 2011 research by US National Library of Medicine found that even among those who died young – most did not. It's another example of our old friend apophenia.

The lone genius myth is a sort of sub-branch of Thomas Carlyle's 'Great Man' theory (his idea that the history of the world is basically the biography of a series of uniquely talented men). Yes, there have been "lone geniuses" or something akin to them in history and Kafka, Jane Austen and Van Gogh spring to mind, but Isaac Newton did not work out all his theories in a bubble any more than Galileo Galilei did. The problem is that the potent myth of the lone genius is a hugely attractive and romantic ideal. In much the same way that we want to buy into the idea of religious saints, heroic guerrillas and great war heroes, we want to believe that there are semi-divine artists, imbued with a mythical talent that transcends the boundaries of heaven and Earth.

And nowhere is the idea of the tortured genius myth more prevalent than in music and art.

One of the great problems with the market in Old Masters is that most of the paintings that came out of the period (spanning roughly 1300–1800) were collaborations. That presents a headache when they come to be sold because many collectors want paintings that are "by the artist's hand" and by their hand alone. But examples of that, in its purest sense, are rare. In *The Agony and the Ecstasy*, the Oscar-nominated 1965 film of Michelangelo's life, we see the lonely artist (played by Charlton Heston) condemned Sisyphus-like to complete the painting of the ceiling of the Sistine Chapel. As the 138 minutes tick by, Heston labours away on his back, collapsing through fatigue, only finally completing his masterpiece when threatened by the Pope (Rex Harrison) that the younger artist Raphael will replace him.

The more you think about it, the more the idea that one artist, who until that moment had mostly been famous for sculpture, would be capable of filling 1,100 square metres of ceiling by himself and complete what is widely deemed to be one of the great masterpieces of fresco art in just four years (1508–12) sounds unconvincing. And that's because it didn't happen. Michelangelo had a whole team of people working for him and key among them were his friend Francesco Granacci, Agnolo di Domenico del Mazziere (known as the "Master of Santo Spirito") and at least four other assistants from the Florentina workshops of Ghirlandaio or Cosimo Rosselli.

The most famous workshop of all in Florence at the time was that of Andrea del Verrocchio (c. 1435–1488). In its day, Verrocchio's workshop was the creative hub of Florence – a veritable Renaissance Factory – and many other artists, most notably Perugino and Leonardo da Vinci, were apprenticed to him, learned from him and, in the words of the Florentine poet Ugolino Verino, "drank from Verrocchio's spring". It was in Verrocchio's workshop that the young da Vinci learned his craft. It is where he was taught to model clay, to draw, to paint and to sculpt. His hand is ascribed to Verrocchio's *Baptism of Christ* along with that of his master – and there may be other hands at work in it too.

From 1490 onwards, Leonardo himself had pupils, known as the *Leonardeschi*, and they helped him with his own works. And yet for most people, outside of the art world, when they think of Leonardo da Vinci, they think of the very model of the lone genius, knocking out helicopter designs and the *Mona Lisa* all by himself in between dabbling in astronomy, alchemy and palaeontology.

The enduring romance of the Renaissance and resonance of towering figures like da Vinci himself helped spawn the idea of the "singular genius", meaning that subsequently the role of others was reduced to a mere mention in the footnotes or even edited out altogether. No actors represent Francesco Granacci or Agnolo di Domenico del Mazziere in *The Agony and the Ecstasy*, and the film's prologue, which shows Michelangelo's greatest sculpture, makes no mention of the help he received in making those either.

In the churches of creativity, the worshippers at the high altar of art want to believe in monotheistic Gods. They want to have faith in the authenticity of the true creation; they want to believe that their idols are "mavericks" and "lone geniuses" toiling away in agony and ecstasy but, most of all, they want to believe that they are possessed of a singular, otherworldliness and not simply fellow human beings.

Despite being hailed in his lifetime as yet another lone genius, the brilliant work produced by Nat Tate's co-enabler, David Bowie, was always a result of collaboration. Bowie was, like many, a great artist, a supreme collaborator. His most commercially successful record, *Let's Dance*, owed much of its fortune to the distinctive... er, let's make an exception, lone genius... of producer Nile Rodgers. Bowie accepted that and made no secret of the fact that he didn't play any instruments on the album. The distinctive piano arrangements on *Hunky Dory* are entirely the work of the celebrated keyboardist Rick Wakeman. The similarly brilliant backing singing is provided by the vocalist Dana Gillespie. The guitar riffs come courtesy of Mick Ronson. The most famous track on that album, 'Life on Mars', has the same chord sequence as the Frank Sinatra standard, 'My Way', originally a French song called 'Comme d'habitude'. Before Paul Anka got his hands on the song in 1969, Bowie had been approached and asked to write the first English-language lyrics, and his pre-Sinatra version titled 'Even a Fool Learns to Love' clearly heavily influenced the other song. Yes, Bowie was a brilliant artist, but he was brilliant because he took on board the motto, oft attributed to Pablo Picasso, that "bad artists borrow and great artists steal" and used it to his advantage – although not always transparently. His breakthrough character *Ziggy Stardust* was heavily reliant on the ideas of his then wife, Angie, who had herself been inspired by a production of Warhol's only play, *Andy Warhol's Pork,* which scandalised London during its run at the Roundhouse in Camden in 1971.

Looking at the photos of the production, in between deleting my browsing history, it is easy to understand why audiences were so shocked. There is – and I cannot stress this enough – a LOT of nudity. Characters masturbate, have sex in ways which look likely to put their backs out and, for the most part, wear nothing apart from fabulous make-up.

The pictures and the exotic names of the characters – *Vulva, Pork, Bell Telephone* and the *Pepsodent Twins* are hugely suggestive of Bowie's subsequent work and his shift from hippyish *Hunky Dory* to *Ziggy Stardust*. But even Bowie was plagiarising a plagiarist because despite *Andy Warhol's Pork* bearing his name, it wasn't actually written by him. Directed by Anthony (Tony) J. Ingrassia, the work was devised from an idea conceived by Brigid Berlin. Berlin (aka *Polk* on account of her jabbing people who came near her with Vitamin shots and herself with amphetamines), was one of the "Warhol superstars" and in the late 1960s she developed an act where she would call people up, including her society mother Honey, and then surreptitiously record her outrageous conversations – or broadcast them live to theatre audiences (unbeknown to the people she was talking to). *Pork* was typical of much of Warhol's work at the time. Provocative. Headline-grabbing. Pornographic. Derivative. Outrageous. And not by him. But before we get into his art, let's go back to the beginning.

* * *

Andy Warhola was born on 6th August 1928, just seven weeks after Ernestito Guevara. The youngest of three brothers, his parents had migrated, separately, to Pittsburgh, Pennsylvania from Miková in what was then Austria-Hungary (and after 1918, Czechoslovakia) with his father Andrej arriving in 1912 and his mother Julia following in 1922. Julia was a devout Byzantine Catholic who thrust her faith onto the children and defined her life around it. The Warholas were poor, working-class immigrants in America's biggest steel town. Andy's father worked in the construction industry, for a firm called Eichleay which quite literally "removed" buildings from one place and put them somewhere else. The Fluxus Situationists would no doubt have approved. His mother sold flowers and the family scraped by.

Aged four, Andy was sent to kindergarten, but his mother withdrew him the following day after he complained that another child had hit him. Like his contemporary Guevara, he was a sickly child and aged eight suffered a bout of scarlet fever, which led to him being even more intensely mollycoddled by Julia. Long periods in bed were spent listening to the radio and reading movie magazines. The months off school – immersed in movie stars and radio shows – opened the doors to a world beyond steel-town Pittsburgh, once described by one commentator as "hell with the lid off". It was no place for a kid with such a nervous disposition and Warhol frequently suffered panic attacks.

In 1942, the same year that his older brother Paul went off to join the navy, his father died while working away from home in West Virginia on a project. His cause of death was liver failure, perhaps caused by poisoned water.

In Gary Comenas' *Andy Warhol: From Nowhere to Up There*, an oral history of Andy Warhol's early years, brother Paul recalled how Warhol reacted to the death: "When they brought the body into the house Andy was so scared, he ran and hid under the bed. But we didn't push Andy too much when Dad died because we didn't want him to have a relapse. We were always fearful that his nervous condition might come back. Andy started crying. He begged Mother to let him go and stay (somewhere else)."

Three years later, aged just 17, Warhol went to the Department of Painting and Design at the Carnegie Institute of Technology in Pittsburgh to study commercial art. His reclusive childhood and fear that his homosexuality might be exposed in an era where it could land him in jail, alongside his hatred of his own appearance, meant that he was an exceptionally shy and monosyllabic student, but at art college that curiously worked to his advantage. Warhol was a blank canvas to contemporaries and his near-constant silence created an aura of mystery. He became that guy at college who everyone wonders about simply because they remain aloof. He became the outsider and in it, he found his identity.

Warhol was nearly kicked out at the end of his first year for not applying himself to his exams, but his talent was recognised by his contemporaries, and, despite his debilitating shyness, he was briefly the director of the in-house student art magazine. In 1949, he graduated and left Pittsburgh for New York, changing his name to Warhol, somewhere along the way.

There he very quickly achieved astonishing success in the advertising business and became renowned for drawing shoes, going on to become a designer for the iconic footwear brand Israel Miller, beloved of ballerinas and movie stars.

From 1949 and into the late 1950s, he began to carve out a parallel career as an artist. This began when Warhol was commissioned by the record labels RCA and Columbia to create album covers for the rapidly expanding Long Player (LP) market and managed to show a flare beyond shoes. A full decade before he produced his iconic "banana" cover for the Velvet Underground and Nico's eponymous debut album, he was designing album sleeves for Count Basie, Thelonious Monk and even Tennessee Williams. As he grew wealthy, he began to change his appearance and formed a loose workshop that included friends, co-conspirators and his mother Julia, who had moved to New York. With Julia he created a book called *25 Cats Name Sam and One Blue Pussy*, which he self-published in 1954. Julia did the calligraphy and missed out the "d" in the title, but Warhol liked the mistake and so it stayed. The book had a limited print of just a couple of hundred copies. If you chance upon a copy today, it's worth an estimated $60,000.

Warhol wanted to be bigger than cat books and began plotting his entry into the art world. *Abstract Expressionism* was the dominant scene in the 1950s, with figures like Jackson Pollock, de Kooning and Rothko its major players. But as the decade wore on, other artists like Jasper Johns and Robert Rauschenberg began moving away from it towards art that centred around everyday things. They were dubbed "the new realists" and Warhol followed their lead.

That journey led to his silkscreens, the works for which Warhol is now best known and renowned. Silkscreens are a printmaking technique where ink is stencilled onto a canvas and then covered with paint. The method had been around for centuries and long before the 1960s but Warhol's big idea, which was really gallery owner Muriel Latow's big idea (for which he paid her $50), was to use them to depict everyday things. His first attempts, under the tutelage of Max Arthur Cohn, resulted in the Campbell's soup can paintings in spring 1962, which garnered him some notoriety when they were featured in a *Time* magazine article soon afterwards. Later, in August 1962, in the wake of Marilyn Monroe's death, Warhol produced some of his most famous works, based on her celebrated face and image.

Among them is the *Marilyn Diptych*, which can be seen at the Tate in London today. The silkscreen has the face of the actress across two canvases in 50 identical images. The left panel is in colour, the right in ever more fading black and white. It is a superb piece of art, reflecting the glamorous face of the movie icon, fading into her private self.

The juxtaposition was, in fact, not actually Warhol's idea but suggested to him, when both works had already been completed, by his friends, the art collectors Burton and Emily Tremaine. Warhol took on board their idea and created a masterpiece.*

When the various *Gold Marilyns* were first shown in November 1962 at the Stable Gallery in New York, they caused a sensation. The *Diptych* and the other Marilyns have since frequently been ranked among the most important (and expensive) artworks of the 20th century. In May 2022, one of the paintings, *Shot Sage Blue Marilyn*, sold for a whopping $195 million at Sotheby's in New York, making it the most expensive contemporary artwork and the most expensive American piece of art in history.

For the rest of the decade, Warhol created thousands of works. Or to be more precise, thousands of works with Warhol's name on them were produced and sold as "Andy Warhols", because the number of pictures produced was so great that they were perhaps more than any one person could make in a lifetime. From the late 1940s until his death in 1987, he "produced" over 9,000 paintings and sculptures and nearly 12,000 drawings. He made some 650 films in the period between 1963 and 1968 alone and at least 2,500 videos in the years that followed. On top of that there were hundreds of thousands of polaroids and photographs, as well as record sleeves and bands mentored. That is a properly

---

* The photo itself was to cause the artist all manner of copyright headaches, as he had used a publicity still from the 1953 film *Niagara* and later had to settle with the photographer whose work he had used – multiple times.

gigantic body of work by anyone's standards. There were 13,557 days between 1st January 1950 and Warhol's death on 22nd February 1987. In that period putting his photos, records, plays, cameo appearances in films, including *Tootsie* and everything else aside, "Warhol" was producing roughly two significant artworks or films a day. That is an enormous body of art by any metric and, of course, he wasn't producing it all by himself.

Now even people with just a fleeting knowledge of Warhol will know that this is in a sense what Warhol was about. The very idea of his "Factory" was born out of the notion of industrialising art and turning it into a mass commodity. Warhol opened his first "Factory" at 231 East 47th Street in Midtown Manhattan in 1963 and it was to be one of four premises to enjoy that name. The Factory in all its locations was *the* hip hangout but it was also Warhol's studio and the place where he produced and indeed, mass-produced his art with the help of others.

Warhol once said that "Art is anything you can get away with" and his life's work demonstrates that he clearly meant it, but on several occasions, it landed him in significant trouble.

Brigid Berlin, she of the *Pork* telephone calls, was a key figure at the Factory and unusual in the shifting sands of his inner circle, in that she was to remain a close friend of Warhol's for most of his life. As the author and publisher Stephen Colegrave, who as a young punk hung out at the Factory, explained to me: "The thing you have to understand about Warhol is that he was very elitist. He loved high society and interesting people. But you were either in or out – and you could very quickly be out." Berlin was never "out" because (almost uniquely among the Warhol superstars and hangers-on who craved fame and fortune and everything that went with it) she, as a product of an elite and wealthy background, didn't care about money.

The two spoke every morning at 9 a.m. and between 1967 and 1974, Brigid would routinely tape them – conversations that were then used as the material for *Pork*. But Berlin's presence in Warhol's life was also very nearly responsible for destroying his artistic legacy.

In a 1969 interview with *Time* magazine, in what was later described as a "prank", Warhol told the interviewer that all of his silkscreens and artworks had in fact been made by Brigid and that he had nothing to do with them. The magic spell was broken and the value of his art plummeted. Warhol had frequently talked honestly and openly about the collaborative nature of his work, but people had assumed that he was at least involved in making the pictures. He was forced to retract the statement and lay claim once more to his art, insisting that it was (largely) by his hand alone. But it wasn't true. And it wasn't true that Brigid had made most of them either.

Following the success of the *Marilyns* and with his creative career on the up, Warhol began looking for an assistant and eventually found him in 1963, in the form of a 20-year-old drop out called Gerard Malanga. Malanga looked like a rock star and wanted to be a poet. He took on the job thinking it would last a few months but was to remain at Warhol's side for (much of) the decade. In that period, he became his most important collaborator – not least because he had a knack for creating superb silkscreens. Malanga was to become more than the Francesco Granacci to Warhol's Michelangelo – he practically became Warhol, at least from the point of view that much of the work he did was attributed to Andy. Malanga was, in short, Warhol's Ted Sorensen.

He was young, creative and full of ideas. It was Malanga who suggested superimposing screen prints on top of each other, which created a strobe effect and resulted in works like *Double Elvis* (currently on display in MoMA, New York), of Elvis Presley taken from a publicity shot of him playing gunslinger Pacer Burton in the film *Flaming Star*. It was Malanga too who placed the screen and applied the Liquitex paint on the prints of hundreds of Warhol works. And it was Malanga who stamped Warhol's signature on the works. In fact, he played such a critical role that, according to the art critic Tim Harford, writing in May 2022 for the *Financial Times*, Warhol would ask journalists, during interviews:

"Why don't you ask my assistant Gerry Malanga some questions? He did a lot of my paintings."

Malanga–Warhol were prolific. Following John F. Kennedy's assassination in November they produced 302 *Jackies* – silkscreens of the first lady lifted from press stills in the wake of her husband's death in various stages of shock and mourning.

In a catalogue for a sale in November 2016, Bonhams in New York described one of the images, *Jackie 1964* (which sold for $907,500), as "a captivating exploration into contemporary celebrity culture and the media frenzy that surrounded the tragic events that November", which is one way of looking at it. One could of course similarly argue that Warhol and his team were simply cashing in on the tragedy and the public's unnerving taste for beauty, tragedy and violence.

Warhol viewed his art as a business and made no apology for it. In the mid-1970s he (or more likely a ghost-writer on one of his four books) even spelled it out: *"Being good in business is the most fascinating kind of art. Making money is art and working is art and good business is the best art".*

And ever since, this bullshit phrase has been trotted out as if it is some sort of truth. If 'making money is art' then winning £3 on a slot machine is art, selling dodgy time-shares is art and Che Guevara's profits from his cockroach killing formula made him an artist. If it was true, then Odey, who made a reported £220 million on the falling pound on the night of the Brexit vote, would be the greatest artist of our era and Van Gogh, who sold just a single painting in his lifetime, would rank alongside Hitler as an artistic mediocrity.

Fame gives you influence, and influence gives everything – the words you say, the films you make, the art you produce, the books you write a certain power. If an anonymous boy from Pittsburgh had said that "business was the most fascinating kind of art" it would have been meaningless drivel. But because Andy Warhol, a global art superstar, said it, it becomes a sort of truth. And in all of this we get to the nub of Warhol's talent. His greatest skill, undoubtedly, was branding, in knowing how to market himself and his image and make his art famous by dint of it.

Warhol was almost unique when he appeared on the New York art scene, in that he both had money to support himself and was well practised in marketing. In a sense he was extremely modern in that regard and throughout his career behaved much like an extremely powerful "influencer". He knew what buttons to press and how to get noticed, and gambled that the public would always be interested in death, fame, despair, sex and glamour. That is why he made the *Marilyns* following her death and why he cashed in too on that tried and tested formula for getting attention – outrage.

Warhol produced a whole series of paintings about death including dead victims of car crashes and plane crashes. And in one, *Suicide (Fallen Body)*, he reproduced press stills of a young woman, Evelyn McHale, who had jumped to her death off the Empire State building on 1st May 1947. Now you don't need a degree in the history of art to know that the medium has always – from its very origins – been obsessed with death and brutality. After all, practically the entire history of Western art right up to and beyond the Renaissance, is predicated on images of a man bleeding to death on a cross.

Just look at the work of any artists spanning the era from 1400 onwards and you've got massacres of innocents, Icarus falling out of the sky, John the Baptist's head on a tray and Jesus getting crucified over and over again. But that work had meaning – and religious significance. It was created with the purpose of evoking a response from those who gazed upon it and getting them to reflect on the meaning of their faith.

What was Warhol saying in his images of McHale? He may have been inviting us to reflect on the press's gory obsession with death and through it our own voyeurism perhaps. But hadn't that been done a million times before, and even relatively recently in films like Michael Powell's *Peeping Tom* (1960) or Hitchcock's *Rear Window* (1954)? And anyway – once again he was really borrowing very heavily from someone else – someone who nowadays is far less well remembered.

Since the 1930s, the tabloid photographer Arthur Fellig (known as Weegee) had been taking noirish photos of death and disaster on the streets of New York, and Warhol's images were a clear appropriation of that style. Warhol accepted that he was all about surface and that he liked to play with "ideas of originality and authorship", but how much was that a cover for his own lack of originality?

"I want to be a machine," Warhol famously said, but the machine was mostly other people – and for much of the time, he wasn't even at the controls.

* * *

In 1967, after five years of churning out Warhols, Malanga got fed up with the Factory and went on holiday to Italy. By the beginning of 1968, he had run out of money and when wiring Warhol failed to elicit any response, his Italian girlfriend suggested that he might like to turn a then hugely popular photograph, of a certain recently deceased Argentinian revolutionary hero, into a silkscreen. The Che series was born, created by Gerard and knocked off in his girlfriend's flat in Italy. Having given her one as a present, Malanga then began soliciting interest with galleries before the Tartaruga in Rome agreed to sell them, believeing they were "Warhols".

Now arguably they were as much Warhols as many of the other silkscreens made by Malanga, but as the February exhibition approached, the young poet began to get cold feet and tried to contact Warhol to check that he was OK with his assistant making pictures "by him" that he didn't even know existed. His wires were met with silence and when the gallery owners began demanding to see proof that would demonstrate that the pictures were genuine, he began, understandably, to get extremely jumpy.

In her book *Authenticity*, author Alice Sherwood explains what happened next:

"Eventually Andy broke his silence. He agreed to authenticate the pictures on condition that he received the proceeds of sale.

'CHE GUEVARAS are originals,' his telegram ran, 'however Malanga is not authorised to sell. Contact me by letter for adjustments. Andy Warhol.'

When the Malanga 'Warhols' became Andy Warhols by a process of retrospective authorisation, it marked a shift from the artist's hand to the artist's brand".*

It's an incredible story and one which neatly demonstrates the conundrum that sits at the heart of Warhol's body of work. In the early years of his career, the issue of authorship had not been much of a problem and Warhol had even revelled in the superficiality of it all saying: "If you want to know all about Andy Warhol, just look at the surface… and there I am. There's nothing behind it."

By any measure, Warhol was being deeply exploitative of the people around him, and Malanga most of all. While outwardly celebrating the brittle nature of it all, he was also beginning to make serious amounts of money off the ideas, talent and creativity of other people, while passing it all off as his own work. His "get out of jail" free card was his very USP. But does it really fly? If someone else is having the ideas and doing the work and making the silkscreens 4,000 miles away, can they still be Andy Warhols?

Bendor Grosvenor, art historian, art critic, former art dealer and an actual expert in the area, tells me that the Che pictures demonstrate some of the "madder aspects of the art market":

"Warhol's art is mostly to do with branding. The nature of the creative element is as he acknowledged very limited. It's other people's photos presented in bright colours. And since his own involvement with even the authentic work is very limited, then he (could) get away with declaring pretty much anything he liked authentic".

And this is how the Che pictures have come to be seen as a part of the canon, but as Bendor adds: "Where it collides with reality is when people want to buy that idea in order to demonstrate their wealth and

---

* Sherwood, A, *Authenticity*, 2022, p184–5.

taste. So, a market has to be created which then doesn't place value on the idea – because then anybody in the world could print out a Warhol and say they have one – but the object itself."

And that has consequences in the sale and value of the works because Warhols, by their inherent repetitive nature, are essentially commodified. If an Elvis print sells for $50 million, then it sets the value for all the others.

The "market" is critical to Warhol because the extortionate value of his paintings has a huge impact upon how we perceive them as works.

Art auctions are a curious thing. In the world of finance and banking, there are regulators and strict rules, but no such travails bother the art market. Auctions give the appearance of transparency, but all that is needed is for two bidders to set a price and it can be artificially inflated before the gavel hits. There is absolutely nothing illegal about any of that – but it does beg the question as to whether Warhol's works are really as valuable as the prices they command.

Warhol is probably the most famous artist of the last century and ranks among the biggest names of all time. That means that almost any work of his, automatically, has significant value as an investment. Warhols have, in short, become yet another commodity, like cattle, oil, property and Bitcoin. The artworks make a particularly solid investment because the brand doesn't look like it's going to diminish in value any time soon. But what does that say about Warhol's work itself?

It goes back again to what Ben Lewis said: the notion that the biggest and most famous artists are not necessarily the best. And in the case of Warhol, it is tempting to believe that ultimately, the value of his art is down to its accessibility, its ubiquity and the genius of this very quiet ad man to turn anything he touched, Midas-like, into gold.

* * *

Four months after the Malanga "Ches" were sold, Andy Warhol almost died. On 3rd June 1968, Valerie Solanas – author of the self-published *SCUM (Society for Cutting Up Men)* Manifesto (1967) which had called for the total elimination of men – walked into Warhol's office on the 6th floor at 33 Union Square West New York, above the new Factory, and shot him and the London gallery owner Mario Amaya. Warhol was hit twice, with the bullets passing through his spleen, liver and both lungs. Amaya was lucky and received only superficial wounds.

Solanas had known Warhol since 1965 and had appeared in one of his experimental films *I, A Man* (1967); she had also tried, repeatedly, to get him to read and produce her play *Up Your Ass,* only for Warhol to lose (so he claimed) the only copy. Her motives for subsequently shooting him remain opaque, but it has been suggested that she believed that he intended to steal it and pass it off as his own.

Warhol survived the incident but spent weeks recovering in hospital and was obliged to wear a surgical corset for the rest of his life. The shooting left him even more deeply paranoid than he had been beforehand, and he developed a significant phobia of hospitals.

As the 1970s dawned, Warhol became ever less the artist and ever more the entrepreneur with a sideline in photography. He co-launched a magazine *Interview* (1969), which became an iconic and influential pop and arts magazine, in part by his reputation as the manager of ever more influential the Velvet Underground.

With the death of his mother in 1972, Warhol was liberated from her apron strings and began to live as an openly gay man – while claiming he was a virgin. At the same time, he became ever more interested in video.

Warhol had in fact been making experimental films since the early 1960s.

One of the first, *Eat,* which consisted of 45 minutes of footage of a man eating a mushroom, set the mood for the oeuvre. *Blow Job* (1964), has an actor called DeVeren Bookwalter, gurning at the camera for 35 minutes and achieves the extraordinary feat of making a blow job look less interesting than a man eating a mushroom. *Sleep* (1964) is a five-hour film of Warhol's lover, John Giorno, sleeping.

The Life of Juanita Castro (1965) is more watchable in that it has Fidel and Raúl Castro, as well as Che Guevara, being played by women in an improvised performance that challenges the Castro regime and the tales of homophobic persecution that were coming out of the island.

Perhaps the most challenging aspect of Warhol's films is ultimately the challenge to stay awake. Warhol once said: "I like boring things. ... But that does not mean I'm not bored by them."

In Poor Little Rich Girl (1965), named after a Shirley Temple film and featuring Edie Sedgwick, he put that challenge to the test. We watch an out-of-focus Edie Sedgwick applying make-up, smoking joints and listening to Everly Brothers records, but is it art? Is it film? Or is it indulgence?

As the 1970s progressed, Warhol became a sort of latter-day Louis XIV of Downtown New York. A very wealthy and powerful man who dispensed cash to the fly-by-nights who caught his eye and who just as quickly turned his back on them. People were forever in and out of favour – and the boy from Pittsburgh lorded it over them all. Although he could be charming in private, the public Warhol, particularly of the Studio 54 era in the late 1970s, could be very waspish and toxic indeed.

"He was very manipulative," says Stephen Colegrave, "because he had money, he had power... he'd watch people... draw people in... but you got the impression that he was not a very nice man."

"Warhol didn't allow drugs in the Factory in the 1970s," Stephen adds, "so you'd have these extraordinary scenes in the period where everyone was just outside the doors injecting themselves with heroin."

The rules did not apply to Andy himself, who was constantly taking speed in the form of little orange pills. He never seemed to sleep. He was always working or watching or signing things off in his name. The 1970s saw his stock diminish and his work taken less seriously, as art critics turned up their noses at his pictures of his celebrity acquaintances. But as the 1980s dawned, he made something of a comeback, promoting graffiti artist Jean-Michel Basquiat and appearing in weird cameos – most notably in an episode of *The Love Boat* in 1985.

Andy loved the tacky but extremely popular show, set on a cruise liner, and had been trying to get on it since 1979. But as filming began, he had the jitters, writing in his diary that: "One of the lines I have to say is something like 'Art is crass commercialism', which I don't want to say."

A year later, in the early winter of 1986, Warhol began to suffer significant stomach cramps, but his fear of doctors and hospitals delayed treatment and by the time he got to hospital his gallbladder was infected. The operation cost him his life and he died on 22nd February 1987 aged 58.

Almost 40 years after his death his legend has only grown. His artworks sell for millions and his retrospectives are guaranteed box office fodder for galleries around the world. They, like art dealers, auction houses, fridge magnet makers and T-shirt sellers, are all heavily invested in the global business product that is the Andy Warhol brand.

There's much to like and admire about the artist. The strong satisfying whiff of the American Dream that took Andy Warhola, the poor, shy, boy of immigrant stock from Pittsburgh to the very heights of commercial and critical success. But his story too raises many questions about our collective notions of genius and our obsession with value and genius together. Is Warhol's art really worth hundreds of millions of dollars and by dint of it, is it greater than his contemporaries?

Warhol's most famous saying was that "in the future everyone will be famous for 15 minutes" but like so many other attributions in his life and work, the line was not his. Quite who said it first of all is disputed and the Swedish curator Pontus Hultén, artist Larry River and photographer Nat Finkelstein all have a claim. Warhol himself admitted it was not him, but despite that, it was attributed to him in life and long after his death.

"We've decided it's by Warhol, whether he likes it or not," art critic Blake Gopnik was quoted as saying in the *Smithsonian* magazine in 2011, continuing: "We've created and continue to create the Warhol brand for ourselves." And that, in a sense, that's Warhol in a nutshell. Or rather a can of Campbell's soup.

* * *

Even as that nebulous art market continues to lionise and idolise a handful of globally famous big names pushing their stock higher in the process, the work of 99% of history's artists gets largely overlooked. Many of these people are not so much ignored as invisible and nowhere is that more apparent than in the long, near total absence of women in art history – along with any interest in their work.

A 2018 data analysis of 18 major US art institutions found that their collections were 87% male and 85% white. As of writing, the National Gallery in London has just 20 works by female artists in its collection – out of a total of 2,300 paintings owned by the gallery.

Women's art remains significantly undervalued. The most expensive painting by a female artist is *Jimson Weed/White Flower Number 1* by Georgia O'Keeffe, which sold for $44.4 million in 2014, but that is less than a tenth of the value of the most expensive painting in history – Leonardo's *Salvator Mundi* – which went for $450.3 million in 2017 (and of which more in a moment.).

The absence of women's art at sales and exhibitions in their honour gives weight to the lie that female artists didn't really exist before the twentieth century. But it really is not true. The sixteenth-century Flemish Renaissance painter Catherina van Hemessen left a small but significant body of work, including a self-portrait which is often claimed to be the first example of the genre.

Three hundred years later, the French artist Marie-Guillemine Benoist was producing paintings of her own and gave an exhibition in Paris in 1791. Her best-known work, *Portrait of Madeleine* caused a sensation when it was put on public display at the Louvre Salon in 1800, as part of an exhibition of state-sponsored paintings by revolutionary-era artists.

The painting still hangs in the Louvre today and shows a Black woman, half clothed, with her body oriented towards the left while she stares straight towards us. Unlike many portrayals of Black people at the time there is nothing patronising or demeaning about it and nor is she some peripheral dressing to another figure. The picture is of her and nobody else and in her face there is both a weariness and a defiance. It is an extraordinary and powerful work of art.

216

Regrettably, we do not know the name of the sitter, but it has been speculated that she was formerly enslaved and brought to France, from the colony of Guadeloupe, in the Eastern Caribbean, by the artist's brother-in-law who was a colonial civil servant. A decree of 1794, by the French Revolutionary government, had freed all enslaved people from France's colonies, but that did not necessarily mean that she was entirely at liberté. Though technically a servant, she may have been in indentured service and likely had little actual say over her movements, her life or even whether she wanted to appear in the painting that has made her posthumously famous.

The emancipation of enslaved people in the colonies was a hotly contested issue in late eighteenth-century France. Many landowners in the Caribbean were openly lobbying for its return and that, depressingly, would happen following Napoleon Bonaparte's ascendancy in 1802. So, to display a Black woman at the Salon was a provocative move, and all the more so, because the artist herself was also a woman.

In her book, *A Little History of Art*, the art critic, author and historian Charlotte Mullins explains:"It was unprecedented to present a black woman in this way, as a subject in her own right and not playing a role (slave or royalty). Could she be symbolic of Mother France, nearly liberated from the monarchy, a country reborn with equality at its heart, a country that had abolished slavery? Did she symbolise emancipation for black people and for women?"

The answer is that we don't know because Benoist never left an explanation or wrote about the work. Like so much else in the missing gaps of women's lives in history, we are obliged to fill in both her and her sitter's biographies with guesswork.

The twentieth century may have seen more prominence of women in art, but beyond the big names of Kahlo, O'Keeffe, Hepworth and Riley, most women artists continue to linger in relative obscurity.

Even names of relative renown in the art world, like Hannah Höch, aren't familiar to a broad swathe of the public in the same way that Warhol, Picasso and Dali are. She was one of the originators of the Dada movement, whose shifting androgyny and innovative use of photomontage stunned and shocked the Weimar art scene in the 1920s. "Cancelled" by the Nazis, who viewed her art as degenerate, she lived in quiet anonymity in wartime Berlin and continued to produce art up until her death in 1978.

Höch is increasingly recognised and a Google doodle was created in her memory in December 2017 – the very height of digital fame – but like many great female artists she languishes in relative anonymity in a world that is still viewed as a male domain and driven largely by male collectors and buyers. Estimates suggest that at least 70% of art collectors in Europe and the USA are men and that they are overwhelmingly buying art by men as well.

A report by the Freelands Foundation in 2019 found that 68% of artists represented in major London commercial galleries are male too – and that is despite women making up a clear majority of fine art graduates. In the secondary market, the figures are even worse, demonstrating that 88% of sales were of works by male artists. It is a balance that is hardly being redressed – and for the near future at least it seems highly unlikely that any painting by a woman will scale the auction price of Leonardo's *Salvator Mundi* which is, as of writing, the most expensive painting ever sold.

That picture, sold as an original work by Leonardo da Vinci to Prince Badr bin Abdullah Al Saud of Saudi Arabia on behalf of Abu Dhabi's Ministry of Culture and Tourism for $450,312,500 in 2017, has subsequently created something of an art storm itself.

Many critics have suggested that this "lost masterpiece" isn't actually very good and that the hand of da Vinci may not even be there. Others have even gone as far as to suggest that it was a fake. The Louvre in Paris, which conducted a full analysis of the work in 2019, concluded, according to the makers of the documentary *The Saviour for Sale*, that while the work may have been produced by da Vinci's studio: "The scientific evidence was that Leonardo da Vinci only made a contribution to the painting (and) there was no doubt. And so, we informed the Saudis."

The painting has never been seen again. And its fate, like the art world itself, remains something of a mystery.

CHAPTER SIX

BUSINESS HEROES
COCO CHANEL

When Heroes are Too Big to Fail

In the first weeks of August 1944, as the Allied forces raced towards Paris, the French Resistance rose up against the German occupiers in the city.

Across the capital, buildings were seized, street barricades put up and trenches dug and as skirmishes broke out, the tide began to turn against the enemy invader. General Patton's Third Army arrived on the city's limits on August 19th and for the next three days the Resistance aka the French Free Forces of the Interior (FFIs) gained significant momentum. With Patton's soldiers bearing down on them, on 22nd August, the German Wehrmacht launched a counter-attack on the Grand Palais exhibition centre where the French had established a de facto HQ. When German tanks shelled the building, it caught fire, and a thick pall of smoke suffocated the surrounding streets for days giving the impression that the whole area was in flames.

Matters intensified further when, shortly afterwards, Hitler issued an infamous edict that the city be burned to the ground and ordered that: "Paris must not pass into the enemy's hands, except as a field of ruins."

More German tanks were deployed on the streets and all hell broke loose.

An estimated 1,000 FFIs and 3,000 German soldiers died in the fighting that followed, and it was only when the French 2nd Armoured and US 4th Infantry Divisions stormed into the capital two days later, on the night of the 24/25 August, that the Germans finally admitted the game was up and General Choltitz, the military governor of Paris, surrendered to the Resistance. Choltitz is still celebrated in some quarters as the Saviour of Paris for defying Hitler's orders and refusing to burn the city down.

The next day, General de Gaulle processed triumphantly down the Champs Élysées and shortly afterwards, declared the establishment of a new provisional government. Soon after that, the city turned on its native collaborators.

The *épuration sauvage* (wild purge) was the first wave of violent retribution against those who had fraternised with the enemy. It saw profiteers, informers and anyone else who was thought to have had business with the invader taken from their homes, beaten, tortured and, in many cases, summarily executed.

Since the Allied landings in June, France had been dealing with its collaborators and as the events of that year played out, an estimated 9,000 were killed and many more arrested or publicly humiliated. *Horizontal collaborators* were a particular target of the mob. And in Paris things got particularly vicious and out of hand. Prostitutes and other women who were accused of socialising with German soldiers were dragged into the street to have their heads shaved and clothes torn from their backs. Some were made to parade with the babies they had had with German men. Many were tarred with swastikas and even branded with hot irons. The *femme tondue (shaven-headed women)* were spat at, mocked, bullied and assaulted.

In victory – as would later be witnessed in Cuba in 1959 – the very worst traits of human depravity can rise to the surface.

Emotions were understandably running high. France had suffered significant depravation and humiliation under German rule and even the liberation had taken its toll. In total, 567,000 French people died during the Second World War – over a hundred thousand more than all British wartime deaths. The Occupation had been a national tragedy – and equally a source of considerable shame for a country as exceptionally proud as France. So, even before the first Allied boots landed in France, the French had begun rewriting the story and putting themselves at the centre of the hero narrative. By August 1944, the De Gaullist myth of what the author Henry Rousso later dubbed *résistancialisme* had already taken hold.

Like the unifying British wartime myths of Dunkirk and the Battle of Britain, *résistancialisme* contained just enough truth (in 1944) to give it legs, but like those British tales, it was wildly exaggerated for effect. Central to the semi-fictionalised saga was the notion that throughout the occupation, the FFIs aka Maquis* had represented the true soul of France and majority of people and that only the Vichy regime and a small minority of traitors had let the side down. There were indeed extraordinarily heroic people in wartime France and none more so than many of those who made up the Maquis. Thousands gave their lives to the cause of *Liberation* and the deeds of the greatest figures of the resistance like Jean Moulin, Marie Madelaine-Fourcade and Lionel Dubray are rightly celebrated today. But the cliché of the beret-wearing, Gauloise-smoking freedom-fighters, being representative of the majority sits at some odds with the truth.

The ramshackle FFIs were no unified force. They were riven with factionalism, and their activities were, in some cases, little more than a cover for criminality. The even more unpalatable truth is that for most of the war these resistance movements represented just a tiny fraction of the population.

---

* The Maquis were rural resistance fighters in Belgium and France, made up largely of young men who had dodged conscription.

Estimates suggest that following French capitulation in June 1940, roughly 90% of the French public simply accepted the situation and did the best they could to muddle on through in the hope of better times ahead. That mood only really changed following Operation Overlord in June 1944 when the FFI ranks swelled to around 400,000 volunteers; but just one year earlier they had numbered no more than 25,000 people. The fact is, that for most of the war, most French people simply kept their heads down and, in the process, quite a few, inevitably, had dealings with the Germans.

There is another bitter truth, and it is that many of those engaged in the mob justice of the *épuration sauvage* were likely as guilty as the people they were targeting. Undoubtedly, a lot of last-minute side-switching went on, with some French citizens suddenly becoming *plus résistants que les résistants* (more resistant than the resistance). And, as happened elsewhere in liberated Europe from 1944 onwards, in the frenzy of violence, scores were settled that had nothing to do with the war.

De Gaulle's new government quickly sought to restore order and formalise proceedings against the accused. The *épuration légale* (legal purge) which followed brought cases against thousands of collaborators. Most famously, Marshall Philippe Pétain, hero of the First World War and one-time mentor to the young Charles de Gaulle, who had led the Vichy government in the south of France from July 1940, was put on trial and sentenced to death (later commuted to life imprisonment). Pétain was the highest-profile case, but many collaborationists were charged with breaking Article 75 – the treason clause in the French Penal Code – and also tried. In total 300,000 suspects were investigated, 6,763 sentenced to death and 791 executions carried out. Among them was Pierre Laval, twice Prime Minister of pre-war France, who was shot by firing squad on 15th October 1945 at Fresnes prison, south of Paris, as a traitor.

Lesser offenders were judged in Courts of Justice and the guilty sentenced to *dégradation nationale* (national demotion) which saw them lose their civic rights and essentially become second-class citizens in their homeland. Roughly 100,000 French citizens received the penalty, and the lingering taint of dishonour haunted many a life to its end.

There was another tier of retribution too – and it was called the court of public opinion.

Maurice Chevalier, the pre-war entertainer, who had packed out the houses at the Casino de Paris right up to the fall of Paris, was one of its most famous victims.

Soon after the occupation Chevalier had fled Paris with his Jewish partner, Nita Raya, to La Bocca on the Mediterranean coast. There he was approached by theatre investors and carrots and sticks were dangled in front of his eyes. Chevalier refused all offers, including one from Broadway that would have enabled him to leave France, but the pestering did not stop.

Eventually and with some reluctance he travelled to Paris for a short run at the Casino and later sang at a POW camp holding French prisoners on condition that the German authorities release ten of them. Around the same time, a collaborationist newspaper, *Le Petit Parisien*, which was to all intents and purposes a front for Nazi propaganda, published an article titled: "Maurice Chevalier preaches collaboration between the French and the Germans".

The story leaked across the Channel where the British popular press claimed, wrongly, that Chevalier had given concerts all over Germany and the whole mess of misinformation resulted in his name being added to a list of collaborators to be targeted at war's end.

Chevalier's wife and family all had false papers that hid their Jewish identity and clearly, in all of this, the performer was trying to protect her and them, while appeasing all sides. But it caused him immense problems with both the Nazis and the Free French and with the Allied landings, the police and the FFIs set out to capture him. German propaganda, seeking to sow fear, jumped on the story and claimed that he had been killed by a mob, but it was not true, and the singer had simply gone into hiding.

A few days later Chevalier was arrested by three armed members of the Maquis and taken to Toulouse, where he was told he would be executed.

Fortunately, a British newspaper, the *Daily Express*, was on the story and a reporter managed to rapidly untangle the web of lies and propaganda around his wartime activities and publish the truth before he could be shot. Chevalier was released and later whisked out of the country by Paramount News and flown to America.

Similar accusations dogged Charles Trenet, singer of 'La Mer', who also performed at a POW camp under pressure from the Germans. He managed to get away with a slap on the wrist, but the "collaborationist" shame hung over his career for decades.

The famous French actress Arletty, who had lived with a German Luftwaffe officer Hans-Jürgen Soehring during the Occupation of France, was similarly targeted. Arrested by the Maquis in 1944, Arletty allegedly delivered the immortal line "My heart is French, but my ass is international" before being tried for treason and sentenced to 18 months. Her film career never fully recovered although she did briefly and incongruously appear in the 1962 D-Day epic *The Longest Day*.

British intelligence were busy hunting down war criminals of their own too. One of the first MI6 officers on the scene in Paris at the time was a former journalist turned MI6 agent attached to de Gaulle's Free French army, who went by the name of Malcolm Muggeridge.

Muggeridge's list of suspects included the creator of *Jeeves*, P.G. Wodehouse, who had been trying to finish a novel when France fell in 1940. Wodehouse, 58, had been sent to a Nazi internment camp* where he rashly agreed to make five broadcasts on German radio to US audiences. Aired in June 1941, these saw the novelist branded a traitor in the House of Commons in London, but having interviewed him in 1944, Muggeridge concluded that Wodehouse's only crime was to have Bertie Woosterish levels of naivety.

Muggeridge had bigger fish to fry anyway because he had been

---

* In Tost, Upper Silesia – thus perhaps inspiring his line: "If this is Upper Silesia then what must Lower Silesia be like?"

tipped off about a wartime German plan, codenamed Operation Modellhut (Model Hat), which had seen the Abwehr (German Intelligence) try in 1943 to contact members of the British aristocracy in the hope of ending the war. Muggeridge's lover, an MI6 informer known only as "F", knew one of the suspects – so in September 1944, "F" and Muggeridge went to the Ritz Hotel, in Paris, to interrogate her.

The Germans had given their agent a codename, "Westminster", but she was better known to the rest of the world as Coco Chanel.

The businesswoman and world-famous designer had more wartime secrets up her elegantly tailored sleeve than lines at a busy fashion week. Her behaviour, as we shall see, had been far worse than that of the actress Arletty, and as the *épuration* had played out in the streets beneath her rooms she must have been making her calculations. Seeking to curry favour, she had declared that every GI in the city was entitled to a free bottle of No. 5 at her store on Rue Cambon. As Muggeridge and "F" walked towards the Ritz, they would have passed the line of US soldiers snaking around the block.

Two years before he died in 1988, Muggeridge burned his notes from the meeting that followed, fearing perhaps that his affair with "F" might dent his new-found reputation as the holier than thou "St Mugg". But fortunately, an abridged version survives and is available to read in full on the Baudelaire Society website. That Muggeridge admitted it had been edited should of course ring some alarm bells, but it remains an extraordinary document, not least because Coco Chanel sounds as if she has sprung from the pages of fiction.

"I have heard so much about you, Mr. Muggeridge," Chanel begins, adding, "I believe you have come to liberate us. How very solicitous of you."

She then launches a prolonged assault on the events of the *épuration* playing out all around and is dismissive of the FFIs, telling Muggeridge: "At first, their conduct incensed me. Now, I feel almost sorry for those ruffians. One should refrain from contempt for the baser specimens of humanity."

She reserves particular contempt for de Gaulle and his rewriting of the narrative: "Have you listened to him lately? He will soon be claiming that the Resistance has liberated the world. And why shouldn't he? A countless following of French half-wits will believe him."

Muggeridge pushes her on her wartime relationships and Chanel tells him that her perceived spying activities were simply cover for her trying to get back to London and "make it my home". She claims she has been misunderstood and that she has been betrayed by her friend Vera (we shall meet her later) and denounces her as a "fascist". She deliberately name-checks her "close friendship of Winston, the hero who (has) brought hope to the world". And then, challenged as to which side she was on during the occupation she replies: "Why neither side of course. I stood up for myself as I have always done. Nobody tells Coco Chanel what to think."

There is a defiance in the interview and her many apologists have mistaken it for candour, but Chanel was cornered, bluffing and blaming everyone else, perhaps simply seeking to save her own skin. Coco Chanel was a woman of many skills and talents and telling whopping lies about herself was one of them.

It's easy, with hindsight, to judge people caught up in events of war beyond their control who might have transgressed or collaborated. While we might all hope that we might have behaved better in the same circumstances, it is likely that many of us would have behaved as most of those in the occupied territory did and kept our heads down, looked the other way and perhaps even had dealings with the invaders.

But by any metric Chanel was no innocent bystander. Her behaviour had been absolutely appalling. She had actively feathered her nest at the Ritz in Paris, while seeking to use antisemitic laws to wrest back control of her perfume from her Jewish business partners. She had willingly colluded with the German regime in trying to broker peace with her high-level contacts in Britain – and for most of the time she had, quite literally, been sleeping with a Nazi spy.

Muggeridge did not pursue the line of enquiry and made no mention of it in his memoirs, although he did tell biographers that he had deeply disliked her. In time all would be revealed, but, even so, decades after her death, a discreet veil is still drawn over Coco Chanel's wartime behaviour along with many other deeply unfavourable aspects of her life as her legend continues to be bolstered.

Chanel remains a huge icon and is arguably France's most famous business hero. The brand that bears her name remains the first and last word in fashion and perhaps every other word in between.

But her exquisitely cut myth hides a truth, darker than any one of her little black dresses.

* * *

Born in the charity hospital in Saumur, Maine-et-Loire on 19th August 1883 (she would later play hard and fast with the year) the girl christened Gabrielle Chasnel* came into a life of abject poverty and chaos. Her father, Albert, was a habitual liar and a womanising drunk who tried to make a living as a travelling salesman and would often disappear for months on end, leaving no clue as to where he had gone. Chanel's mother, Jeanne, was a laundry woman – the bottom of the social hierarchy – although her daughter would later claim that she had inherited her father's carpentry business and was a lady of means. The couple already had one daughter, Julia-Berthe, but were still unmarried at the time of Gabrielle's birth.

Deeply ashamed of her humble roots and in a familiar trope, Chanel would constantly re-edit the narrative of her childhood, claiming that her parents were successful, that her father had been a horse trader and that she was only born in a poor house because her mother happened to be passing and fell into labour there while on the way to meet her father. In Axel Madsen's *Chanel: A Woman of Her Own* (1991), the author quotes Coco as saying:

---

* The name in which she was registered – a spelling mistake but one which she kept for the rest of her life. French bureaucracy was such that to change it, she would have had to have revealed the circumstances of her birth in a poor house – to an unmarried couple.

"I won't tell this sober story because it's terribly boring, but my mother suddenly felt faint. With the fashion of the day, it was hard to see that the woman was going to have a baby, so some very nice people brought her home with them...(then) she was taken to the hospital where I was born. At hospitals, they christen you right away. They gave me the name of the nun who took care of my mother."

It was untrue. The first lie in a very long lifetime of whoppers and unreliable narratives about her that would see Coco constantly alter and edit even the very basic facts surrounding her birth. Later, she was to tell friends, among other things, that she had been born in a railway carriage and that her father had been a wine merchant and not a horse trader. As other siblings arrived in quick succession, the child jostled to get attention from her sickly mother and wayward father. The family lived, quite literally, on top of each other and while Chanel would later claim that they were brought up in a large house, in fact they inhabited just one rented room in Brive-la-Gaillarde, a town midway between Lyon and Bordeaux.

Distant from her elder sister, who was described as "troubled", she formed a stronger bond with younger brother Alphonse (born 15th March 1885) and later with her baby sister Antoinette (known as Ninette). The familial chaos was such that she frequently retreated into a make-believe world of toy dolls and... gravestones, as Chanel later claimed that she spent much of her childhood in cemeteries.

"Because I lived with people who were insensitive, I wanted to be sure that I was loved. I liked to talk to myself, and I didn't do what I was told. That, no doubt, comes from the fact that the first beings to whom I opened my heart were dead people."*

Her longing for the company of the dead may have been a mis-remembrance of her childhood. Because when she was just 11 years old, her mother suddenly died.

---

* Madsen, A, *Chanel: A Woman of Her Own*, 2015, p13.

One of the curious similarities among the characters thus far in the book is that more than half of them lost a parent in childhood. Bader was 12 when his father died, Mother Teresa was 8 when she lost hers, Warhol's father died when he was 13 and Coco lost her mother when she was 11. The absent parent is key to many a legend and myth – Luke Skywalker, Wonder Woman, Spiderman, Batman, Hulk, Harry Potter and even Kung Fu Panda, are all orphans. There's perhaps a good reason for that, at least in fiction. The fear of losing a parent, taps into the primordial soup of childhood terror. It is the thing many of us have at one time or other worried about more than anything else.

And there's something else. An orphaned protagonist is the greatest shortcut possible to the transformational journey of the *monomyth* – it immediately sets the lonely hero against the world, forces them to adapt and grow up... and propels them forth onwards to adventure.

In 1978, a French book called *Do Orphans Lead the World?* built on the findings of clinical psychologist Martin Eisenstadt, who had analysed all 578 biographical entries in the *Encyclopædia Britannica* over half a page long, to find that dozens of significant "hero" and "anti-hero" figures lost a parent in childhood or early adulthood.

The list includes Churchill, Hitler, the Brontë sisters, John Lennon, Paul McCartney, Abraham Lincoln, Lenin, Michelangelo, Newton, Washington, Alexander the Great, Genghis Khan and Virginia Woolf. Now of course, premature death was far more common in the "good old days", but while there is a lot of confirmation bias afoot in any list, clearly losing one or both parents can be a "primal cue" on a young mind. Studies demonstrate conclusively that the premature death of a mother or a father in one's early years can, not surprisingly, have significant psychological impact later in life and often with negative outcomes. Orphans are more likely to experience PTSD, suffer low self-esteem, and can suffer higher degrees of attachment insecurity in relationships.

The early realisation that the world is a godless and uncaring place, and that death is real, is a sobering lesson and it is perhaps understandable that Chanel tried to spin her own fairytale from the misery of her childhood poverty and loss.

According to her favoured version of events, Chanel was originally brought up by two aunts while her father sailed off to America to make a fortune. But no fortunes were made and while aunts were present, she was essentially abandoned, by her feckless father, along with her two sisters, Julia-Berthe and Ninette, to a convent orphanage in Aubazines, Nouvelle-Aquitaine, while her two surviving brothers, aged 4 and 9, were sent to work as child labourers on a farm.

As a "destitute child", she slept in an unheated dormitory and was ostracised by fellow students who lived by a strict code of hierarchy based on what degree of orphan they were. If you were abandoned by a parent, you basically sat on the lowest tier, so perhaps it's understandable that Chanel changed her backstory during her long, steep climb out from the gutter to turn terrible misfortune into a fairy-tale. That was no easy matter because *fin de siècle* French society was not only horribly class-ridden but also deeply sexist. As a working-class orphan of illegitimate birth, Gabrielle came from the bottom rank of the bottom ladder of the bottom tier of society. Fortunately, beneath her demure, outward appearance, Chanel had steel running through her veins. Convent life could have broken her spirit– but it hardened her instead.

In her 1946 memoir, *The Allure of Chanel*, as dictated to her friend Paul Rand, Coco summed up her time as an orphan child. "I was a pest, a thief, someone who listens at doors. Today like back then arrogance is in everything I do, it is in my gestures, the harshness of my voice, in the glow of my gaze, in my sinewy tormented face, in my whole person."

At 18 Chanel left Aubazines and went to live in a boarding house in Moulins that was funded by wealthy local families and served as a sort of finishing school for destitute young women. She joined her aunt, Adrienne, just a few years older than her and learnt to sew while receiving an apprenticeship as a haberdasher's assistant. The Catholic institution had strict rules on "going out" and mixing with men, but the two young women had a healthy disregard for them, and Chanel began singing in a local cabaret for cavalry officers. It was there that she got the nickname Coco perhaps on account of a song she loved to sing called "Qui qu'a vu Coco?" ("Have you seen Coco?") about a woman who has lost her dog, or more likely as shorthand for the French word *cocotte* meaning "kept woman".

Chanel later insisted that both versions were wrong and that her father had given her the name as a child. She was also to play down her time at the cabaret, while playing up her credentials as a seamstress, and with good reason, because by the age of 23, Chanel was in effect, a courtesan; a bright and attractive woman, willing to use her charm to attract the attention of handsome and wealthy men, who in her case was a playboy called Étienne Balsan.

Balsan would be the first of a series of rich individuals, bewitched by her beauty and charm, who would fund her early business ventures. Balsan was heir to a vast fabric empire and lived in lavish style at a chateau called Royallieu in Compiègne some 45 miles west of Paris. He was a catch and he taught her how to act like an aristocrat. From him she learned to ride horses and became accustomed to a life of servants, fine food, fine wine and the company of the educated, indolent upper classes, who flocked to the estate for parties and weekends. The young Chanel was witty, stylish, defiant, resolute, alive, extremely beautiful and equipped with a fiery temper, an enormous talent for design and an urgency to make something of her life and build a fortune of her own.

In 1909 she convinced Balsan to turn the ground floor of his home on 160 Boulevard Malesherbes, Paris, into a millinery shop. Her business prospects were taking off, but her private life was getting ever more complicated because Coco was embroiled in a de facto ménage à trois with Balsan's English friend Arthur "Boy" Capel, after meeting him in 1908. Capel was even wealthier than Balsan and, impressed by her business acumen and perhaps trying to lure her from his chum, he funded her next venture, *Chanel Modes,* on the fashionable Rue Cambon in Paris's 1st arrondissement.

One of the quirkier aspects of the Chanel story is that Capel, then 28, and on the face of it, the very epitome of an aristocratic English country gentleman, was Coco's muse. Capel, unlike Balsan, was a largely self-made man and again unlike Balsan, he had innate style and flair. Chanel used one of his old sweaters as the template for her early knitwear dresses and Capel's wardrobe was to continue to inspire her for the next nine years and well beyond.

The wealthy Englishman funded more than just her shops and her lifestyle. When her older sister, the wayward and troubled Julia-Berthe, slit her wrists and died in 1912, Coco adopted her 6-year-old son André Palasse, and Capel offered to fund his expensive English boarding school education. In fact, there were some doubts as to who André's mother was and surviving photographs from the 1920s of Chanel and André larking about show that the young man bore more than a passing resemblance to his aunt and adopted mother. Throughout her life, Coco Chanel could be cruel and distant to those around her, but her love for Capel and André cannot be doubted. When she died in 1971, she left almost her entire fortune to her son and his two daughters.

Capel funded the expansion of her business into Biarritz, Deauville and elsewhere, and by the start of the First World War, Coco was the most fashionable up-and-coming designer in France.

A year later, in 1915, the 32-year-old had become so well-established, that even with the country in the throes of a miserable war and partial occupation, French *Harper's Bazaar* suggested that any woman "who hasn't at least one Chanel is hopelessly out of fashion".

Capel and Chanel were properly, deeply in love, but there was no chance of marriage. An aristocratic gentleman, even one of largely self-made means, needed to wed someone of their own social standing. Someone posh. Someone with a ludicrously long family tree, inherited silver and an absurd accent. So, in 1918, he married Diana Lister, daughter of the 4th Baron Ribblesdale, although it didn't stop him seeing Coco.

The following year brought double tragedy for Chanel. War's end had seen her younger sister Ninette marry a Canadian army officer rather too hastily and then move to North America, a choice she swiftly regretted. The vast, unforgiving, empty wilderness of Ontario pretty much matched her feelings for her husband, and she sought a way out. Ninette begged her sister to send enough money for her to return to Paris, but Coco, somewhat sanctimoniously, refused and encouraged her to patch up the marriage, only for her younger sister to elope with an Argentinian playboy to Buenos Aires.

Ninette died there of Spanish flu shortly afterwards.

Just a few months earlier, on 22nd December 1919, Capel had crashed his car, while driving to a rendezvous with Chanel – or, at least, so she claimed, and been killed. A news item in *The New York Times,* printed on Christmas Day 1919, related that Capel was a friend of Lloyd George and married to Lord Ribbesdale's daughter. There was no mention of Chanel, but to his credit, she was not forgotten in his will and Capel left her a considerable fortune, with which she went on to expand her business empire.

"In losing Capel, I lost everything," Chanel later told her biographer Morand, "what followed was not a life of happiness".

Capel's death and that of her sister inspired her most famous enduring design, the little black dress. The shade was already, albeit somewhat morbidly, in vogue in 1919. France had lost 1.4 million people through war and an additional 250,000 in the on-going flu pandemic.

"Fashion should express the time, the moment..." Chanel once said and the colour of mourning well fitted that sentiment in 1919. On a visit to the Paris Opera, mired in grief, she later told Morand, "I remember contemplating the auditorium ... those reds, those greens, those electric blues made me feel ill...(so) I imposed black."

Some weeks after Capel's death, Coco met a medium, who claimed Capel was "living in a place of happiness, in a world where nothing can trouble him any longer". It momentarily lifted her spirits and she fell back, as she often did at times of tragedy, into hard work.

As such, Chanel's impact on immediate post-war fashion went way beyond the little black dress.

"I don't do fashion, I am fashion!" she once said – and in the 1920s at least, it was largely true.

Throughout the Jazz Age (as that decade was dubbed by the writer F. Scott Fitzgerald), Chanel liberated women from corsets and lace and put them in sailor shirts and trousers instead. She created an androgynous and fluid style that can still be seen 100 years later on the streets of the world's great cities and catwalks. Whatever her personal flaws and whatever criticism is levelled at her, that extraordinary talent and vision is not in doubt. She was, by any measure, a one-woman fashion revolution and a bona fide couture legend.

It wasn't just her work that made her famous but her public personality too, and over the course of her life almost as renowned for her waspish observations or "Coco-isms" as she was for her style. Her 1944 interview with Muggeridge is littered with dismissive one-liners – and her famous sayings which include, "Elegance is refusal", "Luxury must be comfortable otherwise it is not luxury" and "fashion changes but style endures" have an almost Zen-like quality.

These legendary soundbites were not in fact throwaway lines but were frequently, carefully rehearsed. Nor were they entirely her own work.

Chanel hated to be alone and in 1921, following the death of Capel, she fell into the arms of the poet Pierre Reverdy. Somewhat inconveniently, Reverdy was both married and extremely religious and his infidelity tortured him, eventually leading to his and Coco's separation in 1926. But their friendship endured to his death in 1960 and he was to become as much her teacher and friend as her lover. He undoubtedly crafted, or helped her craft, many of her most famous lines and was thus, in a sense, Coco's Ted Sorensen.

Chanel spent much of the rest of her time with her hedonistic best friend, Maria "Misia" Sophie Olga Godebska. Misia was, like Coco, a rebel convent girl who had shocked and delighted Bohemian Paris in the pre-war years with her wit and beauty. She had been a muse to painters Renoir, Bonnard and Vuillard, Toulouse-Lautrec had immortalised her on the cover of art and literary magazine *La Revue blanche*, while Marcel Proust had used her as the inspiration for at least two characters in his book *A Remembrance of Things Past*. She was also a close friend of Sergei Diaghilev, the ballet impresario and arbiter of taste in France who had stayed there after the Russian Revolution in 1917, and through him she knew all the Russian émigrés in Paris.

When the two women first met, Misia was almost 50 and attempting to settle down with her third husband, the painter José Maria Sert, but she was instantly drawn to and almost infatuated with Chanel. Their intense friendship was to last the rest of Misia's life (she died in 1950). There has been speculation that the two women may also have been lovers, which would have been ironic, as Coco was a rampant homophobe.

Her various public pronouncements on gay men included dubbing them "cynical paederasts" and "the whores of high society", but in private her slurs were said to be far worse.

A year after Capel's death, Misia and Sert introduced Chanel to Ernest Beaux, an émigré who had been a spy for the British during the Russian Civil War between 1918 and 1920, and then moved to Paris. Ernest and his brother Édouard had worked at the famous A. Rallet & Co. soap factory in Moscow in pre-revolutionary Russia, where Ernest had gained a reputation as "a nose" for his work as a master perfumer. He had created a celebrated fragrance, the "Bouquet de Napoléon" cologne in 1912 – as a tribute to the French Emperor on the 100th anniversary of the invasion of Russia. His follow-up perfume for women, "Bouquet de Catherine", dedicated in 1913 to the legendary Russian Empress on the tercentenary of the foundation of the Romanov dynasty, didn't fare so well in a country that was rapidly falling out of love with its royal family.

France was full of Russian migrants and refugees in the early 1920s and Ernest Beaux was well-connected. Through Grand Duke Dmitri Pavlovich of Russia, a cousin of the murdered Tsar Nicholas II, he met Diaghilev. Through Diaghilev he met Misia and, through her, he was introduced to Coco Chanel – now the biggest name in fashion.

Meeting Chanel in Cannes, on the French Riviera, in 1920, he presented her with a series of bottles containing his latest scents and she picked "number 5", which had been her lucky number since her childhood. Chanel was deeply apophenic. She saw the number everywhere and at the convent at Nouvelle-Aquitaine had daily counted the five groups of stones that made up the five paths that led to the chapel. She was so superstitious about it that she would always launch her collections on the 5th day of the 5th month and there is the strong suspicion that she picked vial 5 because of the number on the front of it. Coco played no part in the creation of her most famous product beyond smelling it and choosing it. Although to be fair she did play a huge role in co-designing that extraordinary and game-changing bottle – which is of course central to the Number 5 mythos.

It says something about the power of myth, that even that bottle has its own conflicting origin story. Some say it was based on one of Capel's old whisky decanters and others on one of the toiletry bottles which he carried around with him on his travels.

Most "celebrity" perfumes, even nowadays, are little more than a branding exercise. All those famous scents with pop star signatures on them have been made by people other than the name attached to them and the person they are named after has likely had sweet FA to do with it. Being a perfumer is a skilled and highly complex job that takes years of apprenticeship and requires that all important "nose". Chanel had no expertise in the field. Choosing the scent was less than an afternoon's work for her and while her name played a significant part in its enduring legend, Beaux should perhaps be granted a little more credit than his obscurity allows. It was he, after all, who was the true creator of the world's greatest and most coveted and recognisable perfume – making him, I suppose, the Gerard Malanga of Chanel No. 5.

Initially, Chanel gave No. 5 away for free to clients and friends. But her magic potion swiftly became as highly desirable as her fashion lines, so inevitably on May 5th (5/5) 1921, she launched it as a product in its own right. Demand immediately skyrocketed and three years later, in 1924, its success led Coco to a racetrack-side meeting, with a businessman called Pierre Wertheimer.

Pierre was the head of Bourjois, which had grown from its origins as a theatrical make-up producer to become France's largest cosmetics producer. The firm had expanded in the post-war era into a global company and had production facilities in other many other countries – most notably the USA. The meeting was brief and Chanel, unbothered with the details of the deal and overly weighed down by too many ongoing concerns, signed away 90% of her holding. Of that, 60% went to Pierre and his brother, another 20% to Théophile Bader, broker of the deal and owner of the Galeries Lafayette department store and 10% to Coco herself. It was actually a very good deal for Coco, as it allowed the global expansion and promotion of her perfume – reaping her enormous financial benefits and making her the wealthiest woman in France on the back of almost no effort on her part. But quite quickly, Chanel came to believe that she had been ripped off. As the company flourished under the Wertheimers, she failed to appreciate that it was them and their work that had made it such a global success, and as such she eventually sought to use every means possible to wrest back control.

The Wertheimer-Chanel relationship was a paradox of enduring love and passionate hatred. Coco liked Pierre in person – and he was, like so many other men who met her, clearly slightly more than half in love with her. But Chanel was no longer the faintly naive convent girl who had fallen in love with Boy Capel. She was a ruthless, albeit sometimes reckless, businesswoman, and the extreme wealth and the power and influence that came with it now defined her world outlook.

She was also unremittingly antisemitic – and her enduring belief that the Jewish Bader and the Jewish Wertheimers had "stolen" her creation was in no small part born out of that rampantly racist world view.

Chanel never attempted to hide her hatred of Jews.

In Hal Vaughan's book *Sleeping with the Enemy,* the author records a conversation she had with Marcel Haedrich in 1969. Haedrich had been editor in chief of French *Marie Claire* in the '50s and early '60s and was now writing the book *Et Moïse créa Dieu* (*And Moses created God*), the title of which Chanel took immediate exception.

"You hope the Jews will like your story?" she asked. "They won't buy your book," she said, adding, "I only fear Jews and Chinese; and the Jews more than the Chinese." Haedrich's thoughts were that "Chanel's antisemitism was not only verbal; but passionate, demoded and often embarrassing."

Unfortunately, her views were not uncommon in the France of her time. Antisemitism had a long history in the country, stretching back to medieval times, and French Jews had only been afforded the same rights as their Christian neighbours in the early nineteenth century. To their shame, the Catholic Church actively encouraged antisemitic literature, and in 1884 a bestselling book entitled *La France Juivre* (*Jewish France*) by Edouard Drumont had set the hate ablaze once more. In 1889, Drumont would form the Antisemitic League of France, which campaigned to have Jews removed from society – in a campaign that foreshadowed the narratives of twentieth-century Nazis.

That atmosphere of hatred led in October 1894 to the Dreyfus affair.

Alfred Dreyfus was a Jewish French cavalry officer, who was accused, on circumstantial evidence, of spying for the Germans. Stripped of his rank, he was sent to the French penal colony of Devil's Island, off the coast of French Guiana. Evidence quickly emerged which suggested that a man called Major Esterhazy was the real guilty party, but it was hushed up and Dreyfus remained a prisoner. The case caused a sensation in *fin de siècle* France and the writer Émile Zola and fellow campaigners managed to secure a retrial – only for Dreyfus to be convicted again in 1899. Public anger later secured his release, but it was not until 1906 that he was fully exonerated.

Well into the twentieth century, Catholic conspiracy theories about the Jews ran rife in France and antisemitic and pro-fascist sentiments proliferated in the interwar years. Chanel's hatred of Jews undoubtedly had its roots in her childhood in the convent and the antisemitic conditioning foisted upon her by the nuns, but she never outgrew it. It remained deeply embedded within her and it is no coincidence that many of her lovers shared her racist world view.

In 1923, Coco was introduced to Bendor Grosvenor,* 2nd Duke of Westminster. Grosvenor invited her, and her friend Vera Bate – the woman Chanel would later denounce to Muggeridge as a "fascist" – aboard his yacht, moored in the bay of Monte Carlo, and the relationship went from there.

Grosvenor, a cousin of King George V, was then the richest man in England and one of the wealthiest people in the world. He owned a succession of grand homes and fast cars, hunting lodges, castles and two enormous yachts, the *Cutty Sark*† and the *Flying Cloud*. A close friend of Winston Churchill and Edward, Prince of Wales, later King Edward VIII, he was also a big fan of Hitler and a massive antisemite. One measure of the man is that he had a dog called "Jew". Another is that in 1931, largely out of spite, he set out to destroy the life of his brother-in-law, William Lygon, the 7th Earl of Beauchamp.

Beauchamp, a liberal politician, had married Grosvenor's sister Lady Lettice, in 1902, but their salad days had been brief. Beauchamp was gay and, by the late 1920s, he was conducting an affair with a journalist and prospective Liberal MP called Robert Bernays.

Bernays had a German Jewish background and was a frequent visitor to Berlin in the Weimar years, not least because Germany then, was one of the most tolerant places in Europe for LGBTQ people. As such, Bernays had a window on Germany's shifting political sands and became an early critic of Hitler and a vehement opponent of fascism long before everyone else caught on. Notably, he was one of the first British politicians to warn about the true nature of Nazi concentration camps.

---

* A very distant relative of the Bendor Grosvenor in the previous chapter.

† This *Cutty Sark* was not the same boat as the ship of that name that now sits in dry dock in Greenwich, London. The Greenwich ship was originally called *Cutty Sark*, but was renamed the *Ferreira* in 1895 and listed as such by its Portuguese owners, thus freeing up the name for Grosvenor.

In 1931, Bernays was a rising star of the Liberal Party, but as he stood as the candidate for Bristol North, his candidacy almost got engulfed in scandal. Getting wind of the relationship, Grosvenor had decided to use it against the brother-in-law he hated and the Liberal Party that he despised even more. Without consulting his sister, whose honour he was purporting to defend, he gleefully informed his cousin the King that Beauchamp was gay and in a relationship with Bernays. George V was outraged, not least because Beauchamp's daughter, Mary, was in a relationship with the King and Queen's fifth child, George, Duke of Kent – and was hoping to marry him. King George, who was, even by the very low bar set, one of the most narrow-minded, dim-witted and unpleasant monarchs in the history of the recent royal family, is said to have muttered: "I thought men like that shot themselves." The King did not know that his own son, George, was bisexual and was even then enjoying a lengthy relationship with the playwright Noël Coward.

As the scandal worsened, Beauchamp was obliged to escape abroad or face jail and his life and those of his wife and his children were all ruined in the process. Grosvenor's spiteful parting note to him read:

"Dear Bugger-in-Law, you got what you deserved."

Bernays, untouched by the scandal, went on to become the Liberal MP for Bristol North and later wrote a book about Gandhi called the *Naked Fakir*. The title was a nod to a remark by Winston Churchill,* but it could equally have applied to Grosvenor, who was conducting multiple affairs with multiple women while using other people's private lives to destroy them. The worst kind of hypocrite.

The tale is yet another sorry reminder of that age of hypocrisy and blackmail, when gay men and lesbians were obliged to hide the truth of their sexuality and run for their lives if found out. Beauchamp died in exile in New York in 1938, aged 66. Grosvenor, the smug, bumptious

---

* Churchill actually called "Mr. Gandhi, a seditious Middle Temple lawyer, now posing as a fakir of a type well known in the East, striding half-naked up the steps of the Vice-regal palace". Like many a Churchill misquote, the misattribution sounds better.

King of Cant, continued to cheat on his many wives and prosper in polite British society until his death.

Throughout the 1920s and into the 1930s, this bigot was Coco Chanel's partner, and it was through him in the late 1920s that Chanel met Winston Churchill, then Chancellor of the Exchequer. Like men and women before him, Churchill was instantly besotted with her. Writing somewhat ill-advisedly, to his wife, Clemmie – as he did almost daily – on 11th January 1928, Winston described their first encounter: "The famous Chanel turned up and I took a great fancy to her. A most capable and agreeable woman much the stronger personality Bendor has been up against…. With her is Vera Bate."

A decade later, Vera, Chanel and Churchill would cross paths again, but in the years that led to Operation Modellhut, Churchill would often seek out Coco. In the midst of the 1936 Abdication Crisis, Winston who had done everything in his power to keep Edward VIII on the throne, was witnessed weeping drunkenly in the French designer's breast, bleating that: "A King cannot abdicate."

Grosvenor showered Coco with money and gave her a villa and a piece of land on the Riviera along with whole chests of very expensive jewellery. The couple were the very embodiment of the Roaring Twenties, throwing parties and living the high life, with Coco the undeclared mistress in chief of the palatial Eaton Hall, the country house of the Dukes of Westminster. These were reckless, self-obsessed individuals without a worry in the world, and with something of the Buchanans in Scott Fitzgerald's *The Great Gatsby* about them. Forever smashing up things and creatures and then retreating into their vast wealth and carelessness, while beyond their gilded doors the nations of Europe drifted towards mutual destruction.

As fascism prospered, Grosvenor funded right-wing organisations and privately professed his admiration for the leaders of Germany and Italy.

Claiming to have links with "Nazi moderates", he used his privilege as a hereditary peer, which automatically gave him a seat in the House of Lords, to push for peace with Hitler. As late as May 1939 he was supporting the fascist Right Club, a group that sought to appease the

Nazis while blaming the troubles of the era on its Jewish victims. That organisation's leader, Archibald Maule Ramsay MP of the Scottish Unionist Party, later had the distinction of being the only serving MP in the Second World War to be locked up in prison. MI5 agents, who had infiltrated the group, discovered that Ramsay and his antisemitic wife were planning a fascist uprising, and later he and two of his Right Club associates were found in possession of thousands of documents, including files stolen from right from under the nose of Ambassador Joseph Kennedy at the US Embassy. Clearly, they planned to share them with German agents and two of the men involved were convicted of espionage and sent to jail.

Thanks, in part to his impeccable connections, no such fate befell Old Etonian Ramsay. Interred at Brixton prison, he remained an MP and sent parliamentary questions from his cell, which were dutifully answered by his friends on the green benches.

Ramsay was far from the only pro-Nazi figure in the establishment and his fellow Right Club member, Grosvenor, was at the nexus of a web of aristocratic Nazi-sympathisers in Britain that included the Duke of Windsor (previously Edward VIII), the 12th Duke of Bedford and the Duke of Buccleuch. Together they made up a veritable fifth column of pro-Hitler influencers in pre-war and 1940s Britain.

Buccleuch was related to the King by marriage and was Lord Steward of the Royal Household from 1937 to 1940, but did not think it inappropriate to be the guest of honour at Adolf Hitler's lavish 50th birthday celebrations in April 1939, just five months before the outbreak of war. When it started, Buccleuch was at the forefront of efforts campaigning for a truce with his old friend Adolf – and one which would allow the Nazi leader to keep all the land he had invaded. Sounds familiar, doesn't it. These were Coco Chanel's friends and lovers. These were the people she lived with and associated with and while her antisemitism was not, as some of her biographers have claimed, a by-product of her association with Grosvenor, it was undoubtedly boosted and legitimised by their echo chamber. Grosvenor and Chanel split up in 1931, but the friendship would endure.

Having fallen in and out of love with one fascist, she swiftly fell for another. Shortly after Coco and Grosvenor separated, she met Paul Iribe, a violent, self-regarding, Basque artist who had worked for Cecil B. DeMille in Hollywood and who, in 1924, had ended up directing a comedy called *Changing Husbands*. The film flopped and its failure was a punch in the gut to Iribe's inflated ego. When he subsequently screwed up the set designs for the DeMille picture *The King of Kings* (1927) – a film, incidentally, which was widely criticised at the time for reviving anti-Jewish tropes – he was forced out of the studio and, subsequently, left Hollywood.

Coco too had been to Hollywood, lured by an offer of $1 million (equivalent to $18 million in 2023) by the Jewish studio mogul Samuel Goldwyn. It's not entirely clear what the strategy was beyond her acting as a glorified costume consultant, but setting her rabid antisemitism aside she happily took Sam's money and treated the divertissement as a sort of grand royal visit in the summer of 1930. Meanwhile, Goldwyn, who was himself Jewish, endeavoured to keep his Jewish employees out of her way.

Whether she met Iribe in France or Hollywood is not known, but either way, by the end of the year they were both back in Paris and, by 1931, despite Iribe being married to someone else, they were living together. In France before the First World War, Iribe had edited a satirical magazine called *Le Témoin* (*The Witness*). The magazine was noted for its artwork, witty observations and rabid antisemitism. Soon after his return from Hollywood, he fired up the press and brought it back.

His venture was funded by Chanel, who sometimes featured in the cover art. Thenceforth this supposedly satirical magazine pumped out anti-Jewish conspiracy theories with Iribe's eye-catching artwork appearing on the pages in between. France, according to the editorial line, was being destroyed by a cabal of Jewish "bankers" and "red rabbles" who made up a "Judeo Mafia" and the country needed to "wake up". The usual, depressing, toxic language of hate, but what made *Le*

Témoin particularly pernicious was that it looked good, appeared clever and seemed – to the readership at least – to be a witty modern magazine. Chanel's capital raised it to a high production standard, giving it the sheen of a respectable "alternative viewpoint" rather than the nasty little hate rag it was. And how could Iribe be that bad, when his magazine was so, well… arty and his girlfriend was the legendary Coco Chanel?

Le Témoin was monetising hate long before InfoWars and its imitators – but doing it in tasteful, pastel colours and Art Deco design. A page of the 24th February 1933 edition of *Le Temoin*, reprinted in Hal Vaughan's *Sleeping with the Enemy*, features Chanel as a half-dead, semi-naked Marianne, the embodiment of France itself, being drooled over by cartoonish depictions of Jewish men rubbing their hands. Hatred had never been so artfully and exquisitely rendered.

As bourgeois right-wing French readers lapped it all up, across the border, Hitler was drawing up plans for the anti-Jewish Nuremberg Laws. Decrees that would take away their German citizenship, forbid sexual relations between Jews and non-Jews and eventually rob millions of people of their education, their property, their dignity and, ultimately, their lives. One month before they were enacted, in August 1935, Iribe had a heart attack while showing off on the tennis court and died between the tram lines while Chanel looked on from a deck chair in horror.

Bereaved once again, Coco turned, with the encouragement of her old friend Misia, to morphine. Misia was already an addict, juggling jabs with a significant cocaine habit, and Coco fell into a drug dependency that stayed with her for the rest of her life.

On the plus side she was now the most successful businesswoman in the world, but even that brought problems because being at the top means that you have only one way to fall. New designers like the Italian Schiaparelli had appeared on the scene and, aged 53, Chanel, the Queen of Parisian fashion, was beginning to feel her age. Slumbering in a morphine-induced stupor in her many perfectly furnished homes, she began a long, slow descent into irrelevance and rage.

* * *

In 1936, industrial unrest gripped France and a general strike spread terror among the business classes. As the Jewish French Prime Minister, Léon Blum, the leader of the left-wing Popular Front, appealed for calm and sought to restore order, Coco was not alone among France's wealthiest antisemites in believing that a massive conspiracy was unfolding. Matters deteriorated rapidly and when there was a run on the nation's gold supplies, the mood on the streets took on a distinctly *1789* air.

Even Chanel's workers went out on strike, locking themselves inside her boutique on the Rue Cambon before putting up a sign that read *OCCUPIED*. It tipped Jew-hating, communist-loathing Chanel over the edge and more so because, like capitalists down the ages, she believed that she treated her workforce well and that they should simply be grateful for it. Chanel, like her former paramour Grosvenor, saw communism and not the rising tide of Naziism in Germany as the real threat to France, and determined to make a principled stand against her employees. But before matters could escalate, Blum struck a historic pact. He had been elected PM with the backing of 85% of the then entirely male French electorate on a mandate of reform and a legal agreement known as *Les accords de Matignon* followed, delivering ground-breaking legislation which guaranteed workers paid holidays, a blanket wage increase, the right to strike and a 40-hour working week.

The agreement was signed between the government and the unions, ending the strikes, but Chanel continued to seethe. The "betrayal" by her girls was not forgotten and when war broke out in 1939, she took her revenge, using the moment as an excuse to lay off 3,000 staff. A year later, with the Nazi Blitzkrieg storming into France, she moved back into the Ritz with her retinue of maids in tow.

If she was going to have to suffer a war, she intended to do so in style – and that is precisely what she did.

In *Remembered Laughter*, Cole Lesley's 1977 biography of his former employer Noël Coward, Cole records that in 1940, Coward, who was staying at the Ritz on his way back to London, very nearly got trampled by Chanel while she was making her way to the air raid shelter, with one maid, Jeanne, trailing behind, carrying her mistresses' gas mask... on a cushion.

On 14th June 1940, the German Army marched into Paris. Shortly afterwards, the Ritz became a privileged venue, reserved only for the German High command and certain well-connected French exceptions. Chanel was one of the latter and remained in her apartments and continued to dine in style – even as the France beyond the elegant curtains fell under occupation. It was at the Ritz, in that first summer of 1940, that she met a handsome German officer, by the name of Baron Häns Gunther von Dincklage.

Von Dincklage was an officer in the Abwehr and known to all as "Spatz". He was to be the last man she ever loved and in the words of her former flame and mentor, the poet Pierre Reverdy, he was to become her "damnation".

Spatz had been operating as an intelligence officer and propagandist in France and Switzerland for two decades. In the 1920s, he had worked for Weimar Germany but, much like Coco Chanel, was singularly devoid of moral principles and with the rise of the Nazis became – in 1933 – Hitler's star Abwehr agent in Paris. French intelligence was onto him almost from the start, but it didn't stop Spatz and his half-Jewish wife Maximiliane in their recruitment efforts of propagandists and spies, as well as their funding of pro-German newspapers and magazines. To subvert his work, French Intelligence leaked his identity to the press, and he was forced to flee to Switzerland and then North Africa, divorcing his wife along the way, lest her Jewish heritage slow his career advancement.

In wartime Paris, Spatz and Coco's relationship flourished, and they were often to be seen dining together with the Nazi ambassador to Paris, Otto Abetz, who held elaborate dinners at his palatial homes in Paris and at the Château de Chantilly, some 30 miles (50 km) outside the city. These invitations were the "hot tickets" of collaborationist French society, and guests would dine beneath great art treasures looted from the Jewish Rothschild family.

While the gaiety and frivolity continued in high society, wartime life was a struggle for ordinary Parisians. Post-invasion adult rations in France amounted to 350 grams of bread a day; 50 grams of cheese and 300 grams of meat a week; and 50 grams of rice, 250 grams of pasta, 200 grams of margarine and 500 grams of sugar a month.

That meant that from 1940 onwards, most French people were consuming roughly 1,300 calories a day, well below the recommended average intake of 2,000 (for women) and 2,500 (for men), and things only got worse as the war progressed. In 1942 rations were reduced by 12% and while criminals running the Black Market grew fat on profits, everyone else started to starve.

Meanwhile, the French economy was in tatters: by 1941 inflation was up 50% and the cost of living was up by 65%. To add insult to injury, the Germans were charging France 20 million (£6.63 million in 2023) Reichsmarks a day for the privilege of being occupied and pegged the French Franc at parity to the German currency, making everything cheap for the occupying forces.

Chanel, living at the Ritz and dining out with influential Nazi figures, was almost wholly unaffected by any of this – and that would become a really terrible look in post-war France, so she would later claim that she too had lived a simple life in the occupied city, riding about on the Metro and living off meagre rations. It was, as they say in French, *super grosses conneries.*[*]

And that was far from the only lie she told about her activities. In her 1944 interview with Muggeridge, Chanel suggested that she had only consorted with the Germans to secure the release of her nephew-cum-son André from a POW camp. And yes, she did use her contacts to

---

[*] Massive bollocks.

get him home and it is also true that Spatz may have been playing her. The professional spy and troublemaker was, after all, on personal terms with Hitler – he had been received by the Nazi dictator in 1941 and had also had at least one audience with Goebbels. The idea that he couldn't have used his influence to get André out of the camp seems ridiculous, and he may well have manipulated her for his and the regime's ends.

It was Spatz who introduced her to a French traitor, Baron Louis de Vaufreland. Through him she was introduced to another Abwehr agent, called Neubauer, who told her that he could secure André's release if she ran an intelligence-gathering mission for him to Madrid.

Perhaps naively believing that she could play the Nazis to her advantage, and by all accounts seizing the opportunity to have a bit of time in neutral Spain, Coco agreed and was enrolled as an Abwehr agent with the number F-7124 and given the codename "Westminster" after her well-connected ex-boyfriend.

It's unclear what that first mission to Spain entailed, beyond intelligence gathering of "political information", but Coco and de Vaufreland did dine with a British diplomat, Brian Wallace, who later filed a report to London. Having returned to France, Chanel was delighted to find that the Abwehr had kept their word and André had been released. Now seeking to realise the full potential of her new connections, she set about trying to seize back control of Chanel No. 5. To that end she tried to use Aryan laws, implemented by the Nazis, to rob the Jewish Wertheimer family of the percentage they took from her perfume franchise. This had been a long game for Chanel, who had grown to bitterly resent the Wertheimer deal and believed they had stolen her intellectual property.

With a Nazi spy for a boyfriend and the network that went with it, she might have thought it would be easy.

Through de Vaufreland, Chanel met a Gestapo bureaucrat called Kurt Blanke, who was head of *Entjudung* – the department responsible for stealing money, homes and possessions off the Jews. Seizing back her fragrance by recourse to racist laws did not appear to bother her. But just as the return of the fragrance seemed to be within her grasp, Chanel discovered that she had been brilliantly outwitted and outplayed. Before moving to America, the Wertheimers had made a deal with a Cherbourg businessman called Felix Amior, which involved him effectively being the puppet CEO of the firm until the war's end, when they could return safely to Europe and take back control of the business.

That was not all. In addition, the Wertheimers had engaged in a little corporate espionage. A brilliant 33-year-old employee called Herbert Thomas had been sent undercover to France in August 1940 to retrieve the secret chemical formula for Chanel No. 5 and to bring it back to America. Thomas had succeeded and No. 5 was now being produced outside of the country for the first time.

Without the Wertheimer deal it is unlikely that Chanel No. 5 would ever have become such a highly sought after and hugely successful global brand. But Chanel seemed unable to grasp that any more than the fact that the 10% she received from it had made her very wealthy indeed. She was, in short, greedy, and her willingness to use Nazi, anti-semitic laws to try to take the business of them is in another league altogether. It made her a collaborator, a Nazi fellow traveller and a thief.

By 1943 the tide was turning and so were Chanel's fortunes. Across the English Channel, the Bureau Central de Renseignements et d'Action (Free French Intelligence Service) had marked her card, just as it had those of the actress Arletty and the singer Maurice Chevalier. As the war turned against the Axis powers, a reckoning was coming and the wily fox Spatz, sensed it too. So, he hatched a plan and, in early 1943, he and Chanel travelled to Berlin to convince his bosses that his girlfriend could broker a peace with her old personal friends Winston Churchill and Hugh Grosvenor, the Duke of Westminster, and perhaps end the war.

In the Reich capital, they met Spatz's boss, Walter Schellenberg – Heinrich Himmler's right-hand man, who was also a late convert to reality now that Germany was losing. Schellenberg not only knew the game was up but was also increasingly concerned about Hitler's sanity, fearing, correctly, that he would be willing to take Germany down with him rather than surrender.

At the SS headquarters at Berkaer Strasse, Chanel, Spatz and another German agent (Momm) went to work. They explained that Coco knew the British PM and, what's more, that her ex-lover Grosvenor was a pillar of British aristocratic society, a relative of the King and probably sympathetic to the cause. If Coco could open channels of communication, perhaps a deal could be struck, and the war could be ended. The plan was hugely ambitious, one might even say deluded, but Schellenberg agreed to go along with it. Chanel would return to Madrid and try and establish contact with London via the British Ambassador Sir Samuel Hoare. Spatz would act as intermediary in Paris and pass on any messages to Schellenberg. Chanel agreed to all of this on the condition that her old friend Vera Bate, who was currently residing in a cell in Italy, could come along.

Vera Bate (now Vera Bate Lombardi) was not only an old friend of Coco's but also of the PM's wife, and key adviser, Clemmie Churchill, and it was she who Winston had briefly met on that first encounter with Chanel in 1928 at the Ritz. A bisexual British woman who had remarried a key member of the Italian Fascist Party, Alberto Lombardi, she had come under growing suspicion from Mussolini's intelligence services during the war and in 1943 was imprisoned on charges of spying for MI6.

Spatz went to work and, via a senior Abwehr agent in Paris, got Vera out of prison, before bringing her over from Italy to be recruited into the operation. The mission was codenamed Operation Modellhut – literally "model's hat". Things started well, with Vera and Coco travelling under the guise of a business trip to neutral Spain. But nobody seems to have explained to Vera what she was meant to be doing and once safely across the border, she threw a well-aimed *spaniard* in the works. A post-war MI6 interrogation of Schellenberg concluded:

"On her arrival in that city... instead of carrying out the part that had been assigned to her she denounced all and sundry as German agents to the British authorities ... In view of this obvious failure, contact was immediately dropped with Chanel and Lombardi and Schellenberg does not know whether any communication was subsequently handed to Churchill through this woman."

A year later, Paris was liberated. Late in the summer of 1944, having started to give away hundreds of Chanel No. 5 bottles, Coco was called before a FFI *épuration* committee and treated everyone present with the contempt she felt they deserved. Incredibly, especially given all that was known about her and all that she had done, she was released that same day. It seems incredible. The designer had been assigned an Abwehr codename and number and actively engaged in two espionage missions on behalf of the Nazis. She had tried to use Nazi laws to seize control of a French perfume empire. And yet despite all the retribution going on all around – they simply let her go.

Perhaps it happened on account of all those high-powered friends in the British aristocracy. Maybe the calculation was made that to save everyone embarrassment it would just be better to forget about it all. Or perhaps it was that the multimillionaire businesswoman, the very embodiment of French fashion, was simply too big a figure to fail in the public's eyes.

Chanel knew who was responsible and told her niece Gabrielle that Winston Churchill had personally intervened on her behalf. Churchill's old friend Duff Cooper, a former associate, and now sworn enemy of Grosvenor's, had been installed as the ambassador to de Gaulle's provisional government and in aristocratic circles, like criminal gangs, old friends help out old friends, even when they have behaved like traitors.

So maybe – for once in her life – she was telling the truth.

* * *

Chanel, then, was spared the humiliations of the horizontal collaborators. She faced no abuse, was not arrested or even properly interrogated. Her head was not shaved, and she was not paraded in the streets – she was not even put before Courts of Justice or sentenced to *dégradation nationale* (national demotion) which would have seen her stripped of her nationality.

Even as her Nazi boyfriend Spatz was hidden in Germany and Austria, she continued at liberty, reopened her boutiques and carried on as usual.

Of course, she did. She was rich and powerful and famous. The savagery was at the end and for the most part – only for a few examples and the little people and she was no longer one of those.

By 1945, Spatz and Chanel were living in exile in Switzerland, but the relationship did not last. Post-war investigations, which turned up Chanel's Abwehr agent number, were not taken further and, though branded "deceptive" when called to give evidence against her old fellow collaborator Baron Louis de Vaufreland, she was untouched by scandal. She continued to support Spatz and his old associate Schellenberg. Spatz later fled to fascist Spain where he lived out his retirement, funded by Coco, before returning to West Germany to die there in 1976.

Schellenberg was released from prison in 1952 on account of his failing health and died a few months later in Turin.

Chanel paid for his funeral.

* * *

In 1954, aged 71, and after a gap of 15 years, Chanel reopened her Couture House and made one of the most extraordinary business and fashion comebacks in history. Her new collection, presented on 5th February (she was still superstitious) caused a sensation. It was funded by her old frenemy Pierre Wertheimer and introduced the Chanel jacket, which redefined women's fashion of the time. The era's most famous actress, Marilyn Monroe, had already made it a matter of record (in 1952) that she wore only "Chanel Number 5" to bed and posed with a bottle of the fragrance the same year that the new collection appeared.

Coco's name and signature style were back and in the decade that followed her business empire would flourish once more. With her return came all the usual myth-making that we have seen thus far in the book. Films were made, books written and sardonic interviews given. Her iconic pink suit would even be put centre-stage at the most famous assassination in history, when Jackie Kennedy sported it that November day in Dallas, Texas, in 1963.

There was inevitably, a musical made about her too.

Coco! was written by Alan Jay Lerner, one half of the team that had penned *Camelot*, and the composer André Previn. When told that she was going to be played by "Hepburn", Chanel was apparently delighted, believing she was getting Audrey – but she was mistaken and to her bitter disappointment got 60-year-old Katharine Hepburn instead. The veteran Hollywood star played Coco as a wisecracking New Yorker – and it was a minor hit on Broadway to the extent that when Chanel died many of the obituaries made mention of it.

That end came on Sunday, 10th January 1971, when having returned from her daily walk through the Place Vendôme, Gabrielle Bonheur "Coco" Chanel, began to feel unwell and some moments later died, in understated style, in a suite of rooms at the Paris Ritz, where she had lived itinerantly since 1934. Her last words, to her loyal maid Céline, were: "Well, that's how one dies" or perhaps "You see, this is how you die" – because like all saints and heroes, whether trend-setting, secular on not, the scripture of her life differs subtly depending on the gospel.

On 13th January, *The New York Times* reported that throngs had gathered outside the Church of the Madeleine in Paris to watch her funeral cortège go by. A misprint gave the late designer's age as 37 and Coco, who had lied about her date of birth for 50 years, no doubt would have approved. In his address, The Rev. Victor Chabanis said that she was "universally respected", but behind the scenes uncomfortable memories of her wartime behaviour were already being recalled.

In the years that followed there were more films about her life, although most cut off before the arc of the narrative reached the late 1930s. There was a reason – as you can see – for that. Coco, the lover of racist Dukes and Nazis, and herself an agent of the Abwehr, is not the stuff of which fairytales are spun. Her appalling selfishness, pettiness and greed sit at odds with the sophisticated global brand that bears her name. It is undoubtedly the reason why her wartime activities and personal opinions are kept as quiet as possible. For Chanel the legend and the brand were ultimately too big a name to fail. Like France's own wartime *résistancialisme* myth, perhaps many people simply prefer things that way.

As a businesswoman, Coco Chanel was a capitalist bar none. Her adult life was directed and dictated entirely by her need to be both powerful and rich. It made her a lot of money and by 1971, she was worth an estimated $100 million (about $8 billion today), making her one of the wealthiest business people in history. But, at the risk of going all parabalistic, it most certainly did not buy her happiness. Yes, she had all that so many modern superficial wannabes desire. She was famous, she was ludicrously rich, and she was widely admired, but it is notable that when she died, except for the hired help, Coco Chanel died very much alone.

Compare and contrast the life of Coco Chanel with that of billionaire tycoon Chuck Feeney who made his money selling – among other things – Chanel No. 5.

Born in 1931, in the middle of the Great Depression, Feeney went on to become very rich indeed. From 1960, his Duty-Free Shoppers Group (DFS), based in Hong Kong, began selling Western luxury items to visitors. Expanding into Europe and Hawaii, the company dominated the duty-free sector. But in the 1980s, having read *The Gospel of Wealth* by nineteenth-century philanthropist Andrew Carnegie, he decided to give all his money away – in secret.

In 1982, he created The Atlantic Philanthropies, a charitable trust, and two years later transferred his entire 38.7% stake in DFS into it without telling his business partners. For the next 15 years he anonymously gave his fortune away, but from 1997 onwards, after falling out with his DFS partners while seeking to sell the company, he went public – in part in the hope of encouraging others to do likewise.

Chuck Feeney was not like those philanthropists who make big statements and don't follow through.

By 2020, he had given his entire $8 billion fortune away for the benefit of other human beings. As of writing, Feeney is still alive and no longer has a jet-set lifestyle. He lives in a modest, rented two-bedroom apartment in San Francisco and already leaves a legacy of philanthropy across Africa, Asia, South America and some of the poorest communities in the USA.

In 2014, the billionaire Warren Buffett said of him: "He's my hero… he should be everyone's hero."

And Buffett was subsequently inspired to follow his example. In 2006 he made a commitment to gradually give all his stock to philanthropic foundations and he has since pledged to give 99% of his wealth away, either before or on the time of his death. The so-called "Giving Pledge" formally announced by Buffett and Bill Gates in 2010 has since taken off and currently has around 236 billionaires pledging their fortunes, amounting to $600 billion by the time of their deaths.

Which sounds great, but then, when you're dead, you don't really need your money, do you? And wouldn't it be better still if some of the names on the list and the firms they head up paid a little more income tax in the meantime, owned a few less houses and gave a little more?

It is noticeable that, as of yet, none of these pledgers have come close to giving it all away. And despite their largesse, both Gates and Buffett still have fortunes in excess of $100 billion, while fellow pledge-giver Elon Musk is worth an estimated $180 billion.

That's an awful lot of money that he's never going to spend.

CHAPTER SEVEN

HEROES OF EXPLORATION
CAPTAIN SCOTT

How to be Heroic, even in Failure

My homeland's centuries old love affair with heroic failure is in truth a symptom of that very British disease known as exceptionalism.

People who achieve great things on Britain's behalf and who go on to have long and fruitful lives may eventually, if they are lucky, wind up with a blue plaque on the wall of a childhood home, or perhaps a cul-de-sac named in their honour. But those who die miserable, stupid, deaths, having fucked up spectacularly in a totally futile endeavour, are pretty much guaranteed at least one gigantic memorial, poems, plaudits and enduring fame.

In the very heart of London stands Nelson's column, a tribute to the nation's best-known sailor, who died on 21st October 1805, at the height of the Battle of Trafalgar. It is such a ubiquitous London landmark that most of us who live here barely look up as we walk past, let alone give thought to the fact that if Nelson had survived and lived to a great age, few of us would have ever heard of him. Nelson, you see, got his massive phallic column because, like John F. Kennedy and Che Guevara, he managed to pull off an era-defining premature death* – and like them, it is critical to his myth.

---

* Lord Nelson was 47 when he died – a year older than JFK at the time of his assassination.

Some two hundred plus years after the event, Nelson's death and final words remain one of British history's greatest hits. The story is even more remarkable because when you pause to give it proper thought, this was one very silly end indeed. After all, what sort of idiot, one of the best-known people of their day, presents themselves on deck, in the midst of battle, against the advice of fellow officers, in his admiral's jacket, emblazoned with the Order of the Bath, the Knight Grand Cross of the Order of St Ferdinand and of Merit, the Order of The Crescent and the Grand Cross of the Order of Saint Joachim? The man might just as well have put on a sparkly fluorescent duck costume – cleared a space in the middle of the ship and written TARGET in French, in whopping great letters above his head.*

Nelson sealed the deal on immortality by winning his greatest victory at the very moment that he lost his life, proving once again that moulding a great legend, like delivering a great punch-line, is all in the timing.

Nelson gave posterity not one but two sets of memorable last words. First: "Kiss me, Hardy" (to Thomas Hardy, his close friend and commander of *HMS Victory*), which Hardy did, and secondly, "Thank God I have done my duty", which he is said to have repeated constantly until he drew his last breath. Later in the century, Victorian moralists, fearing that the whole "Kiss me, Hardy" thing was a bit, well... homo-erotic, began suggesting that he'd really said: "Kismet[†] Hardy" which was far more PG-friendly. But Nelson could not have said "kismet" for the simple reason that the word did not enter the lexicon until 1834 and gained currency only following the publication of a book of that title by Mrs. Newton Sears in 1877.

---

* You can see Nelson's coat, musket-ball hole and all, at the National Maritime Museum in Greenwich, a little over a mile away from where I am writing this. A tall man is often to be seen standing in front of the glass containing it mumbling, "what the actual fuck was he thinking". If you do see me, say hello.

† From the Turkish "qismet" and Arabic "qismah/qismat", meaning "portion" or "fate".

In other words, it's fake etymology and Nelson really did want a kiss, which is rather a touching thing.

Many of the stories we still buy into about the Battle of Trafalgar come courtesy of contemporary Admiralty spin. It's quite the rabbit hole but, in short, while the battle was a win, it didn't go quite as well as popular myth would have us believe. The notion that "Britannia rules the waves" after 1805 is also only half true.

Trafalgar came to matter primarily because of Nelson's death, which – like those of Princess Diana, Kennedy and Queen Elizabeth II – became bigger than the man himself. His funeral on 9th January 1806 was a major, emotionally charged cultural happening and until that point probably the largest public event in London's history. It was only the third state funeral ever held for a commoner, and its staging, by the Garter King of Arms, Sir Isaac Heard, set the template for those other grand state funerals that followed, both at home and abroad. Nelson's end was far from being the first stupid death in history, but it was very much part of a trend in the 19th century which saw romantic failure become a sort of British virtue. It's a narrative that has continued well into the modern era with self-taught ski jumper Eddie "The Eagle" Edwards being a case in point. Eddie achieved megastardom and became a global icon by coming last in everything he entered at the 1988 Winter Olympics and was very much the modern embodiment of Britain's love of failure. But this was just a continuation of a very long tradition.

Two months before Trafalgar, in August 1805, the flamboyant Scottish adventurer Mungo Park arrived in Gambia. Pumped on the success of his bestselling book *Travels in the Interior Districts of Africa*, he was looking for material for a sequel and intended to find it... at the source of the Niger.

Ignoring local expert advice that it was a *really* bad idea to travel in the rainy season, Park boldly set off into the interior with 40 men and before they had even reached the river, 29 had died from illness or accident. Once at their base camp, dysentery carried off another six, including, on October 28, his brother-in-law, Alexander Anderson, Park's right-hand man and, among the rabble left of the party, one of the few sane and sensible people.

Park wrote to his parents:"Your son my Dear friend has shut his eyes on the scenes of time & opened them on the Glories of Eternity."

Three days later he wrote to his wife, Anderson's sister, and told her that while "the greater part of the soldiers have died on the march during the Rainy Season... the healthy season has commenced, so that there is no danger of sickness and I have still a sufficient force to protect me from any insult in sailing down the river to the sea."

Having buried his comrades, Park acquired two canoes, tied them together, dubbed the boat *HMS Joliba* and set off down the river for the main event. Unfortunately, he had not only lost his most-trusted lieutenants but also managed to annoy and alienate pretty much everyone else in a wide vicinity. Traders in the region, suspicious of his motives and believing him to have imperial ambitions, wanted him killed and spread word to villages down the Niger delta that he was bringing trouble with him. Park made matters worse by loftily ignoring the local people and their customs and by failing to pay river tolls to tribal leaders. As such, he rolled from one lethal encounter to the next, as his band of men diminished further.

Two weeks into the expedition, having nearly been killed by a hippopotamus, *HMS Joliba* capsized on rocks, and Park and his men were left stranded in the middle of rapids. Local villagers, paranoid about his intentions, arrived shortly thereafter and began firing arrows at the party. Park and the surviving members of his expedition dithered, panicked and jumped into the river, where they disappeared beneath the waters never to be seen again.

For his extraordinary contribution to heroic failure, Park had an enormous memorial raised in his memory at Selkirk on the Scottish Borders and has a medal which since 1930 has been awarded by the Royal Scottish Geographical Society in his name. Impressive stuff.

Park was far from being the only Victorian willing to lose his life in a stupid endeavour, nor was it the maddest bit of self-sacrifice of the time. Major-General Rollo Gillespie's 1814 attack on a heavily defended Nepalese fortress in Kalunga, which he basically undertook by himself, was a particularly strong contender in the category.

Waving his sword above his head Gillespie yelled: "One shot more for the honour of (County) Down!", ran at the ramparts, promptly got shot through the heart and died on the spot.

Gillespie got a whopping great statue in his honour, mounted on a pillar 17 metre high in Comber in County Down, Northern Ireland.

Forty-one years later, in 1854, a new bar of idiocy was set during the Charge of the Light Brigade* at Balaklava, Crimea when a suicidal charge by British Cavalry saw 110 men pointlessly lose their lives. This famous cock-up was caused in no small part by the failure of two warring brothers-in-law – James Brudenell, the 7th Earl of Cardigan, and George Bingham, the 3rd Earl of Lucan – to communicate properly, leading to hundreds of men charging needlessly to their fate.

As he looked on, the French military observer General Pierre Bosquet uttered the immortal lines: "C'est magnifique, mais ce n'est pas la guerre; c'est de la folie."† Heroic stupidity can inspire great words and Alfred, Lord Tennyson penned perhaps his most famous work based on that event. It was one of many poems that romanticised British military hubris in the era and, in the end, Empire poetry would turn into an entire genre.

In 1892, at the peak of Britain's global imperial vanity, the Staffordshire-born poet Sir Henry John Newbolt wrote "Vitaï Lampada", perhaps the most famous example. Based on his own childhood experiences of playing cricket at Clifton College, the poem begins:

---

* The most famous depiction of the charge, the one that instantly springs to mind, and which is most frequently reproduced alongside depictions of the event, is not actually of the Charge of the Light Brigade. That painting, by Elizabeth Butler, is called *Scotland Forever* and depicts a charge by the Royal Scots Greys at Waterloo in 1815.
† "It's magnificent, but it's not war; it's madness."

"There's a breathless hush in the Close to-night —
Ten to make and the match to win —"

But soon the action has switched to Sudan, where the same boys, five years later, are taking on the Mahdist army in a fight to the death.

"The sand of the desert is sodden red, —
Red with the wreck of a square that broke; —
The Gatling's jammed and the Colonel dead,
And the regiment blind with dust and smoke."

The work is a paean to stiff-upper-lippery and courage in adversity. One man's sticky wicket in blinding light is the same chap's jammed machine gun* in East Africa fighting Somalis. But in both cases, if everyone remembers to "Play up! Play up! And play the game!", the boys of the Empire will see it through and if they die – well, the old school's roll of honour will impress visiting parents. Newbolt's poem, like Kipling's "If", became liturgy for generations of British public schoolboys. These were the institutions that had been built for the leaders of Empire – schools which, in the words of E.M. Forster, sent boys "forth into (the world) with well-developed bodies, fairly developed minds and under-developed hearts". Newbolt never actually served in the army, but he did see plenty of action at his desk at the War Propaganda Bureau (aka Wellington House) where he was hired, aged 53, in 1915, to stymie the unforgivable tide of truth that was leaking out from the Western Front. It must have been hell on this particular front line, trying to find a sharp pencil or a decent lunchtime restaurant nearby. For services to cannon fodder and gravestone

---

* The jammed gun is a reference to an actual event at the Battle of Abu Klea in January 1885 when the British Desert Column – hugely outnumbered – took on the Mahdist forces on their way to relieving the Siege and Khartoum. The British won the battle but failed to relieve Khartoum, where Gordon and his men were massacred.

makers, this "poet-propagandist" was awarded a knighthood in 1917 and made Companion of Honour by ghastly George V, in 1922. No doubt, he was very pleased with himself indeed.

The Great War saw many opportunities for pointless deaths, but one notable event – so bizarre that it sounds like a Monty Python sketch – certainly topped the rest.

The seven-day bombardment of German lines on the Somme in the last week of June 1916, had lulled the Allies into believing that the "Big Push" would be a stroll in a (albeit barbed-wire-filled) park. But understandably, new recruits, waiting anxiously for their first engagement, were slightly perturbed about the coming battle and all those German machine guns and shells. To quell such anxieties, a Dover College-educated 21-year-old officer called Captain Wilfred "Billie" Nevill, of the East Surrey Regiment, came up with a brilliant idea.

He would turn the Big Push into a sporting event.

Acquiring two footballs, Nevill told his men that the attack would be part of "The Great European Cup" and that the first Tommy to kick a ball into the German trenches would win a prize. The whistles blew at 7.30 a.m. on the morning of 1st July and the match began. Private L.S. Price of the 8th Royal Sussex takes up the commentary: "I saw an infantry man climb onto the parapet into No Man's Land, beckoning others to follow. As he did so he kicked off a football. A good kick. The ball rose and travelled well towards the German line. That seemed to be the signal to advance."

That infantry man was Private AA Fursey of number 6 platoon – and he was never seen again. Nevill, who had taken charge of the second football, dribbled it expertly to the enemy trenches before getting caught in the mesh of barbed wire and shot through the head. The week-long shelling had failed to break the German defences and 19,240 British soldiers were killed in the first day alone.

The good news was that apart from a few barbed-wire scrapes on their leather, the two footballs survived, and soon this insane event was being seized on as an example of British pluck. By the end of the week, Nevill was being held up as a hero.

Invoking Tennyson and Newbolt, a journalist called Claude Burton, who wrote under the pseudonym "Touchstone" for the *Daily Mail* wrote (yet another) pro-war poem:

> *"On through the hail of slaughter, where gallant comrades fall,*
> *Where blood is poured like water, they drive the trickling ball.*
> *The fear of death before them, is but an empty name;*
> *True to the land that bore them, the SURREYS played the game."*

Touchstone liked to write poems about the heroism of young men fighting and dying in France and even published a rousing anthology of his works called *Fife and Drum*, from the safety of his study in England. A month after penning this particular piece of work, on 1st August, he received a telegram from the War Office telling him that his own son had been killed in action, aged 23.

There is an old saying that comedy is tragedy plus time. And in the absurd deaths of Nevill and Fursey, there is a sort of bleak humour, of the sort so artfully portrayed in the 1989 comedy TV series set in the trenches, *Blackadder Goes Forth*.

It's funny. Or at least it is, until you start to dwell on Nevill and AA Fursey's extreme youth and naivety or poor Claude Burton and his young boy, slain before his life had even begun and for no real purpose. And the millions of other young lives stubbed out before they had had a chance to live – blown apart, drowned in mud or snared like rabbits on the razor wire for the ambitions of politicians, empires and Kings.

And then quite suddenly – it doesn't seem very funny at all.

* * *

Between the death of Nelson and the carnage of the First World War, there was another significant tragedy caused by British people's extraordinary self-belief – one that came to haunt Victorian Britain. On 19th May 1845, renowned naval officer Captain Sir John Franklin, who as a young midshipman had been present at the Battle of Trafalgar, led two ships, *HMS Erebus* and *HMS Terror*, on an expedition up into the Arctic Circle. His mission was to traverse the last segment of the fabled Northwest Passage and open up trade between Europe, North America and Asia.

But three years later, there was no word of the ships or the 129 men aboard them, and fears of the worst crept in. Franklin's wife Jane, with the help of powerful backers, began petitioning the Admiralty to send out search vessels, and a total of 39 attempts were subsequently to be made to find traces of the two ships and their crews. In 1854, that fate was revealed thanks to a much-neglected Orcadian hero called John Rae.

Born in Orkney in 1813, Rae grew up accompanying his father on trips to the mainland and beyond, and in the process developed something of a thirst for adventure. Having qualified as a surgeon in Edinburgh in 1833, he joined a ship, the *Prince of Wales,* and sailed to North-West Canada where the arrival of ice obliged him and the rest of the crew to sit out the winter on Charlton Island (Sivukutaitiarruvik). Captivated by the wild expanse of Northern Canada, Rae decided to stay on and was hired as a surgeon at a Hudson Bay trading fort known as Moose Factory in Ontario. Rae quickly befriended the local Cree tribe and became their student. He learned their language, how to make and use snowshoes, how to live off the land, the importance of keeping dry in Arctic survival, how to hunt caribou, build igloos and other shelters, and how to properly ice the runners of a sled.

He also discovered how to dress properly for the extreme conditions and adopted animal furs and seal skins – which he sported for a contemporary painting.

As he came from Orkney, with its Viking heritage and strong Nordic identity, he appears to have been completely unfettered by the preoccupations of most other, class-obsessed British imperialists of the time, who – if they noticed native people at all – saw them as little more than primitive know-nothings who were part of the scenery. Rae came to love and respect his hosts and their culture – and it was a mutual sentiment. The Inuit dubbed him *Aglooka*, aka Man of Big Steps, on the basis that he could cover distance faster than any other European contemporary and even some of his indigenous friends. Rae was, in short, that scourge of modern right-wing news commentators: woke as hell. And that dreaded, ghastly, wokery was to make him Scotland's, and indeed the UK's, greatest Arctic explorer.

Between 1845 and 1848, he made extensive journeys into the north of Canada and plotted and mapped the coast and course of rivers. That same year, when it became clear that the Franklin expedition had disappeared, Rae was the obvious man for the job and was appointed second-in-command by Sir John Richardson, a fellow Scottish surgeon, who was tasked with leading the mission. In that role, he made three journeys up along the Arctic coast with Inuit guides and interpreters. And then, in April and May 1854, six years after he had first set out to discover the fate of Franklin, Rae came across a group of Inuit people, who told him that while out hunting, four years earlier, they had seen a party of disorientated men, numbering about 40, hauling a boat along the coast of King William Island. The hunters followed them at a distance and watched them turn inland, where they caught up with them and communicated with gestures. Members of the British expedition told the Inuit that their ship had been crushed and that they were intending to keep moving in the hope of finding deer.

The following spring, when the hunters returned, they found graves and dead bodies and not a living soul.

Rae bought items from the hunters that they had salvaged, including a silver plate with Franklin's name engraved on the back, silver cutlery, clothing and a medal for the "second mathematical prize", awarded to John Irving, a member of the expedition when he had been at the Royal Naval College in Greenwich. Irving had been so proud of the award that he had carried it all the way to hell.

From Inuit accounts, Rae learned that: "Some of the bodies had been buried... some were in tents; others under the boat, which had been turned over to form a shelter, and several lay scattered about in different directions."

But then came the shocking detail: "From the mutilated state of many of the bodies and the contents of the kettles, it is evident that our wretched Countrymen had been driven to the last dread alternative – cannibalism – as a means of prolonging existence."

Franklin's surviving men had, in short, started eating their dead friends.

The Inuit were reluctant to take Rae on the ten-day trek to the graves and, respecting their word and the evidence, the explorer returned and filed an honest report of events. But nobody believed it. This, after all, was not how British gentlemen of the Royal Navy behaved. They would surely have died with dignity and grace and, to quote that later poem by Newbolt, played up and played the game. Cannibalism was a deed of savages, of distant unchristian tribes that needed to be converted or killed, not British subjects, with engraved silver plates and mathematical prizes on great missions, under the British flag.

Almost as one, the nation turned on him and Rae was ridiculed and branded a liar by Franklin's supporters, including his widow Jane who called him an "unrefined, coarse man" who had believed the words of "savages". Jane had become something of a celebrity in the wake of her husband's disappearance and popular ballads and poems had been written about her. Jane was much more than just "Franklin's wife" and was an explorer in her own right and in a curious way the disappearance had propelled her to a life that she might not have had, if her husband had returned. In an era when women were not supposed to be explorers, she defied her imposed limitations and travelled the Nile and led expeditions into Canada, contributing, in the process, far more to the understanding of the region than her husband ever had.

All of it made her something of a Victorian influencer and the suggestion that her husband's men had eaten each other risked his and her reputations getting cancelled.

So, Jane fought back, using the power of the press and her celebrity friends and soon, no less a figure than Charles Dickens had stepped up on her behalf to start trolling John Rae. In lengthy diatribes in his weekly column in *Household Words,* the great Victorian writer lashed out at the:

"Loose and unreliable nature of the Esquimax (Eskimo) representations.

We submit that the memory of the lost Arctic voyagers is placed, by reason and experience, high above the taint of this so easily-allowed connection; and that the noble conduct and example of such men... outweighs by the weight of the whole universe the chatter of a gross handful of uncivilised people.

Teach no one to shudder without reason, at the history of their end. Confide with their own firmness, in their fortitude, their lofty sense of duty, their courage, and their religion."

Rae's reputation was destroyed, and Jane spent the remainder of her life organising more futile search parties that bolstered hers. Books were written and statues erected in Franklin's great, glorious honour. Rae would not be vindicated for years.

The process began in 1869 when an American explorer of the Arctic, Charles Francis Hall, began gathering testimony from indigenous North Americans and met an Inuit woman called Eveeshuk who told him that: "One man's body when found by the Innuits had the flesh all on & not mutilated except the hands sawed off at the wrists – the rest a great many had their flesh cut off as if some one or other had cut it off to eat."

But most British people still refused to believe it and it wasn't until the 1980s and 1990s when archaeologists found the remains of that last camp that the truth was revealed. What the Inuit had told Rae was correct. The bones of Franklin's crew bore cut marks – and some had been cooked and broken in half so that the marrow could be sucked out of them.

In the horror of their utter desperation, these refined Victorian British gentlemen had eaten each other.

* * *

For centuries, sailors and navigators had known about a polar region to the north, which they called Arcticus, meaning "the great bear". The fourth-century Greek explorer Pytheas of Massalia* (Marseilles) even claimed to have visited it and, though his account was doubted for centuries, the region he dubbed "Thule" may have been Iceland – or possibly the tip of Norway. As successive ages followed and the Earth was mapped and explored, there was increasing speculation that there might be an "opposite great bear" (or Antarcticus) – to the south.

From the late 1700s, as sealers and whalers ventured south in search of stronger winds, better currents and richer prey, they discovered that the region was riven with dangers that included sudden, dramatic, changes in weather and icebergs the size of Caribbean islands.

Captain James Cook's ship *Resolution* crossed the Antarctic Circle three times between 1773 and 1774 and charted a course that came within 80 miles of the coast, but it wasn't until 27th January 1820 that a Russian expedition led by naval officers Fabian von Bellingshausen and Mikhail Lazarev spotted the mainland continent of Antarctica for the first time. Three days later, in a trend that would persist, the British turned up late when a ship called *William* spotted the Trinity Peninsular – the most northern point of the continent.

Despite having established its existence, it was another 75 years before there was a documented landing on the ice-covered expanse.

---

* Marseilles aka Massalia was a Greek colony. Founded on the East Coast of modern-day France in c. 600 BCE, it is the oldest inhabited city in France and one of the oldest in Europe today.

In 1894, Carsten Borchgrevink, a restless Norwegian explorer and childhood playmate of Roald Amundsen, joined an expedition organised by a Norwegian businessman called Henryk Bull and headed south via Australia, in what was essentially the nineteenth-century equivalent of a journey to the Moon. On 24th January 1895, the crew reached Cape Adare and moored their ship, *Antarctic*, off the coast of Victoria Land. With conditions calm and visibility good, Borchgrevink led a party ashore where a 17-year-old New Zealander, Alexander von Tunzelmann, became the first documented human being to stumble onto the icy continent.

Alex Von Tunzelmann, his great-great-nephew and a British historian, tells me: "My dad knew him growing up in NZ. The family story suggests he was the first man in Antarctica because he fell off (the) boat."

If true, the last continent of Earth was conquered by a teenager who lost his balance, which is not how great legends are meant to be, so Borchgrevink rewrote the tale and had himself planting his feet firmly on the ice first instead.

Like Orcadian John Rae before him, Borchgrevink and his sponsors were considered outsiders by the British establishment – Norwegians no less, who in 1895, came from a nation that had yet to gain its independence. The achievements of these jumped-up "Vikings" annoyed the hell out of the class- and status-obsessed Royal Geographical Society (RGS) and its President Sir Clements Markham. Markham had very strong views on how polar exploration should be conducted and, as the self-appointed headmaster of global exploration, looked dimly on the opinions of far more experienced foreigners who actually had some idea about how to do it. Markham had particularly strong views on man-hauling, the practice of physically pulling sleds across the ice, which he saw as a noble and effective means of travel, and so had a strict "no skis, no dogs" approach.

While he delivered lofty papers on the subject to earnest members of the RGS in dusty London rooms, the Norwegians boarded their ships and set about conquering the poles.

In October 1897, tabloid newspaper owner, cinema pioneer and evangelical vegetarian Sir George Newnes sponsored Borchgrevink's return to Antarctica, giving him £35,000 (the equivalent of £3.7 million as at 2023) for an expedition that would attempt to last a year on the continent and see how far south it could get.

Borchgrevink set sail from the Port of London on 22nd August 1898 on his ship *Southern Cross* and landed at Cape Adare in February 1899, where his party of men put up two prefabricated cabins that still stand today. A month after their arrival, *Southern Cross* left Borchgrevink, a party of nine others and 70 dogs behind and made its way back to New Zealand for the coming winter to avoid the risk of the ship getting crushed in the pack ice. Though a man of great ambitions, Borchgrevink was not a natural leader and the expedition was beset with problems that included fires, fallouts and the death of their zoologist, Nicolai Hansen, along with all the psychological and physical challenges that come with living in one of the toughest environments on Earth.

In everything, Borchgrevink had taken his lead from the formidable contemporary figure that was Fridtjof Nansen. A man who, handily for an Arctic explorer, was unarguably one of the coolest people of his or perhaps any age, Nansen would go on to become one of Norway's (and Europe's) greatest figures, winning the Nobel Peace Prize for his work in leading efforts after the First World War to end humanitarian crises among refugees. In addition to that and his foundational efforts in creating the League of Nations, he was an oceanographer, oracle, innovator, diplomat and fashion icon who looked like a rock star.

Nansen was the towering figure of the heroic age of Arctic exploration and, in 1888, had led the first expedition across the Greenland ice-cap. In preparation, he had invented – almost from scratch – the insulated sleeping bag, snow goggles and a small portable cooking stove and had specially designed clothing made that was suitable for Arctic travel. Seven years later in 1895, aged 34, with his colleague Hjalmar Johansen, he made an extraordinary attempt on the North

Pole and survived, crucially, because he had known what he was doing and when to turn around.

He was in fact a huge admirer of John Rae and was particularly impressed by the Orcadian's willingness to learn from indigenous experts and, like them, use dogs, snow shoes and animal skins. Nansen had largely copied Rae's template and taken pains to learn survival skills from indigenous people and even hired two Sami people for his expeditions. Amundsen in turn took his inspiration from Nansen, and what followed is one of the great paradoxes of the story in that the Norwegians succeeded where so many British expeditions failed largely because of the example of a Scotsman whom the British Establishment had conspired so hard to forget.

Borchgrevink had consulted Nansen at length and, though he lost his zoologist, the other 8 men survived 11 months together and not only gathered critically important scientific data but also proved that it was possible to live in the coldest place on Earth.

It may have been a "British expedition" on paper, but his return was met in England with a positively muted response.

On Newnes's insistence and despite being conducted under a British flag, the mission had been made up almost entirely of Norwegians with just one Australian and two British men on the team. That was bad enough but the published account, with its very un-British bragging, annoyed the cliquish, hierarchical, Royal Naval establishment and – worse – made them fear that the great prize of the South Pole might be snatched by some upstart Scandinavians who were better explorers than them.

Borchgrevink's many successes were known long before his return to London and they gave the RGS the kick up the comp-ass it sorely needed. Soon, Sir Clements Markham had secured funding of £90,000 (£14 million 2023), the patronage of the Prince of Wales, the Queen herself and even Foreign Secretary Arthur Balfour, the future prime minister who saw, in the Heroic Age of Antarctic Exploration, an opportunity to demonstrate British supremacy in the era of rising German power.

For the British, it was a matter of pride that this new frontier of exploration would end with a Union Jack at the South Pole, and Markham had already picked the hero who would make it happen. His name was Lieutenant Robert Falcon Scott and, although he did not know it yet, he was destined to become history's most famous runner-up.

* * *

Antarctica is unique among the continents of the world in having no trees or shrubs or native human beings. Covered in 7 million cubic miles of ice, which is sometimes as much as three miles thick, the temperature can fall as low as -65°C deep in the polar winter. Those who have been there talk of Antarctica's "otherness". Herbert Ponting, the photographer and pioneering documentary filmmaker, who accompanied Scott on his last mission of 1910–12, described it as "nature in her most savage and merciless mood".

Mark Brandon, the polar oceanographer, puts it more succinctly: "the ice does something to you".

Scott arrived first in 1902 at the head of that British National Antarctic Expedition (later better known as the *Discovery* Expedition). Hopes and expectations were high, but there were also unwelcome distractions. Polar expeditions at the time were forever engaged in a tug of war between science and adventure and, though Scott had wanted to concentrate on the pole and have complete autonomy over the mission, he and Markham had been obliged to compromise. The stated aim of the expedition was to be noble and scientific and Scott's men would explore and properly map the Ross Sea region, gather geological samples, measure the atmosphere and study the local wildlife – including the penguin colonies.

The assault on the pole was deemed secondary, but was clearly Scott's main ambition.

For many of us, and certainly those who grew up watching it endlessly repeated on TV, Scott is as synonymous with John Mills, who portrayed him in the 1948 film *Scott of the Antarctic*, as Kenneth More (who also appeared in the film as Lt. Teddy Evans) is with Group

Captain Douglas Bader. But Scott was a far more complicated man than the cinematic portrayal of him.

First let's consider his motivation. In the Heroic Age, leading a grand polar expedition was a surefire path to swift promotion, medals and glory, and Scott was a hugely, hugely ambitious individual who chased after it all. Unfortunately, he came along with a whole trunk load of "issues" and very deep human flaws. Fixated with class and rank, duteous to Markham's curious disregard for skis and dogs, and hungry to prove himself as a "great man", Scott had, in short, been drawn to polar exploration largely out of self-advancement. And in many respects, he was ill suited to the task.

Roland Huntford, author of *Scott and Amundsen* (1979), wrote that the young naval lieutenant's favourite expression was: "'What does it all mean?' because he could not find a meaning in life; perhaps it was the expression of the black depression that regularly descended on him; a hopelessness that alternated with bouts of violent elation".

Possessed of a curious, almost manic fatalism, Scott was incredibly sentimental about people and animals. Apsley Cherry-Garrard, one of the members of his last fateful mission, would write in 1922 that Scott "cried more easily than any man I have ever known".

Obsessed with his mother, governed by his friendship with fellow explorer Edward Wilson, utterly humourless and prone to the notion that heroism was wrapped up in what Huntford calls "wanton self-sacrifice and bungling", Scott lacked what NASA in the 1960s would dub "the right stuff" for the men it sent into space. The writer Tom Wolfe defined that characteristic as "an inexpressible blend of confidence, skill, and machismo" – an almost machine-like quality. The character strengths necessary to be an effective 1960s' astronaut were very similar indeed to those required for early Arctic exploration and the erratic, sentimental Scott was far too governed by his emotions to be the man for the job.

To his credit, he did at least have the good sense to consult Nansen in correspondence at some length before setting out. The expedition's ship, the *Discovery*, was fitted out on specifications set by the Norwegian, and passage to Antarctica went off largely without event – although much slower than anticipated due to a detour made to undertake a magnetic survey. They arrived at McMurdo Sound, Antarctica on 8th February 1902 and remained on the ship through the winter, in a spot they called Winter Quarters Bay, conducting scientific experiments and practising for the adventure ahead.

While Scott was preparing for the attempt on the pole, many of his existing biases were confirmed and particularly his dismissive opinion of his pack of 25 dogs, which he had acquired on Nansen's advice from a Russian handler. Despite dutifully buying the dogs, Scott had neglected to hire anyone experienced with Siberian sledge-huskies who was able to run them. Matters were made considerably worse because the animals only understood Russian and were given a diet of fish that saw most of them fall ill.

That failure to handle the dogs correctly or bring along someone with the expertise required was a critical error – and one that Scott only half addressed on his later misadventure.

On 2nd November, Scott and his two companions, Third Officer Ernest Shackleton – later to become famous in his own right – and his friend, the expedition's doctor and zoologist, Edward Wilson, set out for the pole with two four-men supporting parties.

They made good progress and, nine days later, passed Borchgrevink's record for going south.

But from there on it all started going horribly wrong. The diet of rotten fish was making the dogs ill and unpredictable and the party was obliged to kill several of the weaker animals for meat to feed the rest of the pack – much to Scott's sentimental disgust. The far greater problem was that in addition to frostbite and exhaustion, the three men were almost certainly suffering from scurvy, even before they started running out of food. The pressure got to everyone, and Shackleton and Scott fell out badly. As Shackleton's health began to deteriorate, his leader made matters significantly more problematic by making it very clear indeed that he had no time for "invalids".

Roland Huntford explains in his book *Scott and Amundsen*: "Survival in extreme conditions depends on judgement and intuition. Conflict, suppressed or not, disturbs both. It is an invitation to disaster. Before the tensions within the party... the dangers of the Polar region paled. Men, as Amundsen liked to say, are the unknown factor in the Antarctic."

The three men were starving and miles from base and in his desperation to reach the pole and achieve glory, Scott was putting everyone's lives at risk. It became clear to the other two men that if they didn't turn around, they were all going to die. With Scott and Shackleton barely on speaking terms it was Wilson who eventually managed to convince Scott to turn around, and something approaching sanity kicked in.

On 28th December, they crossed the 82nd parallel. Two days later, on 30th December, Scott and Wilson went on ahead, leaving Shackleton behind, and having reached 82°17'S made the decision to return to the *Discovery*. The journey back saw open hostility break out between Scott and an ever-weaker Shackleton, with Wilson cast in the role of peacemaker. They made it, but it was a damn near-run thing.

Shackleton was invalided home on the relief ship. Scott remained for another year before returning, on *Discovery*, in September 1904. He had failed to reach the South Pole, but the scientific achievements he had so resisted filled the vacuum where his triumph should have been. The following year the newly promoted Captain Scott published a book, *The Voyage of the Discovery*, which laid the failure in large part, at Shackleton's frostbitten feet. It sold well and Scott became the pre-eminent British polar explorer of the *Heroic Age*. Scott would define what polar exploration was and at its heart was an almost biblical virtue of suffering and pain. Determination and physical courage – the man-hauling of heavy loads over crevices, in horrific conditions – was now the factory setting for indomitable British spirit.

Across the North Sea, Amundsen scratched his head at the curious spectacle of it all and went back to training with his dogs.

* * *

Three years after his return, in 1907, Scott met and then, in 1908, married the British artist Kathleen Bruce, a pupil of Rodin and one of the most significant sculptors of her era. It was to be a brief and tempestuous relationship and his mother-fixation and bromance with Wilson nearly put her off. But she relented and in 1909 the couple had a son, Peter Markham Scott – later to become famous in his own right as a TV naturalist and one of the founders of the World Wildlife Fund.* A year after that, in 1910, Scott set sail once more – for the South Pole, at the head of the *Terra Nova* Expedition.

The greatest monomyth of Edwardian exploration was about to play out and, unlike the adventures of Odysseus, King Arthur or the *Epic of Gilgamesh*, it was sponsored by Oxo, Bovril, Heinz Baked Beans, Fry's Cocoa and Burberry.

The *Terra Nova* mission was to be an entirely privately funded venture and Scott had had to raise £40,000, equivalent to roughly £3.75 million today, which meant taking those sponsorship deals. In addition, in the build-up, there were lecture tours and fundraising efforts and two members of the team, Apsley Cherry-Garrard and Captain Lawrence "Titus" Oates, paid to come along. Both contributed around £1,000 each (around £95,000 today), meaning that – much like Musk-era Twitter – heroes were now able to buy their blue ticks.

All the time that Scott had been busy lecturing, writing books and garnering sponsorship deals, his nemesis Roald Amundsen had been keeping himself busy. A veteran of the Belgian Antarctic Mission of 1897–99, the Norwegian had followed his hero Nansen and John Rae's lead by studying survival skills and living with Inuit hunters he had befriended in the Canadian wilds. Having done so, he set out on one of the most astonishing adventures of the era.

---

* Or WWF, although the initials now stand for World Wide Fund for Nature.

Between 1903 and 1906, and much to the chagrin of the British, he led a mission that finally managed to successfully traverse the North-west Passage. Amundsen – the upstart Norwegian – had achieved what Franklin had failed to do, and without the help of a single silver salver. His success also came with some remarkable timing, for while he was away in 1905, Norway gained her independence from Sweden. The serendipitous timing meant that Amundsen's victory became a matter of immense national pride to Norway, and Arctic travel became synonymous with the renaissance of Norwegian identity.

In 1909, the year before Scott headed south, Amundsen had been planning a trip to conquer the North Pole, but after learning that the American explorers Frederick Cook and Robert Peary had both claimed to have reached the North Pole, in April 1908 and April 1909 respectively, he decided to take Nansen's old ship, the *Fram*, and try to conquer the South Pole instead. Although, critically, he told nobody – not his backers, not his family and not even his crew of his plan.

On 7th June 1910, the 5th anniversary of Norwegian independence and five days (Coco Chanel would have approved) before Scott left Cardiff in the *Terra Nova*, Amundsen quietly set sail for Antarctica, slipping out of Oslo without any of the fanfare that would attend Scott's departure. Those master hunters, his Inuit tutors, had taught him the importance of stealth, and he informed his men of his real intentions only when he reached Madeira, wiring Scott on 9th September:

"Beg to inform you *Fram* proceeding Antarctic – Amundsen".

In Britain and Norway, the announcement resulted in a public backlash with everyone, except Nansen, aghast that someone could behave in such an underhand way. Markham, now late of the presidency at the RGS, was particularly infuriated by the move and fired off angry letters to anyone who would read them. It simply was not cricket for a gentleman to behave in this manner.

But that was OK, because nobody played cricket in Norway and the race was now on.

* * *

The *Terra Nova* Expedition nearly ended before it had begun. On the journey south, via New Zealand, the ship almost sank in a storm and later found itself in thick pack-ice, which hampered the journey further. The expedition arrived at Ross Island on 4th January 1911 and Scott's men started to make a base at Cape Evans. A month later, Scott ordered the *Terra Nova* east to explore King Edward VII Land and the ship sailed with a six-man crew under the command of First Officer Victor L. A. Campbell. Unable to find a suitable mooring point, Campbell continued eastward and some 400 miles from Cape Evans, caught sight of Amundsen's *Fram* in the Bay of Whales. The Norwegians had made camp 70 miles closer to the South Pole than the British.

The *Terra Nova* dropped anchor and went ashore. They were cordially greeted, and the Norwegians and small British expedition ate breakfast and lunch together on each other's ships while garnering some surreptitious intelligence, on each other's plans.

Campbell and his men were stunned by the small scale of the Norwegian expedition.

Amundsen's entire team was made up of just eight men – all hand-picked experts in individual fields. Between them, they had 116 dogs, which would not only provide much of the muscle power but a ready source of fresh meat both for the other animals and hungry human beings. They were heavy on supplies of food and chocolate and light on all bar essential equipment. Unencumbered with pretensions to carry out "scientific research", they were focused entirely on the race for the pole.

The British were impressed and somewhat dismayed by the Norwegians' expertise with their dog teams and general efficiency in the conditions. And it may have led Campbell into trying to mislead and wrong-foot Amundsen. One member of the *Terra Nova*, Tryggve Gran, was Norwegian and in the 1960s, he published an autobiography *Kampen om Sydpolen,* which although never translated in full into English is quoted by Swedish academic Björn Lantz in a Cambridge University paper called "The '*terra firma*' anecdote", published in September 2020. According to Gran (as translated by Lantz), the conversation went like this:

"'How are the motor sledges doing?' asked Amundsen.

'Well, I can inform you, Captain Amundsen,' answered Campbell—and in correct Norwegian, too, because he had spent several years in Norway, as a farmer—, 'our motor sledges are outstanding, and if I am not very mistaken, they are now well on their way over the barrier towards the Beardmore Glacier'."

It was a lie. One of them was already at the bottom of the ocean and the rest were giving the British considerable headaches, but the artfully placed bit of misinformation spooked Amundsen, who knew that if he didn't reach the pole first, he would be bankrupted and ostracised by the polar community, for behaving in such an ungentlemanly manner. If Campbell had intended to psyche Amundsen out then it worked, because the Norwegian would later make an ill-advised break for the pole earlier than he should, in September that year, and have to turn back.

Having said their farewells, Campbell and his crew reported back to Scott, who wrote in his diary, on 22nd February: "Amundsen's plan is a very serious menace to ours... I never thought he could have got so many dogs safely to the ice. His plan for running them seems excellent... (and) he can start his journey early in the season."

The Norwegian also had the significant advantage of agility. The scale of the British expedition dwarfed the tiny *Fram* operation in every regard – and in being bigger and more complex it created a veritable smorgasbord of logistical headaches. Where Amundsen had brought 8 men, Scott's shore and ship party consisted of 65, of whom 12 were scientists. Where Amundsen had brought the bare necessities, Scott had taken everything he could fit into the *Terra Nova* and quite literally – a kitchen sink.

The Royal Navy at the time was obsessed with gadgetry and both of his expeditions had an "all the gear and no idea" feel to them. On the *Discovery* expedition a decade earlier, Scott had taken two massive hot air balloons with him, in part because he wanted to lay claim to being the first person to fly on the continent. He later wrote in *The Voyage of Discovery*: "The honour of being the first aeronaut to make an ascent in the Antarctic Regions, perhaps somewhat selfishly, I chose for myself."

This time he had planned to do so again, but carrying so much hydrogen south was risky and instead he made do with two sizeable weather balloons, which to Captain Oates's growing disquiet, he kept trying to inflate as they sailed towards Antarctica.

Although still dubious about the use of dogs, Scott had ordered 33 from Siberia, which again only understood Russian, and had picked them up in New Zealand along the way. He hoped to rely on the three massive motorised sledges that had so unnerved Amundsen, as well as the 19 Manchurian ponies he had brought along. But both presented significant challenges. The sledges needed specialist fuel and the ponies required huge amounts of fodder, in a land with no grass.

Taking ponies to the Pole was a gamble and one that failed on every count, not least because the horses Scott had bought were not up to the job. Captain Oates, who had been assigned the job of caring for them, was shocked when he saw the animals in New Zealand, believing that they were both too old and too weak. Scott – on purely anecdotal evidence – had come to believe that grey or white ponies were sturdier than black or chestnut ones, but just looking at them, Oates knew they would not survive the conditions ahead. Scott had also failed to provide enough fodder and Oates was obliged to shell out for more.

Lawrence "Titus" Oates was a level-headed, practical and extremely tough man. A product of the self-styled upper classes and an Old Etonian, he had spent his life thus far forever trying to escape the cloying expectations of his background. A hero of the Boer War, he had been mentioned in dispatches and received a gunshot wound to his left leg that had left it shorter than the other. Unlike Scott, he was – perhaps because he could afford to be by the status of his birth – uncon-cerned with status and class. He was an iconoclastic character who, in a very un-British manner, said what he thought. Fragments of surviving correspondence suggest that he despaired of Scott's sentimental attitude to animals and, by contrast, praised Amundsen's practical approach to his dogs and their use as a source of meat. Oates also doubted his commander's leadership, writing:

"Scott's ignorance about marching with animals is colossal", and adding later: "Myself, I dislike Scott intensely and would chuck the whole thing if it were not that we are a British expedition.... He is not straight, it is himself first, the rest nowhere."

The expedition to the South Pole was, in Oates' eyes at least, being run by an emotional egomaniac.

In addition to the balloons, ponies, dogs, men, camera equipment and assorted luxuries, there was the food. Sledging rations and base camp rations for 65 hungry men to last many months included cider, sherry, rum, fruit tarts and Sunday roasts. The ship also carried enough wood and materials to build their winter quarters and make all the furniture inside and enough fuel to keep them warm.

Amundsen had journeyed south with the stealth of a guerrilla commander; Scott's plans resembled those of a flamboyant tour manager taking a pampered overblown rock band on tour. The rider was enormous and the outlandish laser light display was failing to work.

Watching the misadventure unfold 110 years later is a bit like witnessing a very slow-motion pile up of egg trucks in a head-on collision – in a petrol station.

Almost immediately upon arrival, and something that Campbell tried to hide from Amundsen when they met later, one of the precious motorised sledges broke through the ice and sank. Nine of the 19 ponies died before the sun disappeared for four months on 21st April. On one occasion a group of them broke away on an ice floe which began to get circled by killer whales. Oates had to row out and hack them to death with an ice pick, perhaps to save Scott the upset of watching them get eaten alive.

The beasts that did survive the dark months shivered with their legs up to their stomachs and grew ever weaker until the sun came up again.

Conversely, during this same period of darkness, miles away across the ice and snow, Amundsen's 12 years of preparation had come into its own. He and his tight-knit team were all properly kitted out in wolfskin and reindeer fur and had kept perfectly warm. Scott's men were dressed in Burberry weatherproof coats, provided by their sponsor, which would have been fine for a windy walk in the Fells, but which were fairly useless for Arctic conditions. Apart from anything else, they failed to dry out properly, leading to misery and illness all round.

The Norwegian expedition had spent the early months of 1911 laying supplies and practising with their dogs. The British had done depot runs too, but they had also expended much of the time measuring the wind, gathering rocks and minerals, filming penguins, writing lengthy diary entries, listening to shellac records on the two large gramophone players provided by another sponsor (HMV Monarch), playing football and wondering why all their ponies were attracting orcas and why all their dogs were getting so thin.

In summary, the Norwegians were laser-focused on their goal while the British had other distractions on their minds.

Come the summer sun, the main event dawned.

The Norwegians and British had roughly similar challenges ahead. First, they had to reach the Beardmore Glacier, then traverse it and finally cross the plateau above to the South Pole. Then they had to turn around and get back home again alive. The Norwegians had slightly less distance to travel (700 miles to Scott's 766) but they first had to cross the uncharted Transantarctic Mountains, while Scott was following a route pioneered by Shackleton several years earlier.

On 19th October 1911 after an initial false start in September, Amundsen's five-man expedition left with 52 dogs and 4 sledges. His team was made up of a skiing champion (Olav Bjaaland), an expert dog handler (Sverre Hassel), a multitalented navy veteran (Oscar Wisting), Helmer Hanssen – an experienced navigator – and Amundsen himself. All could ski, all were used to operating in sub-zero temperatures, all were supremely fit and confident. They had been selected for their individual skills and temperaments and the small group brought with it a sort of inherent efficiency and comradeship.

Scott's far more cumbersome expedition left in two waves. On 24th October, four men, led by Lieutenant "Teddy" Evans (as played by Kenneth More in the later film), set out on the mechanical sledges. Both broke down a week later, meaning they had to haul 336kg of supplies hundreds of miles to the rendezvous.

On the 1st November, the rest of the party – 12 men, alongside the surviving ponies and dogs – followed. Eventually they came across the abandoned sledges and Scott, with his usual faux bonhomie wrote in his diary:

"Half a mile beyond, as I expected, we found the motor, its tracking sledges and all. Notes from Evans and Day told the tale… They had decided to abandon it and push on with the other alone. … So the dream of great help from the machines is at an end!"

Taking such primitive motorised vehicles to such a hostile environment was an ambitious, one might almost add – recklessly stupid move and there must be a suspicion that the "manhaul mad" Scott preferred things that way. His party lumbered up the Ross Ice shelf and towards the Beardmore Glacier and met Evans' team on 21st November. From there, the whole party, including dogs and ponies, trudged on but by 6th December they were trapped in what Scott called a "tempest" while the captain's mood began yo-yoing from hearty and optimistic to dark despair from one page of his diary to the next. In his entry on 6th December, he wrote:

"Miserable, utterly miserable. Everything in the tent is soaking. People… drip pools on the floorcloth… A hopeless feeling descends on one and is hard to fight off."

After three days, the weather improved slightly and on 9th December, the remaining ponies were shot. "It is hard to have to kill them so early," wrote Scott.

Two weeks earlier, Amundsen had shot 27 of his surviving 45 dogs at the top of the Axel Heiberg Glacier, to provide meat for the other dogs and members of the party. The Norwegians had done so with many of the same regrets as Scott and dubbed the place the "Butcher's

Shop", with the party leader lamenting that: "There was depression and sadness in the air; we had grown so fond of our dogs."

That's as may be, they now had plentiful supplies of fresh meat and were fully ready to take on the last leg of the attempt.

Scott did not know it, but he was losing badly.

On 20th December, the British party reached the Beardmore Glacier and on 3rd January revealed who would be staying for the final leg and who would be going home.

His party were to be: Old Etonian class-rebel Captain Oates, the self-funded pony handler and a hero of the Boer War; Scott's old friend and companion on his last mission south, Dr Edward Wilson; and Welshman Petty Officer Edgar Evans, who had also been on that first polar expedition in 1903. Then in the kind of twist beloved of reality TV producers, he added a fifth man, Henry "Birdie" Bowers, a naval lieutenant with no experience of Arctic travel beyond their recent trek; he was at 28 the youngest member of the group.

The addition of Bowers meant that five, not four men would be making the final attempt on the pole and that meant there would not be enough rations to go round. There were not enough skis either, as Scott had ordered all but four sets to be deposited at the previous depot.

Bowers would have to walk and the team of five would have to sleep in a tent designed to hold four people.

By the time the British team began the last leg of their trek, Amundsen, with his dogs and his hand-picked elite unit, was moving twice as fast as Scott and in the opposite direction. The Norwegian mission had reached the South Pole in good health on 14th December – 11 days before Christmas.

Not realising that they had already been beaten, Scott and his party trudged on. On 16th January 1912 they saw a small black flicker in the distance – about 15 miles away – and the following day, having already seen paw marks in the snow and sensing that they had been "fore-stalled", arrived at the tent and fluttering flag left by their Norwegian rivals at the South Pole.

Amundsen had left a note, addressed to the Norwegian King.

The party "celebrated" second place with gloomy photos and a shared cigarette that Wilson had miraculously managed to keep dry.

"Great God! This is an awful place," Scott wrote before adding, with his usual and – in the circumstances understandable – bravado, "well, it is something to have got here and the wind may be our friend tomorrow."

The wind was not listening and as they made their way back, any dwindling reserves of optimism broke, as the men slogged the 766-mile march home.

Scott's deservedly famous diary makes gut-wrenching reading, as each step takes the men closer to their doom. The earlier flourishes of poetry, written after the arrival in Antarctica, have gone and been replaced by sparse sentences and growing terror not only for their own health, but for the loved ones who will be left behind. Scott quite obviously has another concern too and it is what posterity will make of it all.

"Wednesday 24 January: -8 F (-22C) Things beginning to look a little serious.

Sunday 4 February –22F (-30C) Just before lunch unexpectedly fell into crevasses, Evans and I together – a second fall for Evans."

While the Norwegians had left all the graft to their dogs, Scott and his men were now man-hauling their supplies unaided. It was hard, physical labour, on top of the psychological impact of coming second. At the same time, their boots were giving in, causing them to suffer increasingly from frostbite while their diminished diet began messing with their minds.

Amundsen and his team had made it all the way back to base with an overabundance of food. They had taken dried milk powder, chocolate and crucially wholemeal and yeast biscuits – a rich source of Vitamin B. And, having killed a number of their dogs at the "Butcher's Shop", they had a fresh supply of fresh meat, providing them with the necessary Vitamin C. Amundsen had learned the importance of fresh meat in warding off scurvy from the Inuit a decade earlier.

Scott, by contrast had been appalled at Amundsen's willingness to eat dog meat, writing: "One cannot calmly contemplate the murder of animals which possess such intelligence and individuality, which have frequently such endearing qualities, and which very possibly one has learnt to regard as friends and companions."

So, instead, he and his men were living off Huntley & Palmer biscuits made up of white flour and bicarbonate of soda. The onset of scurvy was inevitable, and the poor diet was hitting their collective mental health. In his diary, Scott blamed the surface for their slow progress back, but it might simply have been that their muscles were wasting away because they hadn't brought any dogs.

The men were burning approximately 7,000 kilocalories (kcal) a day while only eating 3,800 kcal of the wrong kind of food – it was an appalling miscalculation and just one of many.

Incredibly, as they man-hauled their sledges home they continued to gather rock samples, perhaps in the hope that they could prop up the myth that the *Terra Nova* Expedition had been primarily about scientific endeavour and that it had all been worthwhile.

After two consecutive falls, Evans's health, both physical and mental, went into a steep downward spiral. On 17th February, Scott wrote: "Evans looked a little better after a good sleep, and declared, as he always did, that he was quite well."

Later that day, the Welshman fell behind the others and turning back they found him with "a wild look in his eyes" on his knees and dishevelled in the snow. He died just after midnight on the following day.

Oates was next. Frostbite had taken his feet, and some have speculated that scurvy and the failing diet might have stirred up that old war wound as well. Realising he was slowing the others, he told his comrades to leave him behind and when they refused informed them on the night of 17th March that he was "just going outside and may be some time". In a deeply moving, extraordinary act of selflessness and heroism, he disappeared into the blizzard and was never seen again.

His death was to no avail and the remaining three died some time after 29th March. Scott's final message to the public, scribbled in the tent, ended with lines that were to become late Empire scripture to generations of British people:

"Had we lived, I should have had a tale to tell of the hardihood, endurance and courage of my companions which would have stirred the heart of every Englishman*... These rough notes and our dead bodies must tell the tale, but surely, surely a great rich country like ours will see that those who are dependent on us are properly provided for."

Three weeks earlier, Amundsen's *Fram* had berthed at Hobart. Operating once again in secrecy and dodging the local press, the Norwegian relayed the message of his conquest home. When Nansen received the message by telephone, he was, by coincidence writing a letter to his lover, Kathleen Scott, the British explorer's wife.

The couple had met in Norway when Scott had gone there seeking advice from the great sage of polar exploration and their affair had later been consummated in a Berlin hotel, while Scott was racing south. Nansen confessed of his mixed feelings about the Norwegian victory – and professed to his mistress that he had wished "that Scott [her husband] had come first" adding, with the understatement of the century, "yes, life is very complicated indeed."[†]

Eight months later, on 12th November 1912 the men's bodies were found by a search party, just 11 miles from Scott's One Ton Depot and supplies that might have sustained them further. Scott's diary, letters and mementos were recovered, but the bodies could not be moved as they were frozen solid. The bodies remain there – even now – locked in time beneath the canvass and the ice.

* * *

In the following decades, Scott's myth and those of his men came to far eclipse those of Amundsen and Nansen – at least in the Anglophonic world. In the era after the First World War, his "clean" and heroic death

---

* Evans was Welsh and Bowers was Scottish, but no such considerations were made by Englishmen in 1912.
† Huntford, R., *Scott and Amundsen*, 1979, p528.

was in marked contrast to the horrors of the trenches and the violence and mud of the Somme and elsewhere. Captain Oates too became a sort of paragon of Englishness. Collectively, the grit and hardiness of these undoubtedly brave men became nothing short of a gospel in the Bible of British (and particularly English) exceptionalism.

The *Great White Silence* – the 1924 documentary masterpiece of the expedition captured by photographer/cinematographer and expedition shore party member Herbert Ponting – was not a commercial success on release, perhaps because of suspicions that he was "cashing in" on the deaths. It ends with a peculiar slide of an angel, in the tent, taking Scott's diary from his hands for posterity and it was Scott's narrative, which went on to be a bestseller, that sealed the expedition's legend.

From the 1970s onwards, the reappraisal began and some, including the controversial account by Roland Huntford, which at times is a bit of a hatchet job, along with the writings of Eric Hobsbawn and Paul Theroux, attributed the status of Scott's legend to declinism (the notion that as the Empire spiralled downward, the nation sought out heroic stories of failure that reflected its declining status).

But I'm unconvinced by the declinist myth because really it just lets the crimes of the Empire off the hook. In trumpeting the so-called heroic failure of Scott, Park, Franklin and others, it's easy to ignore that what the British were really doing was perpetuating their self-re-inforcing narrative of inimitability. It was a means of saying "yes, Scott screwed up – but wasn't it magnificent! Look at us – even in our abject failure, we British are supreme."

The British may have lost the race to the South Pole, but in their heads they had won the moral and poetic victory. For them, Amundsen had cheated by eating his dogs and as he didn't write anything to rival Scott's diary his victory was inconsequential. In the 1948 film it is telling that Amundsen and his men do not even feature. They are entirely off-stage characters – a group of invisible sprites rather than actual people.

In recent decades, Scott has been eclipsed by the man who dwelt in his shadows, Ernest Shackleton. His and Scott's polar contemporary,

Sir Raymond Priestley, put it like this: "For scientific leadership, give me Scott. For swift and efficient travel, give me Amundsen. But when you are in a hopeless situation, when there seems to be no way out, fall on your knees and pray for Shackleton."

And books by the likes of Ranulph Fiennes and a popular TV 2002 miniseries called *Shackleton*, starring Sir Kenneth Branagh, have told the story of Shackleton's remarkable leadership in the failed 1914–1917 Imperial Trans-Antarctic Expedition, when he managed to save all 27 of his men after their ship was crushed in 1915 and get them back home to Britain alive.

In 2011, a hefty popular history book called *Made in Britain* by Adrian Sykes appeared in bookshops and went on to be a hit with traditionally minded British readers seeking to be reminded of just how exemplary UK history was. The book had a foreword by the right-wing historian Norman Stone and was praised by Conservative commentators, including the historian Dominic Sandbrook, who gushed that it made "A wonderfully old-fashioned introduction" to British history.

Prime Minister David Cameron, who at the time was seemingly ever ready to back books that shored up a sort of simplistic Ladybird narrative of history added, "I'm reading something called *Made In Britain*. It's a very nice, rather old-fashioned history book about the great figures and inventions of British history."

So, it was interesting that Sykes picked Shackleton, not Scott, as the greatest figure of the Heroic Age, although it seems to have been on the basis that: "Shackleton is the model for many leadership courses – he is also cited as the perfect example of a great leader by the US navy."

Americans! What an endorsement!

In fact, the raising up of Shackleton in Scott's place was simply the rearranging of British polar heroes on the frigid poop deck. For despite his remarkable heroism and leadership in saving his men, he was, arguably an even more flawed man than Scott. Shackleton was an individual of infinite flaws. Capable of vindictiveness and spite, he was willing to hold grudges like perhaps no other – and while he saved his men in that famed *Endurance* cock-up of 1914–1917 the actual expedition failed before it had begun. It was one of many failures. Shackleton's business ventures failed, his many relationships failed, and when he died in his cabin on yet another expedition in 1921, horribly in debt, his heart had finally failed too.

The awkward truth – for Britons at least – is that however much patriotic historians and latter-day British Antarctic adventurers might shuffle the Top Trumps pack of the Heroic Age, those Norwegians who don't even get portrayed in our movies about the events – were the great figures of the era. They moved with stealth and speed and were possessed of a willingness to learn from the true masters of Arctic survival – the indigenous people. They had, critically, taken that lead from John Rae, arguably one of the most neglected heroes of our history; a man well before his time who was not only willing but eager to learn from the "savages" in the Canadian Northwest, appreciate that they were very far from savage, and in the process, unlock the key to Arctic exploration.

John Rae was by any measure a man of fortitude and courage, whose insistence on telling the truth about the Franklin expedition effectively saw him erased from British history. It is testament to him that he inspired so many others and chiefly, Nansen and Amundsen, so in a way it could be argued that he was the Godfather of the Heroic Age.

A statue of Rae was unveiled on Stromness Pierhead in September 2013, but it seems remarkable, to me at least, that a nation so in thrall to failed polar heroes has – in the process – neglected the greatest home-grown Arctic hero of all.

CHAPTER EIGHT

ROYAL HEROES
HENRY V

The Power of Status

As with the death of Princess Diana and JFK before it, those of us alive on 8th September 2022 will long remember where we were, when we heard that the Old Queen had died. I was at a meeting for one of my children's exam options and as the news broke on parents' phones a strange mood swept through the room. Nobody present seemed particularly shocked. After all Queen Elizabeth II was 96 years old and in rare public appearances had looked increasingly frail in recent months, but still, there was an unsettling sense that an era had ended.

Like the sky above our heads and the earth beneath our feet, the Queen had been a constant – a sort of supranatural grandmother opening train lines and interrupting our Christmas lunches with her annual speech – seemingly forever. Indeed, it was forever for most of us. You would have had to have been well over 75 to even dimly remember a time before her reign and more than 100 years old to recall life without her altogether.

Whatever your views on monarchy, there had been something permanent and even curiously reassuring about her presence, and now, she was gone.

Gripped in multiple political, financial and post-COVID crises and awaiting the economic miracle that the new PM Liz Truss was promising would come, Britain ground to a halt as the country entered a 12-day period of national mourning. Most noticeably, everything turned black and even the bright neon signs in Piccadilly Circus drained of their colour and were replaced with a sombre portrait of the late Queen. It was a reminder, that even in the twenty-first century, the United Kingdom remained, at its heart, an essentially feudal kingdom.

The nation's broadcasters adopted black dresses and hats and solemn tones as the same handful of guests in matching sombre attire shuffled between the various television sofas and talked reverently of the times they had met or glimpsed Her Majesty.

At the same time, firms across the land tried to prove that they were mourning harder than anyone else. Greggs, Domino's Pizza, Cash Converters and B&Q were among the first big brands to put out condolence messages. Center Parcs announced that it would close on the day of the funeral and require guests to leave the premises "out of respect" – although they later withdraw the plan. Morrisons supermarket caused considerable confusion for customers by turning down the beeps on its self-scanning check-outs, Transport for London banned buskers from the Tube and Heathrow Airport diverted planes away from Central London.

Those wishing to escape it all were frustrated in their efforts. Leading up to the state funeral, many shopping and betting channels went off air. So did the nation's best-known pornography* providers, who replaced their usual content with respectful notices.

Dan Wootton, a presenter on the right-wing, "patriotic" news channel GB News, was among hundreds of celebrities who made sure that their pilgrimages to Buckingham Palace to lay flowers did not go unnoticed. Taking to Twitter he wrote: "I wanted to return to Buckingham Palace today, for some quiet reflection and (to) lay my own

---

* An event dubbed "mourn hub". A rumour that the channel Babestation would actually broadcast the funeral was an internet myth.

tribute. Crowds young, old, from all ethnicities and backgrounds. Truly the best of British doing her justice."

Wootton, whose career had largely been built out of attacking "virtue signalling" do-gooders, was widely mocked for having apparently brought someone along to film him laying his posy, in what was perceived to be an act of performative social media mourning. The political response was similarly unrestrained. In the House of Commons, Prime Minister Liz Truss told fellow MPs that the Queen was "one of the greatest leaders the world has ever known". Labour leader Sir Keir Starmer described her as "this great country's greatest monarch".

Twelve days is a long time in broadcasting and as the scale of the content black hole became evident, news reporters took to the streets to ask ordinary people their thoughts. The answers were all very similar. People told interviewers that they had come up to lay flowers and visit the gates of Buckingham Palace because it was "history" or more opaquely because "we felt we had to come", along with "the Queen had been an important part of people's lives", "my mum was the same age as her", "we brought the children", "we wanted to pay our respects", "we wanted to mark the moment", and "it was the end of an era". Nobody, as far as I am aware, simply said that they had come to gawp.

Not everyone played along. In one spectacularly ill-judged contribution, a fish and chip shop owner called Jacki Pickett, of Muir of Ord, Inverness-shire, not only celebrated the Queen's death but posted a video of herself doing so online.

Jacki's belief in conspiracy theories was well-known locally. Conducting most of her research on Facebook, she had become an avid QAnoner* and anti-vaxxer, and spent the previous two years haranguing customers with signs claiming that Walt Disney was a "pedo" (sic) responsible for "organ harvesting" and "kiddie trafficking" and that government was "made up of the cabal, deep state satanic morons". "Do your research" proclaimed one sign and "Save the Children" said another.

---

* US-origin conspiracy movement who believe that Donald Trump is an undercover spy fighting child paedophile rings. Really. There are people who really believe that.

When news of the Queen's passing reached Jacki, she promptly knocked up a sign proclaiming: "Lizard Liz dead, London Bridge has fallen"*, opened some fizzy wine and began dancing in front of her premises, only for an angry mob to turn up and start pelting her with eggs. Jacki was later spirited out of town by the local constabulary and as her infamy spread, the National Federation of Fish Fryers announced that it would be revoking her membership.

On 14th September, the late Queen's body was taken to Westminster Abbey to lie in state and over the next few days an estimated 250,000 waited in line to see her coffin. Soon the queue had become a sort of spiritual endeavour that was very reminiscent indeed of Medieval pilgrimages. Hyperbole abounded. The *Daily Mail* went as far as to claim that the line was visible from space, which was patently and absurdly untrue. But nobody could doubt that the queue had taken on a sort of life of its own and, as people waited upwards of 30 hours in line, friendships and relationships blossomed. There were even tales of passers-by finding themselves almost miraculously drawn in on their way to do something else.

Every mass event, like every pantomime, needs a villain and this one had two. When rumours spread that television hosts Phillip Schofield and Holly Willoughby had "skipped the queue" (something they both vehemently denied) a backlash followed, and a petition was signed by 67,000 people demanding that they be sacked. The episode hinted at the darker instincts that come with any mob and you could almost hear the pitchforks being sharpened.

Signs of republican sentiment were initially muted but when a man was led away in Westminster for holding up a small banner saying: "Not My King" other protests followed. Soon sporadic groups of demonstrators were descending on public places and holding blank pieces of paper before being led away – a chilling echo of recent protests

---

* Operation London Bridge was the long-established term (used by civil servants and broadcasters) for the protocol in the event of the death of the Queen. In fact, as she died in Scotland, it became Operation Unicorn instead.

in Russia against the dictator, Vladimir Putin, and his invasion of Ukraine – although at least these people were quickly released.

But overall, the tide of press and sentiment was firmly in the late Queen's favour.

In his 1938 poem "Musée des Beaux Arts", the poet W.H. Auden writes admiringly of the Flemish Masters of the sixteenth and seventeenth century. These were artists who understood the true nature of tragedy and as such, when they painted scenes of great martyrdom or suffering, they would place the subject matter within huge crowds.

As Christ is crucified, in Brueghel the Younger's 1617 painting *Calvary*, you see people fighting with each other, or looking bored, or resting lazily on a hillside, while two uninterested dogs dig a hole in the ground to the right. Auden insightfully wrote:

"How, when the aged are reverently, passionately waiting
For the miraculous birth, there always must be
Children who did not specially want it to happen."

London that week was positively Brueghelian. And, contrary to the media narrative and the sombre news reports, not everyone who came to witness events was sad and or even there, simply to lay flowers. In St James's Park, people had picnics and queued for ice creams with their kids. Toddlers cried and pulled at the straps on their buggies as their mums and dads tried to find a path out from the throng. An elderly woman collapsed in the middle of the crowd along The Mall and medics struggled to get to her past irritated onlookers clutching bouquets of carnations for someone they had never met.

Men sat on benches drinking lager from cans. Someone had tied a laminated poem to a tree – it included a verse that ran:

"We will all remember
That for comedy she had a flair
The 007 helicopter landing
And tea with Paddington Bear"

Many of course had come to pay their respects to the Queen but many others had come to be part of the cavalcade, to see what was going on and to promote their poetry, by tying it to trees. The motives of crowds – like the mystery of monarchy itself – is a complicated business.

In the weeks that followed, in my day job as a journalist, I crossed paths with several people – a former diplomat, a former government minister and a television personality, who had all met the Queen. In each case they positively lit up when I asked what she was really like and then struggled to define it. She had had a "sense of humour" was a common thread, but I was also told that she was "highly intelligent", "well informed", prone to making "throwaway but meaningful remarks" and had "an aura" that none of them could define.

Scriptwriters and directors obsess over something called "status", which is the sort of pecking order of characters on a stage or in a film. "High status" can be projected through factors including body-language, accent and profession, but give a character the title of a king, queen, president or prime minister and it's a case of "job done". Most of us, through conditioning, are in awe of presidents, kings and queens simply because of their titles. The very terms elevate them, making them instantly interesting and powerful. It puts them on a pedestal and infers honour.

Her Majesty the Queen met almost all the big names of the twentieth century. Everyone from John F. Kennedy to Winston Churchill, Morecambe and Wise to Charlie Chaplin, Margaret Thatcher to Nelson Mandela. In a world of kings and queens, she was "The Queen", the Top Trump of the pack, and came as a result, fully loaded with an extraordinary degree of status. Perhaps the awe she instilled in those highly educated and successful people I met in the wake of her death was real, but it is hard to escape the suspicion that it was primarily down to that unfathomable degree of status that she carried purely by dint of her title.

As with so many memorable names in history, from Che Guevara to Alexander the Great, from Elton John to Coco Chanel, the Queen worked hard at maintaining her image, and critical to her success was the virtue she made out of her silence. In her entire life, she never gave an interview, never leaked stories about her private life to the press and, with help from advisers only rarely misread the mood of her subjects. Aided and abetted by a fawning media and political class that never questioned her role, there was little material for even the most hardened republican to use against her. Elizabeth's greatest triumph was to maintain the mystery of her role and at times this required absolute ruthlessness.

In the 1930s, young Princess Elizabeth and her sister Margaret acquired a governess. Scots-born Marion Crawford was in her twenties when she went to work at the Palace and remained in the service of the Windsors until Elizabeth married Philip in 1947. By then, "Crawfie" was 39 and she had effectively forfeited her own happiness and chance of having children in service of the future Queen.

In childhood, the royal princesses saw their parents only once a day and during the Second World War, they lived in Windsor while King George and their mother were in London, so hardly saw them at all. "Crawfie" and another servant, Margaret MacDonald (aka Bobo*), effectively became surrogate parents and confidantes to the girls. Having been pensioned off in 1947 and seeking purpose, Crawford began writing articles for an American publication, the *Ladies' Home Journal,* and in 1950 and with permission from Queen Elizabeth (the future Queen Mother) penned a book called the *The Little Princesses* about her life with the girls. But even before it had appeared, the Royal Family had had second thoughts and turned on her. Something had triggered Queen Elizabeth (the future Queen Mother) and she declared that the governess had "gone off her head". Henceforth this woman, who had quite literally sacrificed the best years of her life to the royal family, was "ghosted". What secrets had she revealed to deserve such treatment? Well – it's a bit of a mystery. The book was not just affectionately written but sycophantically so. There was

---

* Bobo was perhaps the Queen's closest friend and confidante. She did the job so well and loyally that most people have never heard of her.

one suggestion that the king sometimes got a bit grumpy during the war and another that the Queen Mother didn't think much of Wallis Simpson, wife of Edward VIII, but these were hardly scandalous accusations and indeed, Edward was to bring out his own (ghostwritten) memoir the following year which hinted at much the same.

No – what Crawfie had done was to break the covenant of the "master and servant" relationship. The notion that working for the royals was reward enough and that to reduce them to the status of actual human beings by talking about them was an unforgivable betrayal. The Christmas and birthday cards stopped. Crawfie's correspondence went unanswered, and she went on to attempt suicide twice. Later, she moved close to Balmoral in the hope that she might one day meet her old charges and patch things up, but the moment never came.

Crawfie died in 1988, but no wreath was sent and no acknowledgement made. She was edited out of the Queen's story with an efficiency and ruthlessness that would have put Soviet propagandists to shame. The callous dispatching of such a loyal servant says much about the power and modus operandi of "The Firm", as they are sometimes referred to in the UK. Their self-preservation requires ruthlessness and at times even family members have been dumped for the sake of the institution. When exiled Prince Harry brought out his own autobiography, *Spare*, in 2023, the Establishment went after him with a mercilessness that it usually reserves for foxes. In a Comment leader, the Conservative newspaper the *Daily Telegraph* blasted "The Duke of Sussex's self-pitying whinge" and demanded that it "must not overshadow the coronation", and royal commentators lined up to attack the wayward prince and pour scorn and blame for it all on his American wife.

The prevalence of monarchy requires stoney hearts, the preservation of myth and an army of obsequious lackeys. It also requires a lot of smoke and mirrors and the promise of reward. There were few occasions in the Queen's reign when a miscalculation was made but one came most definitely in 1969, when the smoke machine was deliberately switched off by the royal family themselves.

That year, to mark the ascendancy of Prince Charles to his role as Prince of Wales which culminated in a bizarre, made-up investiture at Caernarfon Castle on July 1st, the Royal Family, on the suggestion of their Press Secretary, William Heseltine, allowed a TV crew to make a fly-on-the-wall documentary about their lives. The idea was that the monarchy, then deemed to be out of step with Swinging Sixties' Britain, might be assessed in a fresh light and that new relevance might be injected into The Firm.

But it was – at least from the Windsors' perspective – a sceptre-acular disaster. In one fell swoop, the mystique of the Queen was shot to pieces, like a pheasant at close range with an anti-aircraft gun, as the Windsors showed themselves to be very normal, if wildly eccentric human beings. In one excruciating scene, Philip complains loudly about his wife's food at a barbecue in a Scottish field. In another, a young Edward bursts into tears when Charles accidentally hits him with a sprung cello string.

Like the moment at the end of *The Wizard of Oz* when the curtain is drawn back on Oscar Zoroaster, Elizabeth Windsor was shown to be a likeable, albeit detached and very posh, Home Counties mother, who drove a Land Rover chaotically and watched herself on TV. Behind the walls of her big homes, she was in fact just another otherwise ordinary human being who by dint of birth had ended up being the hereditary head of state of the United Kingdom and 32 other countries.

Following one more outing during the Queen's Silver Jubilee in 1977, the film was canned. The notion of royalty lives and dies by its mystery and by airing their dirty Crimson Surcoat in public the House of Windsor had risked doing to itself what the Queen had done to Prince Philip's barbecue steak.

* * *

One of the great arguments against republicanism in the UK is that "nobody does it better" than the current royal family whose thousand plus years of breeding and service to the people could never be replicated by mere "politicians". It's a very convincing argument indeed, or at least would be, if British monarchical history was not brimming with such a long list of dreadful Kings and Queens.

The late Elizabeth II was very much the exception, not the rule and if you go back beyond her reign it's hard to find anyone who comes close to reflecting her extraordinary time on the throne.

Her father George VI (known as Bertie to his family), had the crown thrust onto his head by circumstance and did his best in the war but had never wanted the job and was out of his depth. A miserable childhood and his dreadful, bullying father, twinned with the extraordinary pressures of the job in wartime, made his debilitating stammer worse and resulted in an ultimately fatal chain-smoking habit that sent him to his grave aged just 56.

Bertie was also a heavy drinker with his mammoth whisky intake causing concern long before he stepped up to be King. Prone to fits of uncontrollable rage, he was once described by the court photographer Sir Cecil Beaton as "a backward young man" even as Cecil himself took the money to promulgate the imagery that propped up the feudal kingdom.

The King's older brother, the dashing Edward VIII (later Duke of Windsor) – long sold to the world as a man of the people, who gave up his throne for the love of Wallis Simpson – was in fact an antisemitic, Hitler-admiring drunk, who did not so much walk away from the throne as was pushed. And as for that great love affair? Well, Wallis herself didn't much love him and did everything she could to duck the relationship.

In Andrew Lownie's comprehensive take on the abdication and Windsor marriage, *Traitor King*, the author relates that Wallis "suggested they break off the marriage" and quotes her friend, Constance Coolidge, saying at the time: "Can you imagine a more terrible fate than to have to live up publicly to the legend of a love you don't feel? To have to face… A middle-aged boy with no other purpose in life than a possessive passion for you?"

Having failed to dodge marriage to Edward, his wife sought excitement elsewhere. Mrs Simpson had already been conducting an affair with a second-hand car salesman, Guy Trundle, simultaneous to her relationship with the King and two years after the abdication, embarked on another with William Bullitt, the US Ambassador to France. Trapped in the existential myth of their great "love story", this ghastly couple went on to make friends with the Nazis and – as Lownie documents in *Traitor King* – frequently eulogised Hitler behind closed doors.

In June 1940, Don Javier Bermejillo, a Spanish diplomat, reported to his superiors that Edward blamed "the Jews, the Reds and the Foreign Office" for the war and believed that future PM Anthony Eden should be put "up against a wall" and shot. On New Year's Eve 1962, as German documents were released that revealed the full extent of Edward's collusion with the Nazis, the ever-reliable Noël Coward wrote in his diary: "Secret papers have disclosed his pro-Nazi perfidy which, of course, I was perfectly aware of at the time. Poor dear, what a monumental ass he has always been."

In the post-war years, these dreadful, entitled people travelled the world, showing disregard for hosts, loyal friends and servants while thinking up ways to fleece them and get Wallis the HRH title she craved. Like Coco Chanel, their status and friends in high places, including Winston Churchill, protected them from accusations of wartime collaboration and their connection to the royal family continues to do so long after their deaths.

The pernicious myth of Edward and Mrs. Simpson and their "great romance" that was not, continues to eclipse their repellent truth for no other reason than that most British people are encouraged to be in thrall to monarchy and even its very worst examples.

The apple doesn't fall far from the tree and George V – Edward and Bertie's sclerotic father – was even worse than his sons. Embarrassed by his fifth boy John's epilepsy, he hid the child away. Refusing to give asylum to his cousin the Tsar Nicholas II and his wife Alexandra and their five offspring, lest it dent his own popularity, he left them to be murdered by the Bolsheviks instead in July 1918. In his spare time, he was a snob, a bore, an ignoramus and a bully.

Winston Churchill once overheard him telling the Earl of Derby: "My father was frightened of his mother, I was frightened of my father, and I am damned well going to see to it that my children are frightened of me."

George V, like almost all the royals of his century, was not well-educated, most certainly not well-read, lacked any discerning characteristics and was singularly devoid of wit, charm and even the ability to tell a half decent anecdote. Because he happened to be the King at a moment of national crisis, he was promoted as a rallying figure of the Empire during the First World War, but it was all just iconography. He despised the arts, hated sitting for portraits and, having rashly decided to give up booze for the duration of the war, sulked his way through the four years of it. His famous last words "bugger Bognor" were in fact delivered almost a decade earlier when he churlishly turned down that town's first attempts to add "Regis" to its name.

His father, Edward VII, aka Edward the Caresser, was a feckless, hedonistic, crowd-pleasing playboy who slept with friends' wives, fathered dozens of illegitimate children and spread misery in his wake. His mother, Victoria, had her charms and strengths – but spent some 40 years in self-indulgent mourning following the death of her husband and was rarely seen in public at all. Notoriously quick-tempered, she could be obstinate to a degree unrivalled even by her descendants and was hugely politically partisan in favour of the Conservatives. Her instincts were jingoistic and tyrannical. And it says a lot about her fellow monarchs that despite all that, she was probably one of the best of the bunch.

Her uncle, William IV, was a supporter of slave owners' rights in the West Indies and deserted his wife and children. George IV was a lazy, debt-plagued gambler and inveterate drunk, who took credit for beating Napoleon, even though it had nothing to do with him whatsoever. In between opposing Catholic Emancipation, he spent money he didn't have on vanity projects and fripperies.

Even before he became King in 1820 he had ratcheted up debts of roughly £630,000 in 1795, equivalent to £60,000,000 in 2023.

The Duke of Wellington dubbed him: "the worst man (he) ever fell in with his whole life, the most selfish, the most-false, the most ill-natured, the most entirely without one redeeming quality."

And so, it goes on. George III: likeable and devoted to his duty but mad; churlish George II who spent most of his time in Hanover; and George I, a gold-digging, wife-cheating, rat who only won the throne on a technicality.

Before becoming King of England, he may also have been responsible for a murder. When his young wife Sophia repaid his infidelity by taking a lover of her own, the Swedish adventurer Count Philip Christoph von Königsmarck, and then made the mistake of falling in love, she and Philip planned to elope. That was too much for George, the Elector of Hanover, and he plotted to stop her: before they could flee, George's courtiers had Philip killed. His body was then weighed down and thrown in the River Leine. To add insult to injury, George's marriage to Sophia was dissolved on account of her "abandonment" before Sophia was locked up in a house near Hanover, while George married someone else. Sophia spent the rest of her life under house arrest while her ex-husband went on to be King of England.

Keep going back further and for every well-meaning but utterly useless incumbent of the throne, like the unremarkable and painfully shy Queen Anne, there are a dozen incompetents, playboys, charlatans, psychopaths, slave owners or mass murderers. William and Mary invaded – albeit with an invitation to do so – to take power from the incompetent James II and brought misery and bloodshed to Ireland, the impact of which, still resonates to this day. The Stuarts were, to a man, entitled bunglers who plunged the nation into a series of protracted civil wars that scarred the nation for centuries.

The English Civil Wars alone, which were fought between 1642 and 1651, saw roughly 150,000–200,000 deaths in a country of just 5 million people.

Queen Elizabeth I is such an iconic figure today that it's easy to forget that she was very much an enigma in her time, hard to read and often deliberately opaque – perhaps fearing that she was never entirely secure on the throne. And her reign was every bit as bloody as her half-sister Mary's. Most Britons, basking in the cult of the nation's inimitable history, don't really give it much thought. And for many generations the bowdlerised pre- and post-war Ladybird book tradition of "Kings and Queens" history has rendered even the ghastliest monarchs if not heroes, then at least "interesting characters".

Take Elizabeth and Mary's psychopathic father, Henry VIII, undoubtedly one of the worst people out of a very bad bunch, to ever sit on the English throne. Despite that, he remains a favourite subject for film-makers and is often sold as a sort of colourful king and a romantic Renaissance man. That's tyrannical Henry VIII, beheader of wives and murderer of friends, whose 36-year reign left a legacy of isolationism and civil war and who ordered the execution of an estimated 57,000 people. Henry VIII, whose dissolution of the monasteries left thousands unemployed and wandering the countryside and whose 1536 Act for Punishment of Sturdy Vagabonds and Beggars resulted in thousands of them being executed.

It is no stretch to argue that Henry VIII was Stalin in a doublet and hose, and perhaps we should start to view him as such rather than a sort of cheeky chappy who liked jousting, carousing, wenches and chicken drumsticks.

So, thank God then for King Henry V. The king that the historian K. B. McFarlane dubbed: "the greatest man that ever ruled England". This island's towering Medieval-era monarch. That great general, man of the people, defeater of those dastardly French, who was loved by all and gave magnificent speeches to boot.

Can you guess what's coming next?

* * *

Well probably not, because we are going to start with his son, Henry VI.

Heroes, like camel coats and fondue sets, go in and out of fashion. Nowadays Henry V is seen as one of England's most remarkable monarchs, but for years after his death, his fame was eclipsed by the cult of his son. Henry Junior came to the throne of England aged 9 months on his father's young death in 1422 and just three months later became King of France as well when Charles VI died. He was the first and only monarch to rule both countries, but the high hopes for a new age soon went awry and as he grew up, he began to show signs of a debilitating, possibly genetic, mental health condition.

In his childhood the kingdom was governed by a squabbling council of regents, which caused chaos enough, but on taking power himself in 1437, it swiftly became apparent that he had none of his father's skills of leadership and was far more like his French grandfather, Charles VI of France, who had, in his later years, been known as Le Fou (The Mad). Paranoid and delusional, Charles had variously believed that he was Saint George and that his body was made of glass, leading him to wear clothes rammed with iron rods, to protect him against shattering.

By turns unpredictable, paranoid and pious, Henry VI's unhinged behaviour began with him founding Eton College in 1440 and peaked, following defeat at the Battle of Castillon in 1453, when all his possessions in France, bar Calais, were lost. The 31-year-old king then had what was obviously a significant mental health breakdown and having turned mute, he began to suffer hallucinations, which some historians have taken to be signs of catatonic schizophrenia.

Into the vacuum stepped his cousin, Richard, Duke of York, and the 32-year dynastic struggle between the Houses of Lancaster and York, known to us as the Wars of the Roses, followed. Richard was killed at the Battle of Wakefield in 1460. A year later, York's son Edward was crowned King Edward IV. Henry went into exile, was restored briefly in 1470 but ended up being murdered in May 1471 at the Tower of London.

Henry VI's only gift to posterity, thus far, was to demonstrate that primogeniture is a really very bad idea indeed. But despite his complete lack of leadership and wholly disastrous chaotic reign, a decade after he died, he nearly became a saint.

On 7th February 1486, a girl called Alice Newnett, who it was believed had died of plague several days earlier, sat bolt upright in her shroud and started gasping for breath. Her parents ascribed the miracle to prayers offered up to the late King. The same year a baby called Miles Freebridge swallowed a Pilgrim badge of St. Thomas Becket and nearly choked to death, only to spit it out when Henry's name was invoked. In total there were 300 miracles accorded to "Holy King Henry" in the period 1481–1500 and as his cult grew, pilgrimages were made to his tomb at St George's Chapel in Windsor where many more were ascribed to him.

The elevation of this man's cult was, in part, a piece of artful propaganda by the new Tudor dynasty. Devotion had started on the back of his perceived martyrdom in the 1470s, but it later served the interests of the deposed King's nephew, the anti-Yorkist Henry VII, who had seized power back from the Lancastrians in 1485 to become the first Tudor King of England. In an age of short lives and no journalists or fact checkers, Henry VI's myth prospered, and his reign of chaos came to be seen, retrospectively, as a sort of golden era. Another golden era.

Henry VII's son, who became King Henry VIII in 1509, upset his great uncle's chances of becoming a saint by enacting the Reformation and, with all the subtlety of an outsized, comically suggestive codpiece, began hammering home the similarities between himself and Henry V instead. Enraptured by his predecessor's perceived dynamism and seeking to capitalise on it, Henry VIII even plagiarised his greatest hit by invading north-eastern France in 1513 and, while the new king's adventures in France were, in the words of historian Keith Dockray "a pale shadow of the Azincourt [Agincourt] campaign" they did at least result in an English biography, *The First English life of Henry V*. That anonymously written book, published in 1514, was later attributed to "The Translator of Livius" as it was clearly a rip-off of Tito Livio's mid-fifteenth-century Latin history, *Vita Henrici Quinti*. The work praised Henry V's "Virtuous manners, victorious conquests and excellent maxims" and claimed to be part-based on the testimony of James Butler, 4th Earl of Ormond, who had fought alongside the King in France. The book was the main source of the legend of wayward Prince Hal – of which more in a moment.

A 1540s biography by Edward Hall followed, with the less than snappy title *The vnion of the two noble and illustre femelies of Lancastre [and] Yorke*. Hall portrayed Henry as an explicitly Christ-like figure who transforms from troubled son of a king to a greater one in his own divine right: "This prince was a shepherd whom his flock loved and lovingly obeyed."

By the time Elizabeth I ascended the throne in 1558, Henry V's legend as one of the greatest of English kings, if not the greatest, was established. The hugely influential *Raphael Holinshed's Chronicle*, first published in 1577, served as the source material for the anonymously written play, *The Famous Victories of Henry the Fifth*, which was performed in London in the mid 1580s. Shakespeare's more famous trilogy, written between 1597 and 1599 followed, consisting of *Henry IV Parts 1* and *2* and Henry V. Those tales popularised and cemented Hal's place in the English psyche.

Shakespeare's take on the story has indelibly imprinted the King in British minds, largely because many of us were taught it in school or saw film versions on the TV, but in case you are unfamiliar with it, here's a very short summary of the plot:

King Henry IV has problems, both domestic and political. His wayward son Hal boozes his life away in seedy pubs, while a Welsh rebel called Glyndŵr causes him headaches in the West and his one-time allies, the Percy family, stab him in the back up North. Harry Percy aka Hotspur is everything the King wishes his own boy would be: noble, virtuous and brave – but the feckless son and heir is oblivious to it all and spends his days getting pissed with a layabout called Sir John Falstaff. But – plot twist – it's all an act and Hal, is intending to "uphold the unyoked humour" of his idleness (aka do the right thing in the end), which happens, when Hal saves his father's life at the victorious Battle of Shrewsbury. *Part 2*, very much *The Empire Strikes Back* of the saga, sees father and son reconciled before the old king dies, Hal becomes King Henry V and then turns his back on Falstaff to settle local uprisings before setting out to conquer France.

Henry V sees Henry raise an army of rogues and misfits and, against all odds, defeat the stuck-up French at the Battle of Agincourt, before winning the heart of a princess and returning home triumphant as de facto King of both lands. It's a cracking monomyth made better by Shakespeare's rendering of Hal as a rounded and likeable character. One-part Hamletish rebel without a cause, one-part late sixteenth-century James Bond and one-part inspirational orator.

It's unsurprising that he persists as a figure in the political and cultural sphere and is still often alluded to by politicians and sportsmen. More critically, in a very long line of singularly psychopathic, self-serving or deeply underwhelming English Kings and Queens, this attractive man of action is someone to make the English proud. Someone, like all the best national heroes, who makes the people who share the land that was the place of his birth over 500 years ago feel good about themselves by dint of occupying the same space.

His reputation dimmed a bit between the seventeenth and eighteenth centuries (although Charles Dickens was a fan), but when his story was included in a hugely successful series of popular books called *Heroes of the* Nations (No.34 in the series was *Henry V: The Typical Mediaeval Hero* by C.L. Kingsford, published in 1901), his fortunes were restored.

Like Captain Scott, Henry V and his campaign against the dastardly enemy across the sea became a fitting hero for a nation at war in the twentieth century. In September 1914, just a month into the First World War and following the British Expeditionary Force's first major engagement at Battle of Mons, the novelist Arthur Machen – another of those writers hired to work for the War Propaganda Bureau at Wellington House – wrote a short story for the *London Evening News*. Called *The Bowmen,* Machen told of giant ghostly archers miraculously appearing behind the heavily outnumbered British troops at the engagement and how they had begun firing giant ghost arrows at the German lines.

Written from a first-person perspective and not marked as fiction by the newspaper, many readers were *spaghetti treed** and began believing that Henry V's army from Agincourt had pitched up to help the boys.

---

* No need to flick back: *spaghetti treeing* was the term coined to describe mass tomfoolery after the hoax report by the BBC on April Fool's Day 1957 about harvesting spaghetti from a spaghetti tree

The story was picked up by local newspapers and parish magazines and later featured in a collection by Machen, called *The Bowmen and Other Legends of The War*. But by then, and despite the author making it very clear in the introduction that it was a fictional story, it had taken on a life of its own and some people even began to start claiming that they had seen them. Decades later, the fictional event was still being reported as fact by believers in angels and the myth is still being propagated today on YouTube channels and in magazine articles.

"People are strange" as Doors front man Jim Morrison so trenchantly observed.

Thirty years later, Laurence Olivier's 1944 colour film version of Shakespeare's *Henry V*, part- funded by the wartime propaganda unit – the Ministry of Information – was made, explicitly to rally British hearts in the final years of the war. The film portrays Britain (specifically England) as a country that has long stood against tyrants and "foreigners". The morally upright protagonist, played by Olivier, then the country's most respected actor, leading a plucky band of British brothers (including Scots and Welshmen) against continental forces, which resonated strongly in the wake of D-Day. It was a big hit and inevitably linked wartime national endeavour with the idea of a sort of intrinsic "spirit" that resonated back into time.

Since then, millions of us have grown up studying one or more of these plays and millions more have seen the theatre, film and TV versions in which Henry V has been portrayed not only by Laurence Olivier but also Kenneth Branagh (1989), Tom Hiddleston (2012) and Timothée "Hal" (yes, really) Chalamet (2019), and, even – in a curious performance in his 1995 audiobook *A Prince's Choice* – King Charles III.

Shakespeare's Hal is a hugely enigmatic character and very much a man for all seasons. The kind of king you could have a drink, a bag of nuts and a laugh with – before following him once more unto the breach. Like all the best Fake Hero myths in this book, there's just enough historical validity to give the characterisation merit too. It is true, for example, that Henry (Hal) had beef with his father, although it had nothing to do with the boy's wayward behaviour.

In 1398, when Hal was 12 years old, his father, Henry Bolingbroke, was forced into exile and his father's cousin, King Richard II, took him as a hostage. The relationship between boy and second cousin blossomed and some historians have speculated that when Henry Senior came back, seized the throne and in February 1400, killed Richard, Hal took exception to the murder of his mentor. Five years later, in June 1405, in the wake of one of many failed uprisings against his reign, Henry IV ordered the execution of the Archbishop of York, Richard le Scrope. Shortly thereafter the King's skin broke out in a "mystery" illness, which was probably leprosy, but many in the superstitious world of the era took it to be a "sign". Bolingbroke had committed regicide and was now killing archbishops – these strange lesions on his skin were surely no coincidence.

As the King's condition worsened, Hal's star rose and from 1408, aged 22, he became de facto regent, much to his father's consternation. Biographers and Shakespeare both have Henry IV and his son reconciled on his deathbed in March 1413, but in the race to secure succession such Prodigal Son-like bedside goodbyes almost certainly never happened.

Henry was crowned king on 9th April 1413 and thereafter, according to his early biographers, Hal changed.

Chronicler Thomas Walsingham, who lived through the events, wrote that as soon as the new king was anointed, he transformed into "another man, zealous for modesty, honesty and gravity" and the works of Hall and the anonymous translator of Livius follow the same line.

The myth of drunken and hedonistic Hal hanging out with wayward pisshead and part-time highwayman Sir John Falstaff is largely a fiction. But Shakespeare did base Falstaff on a real person, Henry V's friend, Sir John Oldcastle, who had campaigned with him in Wales, and like Falstaff, Oldcastle did bring trouble to the prince, but not of the sort depicted in the plays.

Oldcastle was a *Lollard*, part of a proto-Protestant movement that attacked Catholic doctrines, including the sacred notion of transubstantiation (the belief that bread and wine turn into the actual body and blood of Christ at Eucharist). Lollards were viewed as heretics who, among other things, believed that baptism and confession were unnecessary – an extremely radical position at the time. As the movement became more militant and explicitly political in character, it put itself on a collision course with church and state, but Oldcastle's close friendship with the prince at first protected him. That changed in 1413 – two years before Agincourt – when Sir John was indicted by the Archbishop of Canterbury, Thomas Arundel, for heresy. The new King intervened, and Oldcastle managed to escape, only to lead a failed and rather lacklustre insurrection against his old friend.

Oldcastle escaped again but four years later was captured at Welshpool, taken to London and hanged above gallows that were then set on fire. In his book *Foundation: The History of England*, Peter Ackroyd relates that: "In his last words before his painful death, he declared that he would rise again after three days. In truth his resurrection took a little longer than that. In the sixteenth century he became a proto-martyr of Protestantism… one of the reasons why Shakespeare felt obliged to change his name to Falstaff."

Oldcastle, then, was no comic foil but a hugely complex figure and Hal was no loveable kind-hearted rebel prince but the sort of chap who roasts people alive while hanging them. Getting burned alive on the gallows is not exactly ripe comedy material, so Shakespeare turned Oldcastle into trouble-making Falstaff, who sets the prince up for his narrative of redemption instead.

Just as Paul the Apostle (later Saint Paul) comes to his senses on the road to Damascus and the Very Hungry Caterpillar turns into a beautiful butterfly after pigging out on cake, the transformative element is critical to any monomyth but particularly one of a religious bent. Central to the fictional Henry V is his moment of revelation and call to destiny, but in fact the real-life Hal was more pious priest than potty-mouthed party animal. Contemporary portraits render him as a clean-shaven, harsh-looking character, with hair closely cropped in the style of a monk as an indicator of his piety.

Despite what some movie versions might have you believe, Hal was no peacenik either. Aged 17, he had his first taste of war, fighting in Wales against Glyndŵr and in 1403 got an arrow in his face at the Battle of Shrewsbury for his trouble. It left him with a distinct scar on his right cheek just below the eye. Like many princes in the age before social media, he enjoyed campaigning and though his subsequent invasion of France in 1415 was long sold by historians as a necessary distraction from domestic problems, most of those had already been resolved. Henry undoubtedly would have seen the invasion as an attempt to get loot and land while taking advantage of the discord and civil wars that had broken out in the reign of mad Charles VI's reign.

While claiming a divine right to rule, medieval kings were little more than glorified gangsters – forever taking out weaker hoodlums while extending their patch and protection rackets and killing anyone who got in their way. But depicting Henry V as a fifteenth-century godfather whacking his rivals to steal their stuff doesn't exactly put him, or monarchy, in a great light, so instead Henry has long been portrayed as a sort of military healer seeking almost altruistically, to reunite the kingdoms of England and France for the good of all.

That is – and let me be very clear about this – utter, pernicious bullshit – but for some, it's pervasive and attractive bullshit and an awful lot of people cling to it.

In *Made in Britain*, the book so beloved of recent Conservative politicians and historians, Adrian Sykes even has Henry "pursuing his claim to the French throne – and righting the wrongs which he passionately believed France had inflicted on England". That claim on the throne was very tenuous indeed. It stemmed from his great-grand-father Edward III's belief that he was heir on his mother's side – despite there being no precedent for it – and a woolier case that the lands of the Dukes of Normandy, who had invaded England in 1066 plus later gains, meant that large tracts of France belonged in perpetuity to the English kings, for no other reason than that they once had.

That belief became so entrenched in the psyche of English and later British Kings and Queens that it wasn't until the middle of the reign of George III in 1800 that monarchs agreed to stop being crowned kings of France.

Shakespeare and the chroniclers who inspired him gave a nod to those claims but also found a more poetic excuse for the invasion and had Henry V deciding to act after being insulted by a gift from the French Dauphin.

L. du Garde Peach, author of the children's Ladybird book *The Story of Henry V,* a staple of British children's home history libraries from the 1950s to the 1980s, takes up the narrative: "He sent a box of tennis balls to Henry, scornfully telling him that he had better stay at home and play tennis and not try to conquer France. This made Henry very angry. He sent back a message that he would reply with cannon balls."

This story has done the rounds since the very first chroniclers and their biographies of King Henry and even features in the 2019 film *The King*, but is unlikely to be true since there is little evidence that real tennis was played in England until the reign of Henry VIII.

Henry V saw the invasion of France, not as a reason to take revenge on a crappy accession gift but as an opportunity to make himself wealthy and even more powerful. Like the twenty-first-century tyrant Vladimir Putin, he essentially orchestrated an excuse to invade neighbouring Normandy by siding with the breakaway Burgundians and made a list of outrageous demands, including the restoration of the Angevin Empire. That was the empire established three hundred years earlier by the House of Plantagenet during the twelfth and thirteenth centuries, in a process started by another of England's "great Henrys", Henry II, who inherited three dynasties and ruled over a realm that covered nearly half of France, along with England and parts of Wales and Ireland.

The very idea that the French king would hand Henry V back the French possessions of the Angevin Empire was ridiculous. The territory had been lost almost two hundred years previously at the end of the reign of King John and Henry had no claim on it. The young king knew that, knew his demands would be rejected and also knew it would all make a good pretext for invasion. While awaiting a reply, he started preparing for the campaign. Enjoying an unprecedented level of support from parliament, he levied taxes and borrowed heavily from merchants, including the Lord Mayor of London, a certain Richard "Dick" Whittington, who was the go-to loan shark to royalty in the era.

With all the stage set and all the characters in place, the pantomime could begin.

Rather undermining the narrative of the underdog English taking on monsters, the first chroniclers of King Henry's life boasted of a huge fleet of 1,500 ships carrying 11,000 men that crossed the Channel in August 1415. Those numbers seem to have been rather inflated and in her 2006 book *Agincourt: A New History*, the medievalist academic Anne Curry suggests that just 700 boats and some 8,500 men were sent across the sea. Having landed safely in Normandy, the army marched inland to besiege Harfleur.

There, Shakespeare has Henry deliver the immortal words: "Once more unto the breach, dear friends, once more" as he seizes the city. Glorious stuff in fiction, but hell on Earth for the hapless, ordinary men, women and children of the city, who had not invited this miserable conquest upon themselves and were now the focus of the English king's ambitions. On 22 September, after a month of destruction and terror, Henry V marched triumphantly into the city and demanded that all the women and children be rounded up and separated from the men. On 24th September, these war refugees were forcibly marched to the city of Lillebonne and handed over to renowned French knight and military leader Marshal Boucicaut aka Jean II le Meingre.

Henry's perceived clemency is traditionally used to shine a light on his inherent English decency with Ladybird's L. Du Garde Peach arguing: "Very often in those days, when a town was captured, all the defenders and sometimes even the citizens were killed. Henry was more merciful. All who wished were allowed to go in peace."

But "go in peace" in this case meant being expelled from their homes and, as Ian Mortimer puts it in *1415: Henry V's Year of Glory*:

"For a full month they had suffered from a lack of sleep and food; they had lived in fear that the English siege engines would destroy their homes and families. Then at the end... they were driven from their homes and husbands and sons losing all they owned... it was a far worse fate... what lay before them was hardship, penury, alienation from their husbands and the unknown."

The uncomfortable parallels between fifteenth-century Henry V and twenty-first-century Putin are there; Hal had not only invaded France on spurious grounds, he was also now destroying a city while claiming to liberate it and expelling people from their homes, rendering them refugees. He was no liberator or a hero – he was a tyrant – upturning other people's lives and burning their homes in his quest for land and thirst for glory. Henry, like Putin, and indeed like every tyrant in history, no doubt convinced himself that it was otherwise. This land was his "birthright" and he was "on a mission from God". And Henry, like Putin and indeed as with all despots through time, had and has his apologists willing to argue that he had "just cause" in destroying cities, killing innocent people and separating loved ones on a whim. Nothing could have been further from the truth.

Almost as soon as Hal had achieved his first victory, dysentery took hold among his men, and as even his most trusted lieutenants succumbed, so he decided it was time to cut his losses and retreat north to the English enclave at Calais. Some 76km (47 miles) from that goal, having crossed the river Canche, his scouts met French men-at-arms near the town of Azincourt. Henry realised he would be cut off or killed and that he had no option but to stand and fight. On Thursday 24th October, the day before St Crispin's Day, the French and English armies camped opposite each other in preparation for battle.

In Act IV, scenes 1 and 2 of *Henry V*, Shakespeare has Henry spending the evening before battle boosting morale among his men. It's a lovely story of the "man of the people" hanging out with the gang and lifting their spirits. What actually occurred, was somewhat less prosaic. In reality, he ordered silence in the camp and threatened to cut off the ears of anyone who made a sound.

The following morning the two sides met.

The anonymously written Medieval chronicle *Gesta Henrici Quinti* (Deeds of Henry V) has the English heavily outnumbered with just 11,000 men facing the French force of 60,000. Adrian Sykes' *Made in Britain* has: "25,000 men, including heavy cavalry, outnumbered Henry's by at least a factor of five to one." Anne Curry has the far more sober and realistic figure of 8,500 English soldiers facing 12,500 French, so still outnumbered but by nowhere near as much as the odds of history would have you believe.

What everyone can agree on is that the French were defeated, and that brilliant strategy by the English played an enormous part. Henry had chosen the site of the showdown well. Newly ploughed fields, the narrow width of the battlefield (between two dense woodlands) and the sodden conditions gave the lightly armed English, with their 7,000 expert longbowmen, a huge advantage over the cumbersome French knights in their heavy armour and all the rest of their fancy gear.

The eventual winners were also aided to victory, as is so often the case in war, polar races and football, by their enemy's mistakes and bad weather.

Despite their horses sinking up to their knees in mud, the French decided that it would be a good idea to launch a cavalry charge, largely on the basis that this was what they always did. As they advanced, thousands of arrows rained down on them, cutting their horses from underneath them and, as the heavily armoured knights lay on their backs in the mud, like helpless turtles, they were slaughtered en masse. The French men-at-arms who followed faced the significant psychological torment of more arrows and the sight of wounded knights being butchered ahead of them in the mud.

Having won the initial advantage and perhaps spooked by his good fortune and a commotion among his prisoners, Henry then committed a war crime. For reasons that remain opaque, he ordered that his men cut the throats of his remaining hostages lest they suddenly rise up. It was a shameful and callous act that broke every single contemporary law of chivalry.

The French monk of Saint Denis wrote: *"This order was executed quickly and carnage lasted until he had realised and seen with his own eyes (that the threat had passed.)"**

Shakespeare does not shy from the event with Henry proclaiming (in Act IV, scene 6):

"But, hark! what new alarum is this same?
The French have reinforced their scatter'd men:
Then every soldier kill his prisoners:
Give the word through."

But it's interesting to note that both Olivier and Branagh cut the line and the event itself from their film versions, presumably on the principle that great heroes don't slit hundreds of unarmed men's throats because they're feeling a bit paranoid about how things are going.

Having lost fewer than 600 men in defeating the French army in battle, Henry returned via Calais to England. The adventure had achieved little in practical terms, but it had made him a hero back home and paved the way for further campaigns. Ever more zealous, fanatical, misogynistic and ever more imbued with the notion that he was on a mission from God, Henry returned to France in 1417 and besieged Caen. Having overrun the city, he ordered that every male over the age of 12 be executed and 1,800 men and boys were butchered.

---

* Dockray, K., *Henry V*, 2004, p154.

Challenged by a Dominican friar, Henry is said to have replied: "I am the scourge of God, sent to punish the people of God for their sins."

These are the words of a murderous, religious extremist who believes himself to be on a divine mission. But again – Henry V is rarely if ever seen in those terms in popular versions of the story.

The Treaty of Troyes in May 1420 saw him secure his French bride Catherine and the agreement that any future heir would be King of France. But the atrocities and campaigning did not end, and more killings followed at Rougemont in 1421 and Meaux in 1422. Henry died shortly after the latter at Vincennes on 31st August 1422, aged 35.

Henry had spent a third of his nine-year reign waging unprovoked war. Little of what Henry V achieved had any lasting impact and his great bequest to posterity was the legend of the man himself. He became an icon of Englishness, the hero and role model to tyrannical Henry VIII and a rich seam of propaganda and nationalist identity well into our modern age.

Dickens and Winston Churchill went further and promoted his contributions to the English language and his role in making it the *lingua franca* of government and literature. But language, like the dinosaurs in *Jurassic Park*, always finds a way without the help of kings and Henry was in fact less "promoting" English than, by speaking it, reflecting its irresistible rise. Hoodlum Henry was no proto-lexicographer, any more than he was lovable Hal. As Ian Mortimer argues, he was instead: "A deeply flawed individual. He lacked the simpler qualities of compassion, warmth and the understanding of human frailty that one looks for in all men – yeoman and paupers as well as kings."

And yet, in an age when autocrats invade their neighbours and kill innocent people who get in their way, it seems remarkable that this religious fanatic and warmonger, whose pursuit of land and power destroyed cities and took innocent lives, remains a national hero. The very victories and methods of our hero King Henry V are, after all, uncomfortably similar to those of tyrants of this and our last century from Nazi Germany to Russia and modern China.

Henry V sits at a cornerstone of the Kings and Queens narrative that still dominates both our island story and how millions of us view our past. It is, in many ways, a deliberately false and poisonous myth of fictional blue blood, the lie of caste superiority and the long-propagated notion of divine right that was long maintained to prop up the power and status of a tiny, privileged band of people while everyone else was kept in their place. But undoubtedly the most astonishing thing about it all is that on-going conspiracy to pretend that our long line of monarchs has, for the most part, been full of remarkable people, rather than the lacklustre human beings who have sat on the throne. It is somewhat bizarre that some of the most God-awful people in this nation's story are still being deified and lionised centuries after their deaths despite the deeds of their life stories.

Should we really be buying so blindly into this stuff in 2023?

The problem with traditional "Kings and Queens" history, as personified in the legend of Henry V, is that it is used to validate the activities of many of history's worst despots, land grabbers, tyrants and oppressors. It has modern implications too because the weaponisation of heritage is still used to legitimise a wider still-prevailing system of class, power, nepotism and privilege that seeps into every nook and cranny of British society. It is a system that continues to exist for the benefit of just a tiny number of largely unelected, still-powerful people and one long ago rejected by other people.

* * *

The "First Fleet" of 9 transport ships, escorted by two warships and carrying 850 convicts, officers and guards arrived at Botany Bay on 20th January 1788 and over the next few days, discharged its cargo of men. The local area was known by its Aboriginal inhabitants as Warrane, but the following year the ship's captain, Arthur Phillip, dubbed it "Sydney" after the then Home Secretary, Thomas Townshend, who was made Viscount Sydney that year– and the name stuck.

These first transportees arrived on a continent that had flora and fauna the likes of which they had never seen. Pouched marsupials bouncing about on hind legs, giant flightless birds, spiders the size of a convict's hand and amphibious mammals that looked like they'd been stuck together with the leftover parts of other species.

The Aboriginal Australian people, who had already been living on the continent for some 50,000 years, spoke of other, even odder beasts lurking in the outback and they included the most feared beast of all. The Bunyip was a child-eating monster at least 12-feet high with an emu's head, a long, serrated bill, walrus tusks, flippers, the body of a giant crocodile and a long, swishy tail which hugged its prey to death – like a sort of killer Mr Blobby. As soon as the British heard about it, they naturally set out to bag one, murder it and stuff it with sawdust for a museum. But frustratingly, they didn't have much luck. In the 1830s, remains were found, but it was later deduced that they were probably those of a cow. In 1847 an oddly shaped skull was found in the bed of the Murrumbidgee River in New South Wales, but again it was inconclusive and most likely a dead kangaroo.

Either way, the thought of this weird monster freaked out many settlers and pot shots were forever being taken at bushes in the dark, as apophenic fear of every shadow ran wild. In time, with no confirmed sighting, the suspicion began to creep in that the Bunyip was a fictional beast.

In 1871, the eminent naturalist Dr George Bennett went as far as to suggest that the Bunyip might be a cultural memory, a fragment of reminiscence for a diprotodon, or any of the other giant marsupials that had once roamed the continent, but in the meantime, the term *bunyip* had already become Aussie slang for an imposter or criminal.

Mid- to late-nineteenth-century Australia was beginning to forge its own identity and carve its own path and that took many forms – from the development of a distinctive vocabulary, to a shift in accent, to the development of its own literature* and culture. And inevitably, from quite early on questions were raised about its political autonomy

---

* The first Australian novel, *Quintus Serviton*, by convict Henry Savery, appeared in 1831; the first great work of definitively Australian literature was *For the Term of His Natural life* by Marcus Clarke in 1870.

and just how many ties were needed with the Mother Country, the United Kingdom. New South Wales began taking steps towards self-government and achieved it in 1851 with the establishment of an elected Legislative Council*. But there was a problem. In Britain, there were two executive bodies – the House of Lords, a then entirely hereditary upper chamber, and the elected House of Commons – while in NSW there was just one.

How could NSW democracy properly function without its own House of Lords to review the work of the popular assembly?

Into the breach stepped millionaire businessman and adventurer William Wentworth. Wentworth had quite a backstory. He was born to a convict mother, Catherine Crowley, on board the ship *Surprize* that was bound for the Norfolk Island penal colony in 1790; his father, D'Arcy, had been the ship's surgeon and was scion to a purportedly very grand Anglo-Irish family which made damn sure that everybody knew how important they were. D'Arcy later went on to claim, rather confusingly, that he was the "first paying passenger" to travel to New South Wales but it was a big heap of dunny, because court documents suggest that he had gone to Australia as a doctor on condition of avoiding a prison sentence for highway robbery in England instead. In 1813, Wentworth Junior, aged 23, led an expedition that "discovered" a path through the Blue Mountains (that indigenous Aboriginal people had been using for tens of thousands of years) and henceforth opened a route into the continent beyond.

An eight-year sojourn in England between 1816 and 1824 saw him admitted to the bar and in between he wrote epic poetry and political literature, while dreaming up ways of becoming rich and powerful.

On returning to Australia that same year, he co-founded a newspaper, *The Australian*,† and then, having inherited his father's fortune, became a "Squatter" – effectively one of Australia's first oligarchs – who used existing wealth to take advantage of the indigenous population

---

* The council had existed since 1824 but was only (partly) elected from 1851.
† Confusingly there have been two newspapers of that name. Wentworth's closed in 1848; the other one is still going.

and seized massive tracts of land in the outback. Aboriginal people, like most hunter-gatherer societies, did not have a concept of individual land ownership and as such were easily robbed of their ancestral homeland and in many cases their lives by early white settlers. Wentworth went on to become fabulously rich and, as a member of the wealthy Squattocracy, a hugely influential player in burgeoning Australian society as a Conservative politician.

Having been snubbed by English high society on account of his convict mother and colonial roots, he had also grown a massive chip on his shoulder. His youthful instincts as a liberal and enemy of autocracy did not apply to Aboriginal people whom he viewed with uncontained, racist contempt. Comparing them to orangutans, he encouraged the creation of the Native Police and other bodies that were used to subjugate and crush indigenous resistance, and in 1827 successfully defended an officer, Nathaniel Lowe, who had murdered an Aboriginal prisoner.

He was an advocate of indentured Chinese labour and the liberal use of capital punishment, but as his views turned ever more unpleasant and right-wing even his own newspaper eventually disassociated itself publicly from him. A great believer in the notion of "men of substance", he didn't even bother disguising his contempt for the working-class white people of Australia who did not own land and, in 1851, argued: "Those who had no property [should be treated] as infants, or idiots, [as they were] unfit to have any voice in the management of the State."

In 1853, this charmer drafted a proposed constitution for New South Wales which included a plan to establish an Upper Legislative Council based on the House of Lords. His bill would have seen Queen Victoria appointing hereditary peers, who would then bring a little much-needed class to the new country... and a huge amount of hereditary power to the Squattocracy to whom he belonged.

As one of the biggest landowners in the world at the time, this was more than just nation-building. Wentworth wanted an earldom to satiate his vanity, but he also understood that a new Australian aristocracy, with him and his friends at the top, would give them unrivalled power. Unfortunately for Wentworth, meritocratic Australia was not willing to play ball and his grandiose dreams were to be greeted with mockery.

The great Australian satirist and writer Daniel Deniehy was everything that Wentworth was not. The proud son of two convicts, Deniehy wore the badge with pride and was an early product of the Australian Dream. He had risen above the inopportune circumstances of his childhood to become a lawyer, man of letters and statesman. A precocious talent with a gift for languages and words, he blazed brightly through his era and, in 1853, aged just 26, he delivered a blistering speech on Wentworth's proposals, ridiculing the idea of an Australian House of Lords: "Here we all know the common water mole was transferred into the duck-billed platypus, and in some distant emulation of this degeneration, I suppose we are to be favoured with a 'bunyip aristocracy'."

Hinting at the Mother Country's not so glorious origins that had been forged out of blood and conquest, he added:

"The stately aristocracy of England was founded on the sword. The men who came over with the conquering Norman were the masters of the Saxons, and so became the aristocracy… But … by what process would Wentworth and his satellites have conquered the people of New South Wales, except by the artful dodgery of cooking up a Franchise Bill."

Deniehy derided the notion of a Lord of Wollongong, a Viscount of Mount Buggery, an Earl of Camden or a Duke of Vaucluse and questioned the real motives of the Squattocracy, led by Wentworth, in seeking to create a new aristocratic elite. Other writers and satirists piled in and soon the proposition was being so roundly ridiculed that an embarrassed Wentworth was obliged to remove it from the draft constitution, which in 1856 saw the creation of the New South Wales Legislative Assembly, and made plans to leave the country even before it came about.

The absurdity of class had been laid bare and the Bunyip Aristocracy never came about. And yet, 170 years later, in twenty-first-century Britain, that system, so roundly mocked in mid eighteenth-century colonial Australia, persists. The unelected House of Lords remains our upper chamber, ever more stuffed with members of the political chumocracy while "elite" families still cling on to their power and patronage.

Ninety-two hereditary peers, all male and all put there by each other, remain. If a hereditary peer dies or resigns, the remaining 91 select another chum to join them. Twenty-six Bishops of the Church of England also sit on the red benches, and of course, our head of state – the same one shared with Australia – is still appointed by accident of birth, just as happened in the days of Henry V supposedly in an unbroken line dating back to 1066. But if you believe that, then I have a bunyip skeleton to sell you. After all, as Henry V had no living descendants beyond Henry VI's son Edward, who died childless, the line broke there, as it did so many other times. King Charles III is the 1st cousin 18 times removed of Henry V, which sounds impressive until you do a bit of mental maths and realise that you might well be too. If you go back 500 years, almost everyone with a European ancestor is descended from and related to the same tiny group of people, including the kings and queens and the people who emptied their chamber pots.

The class system is a cultural dinosaur, but it is a political one too and one that actively empowers nepotism, the old school network and former prime ministers' friends and siblings. It is as nonsensical and ludicrous now as it was in 1854 and pointing out as much really should not be controversial.

Having been almost literally laughed out of the country, Wentworth retired from the New South Wales Legislative Council in 1854, and went to live in Merley House, a sprawling country home near Wimborne in Dorset, where he died in 1872.

It is a curious thing that if one remains out of sight and out of mind then one's political stature can grow. Dreadful people and land-grabbers can, if they live long enough, rise to the stature of founding statesmen, and this is exactly what happened to Wentworth. When he died, there were plaudits and obituaries galore and when his body was transported back to Sydney by ship, he was afforded Australia's first ever state funeral in a mass event which saw tens of thousands of people lining the streets to honour him. Wentworth had made the arrangements himself and had spent years buying his place in Australian history by giving his money to universities and good causes. It's a time-honoured road to immortality and it is why Cecil Rhodes, one of the monsters of the imperial age, who robbed his way to wealth and power in South Africa, is still celebrated by Oriel College in Oxford today, to whom he gave the equivalent of around £12 million (in today's money).

Wentworth's money built on a fortune made from stolen Aboriginal ancestral lands is the reason why his name lives on in roads and waterfalls, state divisions, postage stamps, statues and buildings. There is a grand statue to him at the University of Sydney which makes him look every bit the grand statesman and towering Victorian political hero. The town of Wentworth Falls and Wentworth are both named in his honour. It's a familiar story and if he were to be aware of all the accolades, one feels quite certain that this tireless racist and disciple at the altar of privilege would be very pleased with himself indeed.

No towns or villages are named after Daniel Deniehy, but there is a stone statue of him in Sydney which is far less grandiose than Wentworth's. Following his Bunyip speech he remained in high demand as a man of letters and public speaker and was a passionate and inspirational thinker who believed, in sharp contrast to pompous and elitist Wentworth that "the first great aim of statesmanship in a new country should be to people the soil, —in a word, to create a great community."

Noble words and a noble ambition are the reason I chose him to be the hero of this chapter. But like so many great people and thinkers throughout history he had a troubled side, a tormented soul and some considerable human flaws too.

He died almost penniless of alcoholism in Bathurst, New South Wales, aged just 37 in 1865. A little over 20 years later, a memorial was erected in his honour over his grave, but he received few of the posthumous plaudits of his political rival and, if remembered at all nowadays, it is mostly for inventing the term *Bunyip Aristocracy*.

And for all Deniehy's grand and noble words about common people and community – he meant white common European people and white European communities. Indeed, Daniel Deniehy, champion of democracy and equality did not believe in the rights of everyone and most notably – the Chinese.

Following the Australian Gold Rush in 1851, around 40,000 Chinese, mostly male, migrants came to Australia and as their numbers increased, the white settler population, who had themselves displaced the Aboriginal people, began to talk darkly of being replaced. In 1860, Deniehy lost his parliamentary seat and subsequently rarely gave public speeches. But he did address a crowd at an anti-Chinese demonstration in Sydney, following the riots at Lambing Flat in May and June 1861.

That outbreak of violence had 3,000 Australian white settlers descend on the Burrangong mining region and attack Chinese labourers, looting their camps and driving them off the land. Thankfully nobody was killed, but when Deneihy later spoke, while deploring the violence he told the crowd:

"We are threatened by an overwhelming influx of barbarians... If this immigration continued on a large scale, it would impart to the country a degraded and barbarous aspect, and the colonial descent would be of decidedly inferior caste. The country stands upon the brink of a great disaster, and ... I see no more injustice in preventing the landing of this degraded race, who would not only lower and demoralise, but also endanger the safety of the country."

Human beings can be a mass of contradictions. Even as radical thinkers talk of a better world and a brighter future, they can simultaneously hold disgusting opinions about other people. Deniehy's life is depressing proof perhaps, that even great heroes can be appalling racists – and have feet of clay.

CHAPTER NINE

SCIENCE HEROES
THOMAS MIDGLEY

When Fake Heroes Kill

It's August 1910 and a woman is driving over the Belle Isle Bridge in Detroit, Michigan, when her car stalls and breaks down. A few seconds later, a Cadillac pulls up behind her and a man called Byron Carter steps out to offer his assistance. The woman has just got extremely lucky because 44-year-old Byron is the owner of *Cartercar*, one of America's leading automobile manufacturers. After exchanging pleasantries, he takes out a lever from his vehicle and begins to turn the engine.

But as he does, disaster strikes. The engine misfires and the crank spins violently from his hands, breaking his arm and fracturing his jaw. Byron is rushed to hospital, but complications set in, he contracts gangrene and, several months later, he dies.

The close-knit automobile industry reels in collective horror at the loss and determines that all shall not be in vain. To that end, one of his closest friends, Cadillac founder Henry M. Leland, hires Charles "Boss" Kettering, inventor of the electric cash register, to design an ignition system that will rid the world of cranks and prevent further tragedy. Kettering's company Delco sets to work on the project and two years later, in 1912, Cadillac begins fitting the new "electric ignition" to their

Model 30.* On 17th August 1915 Kettering's *Engine Starting Device* is awarded patent number 1,150, 523 and the invention, still in use today, makes Kettering rich and famous. But he never forgets the tragedy which inspired his greatest innovation, so when the author Thomas Alvin Boyd is researching a biography of him in 1957, Kettering tells the tale of Byron Carter and the fatal accident that inspired the invention of electric ignition, and the tale passes into mechanical engineering folklore.

It's a story that has been retold many times since in newspaper articles, encyclopedias, books and even a spate of recent podcasts, which is unfortunate, because it's completely untrue. Byron Carter died not in 1910 but in 1908 and his death certificate makes no mention of an accident, attributing the pneumonia that ended his life to "years" of ill health, not gangrene.

There is an earlier version of a hand crank accident inspiring "Boss" Kettering's invention and it features in a history of General Motors called *The Turning Wheel* by Arthur Pound published by Doubleday, in 1934. But Byron Carter doesn't feature in the tale.

Pound relates in Chapter XIX: "An elderly friend of Henry M. Leland ...was driving on Belle Isle bridge when the motor stalled. Forgetting to throw out the clutch before cranking the car, he sustained serious injuries."

So, no Edwardian "damsel in distress", just an anonymous elderly man having an accident with his own car. Hand-cranking did cause accidents but it was also very hard work, as Arthur Pound relates:

"Starting an engine by hand was difficult and often destructive of temper and clothes. It required, usually, a combination of physical vigors not always found in the same individual. The strength of Ajax, the cunning of Ulysses and the speed of Hermes."

Even "electric ignition" needs an origin story, it seems, and the good news is that this accident was probably inspired by an actual

---

* Hand cranks were still supplied as a back-up on cars well into the twentieth century. The last car to have one was the Russian-made Lada Niva in 1998.

incident, in April 1907, reported at the time in the *Detroit Free Press*, when a man called H.O. (not Byron) Carter suffered a "violent blow on the jaw" after cranking his automobile. H.O. Carter was head of the Carter International Automobile Manufacturing Co in Milwaukee, so perhaps this is just a case of mistaken identity. The good news is that H.O. Carter did not die and three months later the paper was reporting that he had made a full recovery. Or rather, good news for Mr Carter but not for lovers of good stories inspiring great inventions.

I suppose you can understand why Kettering and his biographer gave the story a bit of a spin. After all, inventing an electric starter device because 'hand cranking was a pain in the arse and someone once received a slight injury doing it' is hardly up there with *The Epic of Gilgamesh* is it.

Does it matter? I mean who cares about starter motors and engine cranks? And anyway, isn't this particular myth a bit benign?, I hear you cry, and yes, it might sound that way – right up until the moment you discover that "Boss" Kettering's invention caused the deaths of millions of people.

* * *

The Model 30 automobile was a breakthrough for Cadillac. With a V8 engine and a top speed of 60mph, it was not only the first car to have an electric ignition, but the first to come with a closed body too. Unfortunately, Delco's new ignition system had teething problems and chief among them was noise. Sparks from the starter created mini explosions in the engine's cylinders – an effect known as "engine knocking", which not only damaged the engine but also made one hell of a racket. The solution was to find an additive that would change the fuel's octane level and to that end, in 1916, Boss Kettering put a 27-year-old mechanical engineer called Thomas Midgley Jr on the job.

It was already established that adding ethanol to fuel was highly effective in countering "knocking", but it was very expensive and so Midgley sought a cheaper alternative. In 1921, he made a break-through, by instead adding a compound called Tetraethyllead (TEL), which in 1923 won him the prestigious William. H. Nichols Medal. The development revolutionised the motor engine and Arthur Pound eulogises it across pages of his book describing it as an "outstanding development" and celebrating the "liberal licensing policy" that led, by the 1930s, to its being used by "nearly all of the leading refiners". It would lead to Midgley being celebrated as a great pioneer of engineering and widely acclaimed for ending "engine knocking".

The problem was that, despite its fancy sounding name, Tetraethyllead (TEL) was largely made up of lead. And lead is a highly toxic substance, which poisons and kills human beings.

If only they had known! you might think, except that back in 1921, the dangers of lead were very well known indeed. Human beings had, after all, been using it for 6,000 years, so there had been plenty of opportunity to observe its toxic properties and as far back as 200 BCE, the Greek botanist and physician Nicander had ascribed colic and paralysis to the heavy metal. In Roman times, lead plumbing, urns and cooking pots slowly poisoned the wealthier citizens of the Empire, but it was with the dawn of the Industrial Revolution in the mid-eighteenth century that the dangers of exposure became most patently clear.

In 1786, US polymath Benjamin Franklin wrote a letter to a friend with observations he had made during a trip to England and France about exposure to the substance. On a visit to Paris's Hôpital de la Charité, at the time a pioneer in diagnostics, he had been allowed to examine a list of patients who had worked with the metal and who had all developed the same conditions as a result.

Franklin ends the letter with a remark for the ages: "You will see by it, that the Opinion of this mischievous Effect from Lead, is at least above Sixty Years old; and you will observe with Concern how long a useful Truth may be known, and exist, before it is generally receiv'd and practis'd on."

That other Franklin, Sir John (of 1840's Arctic explorer fame), took lead food cans on his expedition and there was long speculation that it may have contributed to the men's bizarre behaviour while trying to find the Northwest passage. By the end of the First World War in 1918, lead was perhaps the best understood toxic substance in nature and everyone knew it was extremely dangerous, which is why the corporation that GM and Standard Oil Jersey* (ESSO) formed to process Tetraethyllead was dubbed Ethyl – to give the strong impression to consumers that it was using ethanol instead. It wasn't. There was no ethanol. They were using lead.

Experimental production started in 1923 at a small plant in Dayton, Ohio, and people began to get sick shortly after that. When large-scale manufacturing moved to a bigger plant in Deepwater, New Jersey, the same problems began and visitors were disturbed to find employees brushing imaginary insects away from around their heads while babbling to themselves unintelligibly. The refinery became known as the "Looney Gas Building" and later the "House of Butterflies".

Two workers died of lead poisoning that autumn of 1923 and four more in the first months of the following year. In April 1924, two employees died at the Dayton plant and it was shut down. Another, smaller processing refinery in Bayway, New Jersey opened in September 1924 and closed just a month later after 44 employees were taken seriously ill. Five of the workers subsequently went insane and died.

Luckily, Kettering, now vice-president of General Motors Research Corporation, had figured out who was to blame and quite obviously, it was the employees. Poor Charles found it was simply impossible to get through to "the boys" the danger of working with lead: "We put watchmen in at the plant, and they used to snap the stuff at each other, and throw it at each other, and they were saying that they were sissies. They did not realize what they were working with."

---

* Standard was broken up in 1911 but in the 1920s Mr Rockerfeller's entity was still commonly called Standard.

And all the while, people kept going mad and dying. On 21st September 1924, a 37-year-old process operator called Frank Durr went home feeling unwell and later died – in a straightjacket. A month later Ernest Oelgert started yelling that figures were "coming at him" and also died. Another employee, William McSweeney, was sent home feeling delirious and Sharon McGrane, author of *Prometheans in the Lab* (2000), explains what happened next: "The next morning McSweeney's sister-in-law had to summon a policeman who needed extra men to subdue (him). Violently insane the Irishman died in a local hospital three days later bound in a straitjacket and clamped to an iron cot."

No longer able to contain the slough of stories coming out of the factory, Ethyl lost control of the narrative. On 24th October 1924, the New Jersey medical examiner intervened, and some of the production facilities were shut down, but the deaths kept coming. And it was only when the newspapers latched on to the story that something was done.

On Monday, 27th October 1924, *The New York Times* splashed events across their front page: "ODD GAS KILLS ONE, MAKES FOUR INSANE; Stricken at Work in Standard's Experiment Laboratory in Elizabeth, N.J."

The following day there was another sensational heading, recording that a "second death from insanity-producing gas at the Standard Oil plant of Elizabeth, N.J., was reported yesterday. The victim was Walter Dyhock, who died violently insane at the reconstruction Hospital in this city". At this point Standard offered one the most jaw-dropping excuses in business history, with a spokesman telling a *New York Times* reporter that: "These men probably went insane because they worked too hard."

Soon the chief chemist at New York City's toxicology department, Alexander Gettler, was on the case and over the course of the next three weeks, he studied the bodies of four dead workers who had been brought into the Examiner's Office.

With Kettering in Europe on business, Thomas Midgely launched a media counteroffensive. Ever the showman, on 30th October 1924, he held a press conference in New York where he produced a jar of TEL and poured the contents over his hands before wiping it off with a handkerchief: "I'm not taking any chance whatever... nor would I take any chances by doing that every day," he told the assembled journalists before taking a second bottle and holding it under his nose, inhaling the fumes for a full minute. The man from the *Herald Tribune* reported that Midgley claimed: "The fumes had no (negative) effect ... if inhaled only a short time."

It was a big fat lie and Midgley knew it, because while developing TEL he had become extremely ill and been forced to take an extended leave of absence, lasting some months, in Florida. Before departing, he had written a letter of apology to the committee of the William H. Nichols Medal excusing himself from the awards ceremony since: "After about a year's work in organic lead, I find that my lungs have been affected and that it is necessary to drop all work and get a large supply of fresh air."

Midgley was, in other words, fully aware that the substance was not just dangerous but potentially deadly, and that it was poisoning everyone who came into extended contact with it, including himself. But TEL was his big moment – his big career break. He was winning awards and getting promoted and the company was relying on him. People were delighted that their engines no longer knocked, and the oil giant was reaping huge rewards. So, Midgley significantly downplayed the danger and instead, like Kettering, blamed the workers for not taking the necessary precautions while risking his own health and even his life to prove that something that was highly toxic was not. It sounds utterly insane, doesn't it? But that was just the start of it.

Gettler's report appeared some days later and provided incontrovertible proof that the victims at the plant had all died from lead poisoning and not "hard work". Heavy deposits of the metal had been present in their brain tissue, lungs and bones. They had been killed by the product. That posed a bit of a problem because obviously if it was killing the employees, it might bump off the consumers too. Rather than stopping production there and then, Midgley and his colleagues sought to cover up the risk and, as 1924 rolled towards 1925, the vested interests rallied. On Christmas Eve 1924, Kettering led a committee that included key figures at Standard, Ethyl, GM and Du Pont to a private meeting with Surgeon General, Rear Admiral Hugh S. Cumming. The business leaders requested that a national conference on TEL be held so that the debate could be aired in the courts of expertise and public opinion. Cumming agreed and a week before the conference, Ethyl withdrew TEL from gas stations to make it look like they were taking matters seriously.

On 25th May 1925, the TEL conference was held in a federal auditorium in Washington D.C. and the Surgeon General presided over events. This was a peculiarly modern corporate stitch-up. The oil and automobile giants had deliberately engineered a scenario where false balance aka "bothsidesism" could be used to their advantage. That phenomenon occurs when "both sides" in a debate are treated as if they have equally strong arguments – even when they quite clearly do not.

In 2021, the ZDF German journalist Dirk Steffens described bothsidesism in an interview with the Teleschau news agency thus: "Suppose an astrophysicist says on a talk show that the earth is a sphere. Then there is someone else who claims that the earth is flat. The truth doesn't fucking lie somewhere in the middle. If one of two statements is complete nonsense, journalism does not have to let the nonsense have its say and grant it equivalence to the truth."

Bothsidesism is a very contemporary plague and in an age when biased TV networks and social media influencers pump out false equivalence and misinformation into the mainstream, we need to be ever more on our guard against it. But it is far from being a modern problem. In 1925 given the threat it posed to the public, there was no possible case for TEL. It had been shown to be obviously and demonstrably toxic and it was also known that safer alternatives were available in the form of ethanol. But the public could not be expected to fully understand that or the science, and the US press let them down very badly indeed by portraying proceedings as a balanced debate between two equally credible authorities. By agreeing to appear at the conference, the *antilead* scientists also walked headlong into a trap.

On the day, Standard's spokesperson, Frank Howard, was up first and went in hard, arguing that progress had its costs: "Because some animals die and some do not die in some experiments, shall we give this thing up entirely? Frankly, it is a problem that we do not know how to meet. We cannot justify ourselves in our consciences if we abandon the thing. I think it would be an unheard-of blunder if we should abandon a thing of this kind merely because of our fears."

He namechecked the war dead and argued that lead was "a natural substance" and more that: "Present day civilization rests on oil and motors... We do not feel justified in giving up what has come to the industry like a gift from heaven on the possibility that a hazard may be involved in it..."

His "common sense" approach, evocation of the sacrifice of the war dead for the freedom to manufacture leaded petrol, and God's grace in providing the raw materials, went down well with the assembled journalists. Howard also had science on his side in the shape of Robert A. Kehoe, who, at 32, was already a leading toxicologist and environmental health expert.

Kehoe argued that TEL should only be banned "if it can be shown ... that an actual danger is had as a result..." and warned against hysteria, insisting very reasonably that everything should be done "on the basis of facts", not "the basis of opinions". This logic gave rise to the term the "Kehoe Rule", which placed the burden of proof not on the manufacturer of the potentially lethal product but on those opposing it. The rule essentially posits that until a product or substance can be proven guilty of harming other people it must be considered safe.

Anyone who has spent any time debating climate change, so-called stolen elections or the efficacy of vaccines on social media will be familiar with Kehoe's Rule which, in essence, is: PROVE IT.

The *antilead* group was up next. Consisting mostly of experts, scientists, university professors and labour representatives who, unlike their opponents, had come at their own expense, it presented its case in a far less flamboyant manner. Their star player was Alice Hamilton. The first woman to ever become an Assistant Professor at Harvard Medical School, in 1911, as Chief Medical Officer at the Illinois Commission of Occupational Diseases, she had been responsible for the landmark, mandatory introduction of health and safety legislation for workers dealing with toxic materials. She was more than just any old authority on lead toxicity, she was *the* acknowledged expert in the field and knew far, far more about the subject than Kehoe. Aged 56, she came armed with science, experience, facts, figures and killer logic.

It was established that TEL was not the only ingredient that could be used to solve the problem, so as *The New York Times* recorded she: "urged the men connected with the industry to put aside the lead compound entirely and try to find something else to get rid of the knock."

Midgley had landed on TEL extremely quickly in what amounted to a scientific stab in the dark. But two years in, he and Ethyl and Kettering were now so heavily invested – financially, professionally and emotionally – in the product that they did not want to risk losing face by admitting that it was dangerous. This was, once again, a classic example of the sunk-cost fallacy. And nobody wanted to walk away despite leaded petrol being a very bad idea.

Hamilton was not just a scientist but also a key figure in the American women's rights movement and a leading peace campaigner – used to speaking to crowds and forcefully making her case. In fact, the *antilead* advocate group on the day prominently included women in their number, with activists Grace Burnham McDonald, founder of the Worker's Health Bureau, and her colleague Harriet Silverman, both there on behalf of the employees and their families. These were remarkable people and Burnham McDonald caused something of a stir by responding forcefully to Frank Howard's opening statement about

God's part in TEL by saying: "It was no gift of heaven for the 11 who were killed by it and the 149 who were injured ."*

The very presence of these extremely smart people may have brought problems of its own and retrospectively, as depressing as it sounds, Hamilton wondered whether their presence had in fact been counterproductive to the cause. America's male-dominated media, industrial and political landscape was not about to be told what to do by a bunch of women and, in Hamilton's words, they gave "an unmistakable aura of Socialism or feminine sentimentality for the poor" which did not go down well with the auditorium full of men. Or to put it another way, the women's presence gave the assembled patriarchy the green light to dismiss the science as the opinionated, hysterical, posturing of some middle-aged women.

The conference was a PR coup for Ethyl because it ended exactly as they had hoped, with the waters muddied and everyone more confused than they had been before. The Surgeon General ordered a federal inquiry, a tried-and-tested method of kicking a story off the front pages, and the news cycle moved on from the negative stories and the fears about lead, in the belief that it would all be OK now.

As the government's panel of scientists began their investigation, Ethyl and Standard went on manoeuvres and commissioned their own research from Robert Kehoe who was, as you have probably guessed by now, deep in the pockets of the oil giants.

After several months of "scientific investigations", Kehoe concluded that TEL could be safely handled with the introduction of proper ventilation, protective equipment and training and his work† was rushed to be published ahead of the much more thorough federal inquiry, in order to put pressure on it. Hurried into producing its own findings, the government panel agreed with Kehoe and said that TEL posed no significant public health threat. Their main recommendation

* Unknown to her, 17 people had died and many thousands had been poisoned.
† Kehoe's research was to define attitudes to TEL for the next five decades.

was that TEL be mixed with gasoline before distribution and not on the premises of gas stations, and then the panel did add that as car numbers grew and roads became more congested, leaded petrol could one day "constitute a menace to the general public after prolonged use or other conditions not foreseen at this time."

But hey, that would be a problem for a future generation to contend with, so let the good times roll. Production resumed and Ethyl, its parent companies and competitors grew massively rich on the profits while a lead-coloured haze crept over the horizon.

Fortunately for us all and for the planet, the story does not end there.

In 1948, a US geochemist called Clair Patterson was part of a small team trying to work out the age of the Earth by studying lead. I appreciate we haven't all come here for a science lesson, but sit up at the back there because it's important to grasp it so that you can understand what happened next. Very basically, the chemistry goes like this: as uranium decays over time to produce lead, it is possible, by studying meteorites and rocks with a known age, to compare the lead found in them with lead found in the core Earth's core and work out the ratio between the two. From that, you can estimate the age of the planet.

Along with his colleague, George Tilton, Patterson began analysing rocks with a determined age, which they could then use to measure against deposits of unknown quantity. But there was a massive problem because it quickly became apparent that something was interfering with the test material. In short, they were finding lead where it should not have been. The stuff appeared to be on everything. Even the lab itself was contaminated.

That made it impossible to accurately read the samples and so the men set about creating what was the world's first sterile lab but despite their efforts, lead deposits still kept showing up. Patterson found lead in the lab tap water, lead in dust, lead on his skin, lead on his hair and even in his dandruff. Extending the search, he found lead everywhere else as well. There was lead in soil, in plants, grass, trees and right across the food chain, in a trail that could be traced back to the exhaust fumes of cars.

In seeking to find a cheap and profitable solution to engine knocking, Thomas Midgley had literally poisoned the Earth.

That terrible truth and the extent of the destruction it had caused would take years to emerge and, in the meantime, Patterson and Tilton managed to calculate the age of the planet. Their final assessment was that our Earth is 4.54 billion years old – give or take a few million years either way – and no better figure has been put forward since. On reaching this figure, Patterson got so excited that he thought he was going to have a heart attack and later wrote: "The discovery electrified my soul. True scientific discovery renders the brain incapable at such moments of shouting vigorously to the world, 'Look what I've done'. Instead, such discovery instinctively forces the brain to thunder 'We did it'."

In 1956, the men published their findings in the peer-reviewed bi-weekly *Geochimica et Cosmochimica Acta* and having filed it, Clair set about trying to save the world. There are many heroes in this chapter, but more than anyone Clair is the man to whom we all owe a remarkable debt, because if he had not dedicated his life to the task many millions more of us would likely be prematurely dead.

You'll be astonished to hear that the oil giants didn't like his findings and began to take sanctions against him. Funding Patterson received from the American Petroleum Association was switched off and a contract he had with the Public Health Service was revoked. One day a group of men in suits appeared at his lab and offered him money to conduct "research" that was favourable to the interests of big business. Patterson took the men into his lecture hall, patiently explained the problem of lead in the atmosphere and then politely invited them to go fuck themselves (my words, not his).

In 1965, Patterson wrote an essay entitled "Contaminated and Natural Lead Environments of Man", which elucidated the problem of leaded petrol and its impact on the environment. The most highly regarded scientist in the field, who had written a definitive paper on the subject in 1925, was then invited to peer-review it.

His name was Robert Kehoe, of the University of Cincinnati and Kettering Laboratories, and you might remember him from such works as "fiddling the data for his masters in the oil and automobile sector" on the previous pages. Kehoe had now spent four decades in the service of his sponsors in the oil and manufacturing industry and had held firm to the Kehoe Rule.

He had successfully managed to convince not just America but the world, that lead was naturally present in the human body and that there was a certain threshold at which it became dangerous. Both hypotheses were wrong, but Kehoe stuck to them like lead deposits to a human lung and, like every other charlatan in this book, he had been showered with awards and praise for his work. It is a depressingly familiar story and so too was his willingness to deploy contempt and ridicule in order to maintain the status quo.

Kehoe portrayed Patterson as an ignorant fool who, as a mere geologist, had no understanding of biology. Patterson was "naïve" and his work was "an example of how wrong one can be in his biological postulates and conclusions, when he steps into this field, of which he is so woefully ignorant and so lacking in any concepts of the depths of his ignorance, that he is not even cautious in drawing sweeping conclusions."*

In an article for *Mental Floss* in 2017, journalist and editor Lucas Reilly adds: "Kehoe could have spiked the paper – he was, after all, lead's foremost authority – but he greenlighted it anyway, believing publication would destroy Patterson's credibility."

In a very recognisably modern way, fellow toxicologists and scientists piled in, pouring scorn on the findings, and Clair Patterson was ostracised by research organisations and public and privately funded bodies. But to his immense credit, this hero plugged on, carrying out

---

* Ad hominem attacks – the last recourse of the Establishment lackey. Much easier for Kehoe to attack and ridicule a rival and dismiss their work than to engage with it

research and lobbying politicians and the US Environmental Protection Agency (EPA) and all the while being led by science not the interests of multibillion dollar corporations. His efforts finally paid off and, in the mid 1970s, the consensus shifted. Conferences and hearings were convened and bothsidesism was indulged once again.

Mr Kehoe held fast to his "rule". No matter that it could be proved that modern human beings were walking around with 600 times more lead in their bodies than their ancestors. No matter that an article in *The Lancet* showed that children with higher levels of lead in their bodies had lower IQs, worse health and a shorter life expectancy. No matter that every indicator showed that Patterson was right and the motorcar and oil industries were engaged in a massive cover-up. No matter that everything pointed to the poisoning of the planet to make a few people very rich.

With weary predictability, Ethyl's vice president, Larry Blanchard, cautioned against any hasty moves to reduce leaded petrol until his company's own biased research was published. Practically holding back the tears, he compared the multi-billion-dollar oil industry to the infamous trials at Salem in 1692, saying: "The whole proceeding against an industry that has made invaluable contributions to the American economy for more than fifty years (is) the worst example of fanaticism since the New England witch hunts in the Seventeenth Century."

Luckily, sanity prevailed. The US Court of Appeals swung against the oil giants and in EPA's favour, and ordered the gradual phasing out of leaded petrol. From 1976, levels of lead in the environment began to fall dramatically.

The evidence from what followed spoke for itself and in 1986 EPA called for a total ban on all leaded fuel in US cars – which came, eventually, in 1996.* The rest of the world gradually followed and in 2021, Algeria became the last nation in the world to ban TEL. Data compiled

---

* Although propeller-driven aircraft received an exemption

by the UN Environment Programme in the years since, shows that the banning of leaded petrol is estimated to have prevented over 1.2 million deaths per year from strokes, cancer, heart disease and lead poisoning.

The benefits to public health and clean air have been immeasurable but some scientists have gone further, arguing that the removal of lead from our environment has even reduced crime. From the mid-1940s onwards, the crime rate in the USA was on constant rise, with violent assaults and homicide on a steady upward curve. But with the end of TEL, and despite what the tabloids and Fox News might have you believe, all crime began to fall, and in areas with higher-than-average lead contamination, it fell fastest of all.

How much that can be put down to lead in the atmosphere and how much it can be attributed to other societal factors continues to be debated. The most recent meta-analysis of data from 2021 available suggests that the ban on leaded petrol could be responsible for little as 7% and as much as a 28% decline in criminal activity. But the deeply disquieting story of TEL is much bigger than mere percentages. For five decades, vested industrial interests conspired to make vast profits while poisoning the Earth. In that endeavour, they were supported by presidents and defended by politicians, newspaper proprietors, unprincipled scientists and any number of useful idiots willing to dismiss concerns about leaded fuel as hysterical scare stories. While the public were fobbed off with lies and distractions and bothsidesism that deliberately obfuscated the truth, millions of human beings were posioned or died. And as if all of that is not bad enough, what makes the story even more depressing is that the same thing happened twice.

And both times Thomas Midgley was to blame.

* * *

The first electric refrigerator was invented by a Hungarian, István Röck, in the 1890s. He began manufacturing and selling the appliances shortly thereafter, but there was a problem. The gas systems on early fridges used ammonia, ether and sulphur dioxide, meaning that when they started leaking in people's homes, the beers inside might stay nice and cold, but there would be nobody around to enjoy them. Because they would be dead.

You'd think that a product that was shown to kill and poison people would have been swiftly removed from the market. But as with cigarettes, machine guns, leaded petrol and the use of asbestos, for quite some time nobody seemed to think that it was too much of a problem. Early refrigerators were prohibitively expensive well into the 1920s and, as such, getting killed by your domestic appliance remained a rich person's game.

In 1926, Albert Einstein and his student Leo Szilárd began trying to solve the problem of refrigerators' inherently lethal nature, allegedly inspired by an event where an entire family in Berlin had been killed by a leak. The pair used water, ammonia and butane for their system and registered the patent in 1930. The design was far safer than existing models but, as with any innovation, it came with other headaches, quite literally, because the German-built refrigerators were inefficient and – like early engines – very noisy. You didn't have to be Einstein (sorry, I couldn't resist) to realise that they were not the answer and, with the rise of the Nazis in the 1930s, work was put on hold anyway as Einstein and Szilárd, who were both Jewish, left Germany.

Fortunately, the two geniuses who had solved "engine knocking" were already on the case. In 1918, one of the founders of General Motors (GM), William C. Durrant, invested in a refrigeration firm called Frigidaire, which, like Hoover, would eventually become eponymous with the product it made. Seven years later, in 1925, and with time on his hands now that lead was being pumped freely out into the atmosphere, Durrant asked Delco to make his Frigidaires safer and "Boss" Kettering soon had his trusted lieutenant, Thomas Midgley, fixing the problem.

Midgley's team mixed fluorine and hydrocarbon to create a synthetic, colourless gas of chlorofluorocarbons (CFCs) called dichlorodifluoromethane which was later given the brand name Freon 12. To stymie fears that the gas might be lethal, once again Midgley stepped up and did something stupid, inhaling Freon 12 in front of reporters before blowing out a candle.

This very foolish man was once again risking his health to prove that something which was obviously extremely dangerous, was fit for public consumption – and once again, it worked. The nation was reassured and, in 1930, a GM and Du Pont subsidiary, Kinetic Chemicals, began to produce the gas commercially. Freon 12 went on to be used in aerosol cans and coolants – and thereafter became a ubiquitous presence in twentieth-century life. When not enjoying homemade ice or a nice cool glass of milk, the developed world busied itself spraying chlorofluorocarbons at their feet, armpits and passing insects – not realising for one moment that a reckoning would come.

With another massive breakthrough on his CV, Midgley was roundly celebrated and was awarded all manner of gongs, including the prestigious Perkin Medal in 1937 by the Society of Chemical Industry. He was now at the top of his game and was promoted and celebrated accordingly. Between 1940 to 1944 he would become a director and vice president of the Ohio State University Research Foundation, and for his string of successes, he was elected to the National Academy of Sciences. Years after his death, he would still be honoured in some quarters and there was even a biography of him snappily titled, *From the Periodic Table to Production: The Life of Thomas Midgley, Jr., the Inventor of Ethyl Gasoline and Freon Refrigerants*. Written by his grandson Thomas Midgley IV, it painted him very much as a scientific hero. The book was published in 2001, but by then, the truth was already known.

Three decades earlier, in 1973, a 30-year-old Mexican-born postgraduate student called Mario Molina was working in a lab at the University of California, when he made an unnerving discovery. While investigating the properties of CFCs, he used an early computer to carry out some hypothetical modelling and discovered in the process, that CFCs could potentially be punching a hole in the ozone layer, the thin layer of oxygen compound in the upper atmosphere that protects us from radiation by absorbing it. By Molina's calculations, the ozone layer might already have been depleted by as much as 7%.

His boss, the celebrated chemist F. Sherwood Rowland, took Molina and his findings seriously, but inevitably there was the usual round of mockery and scorn from vested interests which insisted that it was all hysteria, that everything was just peachy and that there was nothing to worry about.

It was only in 1985, when Joseph Farman and colleagues on the British Antarctic Survey observed that ozone levels in the stratosphere were dropping 35% more in the Antarctic spring than they had been doing 20 years previously, that people began to sit up and take notice. The following year, US atmospheric chemist Susan Solomon travelled to McMurdo Sound in Antarctica – the very place where Scott's Discovery Expedition had built their base camp in 1902 – and began conducting experiments in sight of Scott's still-standing hut.

A year later, Solomon's National Ozone Expedition proved, without any doubt, that there was indeed a hole in the ozone layer, roughly the size of North America and far bigger than even Molina had estimated, and that CFCs were to blame. Molina was completely vindicated, but of course the vested interests continued to complain, aided and abetted by conservative newspapers and ozone hole deniers, even as governments across the world acted. In 1987, the Montreal Protocol for reducing known substances that deplete the ozone layer was established and, by 2009, every country with a delegation at the UN had signed it. In 1995, Mario Molina, Rowland and a Dutch chemist, Paul Crutzen, were awarded the Nobel Prize for Chemistry for the work they had done in recognising the dangers of CFCs and saving the world from even greater environmental catastrophe.

All history repeats and in the case of human-made environmental crises, it repeats with depressing predictability. The unheroic journey goes like this: big businesses do something bad, dangerous and provably detrimental that makes them money, the product poisons the planet, they deny it is dangerous, someone proves it is dangerous, big business and its fellow travellers ridicule them and insist it is not the case; the cycle repeats, going on and on until it is eventually proved that said product is indeed deadly. Discussions follow and decades later that dangerous thing gets banned. In all of it, just a few people benefit both professionally and commercially, while the rest of us suffer. It continues because all too often, people don't listen to the experts who are pointing it all out and listen instead to gobby opinion-formers and the very big businesses that are reaping rewards.

In future decades, there is no doubt that our descendants will shake their heads in despair at our continued addiction to petrol, gas and oil and hold us in the same contempt that we currently reserve for the likes of Thomas Midgley.

Midgley lived out his brief life as a celebrated hero of science and innovation and was not to live long enough to witness the much-deserved trouncing of his reputation. In 1944, while accepting the post of Chairman and President of the American Chemical Society, in recognition of his life's work, the 55-year-old delivered a speech that summed up his world view: "We are the only species of living creatures that even conceives of exerting any control over the environment thrust upon it (although) admittedly, this control is far from complete. Its extension is greatly to be desired."

It was delivered from his home, by telephone, because Midgley was by now very ill. Four years earlier, he had contracted polio and the result of that terrible illness, so common in the days before vaccination, was that he had become increasingly bed-bound. His lack of mobility had frustrated and depressed him, so he designed a complicated system of pulleys, ropes and wires to lift him out of bed.

On 2nd November 1944 he got caught up in the wiring and was asphyxiated.

In more recent years, as his story and his infamy has gained traction, authors, podcasters and features writers have found a sort of grim poetic justice in that. The man responsible for so much environmental damage, was quite literally hoisted by his own petard. But like so many "much told stories" throughout time, this one, I'm afraid, is not entirely true.

As Sharon McGrayne explains in her book *Prometheans in the Lab:* "Death and cemetery certificates… reveal what must have been obvious to his friends: a mechanical engineer of Midgley's prowess would not have strangled himself on his own invention. In despair, Midgley had carefully planned his own death."

Incapacitated and depressed, he had chosen to end his life.

At the funeral, "Boss" Kettering took umbrage at the priest's suggestion that "we bring nothing into this world and take nothing out" and Kettering delivered a long eulogy to his disciple and friend saying: "In Midge's case it seems appropriate to add that we can at least leave a lot behind for the good of the world", though time was to prove that assessment wrong.

To cause one global environmental catastrophe might be considered a misfortune, to cause two leaves everyone reaching for their thesauruses. The American historian J.R. MacNeill has said that Midgley "had more impact on the atmosphere than any other single organism in human history" and, while true, that lets far too many others off the hook. Midgley did not act alone; Kettering, Du Pont, Ethyl, GM and Robert Kehoe, the scientist who was willing to sell his soul to be the pet expert of the oil giants, were all to blame.

The rise and fall of TEL and Freon 12 are both in essence much the same tale of corporate greed, personal ambition and stupidity. Because, despite the biographies and plaudits, despite the praise and honour they garnered in their lifetimes and since – Midgley, Kehoe, Kettering and their various facilitators were all fundamentally stupid people.

We would do well to be wary of stupid people and let me briefly explain why.

In 1976, the Italian economic historian Carlo M. Cipolla self-published a short book called *The Basic Laws of Human Stupidity.* His ground-breaking thesis was that stupid people – like lead in the environment – exist everywhere and in roughly equal quantities. Being stupid has nothing to do with IQ or academic qualifications. By Cipolla's thesis stupid people can be barristers or garbage men, housewives, businesspeople, chartered surveyors, war heroes, politicians, academics, religious pastors or even great explorers. And this, according to Cipolla, was the problem, because since stupid people exist with such prevalence: "Always and inevitably, everyone underestimates the number of stupid people in circulation."

As a "stupid person is the most dangerous kind of person" (as he goes on to say), this can have all sorts of ghastly consequences.

Midgley's stupidity may have been inherent, but it was greatly amplified by his greed and ambition. In seeking to make himself somebody special, in striving to win honours and plaudits and, most of all, to achieve posterity, he was willing to gamble the health and lives of millions of others on the back of his career progression. Worst of all he did it all, knowing it was bad, while purporting to make the world a better place. That, in a sense, makes him one of the biggest villains in this book. The story of TEL and CFCs and all the denialism that comes with it is jaw-dropping and exactly the sort of history and science that should be taught in schools. It's too late for many climate-change deniers lost in their echo chambers and cults of anti-scientific nonsense, but if our children learned the story of Midgley, Ethyl and CFCs, then perhaps... just perhaps... the next generation might not be quite so at risk from stupid and dangerous people as the ones that went before.

* * *

The modern world is stuffed full of gadgets that have improved our lives immeasurably. We take for granted our computers and smartphones, our washing machines, hot water, bathrooms, smart hubs, electric cars, wifi and even such basic things as electric light – invented, as everyone knows, by Thomas Edison in October 1879. That invention, now such an innocuous part of our existence, changed everything. It revolutionised working patterns, altered sleeping habits and made homes and public spaces safer and more comfortable than they had ever been before.

None of this happened overnight. In 1919, some 40 years after its invention, just 6% of British homes had electric light and by the start of the Second World War, just 75% of the country was wired up. But in the realms of secular scientific saints, Thomas Edison's filament continues to burn brightly. The "lone genius inventor" myth by which all others are measured.

There are also, of course, dozens of biographies, kids' books, documentaries and inspirational social media memes telling his life's adventures along with those famous, pithy quotes including:

"Opportunity is missed by most people because it is dressed in overalls and looks like work."

"Showing up is 80% of success."

And everybody's favourite: "Genius is 1% inspiration and 99% perspiration."

There are also, once again, films about his life including, most famously, a much-loved 1940 Mickey Rooney vehicle *Young Tom Edison* and its sequel *Edison, the Man* starring Spencer Tracy that came out the same year. The story of Edison has also served as inspiration to generations of school children and during a brief sojourn in SE Asia, I even taught it myself from an Indonesian school textbook.

The standard version of the tale begins in Port Huron, Michigan in the 1850s with a teacher writing a letter to Thomas's mother describing the mischievous boy as "addled" and suggesting that he will never amount to anything. His mother, Nancy, takes him out of school, teaches him herself and, out of her love and nurturing, he becomes a curious and brilliant young man.

When Edison is 12, he starts working as a "news butcher", selling daily papers on a train out of Port Huron to Detroit. In his spare time, he does experiments in the guard's van, but one day he sets fire to it. By Edison's own account, that leads to the guard lifting him up by the ears, rendering him deaf for the rest of his life. There are, in fact, two versions of the story of how he lost his hearing. In the other, he is running to get up on to the train and is lifted up ear-wards by a passenger.

Another life-defining moment comes when young Tom sees a railroad employee's young son on the line and leaps in front of an oncoming train to save the boy's life. In gratitude, the kid's father teaches him how to use the telegraph and from there, he goes on to become an employee of Western Union, where he invents a system that can send two wired messages at the same time. He finds fame and fortune as an inventor, businessman and creator of the lightbulb, the movie camera and the phonograph. By his death in 1931, aged 84, he holds patents for 1,093 inventions.

It is a properly cracking and inspirational biography and what's interesting for connoisseurs of fake hero narratives, which I hope by now includes us all, is that quite a lot of it is true. The young Thomas Edison really did leave school in roughly the circumstances described and his mother, Nancy, did indeed teach him at home. There was no "letter", but school reports show that his teacher did assess him as "addled" and in recent years experts have suggested that the young Edison's behaviour may have been down to ADHD. Equally, it is quite possible that he was already suffering hearing problems which may have been exacerbated by scarlet fever and/or childhood infection and, as such, he may not always have been able to hear what was going on, which might have all resulted in him being dubbed "stupid". Either way, there is no evidence that his deafness was caused by an angry railroad employee and, given that he himself kept changing the story, it was almost certainly a myth.

Other things are true. Edison really did save the life of a railroad employee's three-year-old child by jumping in front of a train, demonstrating a heroic Autrey Factor in his nature – and he was also taught to use the telegraph in return by J. U. Mackenzie, the boy's father. It is also true that one of his experiments went disastrously wrong and got him fired, but he was nowhere near a train at the time and was in fact aged 19 and working in the Associated Press office in Louisville, Kentucky. The stories behind some of his early innovations are also true.

With his business associate, Franklin Pope, Edison co-invented a system that could send multiple messages at once, and it eventually became the "stock ticker" that will be familiar to anyone who has seen a film set in the period 1871–1960.

But Edison did not invent the lightbulb in 1879.

That honour, like Clair Patterson's estimate of the Earth's age and pretty much every invention in history, is shared by a succession of innovators, who paved the way to its widespread use today. In 1802, the British chemist Sir Humphry Davy used a giant battery to light an electric "Davy Lamp". In 1840, the British astronomer Warren de la Rue used super-thin, high-resistance filaments made of platinum to achieve enough brightness to light a room. Platinum turns liquid at 1,786°C and that high melting point prevented the filaments from burning out as quickly as the electric Davy Lamp. The problem was that, as they were made with the most expensive metal on Earth, they were prohibitively expensive. So, it was back to the drawing board, but that wasn't the end of the tale. Two years later, British politician and science enthusiast Frederick de Moleyns was granted a patent for the first incandescent light bulb – five years before Edison was even born. In December 1878, yet another Brit, Joseph Swan, demonstrated his own vacuum light bulb and in 1881 his firm, the Swan Electric Light Company, fitted out the Savoy Theatre in London's Strand with 1,200 bulbs, using a generator to light them. The Savoy was the first public space in the world to be lit this way and it opened in October 1881, almost a year before New York City, on 4th September 1882, first flicked the switch to light up the premises of *The New York Times*, which had been kitted out by Edison in a PR masterstroke that guaranteed a whole heap of friendly press.

Edison's light bulbs were better than Swan's and lasted longer. But "inventor of the long-lasting more efficient light bulb" does not have the same ring to it as "inventor of the light bulb" so most of us have grown up with his "lightbulb moment", not Swan's or Moleyns'.

That should not dim Edison's achievement in lighting up the world, but here we have yet another case of the person who shouts loudest getting all the acclaim. The lightbulb was no more invented by one individual than the telephone, internet, computer, car, TV radio, vibrator, wheel or electric toothbrush. The same is true of many of Edison's inventions. Yes, he built an early phonograph in 1877 and managed to record sound that could be played back on tinfoil plates, but it was others, including Alexander Graham Bell, improving on his invention, that led to it becoming a practical home accessory. The claim that "Edison (first) recorded sound" – propagated by, among others, Ira Gershwin in the 1937 song 'They All Laughed' – is also not really true.

More than 20 years earlier, a Frenchman, Édouard-Léon Scott de Martinville, managed to do it using a machine called a phonautograph, which he patented in France in March 1857, when Edison was 10. The oldest surviving recording is from 9th April 1860 and features a woman singing 'Au Clair De La Lune'. We don't know her name, but she is inarguably the world's first recording artist and the trembling voice, echoing down a path of 160 plus years, has a haunting quality to it.

As for the movie camera, well, again while Edison took credit and in turn inspired the Lumières' father (back in Chapter One), who in turn inspired them, he did not invent that either. Another Frenchman, Louis Le Prince, was the first person to make what we would call "moving pictures" although he too was standing on the shoulders of giants. Notable among them was an Englishman, Eadweard Muybridge, who made a celebrated sequence of a horse moving in 1878. But Le Prince undoubtedly made the first ever motion-picture camera, and he used it to shoot footage of his family at their home in Leeds, in 1888, making the Yorkshire city the true birthplace of cinema.

In 1890, while preparing for a trip to the USA, Le Prince boarded a train in Dijon, bound for Paris, and was never seen again. That disappearance spawned some unlikely conspiracy theories and a much more probable suggestion that he took his own life. Either way, his disappearance meant that his planned public exhibition in New York City that September never happened and, as such, his name and his legend slipped into obscurity.

Edison's Kinetoscope was first demonstrated in May 1891. The inventor was happy to take the credit for the innovation but really, it was his employee, British-born William Dickson, and his team at the Edison laboratory who had invented and developed the Kinetograph (aka cinema camera) that had made it all possible. Ultimately, Edison was that most familiar of heroic types; a man of huge enthusiasm, ambition and ideas who was a master of PR, a great businessman and an appropriator of other people's achievements. A sort of creative 'ringmaster'. Yes, he invented things, but collaboration is the true mother of invention and plagiarism its father; add a little myth-making into the mix and you are guaranteed immortality as the *Lone Genius Inventor Thomas Edison*.

Edison's most enduring achievement was to create the Menlo Park Research Laboratory and employ dozens of brilliant people, making him, at the end, a kind of Andy Warhol of science, with Menlo Park his Factory. Some extraordinary things came out of the works. They included the carbon microphone, a machine that perforated paper, an early type-writer, a nickel-plating process and the reversible galvanic battery.

But many others reached Cipolla-esque heights of stupidity.

In 1877, Edison decided that what the little girls of America needed more than anything was a two-foot-high talking doll that cost the equivalent of $200 and sang creepy songs. In the process, he created a monster. The tiny records in the doll's back wore out quickly and the little crank handle broke. But this was nothing compared to the toy's singing voice, which (and you can listen to it online) sounded like an eerie ghost child in a particularly terrifying 1970s' horror film. Children were left quivering in mute fear in corners while while their parents were rendered considerably poorer. Production ceased almost immediately.

Another cracker came in 1911 when he proposed the idea of houses, built entirely out of concrete moulds – with concrete tables, chairs, stairs, beds and kitchens. A great idea after six or seven pints of very strong cider perhaps, but it turned out that nobody wanted to live in homes made of concrete, not least because the substance is very unstable and the occupants risked ending up in concrete coffins.

In 1920, in the post-war and post-"Spanish Flu" craze for contacting the recent dead, Edison told B. C. Forbes of the *American* newspaper that he was working on a "delicately responsive machine" that would allow the living to communicate with the dead. He said: "I have been at work for some time building an apparatus to see if it is possible for personalities which have left this earth to communicate with us" and ever since people have taken him at his word. It does seem an extraordinary proposition by one of the greatest minds of his age, but revisiting the interview 100 years later, I'm not convinced he was being entirely serious. Edison clearly does not have much time for spiritualists and says that seances are:

"Unscientific nonsense. I don't say that all these so-called 'mediums' are simply fakers scheming to fool the public and line their own pockets. Some of them may be sincere enough. They may really have got themselves into such a state of mind that they imagine they are in communication with 'spirits'."

It may have been sincere but more likely Edison's sense of humour was at play, perhaps with an eye to landing his company some free publicity in the newspapers. That said, talking horror dolls, concrete houses and hotlines to heaven were not the worst of his ideas – at least not commercially.

The Wizard of Menlo Park's biggest flop, which became known as "Edison's Folly", was his idea of pulverising low-grade iron ore. The idea was to collect the grains using electromagnets and then to melt the dust down and turn it into bars of metal. On paper it may have made sense but it was very impractical indeed and turned out to be an unmitigated disaster. A rare "big" failure, and Edison made matters worse by throwing more money at it, in yet another classic example of the sunk-cost fallacy. It was only when a rich seam of ore was discovered in Minnesota that the great man came to his senses and shut up shop.

"I have not failed, not once. I've discovered ten thousand ways that don't work!" Edison said once and, yes, he really did say it but there's little evidence he ever uttered any of the other pithy quotes attributed to him.

The most famous of those, "Genius is 1% inspiration and 99% perspiration", was actually the work of a woman called Kate Sanborn. Kate, born in New Hampshire in 1839, was a teacher, poet, mathematician and author who published well over 20 books, including an 1885 anthology called *The Wit of Women* which sought to disprove that hoary old, misogynistic lie that women do not have a sense of humour. The book is unfortunately out of print but can be read online at Project Gutenberg and well proves her point. Sanborn quotes the poems, letters, and novels of hundreds of women writers and artists and almost single-handedly resurrected women playwrights, including the seventeenth-century English dramaturg Susanna Centlivre who wrote 19 stage plays. It is an insightful, entertaining and fascinating read.

In the 1890s, Sanborn gave a series of what were essentially nineteenth-century TED talks on the subject of hard work and genius at which she would deliver the famous line about inspiration and perspiration. Many years later, Edison quoted it to a newspaper reporter and inevitably the phrase became inexorably attached to him.

You will not be dropping your phonograph in astonishment, to learn that this was not the first or last time in history that the work of a woman ended up being attributed to a man.

* * *

Matilda Joslyn (later Matilda Gage) is one of those thousands of hugely influential women through time which popular history conspired to forget.

Born in Cicero, New York State in 1826, she grew up being tutored by her father and eventually went on to complete her education at the Clinton Liberal Institute in New York. Aged 19, she got married and shortly after that, she gave her first public speech at a convention on women's rights and suffrage. In the years that followed she raised a family but became a prolific writer of letters to newspapers and campaigned for the interests of freed slaves, indigenous native Americans and women's rights before herself turning to journalism in her forties.

In 1869, she cofounded the National Woman Suffrage Association (NWSA) and became a regular contributor to its newspaper, *The Revolution*.

Gage bristled at the injustice of all types of discrimination but became particularly active in the cause for women's rights and was a pioneering feminist who was not afraid to forcefully speak her mind. She was to fight the campaign right to her end and beyond, as she wrote her own epitaph, emblazoned on her gravestone which reads: "There is a word sweeter than mother, home or heaven. That word is liberty."

In 1870 Gage published a short book called *Woman as Inventor*, attacking the patriarchal narrative of history that had men inventing everything while women sat about raising babies. Gage's case was essentially that women had not simply been "present" throughout history but active participants in it.

The book begins with the story of Catharine Littlefield Greene who had the idea for a cotton gin, writing: "Although the work on the model was done by the hands of Eli Whitney, yet Mrs Greene originated the idea."

Gage then goes backwards through time, arguing that social pressure had pushed the contribution of countless women into anonymity. In a later short publication called "All the Rights I Want", she wrote: "It is sometimes better to be a dead man, than a live woman" and in the case of women scientists, well, never a truer word was written, as we shall see.

In 1893, Gage published another influential treatise, titled *Woman, Church and State*, which argued that throughout recent history, the church had branded "wise, or learned woman," as "witches" to marginalise, persecute or kill them. "What was termed magic, among men, was called witchcraft in women. The one was rarely, the other invariably, punished," she wrote.

It was a compelling argument and one which resonated with her son-in-law, Frank Baum – a male ally of early American feminists, who used his mother-in-law as the basis of the character Glinda in his book *The Wonderful Wizard of Oz*. For that much-loved book (and 1939 film version *The Wizard of Oz*) is in fact a none too subtle feminist parable. All the fairly dim-witted men in the story, after all, whether they be lions, scarecrows, tin or wizards, are led by Dorothy and wise "witch" Glinda, and it is the women who outwit and defeat evil in the godless kingdom.

Gage's legacy stretches well beyond her life and fiction. The Matilda Effect is a term coined in her honour by US science historian Margaret Rossiter, which describes the bias wherein women in science are routinely written out of the story of their own achievements. Rossiter was one of the few women enrolled on a science degree at Yale in 1969 and struggled to get taken seriously. That and her interest in the role of women in science history inspired her book *Women Scientists in America*, published in 1981. The book sought to highlight the contribution of women throughout time and went right back to the contributions of the twelfth-century physician, Trota of Salerno.

For centuries Trota's name was entangled with that of "Trotula", to whom twelfth-century medical journals including *De curis mulierum* (On Treatments for Women) were attributed. It is likely that Trota's own work was contained within it but "Trotula" was long assumed to be a fictional person until Trota's actual work was rediscovered in the twentieth century, proving that she made valuable early contributions to the cause of women's health.

Through the centuries that followed, women faced almost insur-mountable odds if they wanted to work in science or medicine – not least because they were barred from studying it.

In 1794, during the French Revolution, an 18-year-old young woman called Sophie Germain tried to enroll at the newly opened engineering academy École Polytechnique, but this was a revolution too far even for contemporary Paris and she was rejected by the University. Undeterred, she took on the identity of a male student, and calling herself "Monsieur LeBlanc", she reapplied, only to gain entry. She quickly attracted atten-tion from the professors and eventually, the Italian-born mathematician Joseph-Louis Lagrange, requested a meeting. "LeBlanc" was obliged to reveal her identity, but Lagrange was so impressed by her knowledge and enthusiasm that he became her mentor and she continued to study, albeit outside of the institution, under his guidance.

Germain's principal area of research was number theory, the study of the set of whole numbers, but from 1808 her focus shifted in another direction, and she began studying the mathematics of elasticity. Despite Lagrange's guidance, she was largely self-taught and as such there were gaps in her knowledge that allowed fellow, male, contem-poraries to dismiss her and parts of her work, but in 1816 she defied them all and won the French Academy of Sciences prize by producing a mathematical explanation for elasticity. To win it she had been obliged to enter anonymously, meaning that her work was open to plagiarism. So, when the far more famous French mathematician Siméon-Denis Poisson published his work on elasticity, he neglected to acknowledge that Germain's thesis had formed the catalyst for his ideas.

Sophie Germain was just one of thousands of women in history who suffered the Matilda Effect – and most of their names will probably remain forever lost in obscurity. But not all. Take the story of the American chemist, Alice Ball, who was the first woman and first African American, to receive a master's degree from the University of Hawai'i in 1915, when she was just 23.

Ball's great achievement was to develop the first effective injectable treatment for leprosy. It had long been established that chaulmoogra oil, which had been used in traditional tribal medicine for thousands of years, had properties which could be used to treat the infection, albeit with mixed results. The problem was that when ingested it was largely ineffective and when injected it caused lesions under the skin. Ball was one of several scientists working on a solution, but it was she who managed to isolate the beneficial ethyl ester compounds in the oil and modified them to form a soluble extract that could be injected and easily absorbed into the bloodstream.

Clinical trials began two years later, and her discovery would go on to cure thousands of people and reduce the symptoms in many thousands of others. Indeed, Ball's method remained the only proven treatment for the disease until well into the 1940s but, unfortunately, she did not live to bear witness to any of it.

Having made the breakthrough, Ball died, in 1916 aged just 24. The cause of death remains a mystery. It may have been tuberculosis, but others have suggested she was poisoned by her lab, perhaps as a result of chlorine, while teaching a class. Either way, she was unable to publish her findings. Instead, they were "completed" by her mentor Arthur L. Dean who took full advantage of the circumstances and passed her work off as his own. The use of isolated ethyl ester even, briefly, became known as "the Dean Method" until Ball's supervisor, Dr Harry Hollman, outraged by the brazen appropriation of his deceased student's work, complained loudly about it and in 1922 tried to get her the proper credit she deserved.

Hardly anything is known about Ball. Unlike celebrated male scientists of the era, including Thomas Midgley, no mentions were made of her and there were no entries about her in school textbooks. She left no diaries or personal papers, so there is but a faint trace of who she was and what she was like. Despite Hollman's best efforts, Ball did not so much fade from collective memory, she was never there in the first place – and it is only in recent years that her achievements have started to be brought to attention.

Much more is known of the life of Austrian-born Jewish scientist Lise Meitner, the first woman to become a full professor of physics in Germany, who worked alongside the famous scientist Otto Hahn for 30 years studying beta decay and, nuclear isomerism, and discovering the element protactinium.

Hahn and Strassmann spent years bombarding uranium with neutrons, which, in the process produced an unexpected effect. For as they did so, the uranium nuclei seemed to break apart and turned into radioactive barium isotopes. Neither could fathom why that was until Meitner and her nephew, Otto Frisch, stepped in and theorised and then demonstrated that a previously unknown process was at work: the uranium nucleus had in fact split in two due to a process Frisch dubbed "fission". Their findings were published in December 1938, but by then, Meitner had already been forced to leave Germany following the introduction of the Nuremberg Laws and was thus a stateless refugee. Moving to Sweden, she continued her worked with Frisch but her name was to lapse into obscurity.

Meitner's work had been critical to the discovery of fission, but when the 1944 Nobel Prize for Chemistry was awarded to Hahn in 1946, he was the sole recipient. The Nobel Committee did cite his collaboration with Meitner and noted: "The ...important theoretical investigations by Lise Meitner and Frisch, who based their study on the theory of the structure of atomic nuclei developed by Bohr."

But it was Hahn who got the Nobel Prize and Meitner's contribution became little more than a footnote to the event. Meitner's work was recognised by her contemporaries, including Albert Einstein, but was not – and is not – nearly as well known, still, some 55 years after her death.

The list of other women scientists who have been overlooked, edited out or erased makes a very long and very depressing read. It includes Rosalind Franklin, whose work at King's College, London, in the 1950s on the density and spiral formation of DNA molecules, led scientists James Watson and Francis Crick in 1953 to discover that the structure of DNA was a doublehelix (a twisted-ladder-like spiral of two interwoven strands). Franklin's critical contribution to their discovery, which later won Crick and Watson the Nobel Prize in Physiology or Medicine in 1962 (along with Maurice Wilkins), was only acknowledged (by Crick) after her death.

Then there's biochemist Marie Maynard Daly – the first African American woman to receive a PhD, completing her thesis at Columbia University in 1947. She received a grant from the American Cancer Society in 1948, and working in collaboration with her colleague, Dr Quentin B. Deming, broke new ground by establishing the link between cholesterol, clogged arteries and heart attacks. Her pioneering investigations of why heart attacks happen and went on to save millions of lives through both prevention and treatment.

Important work. But had you ever heard of Marie Maynard Daly until roughly 15 seconds ago?

On and on and on it goes: Klára Dán von Neumann, pioneer of computer coding on the ENIAC, the world's first programmable computer in 1945, whose name, guess what, was omitted from the paper announcing the breakthrough in 1947. Or Frances Oldham Kelsey who, in her role at the US Food and Drug Administration, in 1960 refused to authorise the use of the morning sickness tranquiliser thalidomide because she had fears over its safety and was not convinced that it had undergone rigorous enough clinical trials. The drug was in wide use across the rest of the world already, and in countries including the UK, Spain and Australia, it was later discovered to have led to thousands of babies being born with birth defects. An estimated 10,000 women were affected by the drug and some 40% of babies born to them died as a result. But this tragedy did not unfold in the USA thanks to one person – Frances Oldham Kelsey.

Another scientist, Alice Hamilton, the toxicology expert who tried and failed to warn the world of the potential hazards of leaded petrol, was blocked in her efforts by big oil and vested interests. She died of a stroke aged 101 in September 1970 and, while in the years since, she has been honoured with a statue, a 55 cent stamp (in 1995) and a place in the National Women's Hall of Fame in Seneca Falls, New York, her real legacy is the lasting impact of her work. Three months after her death, Congress passed the landmark Occupational Safety and Health Act, which revolutionised conditions for working men and women in the USA. Millions of people owe better, safer or longer lives lived – to Alice Hamilton. The legislation dramatically reduced debilitating accidents or deaths in the workplace. It also, inevitably, provided ammunition for moronic right-wing radio presenters and populist politicians down the ages, who have never been near a factory or building site, and allowed them to bang on about "health and safety gone mad" as they sought to roll it all back again.

But you know when you look at the history of CFCs and leaded petrol, the denial of science and the denial of women's place in it, you really do find yourself asking who the really mad people are in all of this. And more importantly why we continue to listen to people who are so patently and dangerously wrong.

CHAPTER TEN

CHILDHOOD HEROES
JOHN WAYNE

The Emotional Pull of Childhood Heroes

It's a late Sunday evening in the spring of 1980 and I'm 11 years old and counting down the hours to school. I hate my Hertfordshire prep school and the feeling, from the teachers at least, is entirely mutual – but luckily BBC1 is serving up a dollop of cinematic escapism. A John Wayne film, *Chisum* (1970), is coming up in the schedules, and my parents have given me permission to watch it – with supper on a tray.

Despite stiff competition from Harrison Ford and Roger Moore, Wayne remains my number one hero in 1980 and his death the previous year is the first celebrity loss to have affected me. Walking, as I often did, with my dad in the fields behind my house, he broke it to me in the same manner that you might tell a child about the death of a much-loved relative or a pet. John Wayne is, perhaps, a curious role model for a prep school boy from a middle-class rural Essex home, but hero he undoubtedly is. At my first school a teacher asked what we wanted to be when we grew up and I said "cowboy" – to gales of laughter, which haunt me to this day.

Wayne's on-screen personality appeals to something deep inside childhood me. He almost always plays the same character – essentially a non-violent man who is always prepared to use violence but only to make the world a better place; a loner who is never quite alone. Wayne is dependable. He never shirks the final showdown, never runs away when the bad guys turn up. He stands his ground and fights until justice has been done. Heroes like that that shape my outlook on the world, at the age of 11 my notion of masculinity and what a hero is, and it is one that Wayne himself shared: "I want to play a real man in all my films, and I define manhood simply: men should be tough, fair, and courageous, never petty, never looking for a fight, but never backing down from one either."

The movie is good, and we are in the middle of a scene where Wayne is taking on a group of bandits when there is a newsflash. The BBC cuts live to Prince's Gate in London, where the siege of the Iranian Embassy has been going on all week. I'm hazy about events but old enough, I think, to understand that terrorists have stormed into the building and taken a British police officer, PC Trevor Lock, and a bunch of other people hostage. My parents appear and tell me to budge up as the BBC cameras show two black-clad figures moving about on the balconies outside. And then – "bang" – an explosion goes off and a huge pall of white smoke lifts across the facade. A figure scrambles across the balcony and in through a window as flames lick the side of the building.

My parents are quite literally on the edges of the fashionably dark brown '70s sofa and our dog is yapping at the screen. But I am preoccupied with just one thought, and it is this: *When is my film going to come back on?*

The siege of the Iranian Embassy is to become a defining event of the 1980s. The men in balaclavas are members of the elite Special Air Service (SAS) and the storming of the building will make them famous. In 1982, the regiment's motto "Who Dares Wins" will become the title of a movie, starring actor Lewis Collins as an SAS officer who infiltrates the Campaign for Nuclear Disarmament (CND) and then kills a bunch of peaceniks who have laid siege to the US embassy. Yes, really, that's the plot, and in another one of life's deeply regrettable off-brand moments, I will come to love that film as a kid, but I will never come to terms with the siege that inspired it, for the simple reason that it robbed me of *Chisum*.

* * *

Memory is a deeply unreliable thing.

Late in the evening of 5th December 2013, Nelson Mandela, the former President of South Africa, died at his home in Houghton, Johannesburg. Soon after, condolences began to pour in from around the world. Barack Obama declared himself "one of the countless millions who drew inspiration from Nelson Mandela's life", Oprah Winfrey put out a statement saying that he was "everything you've ever heard and more", and in London, Prime Minister David Cameron called him "a hero of our time".

Mandela was 95 and had been ill for years, so the news, like that of the death of the Queen, a decade later, shouldn't have come as a shock; but for the people who thought he was dead already it sure as hell did.

Trawl back through social media posts of the time and you find Twitter and Facebook users across the planet, but particularly in the USA, revealing various degree of cognitive dissonance on hearing of his passing:

"Wait WTF? I thought Mandela died in the eighties!"

"Mandela is dead? I thought he died already."

"Didn't this guy get killed 30 years ago?"

Conveniently, a term already existed to explain this phenomenon and even more conveniently it was known as the "Mandela Effect". In 2009 "author, innovator and paranormal investigator" Fiona Broome coined it to define "powerful memories that don't match our recorded history" after herself mistakenly believing that the former president had died in the 1980s. Broome created a website where people could share similar distorted memories of the past and, despite its overtly "new age" origins, the term has become a useful shorthand for the confusion we encounter when we hit the brick wall of a misremembered past.

Many examples of the Mandela Effect revolve around what look like glitches in our collective memory banks. Ask even dedicated *Star Wars* fans what colour the droid C-3PO was and they'll tell you, with some certainty, that he was gold from top to bottom – despite him having one silver leg. In the same movie series, there is a famous moment (in the second film) where Darth Vader reveals his identity to his son with the immortal words: "Luke, I am your father." Only he doesn't. The actual line is "No, I am your father." Surprising perhaps, but not as surprising as the revelation that the wicked queen in *Snow White* doesn't say "Mirror, mirror on the wall, who is the fairest one of all?" but "Magic mirror on the wall, who now is the fairest one of all?"

The Mandela Effect can significantly impact personal reminiscences of actual historic events too. My late mother used to claim that as a child, in June 1940 she had heard the famous broadcast in which Churchill declared that we would "fight on the beaches". Only that "memory" cannot possibly be true because when Churchill delivered the original speech in the House of Commons, it was not recorded or broadcast. The version with which my mother and all of us are familiar was made by Churchill in 1949, four years after the end of the war.

So, what was my mother remembering? Well perhaps it was a radio announcer reading excerpts from the speech (which happened), or perhaps she had heard nothing at all and later confabulated the memory of the event into her reminiscences of war. There is a third possibility. Perhaps I have made up my own memory of her telling me the story. I honestly do not know and as she is no longer alive – I never will.

Much fun is had with the Mandela Effect, but it is in essence, just a fancy term for our species' weakest collective asset: the reliability of our memory. The reason so many (largely American) people thought Mandela had died in the 1980s, for example, was probably down to them not paying much attention to South African politics. Dim recollections of Mandela perhaps fused with the life of another activist, Steve Biko, whose murder in 1977, was later turned into a celebrated film, *Cry Freedom* (1987), by director Richard Attenborough.

The shakiness of our individual recollections is made far worse courtesy of many a mistaken belief that our memory is actually highly reliable. That disconnect makes us all susceptible and prey to bad actors in politics and the media, and the plague of fake history is down in no small part very largely to our misremembered past. An awful lot of our personal memories are either distorted or just plain wrong. And as the years recede, matters get worse because over time it becomes almost impossible not to sugarcoat our past with anecdotes and self-reinforcing stories. We are all, in conclusion, the unreliable narrators of our own monomyths.

Take that event in childhood when I told my class that I wanted to be a cowboy when I grew up. I can – I think – picture the scene, a classroom in the back of the school with us all sitting around in a circle in the sunlight. But did it really happen? I'm not sure. Would I swear my life on it? Absolutely not.

My memories of the siege of the Iranian Embassy on 5th May 1980, though crystal clear in my head, are likewise unreliable, a mixture of fact and fiction and I know that now because, courtesy of the internet, I can fact-check my own, albeit rather mundane, origin myth.

Let's start at the beginning. Well, events did not happen on a Sunday as I once remembered it, but on a Bank Holiday Monday and the film wasn't *Chisum* – but another John Wayne film of the same year (1970) called *Rio Lobo* which I have subsequently watched many times.* This was the sixth day of the siege, which had started when members of

---

* My thanks here to a whole team of social media users of a similar age with whom I twice went through events. It was particularly fascinating to find that most of us thought it was a Sunday and that for some reason a lot of us thought it was *Chisum* too. The Mandela Effect in motion.

the Democratic Revolutionary Front for the Liberation of Arabistan (DRFLA) had stormed the embassy, taking 26 people, including that British policeman, Trevor Lock, two BBC journalists and the Iranian Charges d'Affaires, Gholam-Ali Afrouz hostage.

Much focus was put on Trevor Lock at the time and that comes back to me as I research events. It must be said too that he more than rose to the occasion, wrestling the terrorist leader, Awn Ali Mohammed, to the ground at the climactic moment and then holding a gun to his head while the SAS stormed the building. For his bravery he was later awarded the George Medal.* The man who I distinctly remember clambering across the balcony was sound recordist Sim Harris, one of the two BBC hostages. The other BBC man, Chris Cramer, had fallen ill a few days earlier and been released.

Shots had been heard just before 2 p.m. and again at 7 p.m. just as the *Little and Large Holiday Special* was drawing to its end. In my efforts to fact-check further I did even approach Syd Little – the surviving half of the comedy partnership – and asked him for his memories but regret to report that none were forthcoming. *Rio Lobo* was having its first showing on British TV, but despite my remembering that it got cut off halfway through, that cannot be the case. The *Radio Times* shows that it was scheduled to begin at 7.10 p.m. and the cameras went live to the events at Hyde Park around then (or even possibly before) with the explosion going off at 7.23 p.m., which was broadcast live.

So, the film had hardly started, if it had started at all, when the newsflash came and as it has a rather lengthy opening credit sequence of fingers strumming a Spanish guitar, all I might have seen that day was a hand plucking guitar strings.

Watching the contemporary footage and BBC news report (available on YouTube), I feel like having words with my 11-year-old self. This is by any measure an extraordinary and hugely dramatic sequence

---

* The highest award for gallantry that can be given to a civilian or police officer.

of events. The explosion goes off. A voice off camera says, "That was a bomb." The fire starts. Screams can be heard. And gunshots. Dogs start barking and horns honking. More shots. There is a second explosion and flames lick up from the blown-in window. A figure appears at another window. Machine-gun fire echoes about. At that age I was absolutely obsessed with war, and here was a real-life military drama playing out on live TV in my living room. But all I wanted to do was watch that John Wayne film.

I may have been scared. Terrorism frightened the hell out of childhood me. A year earlier on 30th March 1979, my mother's former boss, the Conservative MP Airey Neave, had been assassinated by a bomb planted under his car by the Irish National Liberation Army. It had exploded as he drove out of the underground car park at the Palace of Westminster and killed him. My mum, Hannah, had been his secretary for years and despite no longer working for him, had maintained a friendship with him. Indeed, she had had lunch with him just a few months previously where he had whispered – and again this is a recollection of a recollection, so we need to be wary of my memory – that: "I think they'll try to get me."

Neave had been the first British army officer to escape from that famous POW camp Colditz before going on to be one of the small team of people running MI9.* The very loose association was the kind of thing that thrills a boy with a love of war and adventure, and I had signed copies of his books. But his very nasty, very brutal, very real death was no thrill at all. It had shaken my sense of security. Here we were, just a year later, with another real-life, violent, contemporary terrorist event going on. The siege and its dénouement were beyond the control even of my parents – and it was all playing out just 20 miles away from home. The bad guys were off camera but, clad in their gas

---

* MI9 was a top-secret department of the War Office in the 1940s, tasked with helping Allied soldiers get out from behind enemy lines. Neave's colleagues included Michael Bentine ,who would later go on to join the famous comedy group The Goons.

masks and balaclavas, the SAS were, in a sense, invisible and menacing too. These were not comforting heroes. There was no John Wayne present to ride in and save the day. And to an 11-year-old child, an uncertain world, devoid of heroes, is a very frightening place indeed.

* * *

You would be hard-pressed to find a better example of small-town America than Winterset, Iowa. The gridded streets swarm with pick-up trucks and people who look like extras in a Peter Bogdanovich film. Stars and stripes flags flutter, uniformly, outside the town's schools, diners, shops and government buildings that look like they went up not long after the era of the Wild West. It's the kind of Spielbergian community where kids still deliver newspapers by throwing them wildly from their bicycles and where Netflix dramas about missing teenagers are set.

At the junction of John Wayne Drive and East Washington Street, you can find the John Wayne Birth House Museum, the town's biggest attraction. The museum consists of a tiny white clapperboard four-roomed house, where he spent his earliest years, and a much bigger, modern museum and movie theater that tells his story a few metres away. In front of that second building, there is an impressive bronze statue of the man, dressed as a cowboy, with a rifle in his hand, which was gifted by his family to the trust.

Entrance is $20, but military veterans and children under 7 go free. A ubiquitous row of US flags sits along the edge of the grass, while beside both buildings, a much bigger one flaps overhead. There is also a rather peculiar rock sculpture with a massive Union flag on it and images of Wayne as a soldier with the word VALOR written at its side. Even before you have entered the premises, it is clear that you are here to pay tribute to a national hero.

It was in that small white house, on 26th May 1907, that Marion Robert Morrison was born. He was such a big baby that a local newspaper thought his arrival worthy of note: "A thirteen-pound son arrived at the home of Mr and Mrs Cyle Morrison, Monday morning."

Wayne would go on to be a very imposing man indeed, towering over others with his 6ft 4in frame and carrying, particularly in later life, quite a lot of bulk. Like many actors, judged constantly on their looks, he could be vain and was known to occasionally wear a girdle and from 1948, a toupée.

The account of his childhood and career, as told in the small cinema in Winterset, is a saccharine and bowdlerised version of his life that is heavy on his service to his country as an actor and as a supporter of the armed forces. Then it's out into the exhibition itself. Pride of place is given to his very ordinary looking 1972 Pontiac Grand Safari with a slightly raised roof – said to allow him space for a Stetson, but more likely to simply give this tall man extra head room. There is a carriage that was used in the 1952 Ireland-set John Ford romantic comedy *The Quiet Man* and an array of guns known as the "John Wayne Tribute" collection, which are replicas of the ones used in his films. Along one wall sits a case of novelty mugs with the names of his famous motion pictures on them. Wayne had them made and gave them out to actors and crew on his movie shoots. There are costumes, hats, an eyepatch and a gift shop where you can buy key rings, jigsaws, a game called John Wayne-opoly and an American Hero throw-blanket with his face on it for $25.

It's a shrine. Another shrine. One of many that have appeared thus far in the book. But unlike those to RAF pilot Douglas Bader, John F. Kennedy or even Che Guevara, there is one significant difference. This chapel of remembrance is to a man who played heroes in motion pictures – rather than someone who did heroic things by himself.

Right back at the start of the book we looked at the concept of *alief* and how the lives of real people can be conflated with the actors who play them; it is a curse that affected Rudolph Valentino, Cary Grant and Sean Connery (among others), all of whom the public could not – or did not want to – disentangle from their on-screen personas. The story of John Wayne is one of *alief* to the power of 10 because for many conservative Americans, he has to all intents and purposes become the man he portrayed and, through it, a symbol of a certain sort of Conservative Old America and its values.

Disentangling the human being John Wayne from the mythical character he played on the screen is quite a challenge.

John Wayne's early life is a curiously familiar tale of a drunken father and his failed business ventures, and an independent mother hating the confines of her domesticity. The marriage didn't last, and his parents divorced when he was 19. Wayne adored his dad but did not get on with his mother and hated his "girl's name", which caused no end of bullying at school. His was a miserable and unglamorous childhood. Young Marion was jealous of his younger brother, Robert, and spent most of his time with his family dog, a massive Airedale called Duke. In 1914 the Morrison family moved to Palmdale, California, where his father opened a drugstore. Cutting a lonely figure, the boy and his pet were adopted by the town's fire brigade department who dubbed the Airedale "Big Duke" and Marion "Little Duke". The "little" was eventually dropped and friends called him Duke* for the rest of his life.

As he entered his teenage years, Wayne grew tall and movie-star handsome. He became a high school sports star but was unusual in that he had a sensitive side too. He was a member of the debating society, the Latin club and even an amateur dramatics society. Duke wanted to become a lawyer and managed to get into the University of Southern California (USC) on a sports scholarship but was, we are told, kicked out after breaking a collarbone during a bodyboarding accident. Collarbones can heal in 6–12 weeks, and it was not a career-ending injury, so this sounds again like a nifty bit of origin-myth making and it's more likely he lost his place because of his complete lack of application to his studies. Wayne was partying hard and getting rewarded with appalling grades.

---

* In the 1989 film *Indiana Jones and the Last Crusade*, it is revealed that "Indy" took his name from the family dog. A nod, some long speculated, by Spielberg to Wayne and his dog Duke. In fact, Indiana got his name from the film's co-creator George Lucas whose own dog, an Alaskan Malamute, was called Indy.

Around the same time, his parents divorced, and out of college and out of luck, Wayne was obliged to make a living for himself.

Marion had appeared as an extra, along with his USC football-ing team, in three silent movies, and, using connections he had forged while making them, he landed a job as an extra and scene shifter at the Fox studio in Los Angeles in 1927. The John Wayne Birth House Museum repeats the famous story that it was around this time that he met the gunslinger Wyatt Earp. Although yet to be a household name, Earp had legendary status among the cowboy actors and film directors in Hollywood at the time. A lawman of the Old West, he had taken part in the single most famous shoot-out of the era, at the O.K. Corral, in Tombstone, Arizona, when he and his brothers Virgil and Morgan, faced down a five-man gang known as *The Cowboys* on 26th October 1881, killing three of them.

In a 1971 television documentary called *The American West of John Ford*, the celebrated director tells actor Henry Fonda that Earp's third wife, Josephine, was a "very devout religious woman and a couple of times a year she'd go to these religious conventions in Utah" while Wyatt would come to hang out around the movie studios. Whether he had been told it by Earp, or misremembered it, or was making it up for the benefit of the cameras, Ford was talking absolute nonsense. Jose-phine was no churchgoer. An extremely tough former prostitute, who had little interest in her Jewish faith, she had a greater addiction to the card table than the tabernacle and had, by the 1920s, a very significant gambling problem. The "religious conventions" Ford talked of were trips to illegal casinos, the boxing ring and race-track.

It is undoubtedly true that toward the end of his life, her husband was befriended by John Ford, but the story of Earp meeting and inspir-ing the young "John Wayne" is a bit more suspect. Various versions have the old law man informing Wayne's famous walk, the way he carried himself and, most of all, his personal code of conduct. Earp was said to have held fast to a set of unwritten rules, which included the one that you never shoot an unarmed man or one who was running away, and that gunfighting itself was only ever a last resort. It's claimed that John Wayne stuck so rigidly to Earp's Code that he insisted on a re-edit of his last picture, *The Shootist* (1976), when the rough cuts appeared to show him putting a bullet in the back of an unarmed man.

By the time Earp died in 1929, the two men, it has long been claimed, were so close that Marion was selected to be one of the pall-bearers at his funeral and, with his first film role as a cowboy in Raoul Walsh's *The Big Trail* that same year, the torch passed seamlessly from the old lawman to the young actor. It's not true. Wyatt Earp did meet several other actors through John Ford, including the now largely forgotten matinee idols Tom Mix and William S. Hart, who were indeed pall-bearers at his funeral. But there is no evidence that he ever befriended the prop-boy Marion Morrison – and someone either made up the story or fell victim to the Mandela Effect in the years that followed.

The far bigger influence on John Wayne and one that he acknowledged in his lifetime was an actor called Harry Carey, a huge star of the era, who played the lonesome outlaw Cheyenne Harry and variants on him in dozens of silent Westerns. It was those films which served as a prototype for Wayne's on-screen persona, and it was Carey, not Earp, who became a friend and mentor to the young actor for the rest of his life.

The Big Trail was to be Marion Morrison's big break. The untried and untested 22-year-old leading man had caught Walsh's eye and he planned to make the kid a star, but the name was a problem, because, well, it made this rugged man sound like he was a girl. To resolve the problem the executives dubbed him "John Wayne" instead.

"I didn't have any say in it," Wayne later told *Playboy* magazine "but I think it's a great name. It's short and strong and to the point. It took me a long time to get used to it, though. I still don't recognize it when somebody calls me John."

The film flopped and very badly indeed, but the name stuck and, to his credit, so did Wayne, who didn't give up and kept on making films. Over the next decade he appeared in hundreds of B movies, some made in as little as two or three days, and the experience gave him an extensive education in acting and screen craft. The hard graft and rapid turnaround allowed him to perfect his laid-back demeanour that would become his trademark and set up the next act in his life's work.

That break came in 1939 when, aged 32, his close friend and collaborator, John Ford, cast him in the western *Stagecoach*. The movie was a critical and commercial smash-hit and made him, finally, a star. Wayne was inundated with offers but just two years later, on 7th December 1941, his rising fame risked getting torpedoed when aircraft of the Imperial Japanese Navy attacked Pearl Harbor and America entered the war. For a decade, Wayne had slogged away, putting in the hours on awful and forgettable films. The work had finally paid off and he had been rewarded with stardom. He even had the celebrity lover to prove it having, in 1941, tumbled into a highly charged affair with Marlene Dietrich while still married to his first wife Josephine.

Getting drafted overseas in service of his country was not on his "to do" list and Wayne had no intention of throwing it all in to join up, but unfortunately, all around him, big Hollywood stars were showing him up by enlisting. They included James Stewart, Clark Gable, Henry Fonda and even John Ford, and while Wayne claimed he was too old, at 34, to go, it simply didn't wash. Fonda was 36, Gable was 40 and at 47, Ford was a full 13 years older than him.

With his credibility as an "action hero" at risk and desperate to avoid going to the front, Wayne played the "family" card. He had married Josephine Alicia Saenz in 1933 and the couple had four children. Yes, he had had at least two high-profile affairs since and was now effectively living with Dietrich and yes, he was going through the early stages of a divorce, but the draft board didn't know that and when Wayne argued that his family depended on him, he was classified "3-A", meaning: "Registrant with a child or children; registrant deferred by reason of extreme hardship to dependents."

While millions of American men joined up, Wayne carried on making motion pictures and his career went from strength to strength. Indeed, the war turned out to be a remarkable stroke of career luck for him because with so many other leading men overseas, he was able to land a series of stellar parts and, in the absence of competition, also got to sleep with a lot of leading ladies.

In many of those films, including *The Fighting Seabees* (1944), *Reunion in France* (1942) and *Back to Bataan* (1945), Wayne played war heroes, despite having made huge efforts to stop himself getting anywhere near the action. Such naked hypocrisy is, of course, a potential problem for his modern-day fans and devotees, but fortunately, there are those willing to leap to his aid and to prop the legend up with a bit of artful spin.

In 1998, John Ford's son Dan wrote a biography of his father in which he claimed that in 1943 Ford Sr. tried to get Wayne a commission in the Office of Strategic Services (OSS), the forerunner to the CIA. That story has since done the rounds, with apologists insisting that he was only too eager to play his part. But there is an on-going debate as to how serious his intentions were.

In his book *John Wayne's America: The Politics of Celebrity*, author Gary Wills explains:

"[Wayne's] excuses were varied and contradictory. He wrote to Ford that he was trying to fill out the proper forms to enter the military, but he had no typewriter on location; that he left forms with [friend and fellow actor] Ward Bond, who couldn't fill them out; or that his wife, from whom he was separated, would not let him get essential documents he had left at home. In short, the dog ate his homework."

Wayne did do a three-month morale-boosting tour of the South Pacific between 1943 and 1944 on behalf of the United Service Organizations (USO) and made further appearances on behalf of the USO in 1945, but his efforts were not exactly welcomed, and he was booed at least once. In July 1987, journalist and historian William Manchester, who had been wounded in the Battle of Okinawa on 5th June 1945, wrote an article for *The New York Times Magazine* claiming he had witnessed that appearance:

"After my evacuation from Okinawa, I had the enormous pleasure of seeing Wayne humiliated in person at Aiea Heights Naval Hospital in Hawaii … Each evening, Navy corpsmen would carry litters down the hospital theatre so the men could watch a movie. One night they had a surprise for us. Before the film, the curtains parted, and out stepped John Wayne, wearing a cowboy outfit – 10-gallon hat, bandana, checkered shirt, two pistols, chaps, boots and spurs. He grinned his aw-shucks grin, passed a hand over his face and said 'Hi, ya guys!' He was greeted by stony silence. Then somebody booed. Suddenly everyone was booing. This man was a symbol of the fake machismo we had come to hate, and we weren't going to listen to him. He tried and tried to make himself heard, but we drowned him out, and eventually he quit and left."

Four years later, Manchester went to see Wayne's celebrated war film, *Sands of Iwo Jima*, and was similarly unimpressed: "I went… with another ex-Marine, and we were asked to leave the theatre because we couldn't stop laughing."

Was Manchester telling the truth or did his obvious personal dislike of the actor fudge his recall of events? I've looked for another account of Wayne's appearance at Aiea Heights, but Manchester's is the only record and as such, I think, we should probably treat it with some caution. Manchester was a hugely credible journalist with a ferocious reputation for trying to tell the truth. He was even threatened with legal action by Jackie Kennedy when he tried to divulge details of her husband's sex life in a posthumous biography of the President. But at a distance of 43 years, even the very best journalists can have a hazy memory of events and embellish what happened for the sake of good copy. Of all the contemporary photographs that I can find of Wayne on stage for the USO during the Second World War, none show him in cowboy gear. He might well have been booed, but that comical outfit sounds like a bit of a flight of fancy.

A year before that appearance at Aiea Heights in 1945, Wayne received the shock of his life when, in the face of rising casualties, he, along with thousands of other American males was reclassified "1-A", meaning: "Available immediately for military service".

The twenty-first-century Wayne fan club, made up most boisterously of some very active bloggers, claim that at this point Republic Studios stepped in and that Herb Yates, the studio boss, threatened to "sue him for breach of contract" if he left, as he was their only bankable A-list star. But Gary Wills has done a deep dive into the story and found no evidence to support it. Rather conveniently, all records pertaining to the event have been lost.

Now, there is a case, and it is a good one, that propaganda was critical to the war effort and there is an equally valid argument that Wayne contributed more to it through his action films than he might ever otherwise have done. But the grim determination he demonstrated in staying out of uniform and away from the front does not sit comfortably with his image as a symbol of American patriotism and an action hero. Which is perhaps why so much is made of his USO work and, indeed, in 2023, the John Wayne Birthplace Museum even planned to hold a commemoration of their 40th year with "A Salute to the Armed Forces." The event featured a: "Benefit Dinner & Auction [and guests] will enjoy a live Big Band orchestra featuring classic favorites from the 1940s. Also planned is a fly-in breakfast of vintage military aircraft at the Winterset Municipal Airport and an encampment of World War II and Vietnam era reenactors at the John Wayne Birthplace."

For after all: "More significant than any screen performance… was Wayne's real-life commitment to the brave men and women of America' armed forces."

Well, perhaps. But it did not stretch to him joining up himself and the unfortunate truth is that, by any measure, America's greatest hero was, in fact, the coward of the county.

His third wife, the Peruvian actress Pilar Pallette, who Wayne met while scouting locations for his film *The Alamo* in 1952, later claimed that his guilt about not serving led him to become a "super-patriot for the rest of his life, trying to atone for staying at home."

Whatever the excuses, it all sits at odds with the legend. The big screen "John Wayne" would have told the executives where to go, picked up a rifle and gone and fought anyway. The real-life one stayed in Hollywood and made movies. Wayne knew it was a bad look and overcompensated as a result. In the post-war years, his deeply conservative politics and his very right-wing version of American patriotism became as hardened as his drinking – which is not much talked about in his many biographies but probably far more crucial to the story than is acknowledged.

According to a 2001 book called *Cut to the Chase* by Sam O'Steen, Wayne could be a "mean drunk" and although he was always considered "professional" by everyone who worked with him, there were shoots where directors were said to have always started early simply to get ahead of his boozing. A singularly odd, 1966 TV appearance, on the talkshow *The Merv Griffin Show*, drink in hand, shows the actor several sheets to the wind and the very antithesis of the hero he played. He appears detached and unfocused and dare I say it – a little boring – and we have almost certainly all met drunks like that.

When he wasn't drinking and making movies, he was increasingly politicking. In 1944, Wayne joined an anti-communist outfit called the Motion Picture Alliance for the Preservation of American Ideals (MPAPA) and became an active and vocal voice in right-wing politics in Hollywood. He was MPAPA president for four terms between 1949 and 1953 and in that role became an active supporter of Democratic Senator Joe McCarthy and the House Un-American Activities Committee (HUAAC).

In 1952, Wayne starred in the properly bonkers spy film *Big Jim McLean*, playing an HUAAC investigator like a cowboy James Bond, hunting down communist cells in contemporary Honolulu. It was essentially pro-McCarthyite propaganda.

Two years earlier, on 22nd June 1950, an article titled "Red Channels" in an anti-communist right-wing newsletter *Counterattack* had listed the names of 151 artists, actors, film directors, journalists and others connected with the film and media industry who were suspected of planting their "un-American" beliefs in the industry. This was to be the first appearance of the McCarthy-era blacklist. Wayne was deep inside a conspiratorial movement that saw reds under every bed in the industry and he was, as such, contributing to the destruction of the lives and careers of Hollywood colleagues.

Famous victims of the era included the star Edward G. Robinson, the screenwriter Dalton Trumbo, who was so ostracised by the industry that he was obliged to use a fake name to get work, and African American superstar Paul Robeson, who was dubbed "Black Stalin" after attending a peace conference in Paris. Mired in a heap of moral and political controversies and having recently been labelled a 'communist' by Senator McCarthy, Charlie Chaplin, the biggest star of the silent era, sailed to Europe for a 6 month extended break in the hope of avoiding being called to testify. Two days out of America, while crossing the Atlantic on 19th September 1952 he received a telegram informing him that he would be refused entry by the authorities until he could "prove his worth". Chaplin had lived in the USA for 40 years but was still a British citizen. He returned to the US just once after that, when in 1972, aged 83 he received an honorary Oscar. Chaplin received a 12-minute standing ovation in an extraordinary, emotionally charged act of atonement from the industry he had helped create, which had then turned its back on him in his hour of need 20 years earlier.

Another victim was the French actor Maurice Chevalier, who having been caught up in the post-war *épuration sauvage* in France, had fled to Hollywood, only to leap from the frying pan into the fire. Chevalier, like Chaplin, was refused re-entry in 1951 following a trip to Europe because he had signed the Stockholm Appeal, which had called for global nuclear disarmament.

This then was the original cancel culture, and while, following Joe McCarthy's fall from grace in 1954, some degree of sanity began to return, many careers and lives never recovered from events. Wayne was one of the most vocal right-wing bullies and McCarthyite fellow travellers of the time and even with the end of it and the shame and grief that followed, his career was completely unaffected. Indeed, it only went from strength to strength.

Asked in a 1974 BBC interview on *Parkinson* whether he regretted his involvement in the blacklists, a visibly irritated Wayne slurred back: "We were not blacklisting... they were..." before adding somewhat contradictorily: "I think it was probably a very necessary thing in Hollywood at the time because the radical liberals were going to take over our business."

Sounds horribly familiar, doesn't it? And it was, of course, quite untrue. There was no conspiracy of reds, and draft-dodging Wayne either knew that or didn't care. It was dangerous conspiratorial garbage.

Wayne prospered in the immediate post-McCarthy era and made some of his most famous films including *The Searchers* (1956), *Rio Bravo* (1959) and *The Alamo* (1960). He also made one of cinema's biggest turkeys when, thanks to one of the most absurd pieces of casting in film history, he played Genghis Khan in Howard Hughes' 1956 film *The Conqueror*. Wayne's portrayal of the mighty Mongolian leader was done with the same characteristic drawl that he played everything else and the only nod to authenticity was some very unfortunate make up, which, let's just say, has not aged well. Dubbed an "Oriental Western" the film was widely drubbed, and *Time* magazine's review summed up the critical mood: "Wayne portrays the great conqueror as a sort of cross between a square-shootin' sheriff and a Mongolian idiot. The idea is good for a couple of snickers, but after that it never Waynes but it bores."

The increasingly eccentric millionaire Howard Hughes produced just one more film before becoming a recluse. Obsessive and increasingly unwell, Hughes later bought every reel of *The Conqueror* and watched it and another film, *Ice Station Zebra* (1968), on a continuous loop.

With the advent of the 1960s, Wayne appeared in a series of hugely successful films. Like many people who are born into relative poverty only to later make a fortune, he also lived perpetually in fear of losing his money, and this led to his agreeing to a growing roster of highly lucrative cameo roles including D-Day film *The Longest Day* (1962) and the centurion in the Christ fable *The Greatest Story Ever Told* (1965).

Meanwhile, his smoking habit, which consisted of three packs a day, was killing him. In an era when cigarettes were promoted by celebrities, Wayne became the face of the tobacco brand Camel and adverts of the day show him talking up the "toasted" flavour and going on about how good they were for his voice. This habit led to a cancer diagnosis in 1964, of which he later said: "I sat there, trying to be John Wayne."

The line hints at another man beneath the tough guy facade and it was one Wayne was aware of: "That guy you see on the screen isn't really me," Wayne once said: "I'm Duke Morrison, and I never was and never will be a film personality like John Wayne. I know him well. I'm one of his closest students. I have to be. I make a living out of him."

Beneath the movie star lurked small-town-boy Morrison, who was happy to admit that he really didn't like horses and only got on them for money. In many of his surviving TV interviews, he comes across as a bit of a fish out of water, peculiar for a man who had been in the industry so long and been so at ease in front of the movie camera. As a result of his HUAAC activities, many in the largely liberal industry were wary of him and he didn't have many celebrity buddies. But in its place, he did have a very loyal family and old and trusted friends, particularly from the early days, who he liked to act with and, when necessary, support.

In *Out West*, which was episode nine of a 1980 documentary series called *Hollywood* voiced by the actor James Mason, Wayne talked tenderly about the shooting of his final scene in *The Searchers* along-side Harry Carey's widow, the actress, Olive Golden:

"I loved Harry… and he hadn't been dead long and I loved Oli and it was emotional… It was just me in the door and I thought of Harry Carey and he had a stance where he put his left hand on the right arm." Wayne mimicked the movement and "Oli looked around at me (off camera and crying) and it was a lovely dramatic moment in my life."

The interview shows a softer side of Wayne, which occasionally spilled over into his professional life and concern for his fellow actors. Featured among the cast of *The Searchers* was a Native American actor, Beulah Archuletta, who was playing the part of "Look" – a deeply unfortunate, misogynistic and racist comedy relief who ends up married to Wayne's sidekick before getting killed. A story from the time recounts how, one day, Wayne noticed that she was crying on the set and when he asked her why, she told him that her son, James, was getting married and that because of filming commitments she was going to miss the event. According to several consistent accounts from crew and family, Wayne insisted that filming be shut down while she was flown in his jet to the ceremony.

During the same shoot, Wayne was also said to have flown a Navajo child to a hospital after he was found to be suffering from pneumonia.

It's easy to mock and, "Well yes, but he was a millionaire movie star and of course he should have done that." But there are plenty of obstreperous, contemporary actors who would have no such concern for people in the ranks and Wayne certainly saw the crews on his sets as a sort of extended family, hence the mugs he made and gave out to them. Inside John Wayne there was most certainly a man who was capable of largesse.

Unfortunately, he was incapable of extending private compassion to his very public politics.

As the quagmire of the Vietnam War led to ever greater numbers of body bags coming home and as protests became ever louder, Wayne decided to do something for the service of his country. In 1968, he produced, co-directed and starred in a war film, set in Vietnam, called *The Green Berets* in which he played Special Forces officer Colonel Mike Kirby.

The film is a libertarian wet dream in which Kirby challenges a liberal journalist, George Beckwith, played by *Fugitive* star David Janssen, to go to Vietnam and see the truth of the war on the ground for himself. As Beckwith witnesses first-hand that the USA is there to save villagers from the wicked commies and is not the bad guy at all, the two men become friends and the journalist determines to start telling "the truth".

Much is made by Wayne's defenders and online hagiographers of the fact that Wayne went to Vietnam to meet troops. While there he was bestowed with a bracelet by the Montagnard people of Vietnam's Central Highlands, which he subsequently wore in all of his movies. The anecdote and many accounts of the making of *The Green Berets* could – perhaps deliberately – give the unmistakable impression that the film was shot in Vietnam and that, by dint of it, Wayne was near the actual action. But in fact, he went there only briefly, in 1966, before the film was made and was given the bracelet while visiting the troops on yet another (albeit better received) brief USO tour. The film was filmed at Fort Benning in Georgia, which any map will show you is quite some distance from South-East Asia.

The critics panned *The Green Berets* and in response Wayne claimed that patriotic Americans turned out in their droves to "own the libs" and make it a big hit. But that's not true. The film was a modest financial success but did not appear among the top ten box office pictures that year and the passing of the decades has rendered it even more ghastly than it must have been at the time. An unabashed pro-Vietnam war message runs through it and it would be risible had it not been produced in support of a conflict that would eventually kill 1.1 million Viet Cong and North Vietnamese people, at least 200,000 South Vietnamese soldiers and over 58,000 Americans.

In a White House interview on 12th September 1988, Wayne's friend Ronald Reagan, another patriotic actor before going into politics, claimed that the film didn't do as well as it could have because there was a conspiracy against it. He said:

"I remember we called the theatre and it had reserved seats. Nancy and I couldn't get tickets to it… (but when we went by another channel) there were tickets for any night you wanted them… in other words, the people who were supposed to be promoting the picture were literally keeping people away."

Yes, those dastardly commies had somehow seized control of the movie theaters and were stopping people watching good old patriotic films. It was an outright lie. Imagine a modern populist American president making stuff up like that.

In 1969, Wayne's faltering career had a fillip when he starred as ageing, bad-tempered, drunken US Marshal Rooster Cogburn in the movie *True Grit*. It earned him a Best Actor nomination at the following year's Academy Awards and, on the night, up against Dustin Hoffman, Jon Voight and Peter O'Toole, he won his only Oscar.

Though now recognised as a bona fide living American icon, he was unfortunately ever more out of step with the age and showed it when, in May 1971, he gave a famous interview to *Playboy* magazine. This is how that event played out:

Greeting the journalist Richard Warren Lewis, in a "realistic toupee" at his home in Newport Harbor, Orange County the actor drives them to the coast where they enjoy a high protein lunch of steak and cottage cheese on board *Wild Goose II,* a converted minesweeper that Wayne has had refitted as a pleasure cruiser. After lunch, a bottle of tequila appears and from there on in the 64-year-old actor lets it all hang out, while providing ample evidence that he is indeed a "mean drunk". He lambasts the "perverted films" of the era and reserves particular ire for the film that *True Grit* had gone head-to-head at the Oscars with the previous year:

"…*Midnight Cowboy*—that kind of thing. Wouldn't you say that the wonderful love of those two men in *Midnight Cowboy*, a story about two fags, qualifies (as perverted)?" he asked.

It's a very long interview, running to 23 A4 length pages – and all the worse for it. In a dreary and familiar trope that still does the rounds today, he blames teachers and schools for indoctrinating pupils with left-wing ideas:

"The Communists realized that they couldn't start a workers' revolution in the United States, since the workers were too affluent and too progressive. So the Commies decided on the next-best thing, and that's to start on the schools, start on the kids. And they've managed to do it. They're already in colleges; now they're getting into high schools."

With another glass of tequila sunk, he turns his attention to the Civil Rights movement:

"With a lot of blacks, there's quite a bit of resentment along with their dissent, and possibly rightfully so. But we can't all of a sudden, get down on our knees and turn everything over to the leadership of the blacks."

And then comes the truly demoralising bit: "I believe in white supremacy until the blacks are educated to a point of responsibility. I don't believe in giving authority and positions of leadership and judgement to irresponsible people."

Having said "I don't condone slavery", which is almost coming as a relief at this point, he then insists in another familiar racist trope that: "I think any black who can compete with a white today can get a better break than a white man."

He goes on to harangue students and suggests that in the right circumstances they and any other activists should expect to be shot. The interview goes on and on, and you end up feeling like you've been cornered in a bar by a bigoted old drunk who wants you to know that "Enoch was right".

It makes a very dispiriting read indeed. As the interview winds up, *Playboy* asks him what legacy he'd like to leave behind and Wayne answers: "You're going to think I'm being corny, but this is how I really feel: I hope my family and my friends will be able to say that I was an honest, kind and fairly decent man."

Well, they did and still do, but the public legacy is different. In recent years snippets of the *Playboy* interview have gone viral on social media and it was those in part, that led in 2020, to his old college USC removing an exhibit to their most famous drop-out and giving it context in a museum. It should not have come as a huge surprise because Wayne's homophobic and racist views were recognised in his time. In an interview on *The Dick Cavett Show*, shortly after publication of the *Playboy* article, veteran actor Kirk Douglas is forced to deploy all his assets of diplomacy when the subject is raised. Wayne "is one of the most professional actors I've ever worked with…" Douglas says through gritted teeth, but "we have never seen eye to eye on things… we never discuss politics."

So, what is to be done with the legend of John Wayne? After all, he was a superb and intuitive movie actor who made a huge body of work and appeared in some of the towering films of his era. In 169 film roles, he perfected all the notes, and across the decades turned in some astonishing performances. His portrayal of the racist cowboy Ethan Edwards in *The Searchers* arguably ranks among one of the great movie performances in the Western canon. Through his craft, Wayne transcended the bounds of Marion Morrison to become more than just an actor. In the words of his biographer Scott Eyman: "He came to embody a sort of race memory of Manifest Destiny, the nineteenth century as it should have been."

And that is why he still matters to so many right-wing Americans even today. The problem is that he also matters to lovers of the western genre – people like me.

For years I turned a blind eye to his politics and parked it all away, but can I really separate the character up there on the screen from the man he was and more to the point – should I? Can I really pretend that the racism, the homophobia, the misogyny and bigotry of John Wayne, my childhood hero, don't matter? Do I blinker myself to the subject matter of many of his films, and in particular the great ones, which themselves have problematic attitudes to history, women and the treatment of Native American people?

If we "Cancel John Wayne", we cancel that body of work in which he collaborated with thousands of other people. We cancel the mighty *Rio Bravo, Red River, The Man Who Shot Liberty Valance* and *True Grit*. But if we don't address it all either, if we turn our heads from who he was and what he believed – we all but admit that it was all OK.

I don't have the answer to this particular paradox. All I do know is that not so very deep inside me as I write this, a trusting 11-year-old boy is crying out to the adult me, to give his hero a break.

* * *

John Wayne may have been my first hero, but he was far from my last. In the decades that followed it often felt as if I'd placed all the wrong clay-footed heroes on pedestals.

What do you do when you find out that one of your favourite film directors, Roman Polanksi, drugged and raped an underage girl or that another, Woody Allen, aged 56, left his long-term partner for her adopted 21-year-old child? Do you simply ignore John Lennon's appalling treatment of his first wife and the callousness he displayed towards his eldest son Julian? Do the dance beats of 'Thriller' have quite the same appeal as they did when Michael Jackson first thrilled us now that a mountain of accusations has piled up against him? And what of Roger Waters, front man of Pink Floyd, who in recent years has backed all manner of terrible causes and who, while at least condemning Vladimir Putin's invasion of Ukraine, claimed that it was 'not unprovoked.'

Can I really enjoy Pink Floyd records in quite the same way that I did as a twenty-something student when Waters is making apologies for the actions of one of the most egregious tyrants of our age?

Do we ignore the transphobia of bestselling authors whose books our kids devoured? Is it still possible to love Charles Dickens' novels knowing that he trolled the great explorer John Rae and was a domestic tyrant, having tried to lock his wife up in a mental asylum dumped her for an 18-year-old girl?

What of those other heroes of childhood? The stars of the Ladybird books that I loved so much whether they be Nelson, Drake or Bonnie Prince Charlie – all hugely problematic people and none of them much like the heroes in the storybooks. And what about Captain James Cook? A hero who is still held up as a great icon – despite being willing to kidnap people and shoot others, while stealing land off indigenous people. History, much like modern life, is in short full of bullies, self-promoting charlatans, bigots, bastards and liars.

And this is perhaps a good moment to admit that I too, have lied to you – twice. There was no such person as Professor Ivor Fuldya who appeared in the Andy Warhol chapter, and I completely made up his theory about *spaghetti treeing**.

I also lied when I claimed that John Wayne was my first hero, because in fact, I had another, even bigger one in my childhood and his name was Peter Scott.

* * *

Peter was my father, and he was sitting on that brown sofa with me and my mum as we watched the siege of the Iranian Embassy in May 1980. Dad was then 62, having been in his early fifties when I was born, and that was both a curse and a blessing. On the one hand, I knew, even before my teenage years kicked in, that he would not be around forever but on the other, as time went on, he and I tacitly acknowledged the fact and, I hope, valued each other's company even more because of it.

I was lucky in another respect. He was a supremely thoughtful, emotional and demonstrative man and was not afraid to show how much he loved me. Peter was forever throwing his arms about me and planting a kiss on my head. It embarrassed the hell out of me in my teenage years, particularly as a strapping public schoolboy – but I knew his love was never in doubt.

---

* Although the Spaghetti Tree story is true!

Throughout my childhood we would go for walks in the fields behind our Essex home and talk. It was on those walks that he broke the news of the death of John Wayne to me and several of my other boyhood heroes, including Eric Morecambe and Elvis Presley. The age gap meant that our cultural points of reference were forever, slightly out of kilter, but it was OK because it just made life more interesting.

Peter had fought in the Second World War and I was far prouder of that fact, particularly in my 1970s childhood, than he was. Bits of old uniform littered the house, and I'd spend whole days dressing up and setting up lines of toy soldiers on my bedroom floor. He had campaign medals, which sat in a box in my parent's bedroom, but for most of his life he never wore them and certainly not to the Remembrance parade on our village green each year. Sometimes my mother would encourage him to put them on but he'd say: "I didn't do much" and never even got around to having them arranged on a pin.

On those walks, I would often try to mine Dad for stories of war, and he would try to entertain me by telling me how a friend of his used to claim that his life was saved by a bacon sandwich or how much he and Richard, my godfather, liked to liberate Italian villages in 1944.

"It was wonderful because you'd drive in and all the Germans had already left and everyone would come out and greet you like heroes."

This was all good stuff, but it didn't really answer the most important question of all:

"Did you kill anyone?"

"Well, plenty of people shot at me."

"Yes, but did YOU ever shoot anyone?"

It was a strange, and in retrospect rather disturbing question for a young boy to keep asking his father. And it is more unnerving still to admit that I wanted him to say "yes" for the simple reason that for boyhood me, heroism was wrapped up in shooting people. That, after all, was what John Wayne did and it was what happened in the war films that I loved, whether they be *Where Eagles Dare, Reach for the Sky* or *The Longest Day*.

War was about action, a grown-up game of life and death and taking down the enemy. It wasn't about driving about the Italian countryside swapping bully beef for wine or eating bacon sandwiches – it was about scaling castle wars, jumping off cable cars and machine-gunning people who came after you in the snow.

Dad's stories jarred with my internal comic-book narrative, not least because in six years of being on or near the front line, he had fired his weapon in anger – just once. He told me the story a thousand times and for reasons which I hope will become clear, it is a monomyth that I choose to believe. Every family has their own *Epic of Gilgamesh* and this one is mine.

Unlike Marion Morrison, my father signed up right at the start of the war and was bursting to do his bit and get out there to the front. Having wriggled out of his reserved occupation, he joined the Royal Engineers and in 1939, aged 22, went to war. That began with him sitting in a machine-gun pillbox, disguised as a postcard shop near the Sussex coast. Later, like thousands of other British and Empire troops, he was active in the campaign in East Africa and later in the north. By 1943, he was attached to the 10th Indian Division and was blind in his left eye just like the John Wayne character Rooster Cogburn in *True Grit*. Even that was a bit of a disappointment because Peter had lost it to disease, not through some wartime injury.

Dad took part in the Battle of Anzio, landing on the Italian coast in a second wave in January 1944, several days after the start of the operation. He was nervously looking forward to storming up the beach from his landing craft like he'd seen in the Pathé news reels and on the journey over he took some shaky photos inside the boat, but when the front of the lander crashed into the sea and he and the other men ran ashore, there was no enemy there to greet them.

The same was not true of his experience at the Battle of Monte Cassino between March and May 1944, an event that he would rarely ever allude to but of which he would say, "there were a lot of bodies lying about." But that was not the story he repeatedly offered up to me on those long walks in the Essex countryside. Instead, he told me about another event that took place, I think, in the Province of Arezzo in Eastern Tuscany in August 1944.

Having lost that eye, Peter had been obliged to stop building bridges and was instead acting as a glorified scout. He was what was rather grandly called a "forward intelligence officer" and it was his job to go ahead of the advancing army, in the middle of the night, and make observations. As the German army was fleeing north that summer, it was blowing up bridges behind it at a rate of knots, and that the Royal Engineers were having to build replacement Bailey bridges in their place. Dad's job was to identify those crossing points.

On the moonlit night in question, he was scouting a stretch of river, when he noticed a shadow on the opposite bank. It was an officer of the Wehrmacht, quite likely – although he never said this – from the Pioneer Battalion and perhaps doing a similar job to him. Peter paused and pondered what to do next. Taking a potshot at a stranger would have attracted attention and would anyway have been an extremely stupid thing to do. But there was another thing: Dad had been to Germany in the pre-war years and he and his parents had German friends. His sister, my aunt, had been engaged to a member of that same family and they had all spent happy times together. The enemy was not some existential evil entity to him; it included people he knew, living in places he had been. War is not the stuff of *Where Eagles Dare*.

So, he did what most of us would do and began to creep away until he realised that the young man on the other side of the river was staring right back at him. In my head there is a moment where they both look at each other in silence across the moonlit divide of the babbling river, wondering what to do before one of them opened fire. I have probably made that first bit up, but shots were most certainly exchanged.

Peter didn't know who fired first but he was quite clear about what happened next. He ran away, as fast as he could, emptying his gun blindly behind him, as he stumbled away from the river and back up the hill towards the safety of his lines.

Four decades later as we trudged through the fields of Essex, I would interrogate Dad over and over on the details of the encounter:"How many times did you shoot?", "Did you see him fall over?", "What did you hear?", "Did you hit him?", "Were there others?".

He wasn't sure. There was a chance he had managed to hit the other man but he thought it unlikely. After all, in real life, pistols are not very accurate. The Webley Revolver Mark VI, the standard firearm for British officers at the time, had a range of about 45 metres. Dad was blind in one eye, legging it in the opposite direction and in fear for his life.

For the rest of that night, by his account, he lay awake wracked by the anomalous feeling that while he may have done his "bit" and fired his gun, he hoped very much that he hadn't hit someone and that it had all been rather unsettling.

"But how did you feel?" I'd ask.

"Scared."

That didn't satisfy me at all and I for the life of me I couldn't understand why he hadn't acted more like John Wayne or Clint Eastwood. In my young mind, a few random shots in the dark meant that he hadn't really played his part. So instead, I ploughed my grandfather for stories of his experience in the First World War, only to be deeply disappointed by those as well.

Time rolled on. I went to university, got some attitude, grew older and not necessarily any wiser and at some point, I stopped asking Dad to tell me stories about his war.

On the 50th anniversary of VJ Day in August 1995, Peter, Richard, their friend Molly who had been in the Women's Auxiliary Air Force (WAAFs) and other surviving comrades marched down the Mall and took a salute from the Queen and Prince Philip. A service of remembrance was held in front of Buckingham Palace and later, a Lancaster bomber, of the type used in the Dam Busters raid, flew over The Mall, and dumped a million paper poppies on the crowd and the parkland beneath. For the first and only time in his life, Peter wore his campaign medals and for the occasion my Mum, Hannah, bought a hat and summer dress and turned out to watch him. Dad was a bit of a crier, and I imagine he spent quite a bit of the day brushing away his tears.

I didn't witness it because I didn't go, or meet up with them afterwards, despite being in London on the day and being invited. I was now in my late twenties and otherwise occupied. I'd like to say there was some dramatic reason, but in truth I just wanted to see an ex-girlfriend.

If Peter was disappointed, he never let on. I have the pictures my Mum took of the event, and he looks happy with his friends, marching down The Mall, so perhaps he wasn't bothered. Or perhaps I simply prefer to remember it that way and forget that the little boy, who had once pestered his Dad for stories, was no longer much interested in his war.

Outwardly Peter was an old-fashioned, one might almost say typical middle-class Englishman. He voted Conservative, was rarely without a tie and bought British cars because they were British, despite them repeatedly letting him down. But beneath that exterior, there was a sort of rebellious defiance to him which – I think – came out of his experiences of war because his old war chums had it too. It's fashionable nowadays to describe all the people who fought in the Second World War as heroes but neither he nor they would ever have described or thought of themselves as such. They were not some extraordinary generation of super-beings but ordinary young men whose lives had been turned upside down by violent events beyond their control.

Peter died in 1998, with the three of us at his bedside, and his passing left a great big Dad shaped hole in my life.

Some months later, his wartime buddy Mack came on a trip to the UK. Mack was a South American rancher of Scottish descent and one of the 4,000 men who left neutral Argentina in the Second World War to come and fight for Britain. He and his wife stayed at my widowed mother's home and over dinner, he told us other tales of Dad in Italy and ones that put Peter in a far more heroic light. There was one that had him rolling Mack into a ditch as a German convoy approached and another of the two of them being handed a coded note, written on cigarette paper by Italian partisans, which led them to the home of a woman who had information on enemy movements.

But these were not the stories Peter chose to tell me. Dad instead told me repeatedly about a night of terror in the Italian countryside and in doing so, whether intentionally or not, taught me an extremely valuable history lesson. The Second World War for millions on all sides, after all, was not some *Boy's Own* adventure – it was human beings stumbling about in the darkness, trying to survive and hoping for a better future ahead.

I have teenage children myself now and we too go for walks; and like our ancestors before us, stretching back through time, I often tell them the random, shaggy monomyths of our tribe. And sometimes that includes the story of my father Peter and his war and, specifically, the night in Eastern Tuscany in August 1944, when he made all our lives possible – by heroically running away.

ACKNOWLEDGMENTS

So many people have helped *Fake Heroes* blink into the light, but special thanks to my agent Doug Young at Pew Literary and Oli Holden-Rea at Welbeck. Thanks too to Nathan Coonan-Joyce and Annabel Robinson.

Huge thanks to everyone who gave me helpful suggestions in the formative ideas stage, but particularly to Robert Gotts in Canberra for first telling me about the Bunyip Aristocracy and to Guy Parker for being an early sounding board and giving me a couple of great ideas.

Gratitude too to the people who gave me insights into the 'ten' or those around them and particular thanks to Bendor Grosvenor, Charlotte Mullins, Alex von Tunzelmann, Mark Brandon, Stephen Colegrave, Sharon McGrayne, John Carter at the Carter Cars website, Gemma Utting and 'Christine the nun' for talking to me and for filling so many gaps.

Several of the formative ideas in the book sprang from pieces written for *Byline Times*, and my thanks to my friends Peter Jukes and Hardeep Matharu there and indeed to the whole Byline team for being so wonderfully supportive. In the same vein I am also hugely grateful to *Politico Europe* and in particular Stephan Faris who commissioned my work there.

Very grateful to my long-suffering sounding board Per Laleng and the steadfast support of so many friends and family, including the Bradley gang, the Thompson family, the Dalys, Matt Tombs, Alex Pannell, Tessa Fantoni and my wonderful, ever-loyal sister Pippa Fairbanks and her husband Peter.

Finally, I am indebted to my extraordinary core team. To my wife Helen and my two children James and Sophia, who accompanied me on research trips, sat and listened to me testing out chunks of material and were just fabulously helpful and supportive throughout.

BIBLIOGRAPHY AND FURTHER READING

Epic of Gilgamesh – The Babylonian Epic Poem and other texts Anonymous – Andrew George Trans. (Penguin – 2002)

This is the Part Where the Superhero Discovers He is Mortal – Robert Kolker (*New Yorker Magazine* April 13 2007)

SuperCooperators – Martin Nowak (Free Press – reprint edition 2012)

Myth and Legend – Sir Francis Drake and the Spanish Armada (*Look and Learn* magazine issue 873 – 7 October 1978)

The Hero with a Thousand Faces – Joseph Campbell (New World Library 3rd Edition 2012)

Lumiere's Arrival of the Train: Cinema's Founding Myth – Martin Loiperdinger (University of Trier 2004)

Eichmann in Jerusalem – Hannah Arendt (Penguin Classics – originally printed 1963)

Douglas Bader – Dilip Sarkar (Amberley – 2013)

Bader's War – S.P. Mackenzie (Spellmount – 2008)

Fighter Leader, The Story of Wing Commander Ian Gleed – Norman Franks (William Kimber – 1978)

Arise to Conquer – Ian Gleed (Air World – republished 2022)

Fighting Proud – Stephen Bourne (Bloomsbury Academic – 2019)

Reach for the Sky – Paul Brickhill (Naval Institute Press – republished 2001)

The Photoplay, a Psychological Study – Hugo Munsterberg (1916 – Gutenberg Project)

Colditz – Prisoners of the Castle – Ben Macintyre (Viking – 2022)

President Kennedy, Profile of Power – Richard Reeves (Simon and Schuster 1993)

The Dark Side of Camelot – Seymour Hersh (Harper Collins 1997)

Profiles in Courage – John F. Kennedy (Harper Perennial Modern Classics reissued 2013)

Voodoo Histories, How Conspiracy Theory Has Shaped Modern History
– David Aaronovitch (Vintage 2010)

Unbought and Unbossed – Shirley Chisholm (Amistad reprint edition 2023)

Che Guevara A Revolutionary Life – John Lee Anderson (Bantam edition 1997)

The Motorcycle Diaries – Ernesto Che Guevara (Penguin Classics 2021)

Authenticity – Alice Sherwood (Mudlark 2022)

Anne Hamilton-Byrne and the Family – Carole Cusack (University of Sydney academic paper 2020)

Combating Cult Mind Control – Dr Steven Hassan (Freedom of Mind Press reprint 2015)

The Missionary Position – Mother Teresa in Theory and Practice – Christopher Hitchens (Atlantic Books 2012)

Mother Teresa – Come Be My Light – Edited and with Commentary by Brian Kolodiejchuk, MC (Ebury House 2008)

Don't be a Bystander, the story of Mustafa and Zejneba Hardaga – Dr Joanna Sliwa (blog)

Nat Tate, An American Artist – William Boyd (Penguin Random House 2011)

Monumental Lies, Culture Wars and the Truth About the Past – Robert Bevan (Verso 2022)

How I Uncovered One of the Biggest Art Hoaxes of the Nineties – David Lister (Independent Premium Nov 2022)

Andy Warhol, From Nowhere Up There an Oral History – Gary Comenas (Warhol Stars Website)

Warhol – The Biography – Victor Bockris (Da Capo Press 2003)

A Little History of Art – Charlotte Mullins (Yale University Press 2022)

Sleeping With the Enemy, Coco Chanel's Secret War – Hal Vaughan (Vintage 2011)

The Chanel Muggeridge Unpublished Interview – (chanel-muggeridge.co.uk)

Chanel, A Woman of Her Own – Axel Madsen (St Martin's Press 1991)

The Allure of Chanel – Paul Morand (Pushkin Press reprint 2008)

Remembered Laughter – Cole Lesley (Jonathan Cape 1977)

Scott and Amundsen, The Last Place on Earth – Ronald Huntford (Random House 1979)

Scott's Last Expedition (Diaries) – Captain Robert Falcon Scott (Amberley Publishing 2012)

The "terra firma" Anecdote – Björn Lantz (Cambridge University Research paper 2020)

Made in Britain – Adrian Sykes (Adelphi 2011)

A King's Story, the memoir of HRH The Duke of Windsor – Edward Windsor (Reprint Society 1953)

Foundation, The History of England, Volume 1 – Peter Ackroyd (Pan Books 2011)

Henry V – Keith Dockray (Tempus publishing 2004)

1415, Henry V's Year of Glory – Ian Mortimer (Vintage 2010)

The Story of Henry V – L. Du Garde Peach (Ladybird 1962)

Traitor King – Andrew Lownie (Blink Publishing 2021)

The Mountbattens, Their Lives and Loves – Andrew Lownie (Blink Publishing 2020)

Agincourt, A New History – Anne Curry (The History Press 2006)

The Turning Wheel – Arthur Pound (Oxford City Press reprinted 2012)

The Basic Laws of Human Stupidity – Carlo M. Cipolla (il Mulino reprinted 2011)

Prometheans in the Lab – Sharon McGrayne (McGraw-Hill Education 2002)

Women Scientists in America – Margaret W. W. Rossiter (John Hopkins University Press 1982)

Woman as Inventor – Matilda Gage (out of print but can be read online at Harvard Library)

Cut to the Chase – Sam O'Steen (Michael Wiese Productions 2002)

Playboy Magazine interview with John Wayne – May 1971 (available to read online via The Wrap (thewrap.com)

Websites, resources and museums include:
Royal Museums Greenwich
British Museum, London
Tate Modern Museum
MOMA (Museum of Modern Art New York)
New York Public Library
Imperial War Museum Duxford

John Wayne Birthplace Museum
Imperial War Museum, London
John F. Kennedy Hyannis Museum
John F. Kennedy Presidential Museum and Library, Boston
National Library of Scotland Manuscripts (online)
The Douglas Bader Foundation (online)
The National Archives (online)
Mail Online
El Pais
Spectator
British Pathe Archive (online)
Independent
Washington Post
Guardian
New York Times
New York Post
New Yorker Magazine
Time Magazine
The (London) Gazette
Cuban Observatory of Human Rights
Yad Vashem – World Holocaust Remembrance Center
Carter Car website

TV, Filmography, Podcasts, Radio and other media used include:
Reach for the Sky – Director Lewis Gilbert (1956)
The Dam Busters – Directed by Michael Anderson (1955)
The Arrival of a Train at La Ciotat Station – Directed Lumiere brothers (1895)
Battle of the Somme – Directors Geoffrey Malins and John McDowell (1916)
One of Our Aircraft is Missing – Directed by Michael Powell and Emeric
    Pressburger (1942)
The Life and Death of Colonel Blimp – Directed by Michael Powell and
    Emeric Pressburger (1943)
JFK – Directed by Oliver Stone (1991)
PT109 – Directed by Leslie H. Martinson (1963)
November 23-25 1963 – Original Colour Film of John F. Kennedy Funeral
    various (1963)

Motorcycle Diaries – Directed by Walter Salles (2004)

Exposure – the Other Side of Jimmy Savile (ITV 2012)

Mother Theresa – an animated classic Directed by Jon Song Chol (2004)

Something Beautiful for God – Director Peter Chafer – presented by Malcolm Muggeridge (1969)

The Great White Silence – Directed by Herbert Ponting (1924)

Scott of the Antarctic – Directed by Charles Frend (1948)

The Savior for Sale – Da Vinci's Lost Masterpiece – documentary directed Antoine Viktine (2021)

The King – Directed by David Michôd (2019)

This is Your Life – Douglas Bader Thames Television first broadcast 1982 (available to view on YouTube)

Desert Island Discs – Douglas Bader November 1981 (BBC iplayer)

Profiling Evil – podcast The Witch Is Dead (episode 16) – 2022

The Great Contemporary Art Bubble – Ben Lewis (documentary 2009)

The Rebel (film 1961) – directed by Robert Day

The Turning: This Sisters Who Left (podcast)

Cautionary Tales, the Inventor Who Almost Ended the World – Tim Harford podcast

Rio Lobo – Directed by Howard Hawks (1970)

Rio Bravo – Directed by Howard Hawks (1959)

The Searchers – Directed by John Ford (1956)

The American West of John Ford – Directed Denis Sanders, narrated by John Wayne documentary (1971)

INDEX